ENVIRONMENTAL POLICY
IN THE 1990s

ENVIRONMENTAL POLICY IN THE 1990s

TOWARD A NEW AGENDA

Second Edition

Edited by

Norman J. Vig
Carleton College

Michael E. Kraft
University of Wisconsin-Green Bay

CQ PRESS

A Division of Congressional Quarterly Inc.
Washington, D.C.

Printed in the United States of America

Cover design: Paula Anderson

Library of Congress Cataloging-in-Publication Data

Environmental policy in the 1990s: toward a new agenda / edited by Norman J. Vig, Michael E. Kraft. -- 2nd ed.
    p.   cm.
    Includes index
    ISBN 0-87187-765-1 : ISBN 0-87187-739-2 (pbk.)
    1. Environmental policy--United States.   2. Environmental policy.
I. Vig, Norman J. II. Kraft, Michael E.
HC110.E5E49876 1993
363.7'056'0973--dc20   93-2116
                                                    CIP

For
Teddy and Jesse
Steve and David

Contents

Tables and Figures

Tables

Figures

Preface

When the first environmental decade was launched more than twenty years ago, protecting our air, water, and other natural resources seemed a relatively simple proposition. The polluters and exploiters of nature would be brought to heel by tough laws requiring them to clean up or get out of business within five or ten years. The sense of urgency that swept Congress in 1970 as it passed the Clean Air Act with scarcely a dissenting voice reflected the rise of one of the most dramatic popular movements in American history. Since then, despite ebbs and flows, the tide of public opinion favoring greater environmental protection has entered the mainstream of political life. But preserving the life support systems of the planet now appears a far larger and more daunting task than anyone imagined two decades ago.

Two events in 1992 demonstrated the growing reach and maturity of environmentalism. In June the largest international diplomatic conference ever held was convened in Río de Janeiro, Brazil, to address an enormous range of global environmental issues. In November the election of Bill Clinton and Al Gore symbolized a renewed commitment to environmental protection in the United States. Their arguments for environmentally sound economic growth echoed calls for "sustainable development" now heard throughout the world.

Despite the importance of these events, translating symbolic commitments into effective action is no easy task. The making of public policy often resembles an awkward dance between idealistic ends and deficient means. The history of environmental protection is no exception. Implementing the major legislation of the 1970s on air and water pollution, hazardous waste, and preservation of public lands and other resources proved to be difficult and frustrating. Although genuine progress was made, few deadlines were met and results have fallen considerably short of expectations. At the same time, environmental protection has turned out to be a moving target. What appeared to be a relatively straightforward job of controlling a few key pollutants by mandating corrective technologies at the "end of the pipe" has become a far larger and more difficult task that may require fundamental changes in human behavior.

By the end of the 1970s it was evident that many of the most serious environmental problems had their origins in massive use and careless disposal of industrial chemicals whose cumulative health and environmental effects were largely unknown. These second-generation problems required cleanup of thousands of abandoned dumps, leaking toxic waste sites, and military bases and production facilities under Superfund and other programs. By the end of the decade, these programs were plagued by growing controversy over the slow pace and escalating costs of clean-ups. But by then a third generation of even more challenging ecological issues captured public attention: the greenhouse effect and global warming, deterioration of the ozone layer, tropical deforestation, extinction of species, and ocean and coastal pollution. The summer of 1988—with its record heat and drought, destructive fires, and sickening urban and beach pollution—along with the great Alaskan oil spill of March 1989 appeared to confirm that things were drastically wrong and had to be dealt with at a much more serious and fundamental level than in the past. Yet the Bush administration proved unwilling to tackle many of the new global environmental issues of the 1990s.

This book seeks to explain the most important developments in environmental policy and politics since the 1960s and to analyze the central issues that face us in the current decade. Like the first edition published in 1990, it focuses on the underlying trends, institutional shortcomings, and policy dilemmas that all policy actors face in attempting to resolve environmental controversies. This edition contains seven new chapters, and the others have been extensively revised and updated. We have also attempted to place the Clinton-Gore administration in the context of the ongoing debate over the cost and effectiveness of environmental policies. As such, the book has broad relevance for the environmental community and all concerned with the difficulties and complexities of finding solutions to our worsening environmental conditions.

Part I provides a retrospective view of policy development as well as a framework for analyzing policy change in the United States. Chapter 1 serves as an introduction to the book by outlining the basic issues in U.S. environmental policy over the past two decades, the development of institutional capabilities for addressing them, and the successes and failures in implementing policies. The nature of public opinion and the evolution of the environmental movement that has supported these developments are analyzed by Christopher Bosso in chapter 2. One of his most important conclusions is that environmental groups are becoming more fragmented, decentralized, and diversified in their concerns and modes of action in the 1990s. States have also become increasingly important sources of policy innovation and action. James Lester demonstrates in chapter 3, however, that the states vary widely in their commitments to environmental programs and their capacities for effective policy implementation.

Part II analyzes the role of federal institutions in environmental policymaking. Chapter 4 by Norman Vig discusses the role of presidents as environmental leaders, focusing on the two Roosevelts, the Reagan and Bush presidencies, and prospects for the Clinton-Gore administration. In chapter 5 Michael Kraft examines the causes and consequences of policy gridlock in Congress in such areas as clean air and acid rain legislation and national energy policy, and what can be done to overcome these stalemates. Chapter 6 by Walter Rosenbaum takes a hard and critical look at the nation's chief environmental institution, the Environmental Protection Agency. In chapter 7 Lettie Wenner explores the evolving role of the federal courts in interpreting environmental laws, reviewing administrative decisionmaking, and ultimately resolving many environmental disputes. Wenner discusses several new legal trends such as the growing controversy over private property rights affected by environmental regulation.

Part III shifts the focus to some of the broader dilemmas in environmental policy formulation, implementation, and evaluation. In Chapter 8 Robert Bartlett raises the surprisingly complex question of how we should measure the success of environmental policies. He suggests that multiple approaches and criteria are needed to capture the full range of policy consequences, even though some effects are very difficult to assess. The next two chapters focus on criteria that are increasingly being applied to environmental policies. Economist A. Myrick Freeman focuses on economic questions in chapter 9. How can greater economic rationality be achieved in protecting the environment? How can market incentives improve the efficiency and effectiveness of environmental regulation? Chapter 10 by Richard Andrews takes up a parallel set of scientific questions: How can environmental risk be measured? Should comparative risk assessment be used to set environmental priorities? To what extent can science improve environmental decisionmaking? Finally, chapter 11 by Daniel Mazmanian and David Morell examines the so-called not-in-my-backyard (NIMBY) syndrome—how can public policies avoid polarization of local interests over hazardous facility siting and other community-level disputes without sacrificing democratic participation?

International environmental and security issues are the focus of Part IV. Chapter 12 by Regina Axelrod explains the recent development of environmental policymaking in the European Community as perhaps the most advanced model for international environmental cooperation. In chapter 13 Richard Tobin shifts the focus to nations at the other end of the development spectrum, those that are struggling with an even more formidable array of threats brought about by rapid population growth and resource exploitation. Chapter 14 by Marvin Soroos then explores the development of global environmental diplomacy and institution building over the past two decades, culminating with the U.N. Conference on Environment and Development at Río de Janeiro in 1992. The last chapter in this section, by Odelia Funke, takes up a new issue: how environmental destruction is related to military preparedness, war, and our long-term national security interests.

Part V concludes the book with a consideration of environmental values and prospects for the future. Chapter 16 by Robert Paehlke discusses the core values of environmentalism and proposes a variety of ways in which environmental ethics can be incorporated into environmental and economic policies. The final chapter by the editors draws on the contributions to the book and on current reports to define the environmental issues, policy dilemmas, institutional problems, and strategic choices that will confront policymakers in the mid 1990s and beyond. We have attempted to project some of the actions of the Clinton administration based on its first three months in office.

We thank the contributing authors for their generosity, cooperative spirit, and patience in response to our seemingly endless editorial requests. It is a pleasure to work with such a conscientious and punctual group of scholars. Special thanks are also due to Brenda Carter, Nancy Lammers, Shana Wagger, and Chris Karlsten of CQ Press, and to Kristen Carpenter Stoever for her splendid editorial work. Finally, we gratefully acknowledge support from the Political Science Department and Technology and Policy Studies Program at Carleton College and the Department of Public and Environmental Affairs at the University of Wisconsin-Green Bay. As always, all remaining errors and omissions are our own responsibility.

Norman J. Vig
Michael E. Kraft

Contributors

Richard N. L. Andrews is professor of environmental sciences and engineering and director of the Environmental Management and Policy Program, Department of Environmental Sciences and Engineering, University of North Carolina, Chapel Hill. Formerly chairman of the Natural Resource Policy and Management Program at the University of Michigan and a budget examiner at the U.S. Office of Management and Budget, he is the author of *Environmental Policy and Administrative Change* (1976) and of numerous journal articles on environmental policy, impact and risk assessments, and benefit-cost analysis.

Regina S. Axelrod is associate professor of political studies at Adelphi University. She is the editor and contributing author of *Environment, Energy, Public Policy: Toward a Rational Future* (1981) and the author of *Conflict Between Energy and Urban Environment: Consolidated Edison Versus the City of New York* (1982). She is currently studying environmental policy in the European Community.

Robert V. Bartlett teaches environmental politics and public policy at Purdue University, where he is associate professor of political science. He is the author of *The Reserve Mining Controversy: Science, Technology, and Environmental Quality* (1980) and the editor and contributing author of *Policy Through Impact Assessment: Institutionalized Analysis as a Policy Strategy* (1989). He has published numerous scholarly articles and book chapters as well. In 1990 he was a Fulbright scholar and in 1992 a visiting fellow in the Centre for Resource Management at Lincoln University, Canterbury, New Zealand. He is currently writing a book about environmental policy in New Zealand.

Christopher J. Bosso is associate professor of political science at Northeastern University, specializing in American politics and public policy. He is the author of *Pesticides and Politics: The Life Cycle of a Public Issue* (1987), winner of the 1988 Policy Studies Organization award for the best book in policy studies. He also has written on the intersection of environmental values and American democratic institutions, on trends within the environmental community, and on public policymaking dynamics generally.

A. Myrick Freeman III is professor of economics at Bowdoin College. He has also held appointments as senior fellow at Resources for the Future, as visiting professor at the University of Washington, and as Robert M. La Follette Visiting Distinguished Professor at the University of Wisconsin-Madison. He is the author of *The Benefits of Environmental Improvement: Theory and Practice* (1979) and *Air and Water Pollution Control: A Benefit-Cost Assessment* (1982). He is currently a member of the Scientific Advisory Committee of the U.S. Environmental Protection Agency.

Odelia Funke is chief of the Information Access Branch, Office of Pollution Prevention and Toxics, at the U.S. Environmental Protection Agency. She has also been a senior analyst and branch chief at the EPA's Policy, Planning, and Evaluation Office. She received her Ph.D. in political science from the University of Virginia, has taught at George Washington and American Universities and the University of Missouri, and has written widely on environmental politics and policy. In 1991-1992 she was a visiting senior fellow at the Army Environmental Policy Institute.

Michael E. Kraft is professor of political science and public affairs and Herbert Fisk Johnson Professor of Environmental Studies at the University of Wisconsin-Green Bay. He has held appointments as Robert M. La Follette Visiting Distinguished Professor at the University of Wisconsin-Madison and as Visiting Distinguished Professor at Oberlin College. He is the coeditor and contributing author of *Population Policy Analysis* (1978), *Environmental Policy in the 1980s: Reagan's New Agenda* (CQ Press, 1984), *Technology and Politics* (1988), and *Public Reactions to Nuclear Waste* (1993).

James P. Lester is professor of political science at Colorado State University. He is the editor and contributing author of *Environmental Politics and Policy: Theories and Evidence* (1989), coauthor of *Implementation Theory and Practice: Toward a Third Generation* (1990), and author of numerous articles and book chapters on environmental policy, hazardous waste politics, and public policy implementation.

Daniel A. Mazmanian is director of the Center for Politics and Policy, and Luther Lee Professor of Government, at the Claremont Graduate School. He has written numerous articles and books, including *Can Organizations Change? Environmental Protection, Citizen Participation, and the Corps of Engineers* (1979), *Implementation and Public Policy* (1983, 1989), and most recently, *Beyond Superfailure: America's Toxics Policy for the 1990s* (with David Morell, 1992).

David Morell is managing associate at ERM-West, Inc. (Environmental Resources Management) in Walnut Creek, California. The author or coauthor of five books, including *Beyond Superfailure: America's Toxics*

Policy for the 1990s (1992), and more than fifty articles, he has served as an office director in both the air and water divisions of the U.S. Environmental Protection Agency and as director of policy for the California hazardous waste program. He has taught environmental policy at Princeton University, the University of California, Berkeley, and the Claremont Graduate School.

Robert C. Paehlke is professor of political studies and environmental and resource studies at Trent University, Peterborough, Ontario. The author of *Environmentalism and the Future of Progressive Politics* (1989), he is also the coeditor of *Managing Leviathan: Environmental Politics and the Administrative State* (1990). He is a founding editor of the Canadian journal *Alternatives: Perspectives on Society, Technology, and Environment.*

Walter A. Rosenbaum is professor of political science at the University of Florida. He is the author of *Environmental Politics and Policy, Second Edition* (CQ Press, 1991) and numerous other publications related to environmental and energy policy. He has also been a staff member and consultant to the U.S. Environmental Protection Agency, serving most recently as a special assistant to the assistant administrator for policy, planning, and evaluation from 1991 to 1992.

Marvin S. Soroos is professor and head of the Department of Political Science and Public Administration at North Carolina State University, where he teaches courses in global environmental law and policy. He is the coeditor of *The Global Predicament: Ecological Perspectives on World Order* (1979), coauthor of *The Environment in the Global Arena: Actors, Values, Politics, and Futures* (1985), and author of *Beyond Sovereignty: The Challenge of Global Sovereignty* (1986). He has chaired the Environmental Studies Section of the International Studies Association.

Richard J. Tobin is professor of political science at the State University of New York at Buffalo. His book, *The Expendable Future: U.S. Politics and the Protection of Biological Diversity*, received the Policy Studies Organization's Outstanding Book Award in 1991. During 1992-1993 he worked on the Environmental and Natural Resources Policy and Training Project of the U.S. Agency for International Development, which administers the U.S. foreign aid program in developing countries.

Norman J. Vig is professor of political science and codirector of the Technology and Policy Studies Program at Carleton College. He is the author of *Science and Technology in British Politics* (1968) and the coeditor and contributing author of *Politics in Advanced Nations* (1974),

Environmental Policy in the 1980s: Reagan's New Agenda (CQ Press, 1984), *Political Economy in Western Democracies* (1985), and *Technology and Politics* (1988). He served on the staff of Sen. Paul Wellstone (D-Minn.) in 1991.

Lettie M. Wenner teaches public law and public policy in the Department of Political Science at Northern Illinois University. She is the author of *One Environment Under Law* (1976), *The Environmental Decade in Court* (1982), and *U.S. Energy and Environmental Groups* (1990). She has written numerous articles and book chapters on air and water pollution, natural resources conservation, and other environmental issues. Her special interest is how federal courts oversee administrative discretion in environmental policy.

I. ENVIRONMENTAL POLICY AND POLITICS IN TRANSITION

1

Environmental Policy From the 1970s to the 1990s: Continuity and Change

Michael E. Kraft and Norman J. Vig

Environmental issues soared to a prominent place on the political agenda in the United States and other industrial nations in the early 1990s. In June 1992 the United Nations Conference on Environment and Development (the Earth summit) met in Río de Janeiro. The largest international conference ever held, it demonstrated the world's growing consensus on the importance of ecological problems. Environmental issues also played a highly visible role in the 1992 U.S. presidential campaign. George Bush, running for reelection, criticized environmentalists as extremists who were putting Americans out of work. The Democratic candidate, Bill Clinton, took a far more supportive stance on the environment, symbolized by his selection of Sen. Al Gore (D-Tenn.) as his running mate. The leading environmentalist in the U.S. Congress, Senator Gore was also author of the best-selling *Earth in the Balance*, in which he argued for making the "rescue of the environment the central organizing principle for civilization."[1]

On cursory examination, these recent developments resemble events of the 1970s, when rapidly rising public concern about threats to the environment and governments' eagerness to respond to this new political force initiated the "environmental decade." During the 1970s the United States, along with other industrial nations, adopted dozens of major environmental and resource policies, created new institutions such as the U.S. Environmental Protection Agency (EPA) to manage environmental programs, and greatly increased spending for them.[2] Under the Reagan administration, however, these programs were curtailed as the president adopted a conservative policy agenda that included deep cuts in the budgets of EPA and other agencies. That strategy ultimately failed as Congress, the courts, and the American public resisted efforts to weaken or reverse environmental policy.[3]

On closer examination, however, it is clear that the 1990s will not be a replay of either the 1970s or the 1980s. While we can expect to see some continuity in environmental policies over the next decade, they will require careful evaluation and a thoughtful search for more effective and efficient approaches. Industry, the Wise Use movement, and others will continue to be effective political opponents of environmental regulation,

3

despite broad-based public endorsement of environmental protection. Environmental organizations are not likely to receive unconditional support for their agenda, even within the Clinton administration.

Different kinds of environmental problems will make their way onto governmental agendas in the 1990s, and the political responses to them will, likewise, vary. For example, governments are ill-equipped to resolve many global environmental problems; hence, institutional reforms and new methods of decisionmaking are critical.[4] Some of the most promising innovations in U.S. environmental policy will occur at the state or regional level, reversing the pattern of the 1970s when Washington had to force the states to act. At all levels of government emphasis will be placed on integration, and balancing, of environmental protection and economic development.

In this chapter we examine the continuities and changes in environmental politics and policy over the past twenty-five years and speculate on their implications for the rest of the 1990s. We discuss policymaking, the development of environmental policies, and the performance of government institutions and political leadership, paying particular attention to the major programs adopted in the 1970s. Many of the broad questions explored in this introduction are addressed more fully in the chapters that follow.

The Role of Government and Politics

The increased political salience of environmental protection underscores the important role government plays in promoting solutions to the nation's and the world's mounting environmental ills. Global climate change, population growth, the spread of toxic and hazardous chemicals, loss of biological diversity, and air and water pollution each requires diverse actions by individuals and institutions at all levels of society and in both the public and private sectors. These range from scientific research and technological innovation to improved environmental education and significant changes in corporate and consumer behavior. As political scientists, we believe government has an indispensable role to play in environmental protection and improvement. The essays in this volume thus focus on environmental policies and the governmental institutions and political processes that affect them. Our goal is to illuminate that role and to suggest needed changes and strategies for achieving them.

The government plays a preeminent role because most environmental ills are *public problems*—they cannot be solved through purely private action. Although individuals and nongovernmental organizations can do much to protect environmental quality, as demonstrated by the impressive growth of grass-roots groups over the past decade, such efforts are often insufficient by themselves without the backing of public policy—for example, on control of toxic chemicals. Moreover, self-interested individuals and a free economic marketplace guided mainly by a concern for short-term profits create spillover effects, or "externalities," such as pollution. The character, scope, and urgency of environmental problems and the deficiencies in human institutions therefore necessitate large-scale collective action. Typically this means governmental policy—local, state, national, and international.

Political Institutions and Public Policy

Public policy is a course of governmental action or inaction in response to social problems. It is expressed in goals articulated by political leaders; in formal statutes, rules, and regulations; and in the practices of administrative agencies and courts charged with implementing or overseeing programs. Policy states an intent to achieve certain goals and objectives through a conscious choice of means, usually within some specified period. In a constitutional democracy like the United States, policymaking is distinctive in several respects: it must take place through constitutional processes, it requires the sanction of law, and it is binding on all members of society. Normally, the process is open to public scrutiny and debate, although secrecy may be justified in matters involving national security and diplomatic relations.

The constitutional requirements for policymaking were established more than two hundred years ago, and they remain much the same today. The U.S. political system is based on a division of authority among three branches of government and between the federal government and the states. Originally intended to limit government power and to protect individual liberty, this division of power may impede the ability of government to adopt timely and coherent environmental policy. Dedication to principles of federalism means that environmental policy responsibilities are distributed among the federal government, the fifty states, and thousands of local governments (chap. 3).

Responsibility for the environment is divided within the branches of the federal government as well, most notably in the U.S. Congress, with power shared between the House and Senate, and jurisdiction scattered among dozens of committees and subcommittees (table 1-1). The executive branch is also institutionally fragmented, with at least some responsibility for the environment and natural resources located in eleven cabinet departments and in EPA, the Nuclear Regulatory Commission, and other agencies (fig. 1-1, p. 8). Although most environmental policies are concentrated in EPA and in the Interior and Agriculture departments, the Department of Energy (DOE) and the State Department are increasingly important actors as well. Finally, the more than one hundred federal trial and appellate courts play key roles in interpreting environmental legislation and adjudicating disputes over administrative and regulatory actions (chap. 9).

Table 1-1   Major Congressional Committees With Environmental Responsibilities

Committee	Environmental Policy Jurisdiction
House	
Agriculture	agriculture in general, soil conservation, forestry, pesticide policy
Appropriations	appropriations for all programs
Energy and Commerce	Clean Air Act, nuclear waste policy, safe drinking water, Superfund, hazardous waste, and toxic substances
Merchant Marine and Fisheries	National Environmental Policy Act, oceanography and marine affairs, coastal zone management, fisheries and wildlife, wetlands
Natural Resources	public lands, national parks and forests, wilderness, energy, surface mining, nuclear waste policy
Public Works and Transportation	water pollution, rivers and harbors, oil pollution, water power
Science, Space, and Technology	environmental research and development, energy research, science and environmental issues
Senate	
Agriculture, Nutrition, and Forestry	agriculture in general, soil conservation, forestry, pesticide policy
Appropriations	appropriations for all programs
Commerce, Science, and Transportation	coastal zone management; marine fisheries; oceans, weather, and atmospheric activities; technology research and development
Energy and Natural Resources	energy policy in general, nuclear waste policy, mining, national parks and recreation areas, wilderness, wild and scenic rivers
Environment and Public Works	air, water, and noise pollution; toxic and hazardous materials; Superfund; nuclear waste policy; fisheries and wildlife; ocean dumping, solid waste disposal; environmental policy and research in general

The implications of this constitutional arrangement were evident in the 1980s as Congress and the courts checked and balanced the Reagan administration's efforts to reverse the environmental policies of the previous decade. More generally, divided authority produces slow and incremental alterations in policy, typically after broad consultation and agreement among diverse interests both within and outside of government. Such political interaction and accommodation of interests enhance the overall legitimacy of the resulting public policies. Over time, however, the cumulative effect has been disjointed policies that fall short of ecological or holistic principles of policy design.

Nonetheless, when issues are highly visible, the public is supportive, and political leaders act cohesively, the American political system has proved flexible enough to permit substantial policy innovations.[5] As we shall see, this was the case in the early to mid 1970s, when Congress enacted major changes in U.S. environmental policy, and in the mid 1980s, when Congress overrode objections of the Reagan administration and greatly strengthened policies on hazardous waste and water quality, among others. Passage of the monumental Clean Air Act Amendments of 1990 was a more recent example of the same alignment of forces.

Policy Processes: Agendas, Streams, and Cycles

Several models are available for analyzing how issues get on the political agenda and move through the policy processes of government. These theoretical frameworks are useful in explicating both long-term policy trends and short-term cycles of action and response. One set of essential questions concerns *agenda setting*: how do new problems emerge as political issues demanding the government's attention, and why do some important problems fail to achieve such recognition? For example, why did the federal government initiate controls on industrial pollution in the 1960s and early 1970s but do little about national energy issues until well into the 1970s?

There are several hurdles to overcome in an issue's rise to prominence: it must first gain societal recognition as a problem, often in response to demographic, technological, or other social changes; then get on the docket of governmental institutions, usually through the exercise of organized group pressure; and finally it must receive enough attention by governmental actors to reach the stage of decisional or policy action.[6] An issue is not likely to reach this latter stage unless conditions are ripe (for example, a "triggering event" that focuses public opinion sharply). One model analyzes agenda setting according to the convergence of three "streams" that flow through the political system—problems, policies, and politics. Although largely independent of one another, these streams can be brought together at critical times when "policy entrepreneurs" are able to take advantage of the moment and make the case for policy action.[7]

Figure 1-1   Major Executive Branch Agencies With Environmental Responsibilities

President

The Executive Office of the President

White House Office	Council on Environmental Quality	Office of Management and Budget
Overall policy Agency coordination	Environmental policy coordination Oversight of the National Environmental Policy Act Environmental quality reporting	Budget Agency coordination and management

Environmental Protection Agency	Dept. of the Interior	Dept. of Agriculture	Dept. of Commerce	Dept. of State
Air & water pollution Pesticides Radiation Solid waste Superfund Toxic substances	Public lands Energy Minerals National parks	Forestry Soil conservation	Oceanic and atmospheric monitoring and research	International environment

Dept. of Justice	Dept. of Defense	Dept. of Energy	Dept. of Transportation	Dept. of Housing and Urban Development
Environmental litigation	Civil works construction Dredge & fill permits Pollution control from defense facilities	Energy policy coordination Nuclear waste disposal R & D	Mass transit Roads Airplane noise Oil pollution	Housing Urban parks Urban planning

Dept. of Health and Human Services	Dept. of Labor	Nuclear Regulatory Commission	Tennessee Valley Authority
Health	Occupational health	Licensing and regulating nuclear power	Electric power generation

Source: Council on Environmental Quality, *Environmental Quality, Sixteenth Annual Report of the Council on Environmental Quality* (Washington, D.C.: U.S. Government Printing Office, 1987).

Once an issue is on the agenda, it must pass through several more stages in the policy process. These stages are often referred to as the *policy cycle.* Although terminology varies, most students of public policy delineate at least five stages of policy development beyond *agenda setting:* these are (1) *policy formulation* (the actual design and drafting of policy goals and strategies for achieving them), (2) *policy legitimation* (mobilization of political support and formal enactment by law or other means), (3) *policy implementation* (provision of institutional resources and detailed administration of policy), (4) *policy evaluation* (measurement of results in relation to goals and costs), and (5) *policy termination or change* (modification of goals or means).[8] The policy cycle model is useful because it emphasizes all phases of policymaking. For example, how well a law is implemented is as important as the goals and motivations of those who drafted and enacted the legislation. The concept also suggests the continuous nature of the policy process: no policy decision or solution is "final" because changing conditions, new information, and shifting opinions will require policy reevaluation and revision. Other short-term forces and events, such as presidential elections or environmental accidents, can also profoundly affect the course of policy over its life-cycle. Thus, policy at any given time is shaped by the interaction of long-term social, economic, technological, and political forces and short-term fluctuations in the political climate. All of these factors are manifest in the development of environmental policy.

The Development of Environmental Policy From the 1970s to the 1990s

As implied in the policy cycle model, the history of environmental policy in the United States is not one of continuous improvement in human relations with the natural environment. Rather, it is one of fits and starts, with significant discontinuities, particularly since the late 1960s. It can be understood, to borrow from the concept of agenda setting, as the product of the convergence or divergence of two political currents, one that is deep and long term and the other shallow and short term.

Social Values and Environmental Policy Commitments

The deep political current consists of fundamental changes in American values that began after World War II, changes that accelerated as the nation shifted from an industrial to a postindustrial (or postmaterialist) society. Preoccupation with the economy (and national security) has gradually given way to a new set of concerns that includes quality-of-life issues like the environment.[9] These changes suggest that in the coming decades ecological issues will replace, or be integrated with, many traditional political, economic, and social issues, both domestically and internationally.

This integration was evident at the 1992 Earth summit and its concern about sustainable development. It is also championed in *Our Common Future*, an influential report by the World Commission on Environment and Development.[10] Samuel Hays, a historian, describes these changes as a social evolutionary process affecting all segments of American society. Political scientist Robert Paehlke, the author of chapter 16 in this volume, characterizes environmentalism as a new ideology with the potential to alter conventional political alignments.[11] These long-term social forces are setting a new direction for the political agenda.

The shallow political current consists of shorter-term political and economic forces—presidential elections, business cycles, and energy supply shocks—that may alter the salience of environmental issues. These short-term developments may either reinforce or weaken the long-term trends in society that support environmental protection. For example, in the early 1970s the deep and shallow currents converged to produce an enormous outpouring of federal environmental legislation. Yet later in the decade energy shortages and high inflation led the Carter administration to pull back from some of its environmental commitments. The election of Ronald Reagan in 1980 shifted the environmental policy agenda sharply to the right for much of the 1980s. But the two currents converged once again in the early 1990s at the beginning of the Clinton administration.

Thus, the interaction of these two currents helps to explain the fluctuations in environmental policy commitments from one year, or decade, to the next. Over time, however, one can see the continuity of strong public support for environmental protection, expanding government authority, and increasingly effective policy implementation—even if scarce resources limit success. But the near-term discontinuities capture our attention. We focus here on the major changes from 1969 to 1992; the future agenda for environmental politics and policy will be discussed at the conclusion of the book.

Pre-1969 Policies

Until 1969 the federal government played a sharply limited role in environmental policymaking, although public land management was a major exception. For nearly a century Congress had set aside portions of the public domain for preservation as national parks, forests, grazing lands, recreation areas, and wildlife refuges. The "multiple use" and "sustained yield" doctrines that grew out of the conservation movement at the turn of the century ensured that this national trust would contribute to economic growth under the stewardship of the Interior and Agriculture departments. Steady progress was also made, however, in managing the lands in the public interest and protecting them from development.[12] After several years of debate, Congress passed the Wilderness Act of 1964 to preserve some of the remaining forest lands in pristine condition, "untrammeled by man's presence." At the same time it approved the Land and Water Conservation Fund Act of 1964 to fund federal purchases of land for conservation purposes.

During the mid 1960s the United States also began a major effort to reduce world population growth in developing nations through financial aid for foreign population programs, chiefly family planning and population research. President Lyndon B. Johnson and congressional sponsors of the programs tied them explicitly to a concern for "growing scarcity in world resources."[13]

Agenda Setting for the 1970s

Despite this longtime concern for resource conservation and land management, federal environmental policy was only slowly extended to control of industrial pollution and human waste. Air and water pollution were long considered a strictly local matter, and they were not high on the national agenda until the 1970s. In a very early federal action the Refuse Act of 1899 required individuals who wanted to dump refuse into navigable waters to obtain a permit from the Army Corps of Engineers; however, the corps largely ignored the pollution aspects of the act.[14] After World War II policies to control the most obvious forms of pollution were gradually developed at the local, state, and federal levels. With passage of the Water Pollution Control Act of 1948, the federal government began assisting local authorities in building sewage treatment plants, and it initiated a limited program for air pollution research in 1955. Following the Clean Air Act of 1963 and amendments to the water pollution law, Washington began prodding the states to set pollution abatement standards and to formulate implementation plans based on federal guidelines.[15]

The first Earth Day was April 22, 1970. Nationwide "teach-ins" about environmental problems demonstrated ecology's new place on the nation's social and political agendas. With an increasingly affluent and well-educated society placing new emphasis on the quality of life, concern for environmental protection grew apace, and was evident across all groups in the population, if not necessarily to the same degree.[16] The effect was a broadly based public demand for more vigorous and comprehensive federal action to prevent environmental degradation. In an almost unprecedented fashion a new environmental policy agenda rapidly emerged. Policymakers viewed the newly visible environmental issues as politically attractive and eagerly supported tough new measures, even when their full impacts and costs were unknown. As a result, laws were quickly enacted and implemented throughout the 1970s, but with growing concern over their effect on the economy and increasing realization that administrative agencies lacked the resources and the capacity to assume their new responsibilities.

Congress set the stage for the spurt in policy innovation at the end of 1969 when it passed the National Environmental Policy Act (NEPA). The act declared that,

> it is the continuing policy of the Federal Government, in cooperation with State and local governments, and other concerned public and private organizations, to use all practicable means and measures, including financial and technical assistance, in a manner calculated to foster and promote the general welfare, to create and maintain conditions under which man and nature can exist in productive harmony, and fulfill the social, economic, and other requirements of present and future generations of Americans.[17]

The law required detailed environmental impact statements for all major federal actions and established the Council on Environmental Quality (CEQ) to advise the president and Congress on environmental matters. President Richard Nixon then seized the initiative by signing NEPA as his first official act of 1970 and proclaiming the 1970s as the "environmental decade." In February 1970 he sent a special message to Congress calling for a new law to control air pollution. The race was on as the White House and congressional leaders vied for environmentalists' support.

Policy Escalation in the 1970s

By the spring of 1970 rising public concern about the environment galvanized the Ninety-first Congress to action. Sen. Edmund Muskie (D-Maine), then the leading Democratic hopeful for the presidential nomination in 1972, emerged as the dominant policy entrepreneur for environmental protection issues. As chair of the Senate Public Works Committee, he formulated proposals that went well beyond those favored by the president. Following a process of policy escalation, both houses of Congress approved the stronger measures and set the tone for environmental policymaking for much of the 1970s. Congress had frequently played a more dominant role than the president in initiating environmental policies, and that pattern continued in the 1970s, particularly because the Democratic party controlled Congress during the Nixon and Ford presidencies. Although support for environmental protection was bipartisan, Democrats provided more leadership on the issue in Congress and were more likely to vote for strong environmental policy provisions than were Republicans.[18]

The increase in new federal legislation in the next decade was truly remarkable, especially since policymaking in American politics is normally incremental. Appendix 1 lists the major environmental policies enacted between 1969 and 1992. They are arranged by presidential administration primarily to show a pattern of significant policy development throughout the period, not to attribute chief responsibility for the various bills to the particular presidents. These landmark measures covered air and water pollution control (the latter enacted in 1972 over a presidential veto), pesticide regulation, endangered species protection, control of hazardous and toxic chemicals, ocean and coastline protection, better stewardship of public lands, requirements for restoration of strip-mined lands, the setting aside of more than 100 million acres of Alaskan wilderness for varying degrees of protection, and the creation of a "Superfund" for cleaning up toxic waste sites.

There were other signs of commitment to environmental policy goals as Congress and a succession of presidential administrations through Jimmy Carter's cooperated on conservation issues. For example, the area designated as national wilderness (excluding Alaska) more than doubled, from 10 million acres in 1970 to more than 23 million acres in 1980. Seventy-five units, totaling some 2.5 million acres, were added to the National Park Service in the same period. The National Wildlife Refuge System grew similarly. Throughout the 1970s the Land and Water Conservation Fund, financed primarily through royalties from offshore oil and gas leasing, was used to purchase additional private land for park development, wildlife refuges, and national forests.

The government's enthusiasm for environmental and conservation policy did not extend to all issues on the environmentalists' agenda. Two cases of note are population policy and energy policy. The Commission on Population Growth and the American Future recommended in 1972 that the nation should "welcome and plan for a stabilized population," but the advice was ignored. Birth rates in the United States were declining and the issue was politically controversial. Despite occasional reports that highlighted the role of population growth, such as the *Global 2000 Report to the President* in 1980, the issue remained more or less dormant over the next two decades.[19]

For energy issues the dominant pattern was policy gridlock, not neglect. Here the connection to environmental policy was clearer to policymakers than it had been on population growth. Indeed, opposition to antipollution programs as well as land preservation came primarily from conflicting demands for energy production in the aftermath of the Arab oil embargo in 1973. The Nixon, Ford, and Carter administrations all attempted to formulate national policies for achieving "energy independence" by increasing energy supplies, with Carter's efforts by far the most sustained and comprehensive. Carter also emphasized conservation and environmental safeguards. For the most part, however, none of their efforts were successful. No consensus on national energy policy emerged among the public or in Congress, and presidential leadership was insufficient to overcome these basic constraints, although a national energy policy bill of limited scope was enacted in 1992 (chap. 5).[20]

Nevertheless, important changes in energy policy were enacted in the 1970s. These included removal of some price controls on oil and

natural gas, creation of modest incentives for conservation, and requirements that state utility regulators find ways to encourage conservation and
the use of renewable energy sources.[21] President Carter also formulated a
national policy for permanent geologic disposal of high-level radioactive
waste from nuclear power plants, which was submitted to Congress in
1980 and enacted during the Reagan presidency in late 1982. Congress
and both presidents hoped that the waste disposal policy would brighten
the otherwise dismal prospects for further development of nuclear energy.
By early 1993 it had largely failed to do so, and the near-term outlook for
resolving conflicts over nuclear waste is not promising.

Congress maintained its strong commitment to environmental policy
throughout the 1970s, even as the salience of these issues for the public
seemed to wane. For example, it strengthened the Clean Air Act of 1970
and the Clean Water Act of 1972 by amending them in 1977. Yet concerns over the impact of environmental regulation on the economy and
specific objections to implementation of the new laws, particularly the
Clean Air Act, began creating a backlash of sorts by the end of the Carter
administration.

The Reagan Interlude

The Reagan presidency brought to the federal government a very
different environmental policy agenda (chap. 4). Virtually all environmental protection and resource policies enacted during the 1970s were reeval-
uated in light of the president's desire to reduce the scope of government
regulation, shift responsibilities to the states, and rely more on the private
sector. Confidence in the efficacy of "environmental deregulation" was
predicated on the dubious assumption that enforcement of environmental
laws had a major adverse impact on the economy.[22] Whatever the merits
of Reagan's new policy agenda, it was put into effect through a risky
strategy that relied on ideologically committed presidential appointees to
the EPA and the Agriculture, Interior, and Energy departments, and on
sharp cutbacks in budgets for environmental programs.

Congress initially cooperated with President Reagan, particularly in
approving budget cuts, but it soon reverted to its accustomed advocacy of
existing environmental policy, frequently criticizing the president's management of the EPA and the Interior Department under Anne Gorsuch
Burford and James Watt, respectively; both Burford and Watt were forced
to resign by the end of 1983. Among Congress's most notable achievements of the 1980s were its strengthening of the Resource Conservation
and Recovery Act (1984), Superfund (1986), the Safe Drinking Water
Act (1986), and the Clean Water Act (1987) (app. 1). It was less successful in overcoming policy gridlock on acid rain legislation, the Clean Air
Act, and the nation's pesticides law (chap. 5). Only in the late 1980s did
energy policy issues reappear on the congressional agenda, as concern

mounted over the threat of global climate change. The same pattern of policy neglect and rediscovery characterized many other international environmental issues.

As we will show, budget cuts and the weakening of environmental institutions took a serious toll in the 1980s. Yet even the determined efforts of a popular president could not halt the long-term progress of environmental policy. Public support for environmental improvement, the driving force for policy development in the 1970s, increased markedly during the Reagan presidency and represented a striking rejection of the president's agenda by the American public.[23]

Paradoxically, Reagan actually strengthened environmental forces in the nation. Through his lax enforcement of pollution laws and prodevelopment resource policies, he created political issues around which national and grass-roots environmental groups could organize. They appealed successfully to a public that was increasingly disturbed by the health and environmental risks of industrial society and by threats to ecological stability. As a result, membership in environmental organizations soared and a new grass-roots activism developed, creating further political incentives for environmental activism at all levels of government (chap. 2).

By the fall of 1989 there was little mistaking congressional enthusiasm for continuing the advance of environmental policy into the 1990s. Especially in his first two years, President George Bush was eager as well to adopt a more positive environmental policy agenda than his predecessor. Bush's White House, however, was deeply divided on the issue for both ideological and economic reasons. The EPA under Bush's appointee, William K. Reilly, fought continuously with the president's conservative advisers in the White House over the pace and stringency of environmental regulations. By 1992 Bush had lost much of the support of environmentalists he had courted in 1989 and 1990 (chap. 4).

Institutional Development and Policy Implementation

Aside from the enactment of landmark environmental policies in the 1970s and 1980s, there were important institutional developments that were equally essential to effective policy implementation.

Institutionalizing Environmental Protection in the 1970s

The most notable institutional development in the 1970s was the establishment of the EPA by President Richard M. Nixon in December 1970. Created as an independent agency that would report directly to the president, it brought together environmental responsibilities that had previously been scattered among dozens of offices and programs. Under its first administrator, William Ruckelshaus, the agency's legislative mandate grew rapidly as a consequence of the policy process summarized earlier, and it acquired many new programs, offices, and staffs. The EPA's budget (excluding construction grants for sewage treatment plants) grew from about $500 million in 1973 to $1.3 billion in 1980; full-time employees increased from 8,200 to 10,600, with two-thirds of them in the agency's ten regional offices. Even with its expanded budget and staff, the nation's leading environmental agency found it increasingly difficult by 1980 to meet new program obligations with available resources.

During the 1970s virtually every federal agency was forced to develop some capabilities for environmental analysis under NEPA, which required that environmental impact statements (EISs) be prepared for all "major federal actions significantly affecting the quality of the human environment." Detailed requirements for the statements were set out by the Council on Environmental Quality and enforced in the courts. Provisions for public hearings and citizen participation allowed environmental and community groups to challenge administrative decisions, often by filing legal suits questioning the adequacy of the impact statements. In response to these potential objections, agencies changed their project designs—sometimes dramatically. Even the Army Corps of Engineers, which had often been castigated by environmentalists, learned to adapt.[24] Although the EIS process was roundly criticized (indeed, it was revised in 1979 to focus more sharply on crucial issues), most studies show that it forced greater environmental awareness and more careful planning in many agencies.[25]

Established natural resource agencies, such as Agriculture's Forest Service and Interior's Bureau of Land Management, generally made the transition to better environmental planning more easily. Long-standing doctrines of multiple use and strong professional norms of land management were gradually adapted to serve new environmental goals and interests. Wilderness preservation, never a dominant purpose of these agencies, came to be accepted as part of their mission.

Both in their compliance with new environmental laws and in their adjustment to democratic norms of open decisionmaking and citizen participation in the 1970s, some agencies and departments lagged seriously behind others. Perhaps the most striking case is the Department of Energy. Following a series of news reports on severe environmental contamination at DOE nuclear weapons production facilities, Secretary of Energy James Watkins acknowledged in 1989 the department's "years of inattention to changing standards and demands regarding the environment, safety, and health." He went on to announce initiatives intended to strengthen environmental protection at DOE facilities and to restore public confidence in the department. DOE estimates the cost of cleaning up its seventeen principal weapons plants and laboratories at more than $200 billion, spread over the next thirty years.[26] The Department of Energy's record stands as a particularly clear example of the long-term costs of environmental neglect.

Successive administrations also gave modest support to the development of international environmental institutions. The United States played an active role in convening the United Nations Conference on the Human Environment held in Stockholm, Sweden, in June 1972. This conference, attended by delegations from 113 countries and 400 other organizations, addressed for the first time the environmental problems of developing nations. The result was the creation of the United Nations Environment Programme (UNEP), headquartered in Nairobi, Kenya. Although it disagreed with some of UNEP's initiatives, the United States provided the largest share (36 percent) of its budget between 1972 and 1980.[27]

Environmental Relief and Reform in the 1980s

By the time President Reagan assumed office in 1981, the effort to improve environmental quality at federal and state levels had been institutionalized, though not without a good many problems, requiring both statutory change and administrative reform. Implementation often lagged years behind schedule because much of the legislation of the 1970s overestimated the speed with which new technologies could be developed and applied. The laws also underestimated compliance costs and the difficulty of writing standards for hundreds of major industries. As regulated industries sought to block implementation and environmental organizations tried to speed it up, frequent legal challenges compounded the backlog. Other delays were caused by personnel and budgetary shortages, scientific and technical uncertainties, and the need for extensive consultation with other federal agencies, Congress, and state governments.[28]

As a result of these difficulties, an extensive agenda for reforming environmental policies emerged by 1980. It was, however, largely unaddressed by the Reagan administration, which was more concerned with providing short-term regulatory relief to industry.[29] The president's neglect of policy reform was exacerbated by his reliance on an administrative strategy that J. Clarence Davies described as "designed largely to reverse the institutionalization process" begun in the 1970s. This was accomplished through sharp budgetary reductions, weakening of the authority of experienced professionals in environmental agencies, and elimination or restructuring of many offices, particularly at EPA.[30] Staff morale and EPA credibility suffered under the leadership of Anne Burford, although both improved to some extent under administrators William Ruckelshaus and Lee Thomas in the Reagan administration and William Reilly in the Bush administration. Nevertheless, the damage done in the early 1980s was considerable and long lasting. At the end of the Reagan presidency in January 1989, environmentalists still complained that there was no policy leadership at EPA and that little had been done to "restore the momentum of environmental protection."[31]

They also criticized Reagan for failing to pursue regulatory reform, saying he "blew the chance to streamline regulations and use marketplace incentives in an honest way to speed up environmental progress, lower regulatory costs, and foster economic growth." Business groups remained dissatisfied with what they believed was still an unnecessarily expensive and rigid system of federal environmental regulation. And even conservative critics expressed disappointment with what the Heritage Foundation termed a "squandered" opportunity to reform environmental protection laws and reduce their cost.[32] Many of the same reform issues, such as risk-based priority setting and use of market incentives to supplement regulation, continue to be discussed in the 1990s (chaps. 6, 9, and 10).

Institutional Capacity: Environmental Agency Budgets and Policy Implementation

As we try to assess the degree to which environmental quality might improve as a result of present laws and to consider the ability of government to meet the ecological challenges of the 1990s, there is little that is more important than budgets. Although spending more public money does not guarantee policy success, drastic cuts can severely undermine established programs. It is apparent that the massive cuts in environmental funding during the early 1980s have had long-term negative effects on the government's ability to implement environmental policies.

In constant 1987 dollars, the total authorized by the federal government for natural resource and environmental programs fell from $17.9 billion in 1980 to between $12 and $15 billion per year for most of the 1980s before rising again to about $17 billion for fiscal 1993 (app. 2). The declines were steeper in some areas, particularly pollution control, where spending fell by 46 percent between 1980 and 1986, and then rose modestly in the late 1980s and early 1990s. By 1993 pollution control budgets (in constant dollars) were still about 13 percent *lower* than they had been in 1980.

To be sure, overall spending on environmental programs increased substantially from the early 1970s to the early 1990s. In constant dollars, spending rose by some 85 percent (app. 2). Yet the same period saw the enactment of virtually all the major environmental laws. Thus, despite the rise in spending, funding often fell short of what was needed to implement these policies and to achieve the environmental quality goals they embodied.

These constraints can be seen in the budgets and staffs of environmental and natural resource agencies (apps. 3 and 4). In constant dollars, EPA's operating budget in FY 1993 (the funds available to implement its programs) was only 21 percent higher than it was in FY 1975, despite the important new responsibilities given to the agency by Congress. The picture would be far bleaker if President Bush had not increased that budget by more than 50 percent and EPA's staff by about 22 percent during his term of office. Even with these increases, the staff in 1993 (excluding Superfund employees) was only slightly larger than it had been in the last year of the Carter administration in 1980.

A particularly vivid case of declining institutional capacity to implement and oversee environmental policy can be seen in the Council on Environmental Quality. In constant 1987 dollars, CEQ's budget dropped by 86 percent between 1975 and 1985 (app. 3). For all practical purposes, the council had ceased to exist for most of the 1980s as its staff declined from fifty-nine employees in 1980 to thirteen in 1983. It was barely able to produce its mandated annual report on the nation's environmental quality, running several years behind schedule with a much briefer report than those submitted in earlier years. Its budget and staff increased significantly under President Bush. Yet by 1993 CEQ's budget in constant dollars remained at less than half its 1975 level; its staff had risen only to thirty. Shortly after taking office, President Clinton proposed abolishing the council and replacing it with a White House Office of Environmental Policy.

The picture is more mixed for the natural resource agencies. The Bureau of Land Management, the Army Corps of Engineers, and the Forest Service all suffered stagnant or declining budgets (in constant dollars) during the 1980s and early 1990s (app. 3). In contrast, the Fish and Wildlife Service, the Office of Surface Mining, and the National Park Service enjoyed some budget increases during the 1980s, although these leveled off or declined slightly in the 1990s. There is little question that limited budgets and staff have severely affected the ability of many agencies to implement environmental policy over the past two decades. They are likely to be significant constraints over the next decade as well.

Improvement in Environmental Quality and Its Cost

It is difficult, both conceptually and empirically, to measure the success or failure of environmental policies (chap. 8). Yet one of the most important tests of any public policy is whether it achieves its stated objectives. For environmental policy, we should ask if air and water quality are improving, hazardous waste sites are being cleaned up, and wilderness areas are adequately protected. Unfortunately, there is no simple way to answer those questions.

Measuring Environmental Conditions and Trends

Environmental policies entail long-term commitments to broad social values and goals that are not easily quantified. Short-term and highly visible costs are easier to measure than long-term, diffuse, and intangible benefits, and these differences often lead to intense debates over the value of environmental programs.

Variable and often unreliable monitoring of environmental conditions and inconsistent collection of data over time also make it difficult to assess environmental trends. The time period selected for a given analysis can seriously affect the results, and many scholars discount data collected prior to the mid 1970s as unreliable. To improve monitoring, data collection, and analysis, some have proposed a new and independent Bureau of Environmental Statistics to handle these important activities, which are now assigned to the Council on Environmental Quality under NEPA.[33]

Despite these limitations on measuring environmental conditions and trends, it is nevertheless useful to review a variety of available indicators of environmental quality. They tell us at least something about what we have achieved or failed to achieved after more than twenty years of national environmental protection policy.[34]

Air quality. Perhaps the best data on changes in the environment can be found for air quality, although disagreement exists over which measures and time periods are most appropriate. Paul Portney, using data the EPA considers the most reliable for such trend analysis, reports that for the years 1978 through 1987, particulate levels fell on average by about 21 percent, lead concentrations by 88 percent, sulfur dioxide by 35 percent, and carbon monoxide by 25 percent. Improvement was not as marked for concentrations of nitrogen dioxide (12 percent decline) and ozone (9 percent decline).[35] Taken together, these reductions are impressive, especially so in light of the growth between 1970 and 1990 in the U.S. population (25 percent), the number of automobiles in use (59 percent), and in economic activity (nearly 100 percent, adjusted for inflation).[36]

Consistent with these achievements, the EPA notes that the number of unhealthful days due to air pollution has declined significantly in most parts of the country, which it attributes in part to new pollution controls on automobiles and cleaner fuels mandated by the Clean Air Act. The results offer some justification for the estimated $35 billion spent per year (largely by the private sector) to improve air quality.

The EPA reported in late 1992 (using data from 1989 to 1991) that some 86 million Americans still lived in so-called nonattainment areas, which exceeded federal ozone standards at least once a year, and that fifty-six urban areas failed to meet standards for ozone and twenty-nine for carbon monoxide. These figures were much lower than in reports over the past few years, which found more than one hundred urban areas exceeding the ozone standard. In part the decline was the result of cooler weather in 1991 and reduced industrial activity.[37] Hence the figures may rise again as the economy picks up and as temperatures return to normal levels.

How serious are the failures to meet federal standards? In some cities, such as Los Angeles, the impact on human health is considerable.

In the late 1980s Los Angeles violated federal health standards for ozone
on 137 days a year on average, and ozone concentrations were sometimes
nearly triple the maximum permissible federal level. In comparison, New
York, the fourth most polluted city in the nation, violated ozone standards
only 17 days a year.[38] Moreover, in most cities standards may be exceeded
by only a small amount, posing a far lower health risk than that in Los
Angeles. Air quality improvement has therefore been substantial in most
parts of the nation, even if problem areas remain.

One of those problems is toxic or hazardous air pollutants, which
have been associated with cancer, respiratory diseases, and other chronic
and acute illnesses. The EPA has been extremely slow to regulate these
pollutants, and set federal standards for only seven of them by mid 1989.
Public and congressional concern over toxic emissions led Congress to
mandate more aggressive action in the 1986 Superfund amendments.
The amendments required manufacturers of more than three hundred
different chemicals to report annually to the EPA (and the states in which
they operate) the amounts of those substances released to the air, water,
or land. The EPA's Toxics Release Inventory shows that in 1989 some
22,000 companies released 5.7 billion pounds of hazardous substances to
the environment, including 2.4 billion pounds of toxic chemicals emitted
into the air.[39] The publicity generated by these reports has galvanized
environmentalists in many communities. The information has also led
many of the nation's largest chemical companies, such as Dow and
Monsanto, as well as other industrial enterprises, to promise greatly reduced emissions of toxic chemicals. In 1990 Congress stiffened regulation
of toxic air pollutants to speed such changes when it rewrote the Clean
Air Act. Less tangible progress, however, has been made in other areas of
pollution control.

Water quality. With some notable exceptions, the nation's water quality does not appear to have improved significantly since 1972 despite
cumulative expenditures by government and the private sector of some
$540 billion. Although monitoring data are less adequate for water quality
than for air quality, the available evidence shows that most rivers, streams,
lakes, and estuaries maintained their quality, and a smaller number improved (in many cases strikingly so). About 25 percent of the nation's
lakes declined in quality between 1972 and 1982.[40] Prevention of further
degradation of water quality in the face of a growing population and
strong economic growth could be considered an important achievement,
yet it clearly falls short of the goals of federal clean water acts.

Most of the effort since 1972 has been expended on conventional
point sources of water pollutants (where a particular source is identifiable), and most industries and municipalities have greatly reduced their
discharges consistent with the intent of the Clean Water Act. Increasing
emphasis on toxic pollutants and nonpoint sources such as agricultural
runoff (the regulation of which is required by the Clean Water Act

Amendments of 1987) is likely in the 1990s. To date almost no progress has been made in halting groundwater contamination despite passage of the Safe Drinking Water Act of 1974 and the Resource Conservation and Recovery Act (RCRA) of 1976 and their later amendments.

Toxic and hazardous wastes. Progress in dealing with hazardous wastes and other toxic chemicals has been the least satisfactory of all pollution control programs. Implementation of the major laws has been extraordinarily slow owing to the extent and complexity of the problems, scientific uncertainty, litigation by industry, public fear of siting treatment and storage facilities nearby, budgetary limitations, and poor management and lax enforcement by EPA. As a result, gains have been quite modest to date judged by the most common measures. For example, by May 1992 only 84 sites had been cleaned up out of 1,245 on the Superfund National Priorities List (NPL). However, cleanup activities were under way at several hundred additional sites, and progress could be found in the number of sites identified and assessed and in scientific research and technological development.[41]

These limited achievements come at a high price. The EPA currently spends $25 to $30 million per NPL site remediated, with unclear and disputed benefits. Realistic estimates for cleanup of the tens of thousands of hazardous waste sites nationwide range from $484 billion to more than $1 trillion, with the job expected to take three to five decades to complete.[42]

The EPA has set a sluggish pace in the related area of testing toxic chemicals. For example, under a 1972 law mandating control of pesticides and herbicides, only a handful of chemicals used to manufacture the 50,000 pesticides in use in the United States has received full testing or retesting.

The track record over the past fifteen years on these programs clearly suggests the need for reevaluation of federal policy. Congress partially addressed that need in its revision of the Superfund program in 1986, and both government and industry have experimented with promising new approaches on toxic chemicals and hazardous waste (chap. 11).

Natural resources. Significant achievements have been more evident in the protection of natural resources than in pollution control. Between 1970 and 1987 the number of acres of national parks increased by 169 percent (most of it by 1980) and the number of miles of wild and scenic rivers increased by 788 percent. Similarly, the National Wilderness Preservation System increased in total acres by 786 percent from 1970 to 1987, the largest part added in Alaska. By 1989, twenty-five years after passage of the Wilderness Act of 1964, more than 90 million acres of wilderness had been set aside. By 1989 the National Forest System consisted of 191 million acres, of which more than 32 million acres were protected as wilderness.[43]

Other trends in natural resources are much less encouraging. The United States loses an estimated 300,000 acres a year of marshes, swamps, and other ecologically important wetlands to development. Protection of biological diversity through the Endangered Species Act (ESA) has produced only moderate signs of success. After twenty years, only about seven hundred species have been listed as endangered or threatened, although over the past decade the government has added about fifty new species per year to the list. Scores of critical habitats have been designated, and a number of recovery plans have been put into effect, but only a few endangered species have recovered.

Insufficient budgets and staffs slow the process. For these and other reasons, the Fish and Wildlife Service (FWS) failed to protect hundreds of species even where substantial evidence existed to document threats to their existence. Some three thousand species are currently candidates for inclusion on the list, but at the current pace of review, it would take at least twenty-five years to decide their status. Development of recovery plans to protect all of those species would cost an estimated $460 million per year over the next ten years, or about eight times the annual budget of the FWS.[44] An evaluation of the ESA by the National Academy of Sciences is due in 1993 as Congress considers renewal of the increasingly controversial act.

Assessment. The nation made impressive gains between 1970 and 1992 in controlling many conventional pollutants and in expanding parks, wilderness areas, and other protected public lands. Despite some setbacks in the 1980s, progress on environmental quality continues, even if it is highly uneven. In the future, however, further advances will be more difficult, costly, and controversial. This is largely because the easy problems have already been addressed, and at this point marginal gains in air and water quality will cost more per unit of improvement than in the past (chap. 9). Moreover, second-generation environmental threats such as toxic chemicals, hazardous wastes, and nuclear wastes are proving even more challenging than regulating "bulk" air and water pollutants in the 1970s. In these cases substantial progress may not be evident for years to come, and it will be expensive.

The same is true for the third generation of ecological problems, such as global climate change and protection of biodiversity. Solutions require an unprecedented degree of cooperation among nations and substantial improvement in institutional capacity for data collection, research, and analysis as well as policy development and implementation. Hence, success is likely to come slowly as national and international commitments to environmental protection grow and capabilities improve. Some long-standing problems, such as rapid population growth, will continue to be addressed primarily within nation-states, even though the staggering effects on natural resources and environmental quality are felt worldwide. In 1992 the Earth's population of 5.5 billion was increasing at 1.7 percent (or 93 million people) per year, with continued growth expected for another hundred years or more (chap. 13).

The Costs and Benefits of Environmental Protection

The costs and benefits of environmental protection have been vigorously debated in the past decade. Critics believe that the kinds of improvements cited above are often not worth the considerable costs, particularly when regulations adversely affect economic growth and employment or restrict technological development. Advocates point, however, to the improvements in public health, the protection of "priceless" natural amenities such as wilderness areas and clean lakes, and the preservation of biological diversity, convinced that these are well worth the investment of governmental and private funds.

Skepticism about environmental policies led to several attempts in the 1980s and early 1990s under presidents Reagan and Bush to impose regulatory oversight by the White House. It was hoped that costs could be limited by subjecting proposed regulations to cost-benefit analysis (chaps. 4 and 9). The imposition of these controls, most recently by the White House Council on Competitiveness under Vice President Dan Quayle, sharpened debate over the costs and benefits of environmental policies. In January 1993 President Clinton abolished the council by executive order two days after taking office and announced that Vice President Al Gore would be given new authority for regulatory oversight. By this action the president signaled his intention to close what had become a "back door" for business interests seeking to overturn what they saw as excessively costly environmental and other regulations.

The impetus for these kinds of centralized control efforts, and the intensity of the conflict over them, can be seen in the amount of money now spent on environmental protection by the federal government—as well as by state and local governments and the private sector. The federal government spends $21 billion per year in current (1993) dollars for all environmental and natural resource programs, or about 1.4 percent of the total federal budget. However, this is only one-sixth of the nation's annual investment in environmental protection. Overall environmental spending in the United States, including that of state and local governments and the private sector, is estimated at more than $130 billion per year, or about 2 percent of the nation's gross national product (GNP). The figure is expected to rise to about 2.5 percent of GNP by the mid 1990s, in part because of the 1990 Clean Air Act, which will add about $25 billion per year.

The benefits of environmental programs are more difficult to calculate and are often omitted entirely from reports on the costs or burdens of environmental policies. Should one measure only public health benefits of pollution control? What about esthetic values? Or the value of conserving ecosystems—water, soil, forests, wetlands—or of preventing disastrous climate change? These kinds of questions have led to a broad reexamination of the way in which nations account for the value of natural resources (chap. 17).

Making rough comparisons of the benefits and costs of environmental policies, one could fairly conclude that many programs can be justified through conventional economic analysis. That is, they produce measurable benefits that exceed the costs. This was true of the original Clean Air Act, and it would apply to efforts to phase out the CFCs that destroy the Earth's protective ozone layer. Energy conservation also makes good economic sense given the costs of new power plants. Some environmental programs, such as cleanup of hazardous waste sites, however, are so expensive that they would be far more difficult to justify on economic grounds alone (chap. 9).[45]

Debates over the costs and benefits of environmental policies will continue in the 1990s, but with several new twists. Government spending on natural resources and the environment, which rose sharply in the 1970s, is unlikely to increase much in the 1990s because of the persistent deficit in the federal budget, widespread reluctance to raise tax rates significantly, and competing budget priorities. The burden of raising additional funds for environmental programs may be shouldered by the states, but some of them are more able and willing to do so than others (chap. 3). This pattern means that more of the additional cost of environmental protection will be borne by the private sector: by industry and, eventually, by the consumer. Another implication is that the federal government as well as the states will have to seek innovative policies that promise improvements in environmental quality without adding substantially to their budgets. A third conclusion is that some form of risk-based priority setting is essential if environmental regulation is to make economic as well as environmental sense. This argument was advanced regularly by EPA administrator William K. Reilly in the early 1990s (chap. 6).

Recent policy developments reflect these concerns—for example, the passage of the Pollution Prevention Act of 1990, which puts a premium on preventing, rather than cleaning up, pollution. Industry is already actively seeking ways to reduce the generation of waste, spurred on by sharply rising costs for hazardous waste disposal brought on by new federal standards under RCRA.[46] A parallel development among environmental groups, particularly the Nature Conservancy, is a successful venture into private purchase of ecologically important land for preservation. Private efforts to save endangered lands have recently been extended to financially strapped developing nations in so-called debt-for-nature swaps.

At another level the question of whether environmental programs are "worth it" must be answered with another question: what are the costs of inaction? In some cases the risks to the environment and to society's well-being are so great that it would be extremely foolish to delay development of public policy. This is particularly so when prudent measures taken at an early enough date might forestall the enormous costs of remedial efforts in the future, whether paid for by governments or the private sector. That was clearly the lesson of environmental contamination at DOE nuclear weapons facilities, as noted. It is also apparent that such a prudent policy response is called for in the cases of global climate change and deterioration of the ozone layer, where there is great potential impact on the environment, human health, and the economy. Much the same argument could be made for preserving biological diversity, investing in family planning programs, and responding to other compelling global environmental problems likely to be high on the agenda in the 1990s.

Conclusion

Over the past two decades, public concern and support for environmental protection has risen significantly, spurring the development of a vast array of new policies that substantially increased the government's responsibilities for the environment and natural resources, both domestically and internationally.

The implementation of these policies, however, has been far more difficult and controversial than their supporters ever imagined. Moreover, the policies have not been entirely successful, particularly when measured by tangible improvements in environmental quality. Given the country's persistent and severe budgetary constraints, further progress requires that the nation search for more efficient and effective ways to achieve these goals, including the use of alternatives to conventional "command and control" regulation. Nevertheless, the record of the past two decades demonstrates convincingly that the U.S. government is able to produce significant environmental gains through public policies. Unquestionably, the environment would be worse today if the policies of the 1970s and 1980s had not been in place.

Emerging environmental threats on the national and international agenda are even more formidable than the first generation of problems addressed by government in the 1970s and the second generation that dominated political debate in the 1980s. Responding to them will require creative new efforts to improve the performance of government and other social institutions, and effective leadership to design appropriate strategies both within government and in society itself. We discuss this new policy agenda in chapter 17.

Government is an important player in the environmental arena, but it cannot pursue forceful initiatives unless the public supports them. Ultimately, society's values will fuel the government's response to a rapidly changing world environment that, in all probability, will involve severe economic and social dislocations over the next two decades.

Notes

1. Keith Schneider, "For Clinton and Gore, Contradictions in Balancing Jobs and Conservation," *New York Times*, October 13, 1992, A12; and Al Gore, *Earth in the Balance: Ecology and the Human Spirit* (Boston: Houghton Mifflin, 1992), 269. Schneider, who covers environmental issues for the *New York Times*, called Gore's book "the most graphic analysis of the world's environmental condition and the most advanced plan for economic solutions that has ever been written by an American politician." See "Book by Gore Could Become a Campaign Issue, for Both Sides," *New York Times*, July 27, 1992, A9.
2. See Walter A. Rosenbaum, *Environmental Politics and Policy* (Washington, D.C.: CQ Press, 1985); J. Clarence Davies III and Barbara S. Davies, *The Politics of Pollution*, 2d ed. (Indianapolis: Bobbs-Merrill, 1975); and Helen M. Ingram and Dean E. Mann, "Environmental Protection Policy," in *Encyclopedia of Policy Studies*, ed. Stuart S. Nagel (New York: Marcel Dekker, 1983).
3. Norman J. Vig and Michael E. Kraft, eds., *Environmental Policy in the 1980s: Reagan's New Agenda* (Washington, D.C.: CQ Press, 1984).
4. See, for example, the World Commission on Environment and Development, *Our Common Future* (New York: Oxford University Press, 1987); and Jim MacNeill, Pieter Winsemius, and Taizo Yakushiji, *Beyond Interdependence: The Meshing of the World's Economy and the Earth's Ecology* (New York: Oxford, 1991).
5. John W. Kingdon, *Agendas, Alternatives, and Public Policies* (Boston: Little, Brown, 1984).
6. Roger W. Cobb and Charles D. Elder, *Participation in American Politics: The Dynamics of Agenda-Building* (Boston: Allyn and Bacon, 1972).
7. Kingdon, *Agendas.*
8. For a more elaborate policy cycle model, see Charles O. Jones, *An Introduction to the Study of Public Policy*, 3d ed. (Monterey, Calif.: Brooks/Cole, 1984).
9. Ronald Inglehart, *The Silent Revolution: Changing Values and Political Styles Among Western Publics* (Princeton, N.J.: Princeton University Press, 1977).
10. World Commission on Environment and Development, *Our Common Future.*
11. Samuel P. Hays, *Beauty, Health, and Permanence: Environmental Politics in the United States, 1955-1985* (New York: Cambridge University Press, 1987); and Robert C. Paehlke, *Environmentalism and the Future of Progressive Politics* (New Haven, Conn.: Yale University Press, 1989). For a comprehensive review of public opinion surveys on the environment and the evolution of the environmental movement, see Riley E. Dunlap and Angela G. Mertig, eds., *American Environmentalism: The U.S. Environmental Movement, 1970-1990* (Philadelphia: Taylor and Francis, 1992).
12. Paul J. Culhane, *Public Lands Politics: Interest Group Influence on the Forest Service and the Bureau of Land Management* (Baltimore: Johns Hopkins University Press, 1981), esp. chap. 1.
13. Michael E. Kraft, "Population Policy," in *Encyclopedia of Policy Studies*, 2d ed., ed. Stuart S. Nagel (New York: Marcel Dekker, 1993). See also Phyllis T. Piotrow, *World Population Crisis: The United States Response* (New York: Praeger, 1973).
14. Davies and Davies, *Politics of Pollution.*
15. Helen M. Ingram and Dean E. Mann, "Environmental Policy: From Innovation to Implementation," in *Nationalizing Government: Public Policies in America*, ed. Theodore J. Lowi and Alan Stone (Beverly Hills: Sage, 1978); and Davies and Davies, *Politics of Pollution*, chap. 2.
16. Hays, *Beauty, Health, and Permanence.* See also Riley E. Dunlap, "Public Opinion and Environmental Policy," in *Environmental Politics and Policy*, ed. Lester; and Robert Cameron Mitchell, "Public Opinion and Environmental Politics in

the 1970s and 1980s," in *Environmental Policy in the 1980s*, ed. Vig and Kraft.
17. Public Law 91-90 (42 USC 4321-4347), Sec. 101. See Lynton K. Caldwell, *Science and the National Environmental Policy Act: Redirecting Policy Through Procedural Reform* (Tuscaloosa: University of Alabama Press, 1982).
18. Henry C. Kenski and Margaret Corgan Kenski, "Congress Against the President: The Struggle Over the Environment," in *Environmental Policy in the 1980s*, ed. Vig and Kraft, 113-114.
19. Kraft, "Population Policy"; Council on Environmental Quality and Department of State, *The Global 2000 Report to the President*, vol. 1 (Washington, D.C.: U.S. Government Printing Office, 1980).
20. See Dorothy S. Zinberg, ed., *Uncertain Power: The Struggle for a National Energy Policy* (New York: Pergamon, 1983); and James Everett Katz, *Congress and National Energy Policy* (New Brunswick, N.J.: Transaction, 1984).
21. Walter A. Rosenbaum, *Energy, Politics and Public Policy* (Washington, D.C.: CQ Press, 1987); and Michael E. Kraft, "Congress and National Energy Policy: Assessing the Policymaking Process," in *Energy, Environment, Public Policy*, ed. Regina S. Axelrod (Lexington, Mass.: Lexington, 1981).
22. See, for example, Edwin H. Clark II, "Reaganomics and the Environment: An Evaluation," in *Environmental Policy in the 1980s*, ed. Vig and Kraft.
23. See Riley E. Dunlap, "Public Opinion on the Environment in the Reagan Era," *Environment* 29 (July-August 1987): 6-11, 32-37; and Mitchell, "Public Opinion and Environmental Politics."
24. Daniel A. Mazmanian and Jeanne Nienaber, *Can Organizations Change? Environmental Protection, Citizen Participation, and the Corps of Engineers* (Washington, D.C.: Brookings, 1979).
25. Richard N. L. Andrews, *Environmental Policy and Administrative Change: Implementation of the National Environmental Policy Act* (Lexington, Mass.: Lexington, 1976); and Caldwell, *Science and the National Environmental Policy Act*.
26. *Remarks by James D. Watkins, secretary of energy*, June 27, 1989 (Washington, D.C.: U.S. Department of Energy, 1989). See also Michael E. Kraft, "Making This World Intelligible: The Politics of Site Remediation," *Environmental Professional*, forthcoming 1993; and Milton E. Russell, William Colglazier, and Bruce E. Tonn, "The U.S. Hazardous Waste Legacy," *Environment* 34 (1992): 12-15, 34-39.
27. John McCormick, *Reclaiming Paradise: The Global Environmental Movement* (Bloomington: Indiana University Press, 1989), 110. This book provides a useful overview of international developments during this period.
28. Alfred A. Marcus, *Promise and Performance: Choosing and Implementing Environmental Policy* (Westport, Conn.: Greenwood, 1980); Lettie McSpadden Wenner, *The Environmental Decade in Court* (Bloomington: Indiana University Press, 1982); R. Shep Melnick, *Regulation and the Courts: The Case of the Clean Air Act* (Washington, D.C.: Brookings, 1983); and Marc K. Landy, Marc J. Roberts, and Stephen R. Thomas, *The Environmental Protection Agency: Asking the Wrong Questions* (New York: Oxford University Press, 1990).
29. George C. Eads and Michael Fix, *Relief or Reform? Reagan's Regulatory Dilemma* (Washington, D.C.: Urban Institute Press, 1984).
30. J. Clarence Davies III, "Environmental Institutions and the Reagan Administration," in *Environmental Policy in the 1980s*, ed. Vig and Kraft. See also Richard N. L. Andrews, "Deregulation: The Failure at EPA," in *Environmental Policy in the 1980s*, ed. Vig and Kraft.
31. See Philip Shabecoff, "Reagan and Environment: To Many a Stalemate," *New York Times*, January 2, 1989, 1, 8.
32. Ibid., 8.
33. See Paul R. Portney, "Needed: A Bureau of Environmental Statistics," *Resources*, no. 90 (Winter 1988): 12-15; and Clifford S. Russell, "Monitoring and Enforce-

ment," in *Public Policies for Environmental Protection*, ed. Portney (Washington, D.C.: Resources for the Future, 1990).

34. Most of the trend data on environmental quality come from Council on Environmental Quality, *Environmental Quality: Twentieth Annual Report* (Washington, D.C.: Council on Environmental Quality, 1990), app. E. For other compilations of such data for both U.S. and global environmental conditions, see *State of the Environment: A View Toward the Nineties* (Washington, D.C.: Conservation Foundation, 1987); *World Resources, 1992-93* (Washington, D.C.: World Resources Institute, 1992); and *State of the World* (New York: Norton, annual).

35. Paul R. Portney, "Air Pollution Policy," in *Public Policies for Environmental Protection*, ed. Portney.

36. CEQ, *Environmental Quality: The Twentieth Annual Report*, app. E.

37. "Air Found Cleaner in 41 U.S. Cities," *New York Times*, October 20, 1992, A17.

38. Philip Shabecoff, "Health Risk From Smog Is Growing, Official Says," *New York Times*, March 1, 1989, 16.

39. Gary C. Bryner, *Blue Skies, Green Politics: The Clean Air Act of 1990* (Washington, D.C.: CQ Press, 1993), 63.

40. Conservation Foundation, *State of the Environment*, 87. See also Debra S. Knopman and Richard A. Smith, "Twenty Years of the Clean Water Act," *Environment* 35 (January-February 1993): 17-20, 34-41.

41. See Daniel Mazmanian and David Morell, *Beyond Superfailure: America's Toxics Policy for the 1990s* (Boulder: Westview, 1992); Roger C. Dower, "Hazardous Wastes," in *Public Policies for Environmental Protection*, ed. Portney; and Kraft, "Making This World Intelligible."

42. Russell, Colglazier, and Tonn, "U.S. Hazardous Waste Legacy," and Kraft, "Making This World Intelligible."

43. Philip Shabecoff, "The Battle for the National Forests," *New York Times*, August 13, 1989, "Week in Review," 1.

44. See Timothy Egan, "Strongest U.S. Environmental Law May Become Endangered Species," *New York Times*, May 26, 1992, 1, 13; Richard J. Tobin, *The Expendable Future: U. S. Politics and the Protection of Biological Diversity* (Durham, N.C.: Duke University Press, 1990); and Jon R. Luoma, "Listing as an Endangered Species Is Said to Come Too Late for Many," *New York Times*, March 16, 1993, A12.

45. Portney, *Public Policies for Environmental Protection*; and Keith Schneider, "New View Calls Environmental Policy Misguided," *New York Times*, March 21, 1993, 1, 16.

46. See Joel S. Hirschhorn and Kirsten U. Oldenburg, *Prosperity Without Pollution: The Prevention Strategy for Industry and Consumers* (New York: Van Nostrand Reinhold, 1991).

2

After the Movement:
Environmental Activism in the 1990s

Christopher J. Bosso

Environmental politics in the United States is promising to be turbulent in the 1990s. American environmentalism is undergoing its most fundamental redefinition in decades—its dimensions only faintly discernible amid the globally induced tremors rippling throughout society.[1] Indeed, as a coherent ideology, it is headed for a collision with long-dominant political and economic values. The outcome will powerfully affect the organizations and activists long at the vanguard of the American environmental community.

This chapter assesses American environmentalism in the 1990s. I begin by looking at the broader societal and political contexts that both shape and limit environmental activism. Next, I examine the organizational challenges facing the major national environmental groups, the dimensions of environmentalism at the grass roots, and the "wise use" and "property rights" backlash. Finally, I discuss whether environmentalism may no longer be a "movement" but a societal paradigm for the next millennium that will reshape environmental politics in the United States, and the world.

Parameters for Environmental Activism

In looking at public opinion trends since the early 1970s, Gillroy and Shapiro noted that "the issue of environmental protection has had its ups and downs," but it "has been a persistent concern."[2] In 1991 Dunlap and Scarce go further, stating, "it is clear that public support for environmental protection not only has persisted but also has risen substantially in recent years."[3] The 1992 presidential election, discussed in chapter 4, in many ways bears out both assertions and in general was an apt metaphor for the murky relationship between public opinion and environmental policymaking in the United States.

What are the dimensions of public support for environmental protection? If one asks about the current *salience* of an issue on the electorate's stated list of priorities, public concern about the environment is fluid. After years of acute concern fueled by such agenda-setting events as the *Exxon Valdez* oil spill or the accident at the Chernobyl nuclear plant, the early

1990s seemed to be one of those "down" periods when the environment takes a back seat to other, arguably more pressing, matters. For example, a January 1992 *New York Times*/CBS News poll asked, "Besides issues like war and peace, the national economy and jobs, what other issues would you like to see the candidates for president emphasize in their campaigns this year?" Health care, mentioned without prompting by 19 percent of respondents, came first, which in itself may have reflected more the extensive media attention to that issue in previous months. Only 4 percent of the respondents mentioned the environment, tying it for fifth place with drugs, the elderly, and abortion.[4] What is more, the Gallup poll in May 1992 found that only 11 percent of respondents listed the environment as the "most important problem" facing the nation.[5] Judging from these data, the environment apparently had fallen on the public's list of priorities.

But survey researchers also point out that environmental issues *never* do that well in such "most important issue" polls, which force respondents to set their own priorities, and only show some strength when media coverage of environmental issues is particularly strong. "Because salience measures are headline-sensitive," says Robert Mitchell, "they are an untrustworthy guide to how the public will respond to policy changes in apparently non-salient issues."[6] So-called issue salience is neither predictable nor consistent, so the more useful indicators of actual public support for environmental protection may be those measuring the *strength* of public concern at any one time, and over long periods of time, in response to actual problems or controversies. Judged in these ways, citizens in the early 1990s regard environmental problems as serious and, suggesting the depths of public unease, believe too little progress has been made in addressing the problems. More important, public concern for the environment has endured, even increased, regardless of fluctuating issue salience.[7]

A frequently cited indicator of the strength of public concern is shown in the *New York Times*/CBS News poll, which gauges agreement with the statement, "Protecting the environment is *so* important that the requirements and standards cannot be too high, and continuing environmental improvements must be made *regardless* of cost." By 1990, as figure 2-1 suggests, most Americans agreed to some extent with what is a rather absolutist view. Equally useful, another poll finds that the percentage of respondents who believe that the nation spends "too little" on improving and protecting the environment has risen from 48 percent in 1980 to 71 percent in 1990.[8] The polling data also suggest that citizens believe increasingly that a healthy environment is not necessarily antithetical to a strong economy. "Only when environmental protection is linked to increased unemployment does its strong majority backing disappear," note Dunlap and Scarce, "and here the proportion willing to accept higher unemployment has grown considerably."[9]

Even so, there are limits. Strong generalized support for environmental protection does not translate automatically into support for specific poli-

Figure 2-1   Support for Environmental Protection, "Regardless of Cost," 1981-1990

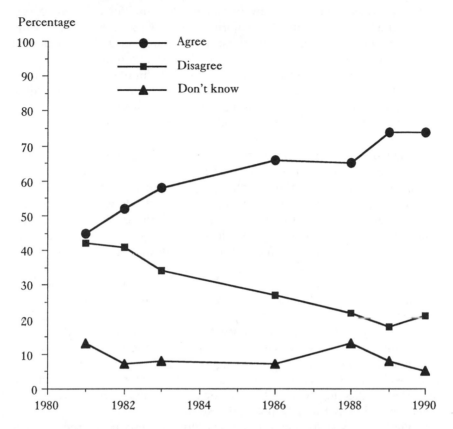

*Source: New York Times/*CBS News. See Riley E. Dunlap, "Trends in Public OpinionToward Environmental Issues: 1965-1990, *Society and Natural Resources* 4 (1991): 285-312.

Note: The question asked was: "Do you agree or disagree with the following statement: Protecting the environment is *so* important that requirements and standards cannot be too high, and continuing environmental improvements must be made *regardless* of cost."

cies. It does not deter voters from rejecting ballot initiatives deemed overly ambitious or from siding with interests defending local industries or jobs. Furthermore, if few candidates today want to be painted as foes of a better environment, says Dunlap, "there is as yet little evidence of a 'green bloc' of single-issue voters comparable to the anti-abortion or anti-gun control blocs."[10] Environmental priorities do compete with other, often more salient concerns during election or policy debates. Even strong public concern does not translate automatically into policy responses. It translates only into opportunities for leadership that may or may not be exploited.

Environmental activism also is constrained, and shaped to some extent, by a constitutional system that purposefully fragments political power, provides remarkably few formal mechanisms for cohesive governance, and often prevents any majority from having its way. This same structure, however, allows innumerable but narrower *publics* to pursue their particular needs through the many distinct and only partially overlapping avenues for representation to be found throughout government. The making of public policy in such a system involves laboriously building "majorities of the moment" from discrete and often self-contained *interests*, not all of which get their demands taken seriously. Indeed, congressional representation itself, which is geographically based, invariably favors parochial economic interests over broader and more diffuse ones. The system also tends strongly toward policy incrementalism, a bias undoubtedly frustrating for those seeking rapid, fundamental change.

These structural constants make it incredibly difficult for environmental groups to match the access and clout of those who rely on traditional resource extraction and land development interests that make up much of the Wise Use movement discussed below. Even for those trying to balance ecological values with more immediate economic needs, the short-term and more risk-averse option almost always prevails, particularly in times of economic dislocation and where fundamental values about the relationship between humanity and nature differ. For example, in 1992 Oregon governor Barbara Roberts was forced into a recall election by the state's timber industry, which accused her of siding with "out-of-state" environmentalists in disputes over logging old-growth forests. Roberts survived with the support of urban and suburban voters, but the episode underscored the clout wielded by narrower economic interests within the niches provided by the U.S. political system.[11]

Public support for environmental values is thus tempered by economic concerns, and refracted through a formal policymaking system where local, short-term interests wield tremendous leverage. These contexts were even less hospitable to environmental activists in the early 1990s because of a shaky economic climate and a hardening of attitudes among those for whom change threatens long-standing economic and political arrangements. The new administration can alter some of these contexts—for example, by making the White House more sensitive to environmental views—although it cannot change them entirely. Many of them simply are constant features of the system of governance itself.

The Environmental Lobby in Washington

The story of American environmentalism is the story of all social movements because, as Snow observes, "even the most grass-roots campaigns of mass mobilization, if they survive, tend eventually to seek their place upon the institutional bedrock. The process is familiar enough: *Ad hoc,* inchoate groups of volunteers harden into chartered organizations, which, if successful, evolve over time into long-standing, stable institutions."[12] In this regard the environmental community is exceedingly diverse. Despite common core values and frequent cooperation among groups, notes Mitchell, "their unity is tempered by a diversity of heritage, organizational structure, issue agendas, constituency, and tactics. The groups also compete with each other for the staples of their existence— publicity and funding."[13] Such competition is more acute today than at any time since the very notion of an "environmental movement" came into being.

The many faces of environmentalism can be seen with the national organizations, which can be sorted into five rough types: (a) large, multi-issue membership groups (e.g., the National Wildlife Federation); (b) their smaller, more narrowly focused, and generally more purist brethren (e.g., Friends of the Earth); (c) education, research, and policy development centers that rarely lobby or take partisan positions (e.g., Resources for the Future); (d) law and science groups that typically promote "rational" solutions (e.g., Natural Resources Defense Council); and (e) real estate conservation groups (e.g., the Nature Conservancy) that focus on setting aside valuable landscapes or ecosystems.[14] This discussion focuses on the member-driven organizations, for it is groups like the Sierra Club and the Wilderness Society where the more compelling evolutionary sagas within the environmental community are being played out.

How Big Is Big Enough?

The growth in public support for environmental causes is reflected in the lives of the large national membership organizations (table 2-1). Typically the oldest and most mainstream in the environmental community, these groups have, as a rule, changed over the years from small, single-issue groups of idealistic volunteers to multi-issue, "full service" entities that recruit a diverse membership, promote broad agendas, employ professional staffs, and utilize virtually every tactic known to traditional lobbying.[15] For the leaders of such groups, the constant struggle is to manage ever-bigger and more expensive operations while holding onto the loyalty and commitment of a heterogenous and often restive membership. These groups almost have to grow to survive, especially as the demands of being active players in the policy arena drive costs.

But growth creates strains. Large memberships and big budgets combined often, if not always, generate pressures toward administration over advocacy, an overt focus on the budgetary effects of agendas and tactics, and a need to be seen as "respectable" so that potential contributors feel their money is spent wisely. Size also creates an emphasis on stricter and more centralized decisionmaking, often at the per-

Table 2-1 Membership Trends Among Selected National Environmental Groups, 1970-1990

Group (year founded)	1970	1975	1980	1985	1990
Sierra Club (1892)	150,000	170,000	181,000	364,000	600,000
National Audubon Society (1905)	105,000	275,000	400,000	550,000	575,000
National Parks and Conservation Assoc. (1919)	50,000	50,000*	31,000	45,000	100,000
Wilderness Society (1935)	44,000*	50,000	35,000	150,000	350,000
National Wildlife Federation (1936)	3.1 million	3.7 million	4 million	4.5 million	5.8 million
Environmental Defense Fund (1967)	nonmember	30,000	46,000	50,000	150,000
Natural Resources Defense Council (1970)	nonmember	35,000	42,000	50,000	125,000

Sources: Encyclopedia of Associations (Detroit: Gale Research Co.); *Buzzworm* 2 (May-June 1990): 65-77; Margaret Kriz, "Shades of Green," *National Journal*, July 28, 1990, 1828; George Hager, "For Industry and Opponents, A Showdown Is in the Air," *Congressional Quarterly Weekly Report*, January 20, 1990, 144; Environmental Protection Section, Congressional Research Service, *Selected Environmental and Related Interest Groups: Summary Guide*, CRS Report 91-295 ENR (March 22, 1991); *National Journal*, January 4, 1992, 30; *Chronicle of Philanthropy*, March 24, 1992, 31.

* Estimated.

ceived expense of local chapters housing the group's most dedicated and least docile activists. Such frictions in turn can generate damaging internal schisms, member defections, and the creation of splinter groups. This tug-of-war between national leaders and local activists, combined with the certain if muted willingness of other groups to recruit the disenchanted—only so many Americans are willing to pay membership dues, after all—makes organizational maintenance an overwhelming burden.

A good example of this dynamic came recently with the Sierra Club, one of the few large groups whose directions and tactics are influenced heavily by the local chapters. This reliance on the grass roots promotes member solidarity and organizational resiliency, and distinguishes it from groups where members merely write checks. Yet it also frequently degenerates into fractious internal politics as influential blocs of members battle over agendas and tactics.[16] In 1991, for example, the Sierra Club helped to forge a complicated compromise with timber companies over cutting old-growth forests in California. The agreement was vetoed by Gov. Pete Wilson (R), who brokered a new bill that was eventually accepted by the Sierra Club leadership as the best deal possible under the circumstances. However, the compromise only enraged already disgruntled Sierra Club activists in Northern California, who forced group leaders to renege on the deal despite withering criticism from the state's political establishment. The Sierra Club has, in fact, yet to issue a position on clear-cutting in the national forests.[17]

If larger groups like the Sierra Club always careen toward splintering, the issue for the smaller ones is survival. These groups, which are younger, tend to have a narrower issue focus, are less willing to accommodate, and, as a result, have a more limited membership appeal. Many also emerged as offshoots of older organizations after some internal conflict over group goals and tactics. Friends of the Earth (FOE), for example, was founded in 1969 by famed activist David Brower because of conflicts within the Sierra Club over an earlier drift toward the mainstream. FOE quickly pursued an ambitious agenda, but tight resources and loose management soon led to internal chaos and staff defections. In 1972 the group's roster of Washington lobbyists defected to form the Environmental Policy Institute.[18] By the mid 1980s FOE was in dire financial straits and embroiled in a dispute over a controversial plan to move the group's headquarters to Washington, D.C. Brower opposed the move because it would make FOE "just another lobby," and soon left to form the Earth Island Institute. FOE undertook the move to Washington and merged with two similarly ailing groups, the Oceanic Institute and the prodigal Environmental Policy Institute. The path traveled by this former Sierra Club splinter group emphasizes the tough choice facing smaller membership groups: grow, at a cost, or die.

Resources and Agendas: Who Pays the Piper?

The choices faced by membership organizations ultimately go back to money. Membership attrition can run as high as 30 percent annually, requiring constant revenue hunting, yet memberships and budgets have skyrocketed—in some cases doubling every five years—and environmental groups in 1990 alone cumulatively took in some $2.9 billion, almost double 1987 revenues.[19] In the early 1990s, however, a combination of nagging economic recession and war in the Persian Gulf sapped revenues, forcing groups both to make painful budget cuts and seek monies elsewhere. In 1991 the National Wildlife Federation, after seeing its budget triple in less than a decade, instituted staff layoffs, froze salaries, and left positions unfilled because revenues did not grow as projected.[20] Similar tales of woe were heard at the Sierra Club, the Wilderness Society, and every other major group. In response, almost all have tried to diversify their revenue sources by marketing goods and services (e.g., books, travel services), and made wholesale and frequently controversial changes in their magazines, which are essential for recruiting new members and—not coincidentally—advertisers.[21] Forty groups have even formed a quasi-United Way association, called "Earth Share," to allow government and corporate employees to donate more painlessly through payroll deductions.[22]

Again the issue of money reverberates; as the saying goes, "Whoever pays the piper calls the tune." Environmental groups—their organizational governance, agendas, and strategies—are influenced by their donors. Especially controversial of late are efforts by many major groups to seek funding from corporations. Businesses, for their part, want to improve their fragile public images. If real policy changes seem unstoppable, they tend to support organizations whose agendas seem more "reasonable" and "pragmatic." Critics of course charge that corporate money simply is a subtle attempt to buy influence. Many cite as a notable example Waste Management, Inc., the waste collection and disposal giant that donates some $1 million annually to, among others, the World Wildlife Fund, National Wildlife Federation (on whose board the company's chief executive sits), National Audubon Society, Environmental Law Institute, Ducks Unlimited, Sierra Club, Natural Resources Defense Council, Izaak Walton League, and World Resources Institute.[23]

Do such donations actually buy influence? This is hard to say, but threats to *withdraw* funding certainly underscore the dangers inherent in relying on corporate money. The Audubon Society, for example, has had highly public difficulties with corporate sponsorship of its popular "World of Audubon" documentary series, aired on PBS and Turner Broadcasting. In 1991 program sponsor General Electric (GE) withdrew further support, citing recession-induced budget cuts. GE's decision, however, came on the heels of consumer boycott threats generated by the National

Inholders Association, a lobbying group for cattlemen, loggers, and those owning property in or near national parks and forests. The group was furious about a series program critical of federally subsidized cattle grazing practices. Audubon officials expressed fear that advertiser boycotts could have a chilling effect on programming. In fact, GE was but the latest corporation—joining Stroh's Brewing, Ford, Exxon, and Citicorp—to cancel sponsorship for "World of Audubon" after some kind of furor.[24] Boycotts have been an alluring tool of public persuasion for many environmentalists—witness how readily distributors of canned tuna bowed to demands for "dolphin-safe" products—so their potent use by opponents is an ironic twist.

Taking controversial stands can also affect groups that depend wholly on member contributions. Greenpeace, for example, has long been envied for its ability to use its radical but nonviolent image to generate staggering levels of direct-mail contributions. In 1990 in the United States alone, Greenpeace generated about $60 million from an estimated 2.5 million members.[25] Yet heavy reliance on direct mail in particular opens Greenpeace up to charges (often from other environmentalists) that its agenda is driven by the latest eco-crisis it can exploit in the millions of pieces of mail it sends out annually. Reliance on individual contributions also makes Greenpeace acutely sensitive to shifts in public attitudes, such as by its ecologically based opposition to the Persian Gulf War. Whether the controversy mattered more than the recession is up for debate. In any case, in 1991 Greenpeace's revenues declined for the first time in its history, producing the now-familiar reorganizations, staff cuts, and leadership departures.[26]

Tactics and Strategies

Money aside, the great crisis facing the national environmental groups is one of faith in their directions and tactics. To outside observers such ambivalence might be mystifying, for after more than two decades of experience the contemporary environmental lobby is active, technologically sophisticated, and politically savvy. From extensive use of television, phone banks, and direct mail to computer bulletin boards and facsimile machines, environmentalists have copied, and in many cases perfected, techniques used by virtually every other lobby group. Also like in most other lobbying sectors, the major mainstream groups increasingly coordinate their activities to maximize resources and areas of expertise even as they compete (albeit usually quietly) with one another for members and leadership in respective policy niches.[27]

All of this enhanced organizational capacity and coordination means that the green lobby usually has the clout to stop legislation it opposes. A prime example of this "veto power" came in 1991 when the Senate considered a national energy bill that proposed to open the Arctic

National Wildlife Refuge (ANWR) to oil exploration (see discussion in chap. 5). The effort was led by the petroleum industry and backed strongly by Alaskan politicians, the Bush administration, an array of business interests, and, last but certainly not least, the powerful chairman of the Senate Energy Committee, J. Bennett Johnston (D-La). However, a coalition of some eighty groups representing environmentalists, outdoors enthusiasts, indigenous peoples, consumers, and proponents of alternative energy sources prevented consideration of the measure until the offending provision was removed.[28] Johnston later said simply that environmental groups "wrote the textbook on how to defeat a bill such as this, and my admiration is to them for the political skill which they exhibited. . . . They pulled together a tremendous phalanx, which was very effective."[29]

Even so, and for all of the efforts and resources expended, the results have been mixed at best, and leaders of the mainstream groups have begun to more openly question the utility of traditional lobbying activities. Sierra Club executive director Michael McCloskey voiced the general frustration: "Surely the movement could still get statutes enacted, and it could win lawsuits over government refusal to implement them. But could we get them implemented properly in the final analysis? . . . What was the point of great lobbying campaigns in Congress if so little came of the enactments in the end?"[30]

Many activists thus point approvingly to the successful 1989 campaign against the chemical growth regulator Alar waged by the Natural Resources Defense Council (NRDC), a group long considered pragmatic and not known to be publicity seeking. Tired of what it saw as endless White House obstruction on Alar, the NRDC used the popular CBS news program "Sixty Minutes" to air its charges about the chemical's potential health risks. Public concern soon spurred apple growers to stop using the chemical, and Alar's manufacturer withdrew it from the market.[31] Despite controversy over NRDC grandstanding, the message to other major environmental groups was clear: bypass convoluted and often toothless regulations, skirt entrenched industry interests, go directly to the people, and let the market work.

Ironically, this lesson cast doubt on the very tactics most of the mainstream groups had been refining for decades. In the 1990s the emphasis appears to be shifting away from working in government to working on government, from lobbying regulators to influencing consumer choices, from lawsuits to making markets work, from entreating legislators to getting voters to force government to be more responsive. In this sense the mainstream groups are admitting what many activists have long argued: environmentalists cannot compete in the politics of interests. Fighting the moneyed lobbyists is a futile proposition. The future involves going directly to the people and changing the way they think and act. It involves the politics of *values*.

The "Wise Use" Counterattack

This emerging "politics of values" goes far beyond relatively safe issues like saving whales or setting aside important natural landscapes. It instead strongly challenges prevailing societal norms and assumptions. In this fight, environmentalists' most intractable opposition comes from groups loosely organized around private property rights and "wise use" banners. It is a mistake to typify these 250-plus groups as mere fronts for corporate interests, as many environmentalists did early on (though some, such as People for the West!, which is backed by the mining industry, are little more than that).[32] Some are groups of private property owners worried about governmental restrictions on the use of their land (e.g., the Maryland-based Fairness to Land Owners Coalition), while others (e.g., the National Inholders Association) are direct heirs to the Sagebrush Rebellion of the late 1970s.

What unites these groups, particularly in the Rocky Mountain states, is staunch defense of the traditional multiple uses of federal lands, combined with concerns about what they see as misconceived attempts by naive suburbanites to end long-standing ways of life. Those who are part of the "wise use" cause consider themselves the *real* conservationists, lovers of the outdoors who hunt and fish, believe in scientific management of natural resources, and chafe at charges that they are despoilers of the Earth. This battle is in many ways but the latest permutation of a century-old split between conservationists who emphasize the "managed use" of natural resources and the arguably more absolutist dictates of preservationists going back to John Muir.

Like the environmental community, this countermovement has discernible wings. The moderates are generally those who own property in or near national parks and regard the major environmental groups as too powerful and insensitive to basic economic needs. The moderate factions are particularly upset about what they consider confiscatory policies that severely restrict the use of their land and in the process reduce its development or resale value. Such complaints were the impetus behind the 1992 Supreme Court decision in *Lucas* v. *South Carolina Coastal Council*, in which the justices ruled that government in certain circumstances may be required to compensate landowners when imposing environmental restrictions on development.[33] Despite their alarums about *Lucas*, environmentalists will learn how to compromise with these more moderate private property rights groups.

The more outspoken and radical wing of this backlash movement presents far more intractable problems, in no small part because its views dovetail potently with conservative populism's strident defense of private property, its lingering suspicion of communitarian values, and its occasional xenophobia. Many of the most ardent "wise use" activists are core veterans of the Sagebrush Rebellion, while others have extensive prior experience with the Young Americans for Freedom, the National Rifle Association, and other traditional conservative groups. To these true believers, there are few, if any, constitutional bases for restricting any use of private property. Among other things, they seek to open virtually all federal lands to resource exploitation, and oppose reauthorization of the Endangered Species Act.[34] At the fringes reside the John Birch Society, which publicly equates federal land policy with the *Communist Manifesto* and regards U.N. environmental programs as threats to U.S. sovereignty, the Rev. Sun Myung Moon's Unification Church, and others in the traditional anti-Communist right who see environmentalism as the newest threat to private property and American values in general. The stances taken by these groups are starkly opposite to those of even the more accommodating groups like the National Wildlife Federation, and the confrontations between the two hostile worldviews have at times been rough.

Equally important, these groups have adopted tactics perfected by environmentalists, including, as one analyst explains, "wholesome-sounding names, grass-roots lobbying, direct-mail fundraising and even demonstrations and boycott threats," and in 1991 about 125 of these groups formed the Alliance for America to give the countermovement greater focus and national visibility.[35]

Environmental groups are only now beginning to recognize the potency and breadth of this new countermovement. Lulled by the general popularity of environmentalism, and by their own distinct cultural and philosophical values, many activists mistakenly believed that few citizens could possibly espouse the more extreme views. Some observers also note that parochialism and rivalries among environmental groups allowed the backlash to gather steam, especially in the Rocky Mountain states. Whatever the case, the struggle between what amounts to competing worldviews will dominate domestic environmental policy debates through the decade, regardless who controls the White House or Congress.

The "New" Environmentalism?

The Grass Roots and Environmental "Justice"

The "wise use" backlash has been fueled in part by the perception that the major environmental groups—with their huge memberships, multimillion-dollar budgets and legions of policy experts—are emblematic of a governing class far too distant from real people and real problems. Kentucky grass-roots activist Jean True argues that "it's not good when a handful of people in Washington are making policy. It doesn't matter whether it's national environmental groups or national polluters. We need to start making decisions from the bottom up. Most of these issues are easy to understand, and the people who live close to a problem learn in a hurry."[36] Her view represents the epochal transformation under way in the environmental movement. Accordingly, the relations between local activists and their national brethren will have to change.

The scope of grass-roots environmentalism is both immense and inchoate. The thousands of groups include large, well-organized, multi-issue state and regional groups (e.g., the Florida Audubon Society—not affiliated with the national organization); highly professional law and science institutions (e.g., the New England-based Conservation Law Foundation); loose, issue-specific coalitions (e.g., the six thousand-member Silicon Valley Toxics Coalition); and, finally, small volunteer groups driven by single disputes. This range suggests also the diversity of values and tactics within American environmentalism generally, possessing many of the same dynamics and tensions as those found in the national advocacy community.

Of special interest here is the emergence of groups that have not traditionally been part of the environmental movement. They constitute, to some extent with the greens (discussed below), a "new environmentalism" that Robert Gottleib and Helen Ingram argue "is gradually coming to the fore in the United States. It is a grass-roots, community-based, democratic movement that differs radically from the conventional, mainstream American environmentalism, which always had a strong nondemocratic strain."[37] The new environmentalism is exemplified by Kentuckians for the Commonwealth (KFTC), begun in 1981 by two housewives to fight against the coal industry's control over the mineral rights beneath residents' property. KFTC members usually are poorer and less educated, and are concerned primarily about what they see as the economic and environmental inequities foisted on them by big institutions of all kinds. KFTC's biggest success came in a 1988 referendum to overhaul state mining laws, a victory over a major industry that gave the group enormous clout statewide. Arguing that the poor and less influential too often become the bearers of society's environmental burdens, KFTC has since become forceful on such issues as the importation of garbage from other states.[38]

Those active in KFTC, Mothers of East Los Angeles, or the various local groups comprising Lois Gibbs's Citizens Clearinghouse on Hazardous Waste (CCHW) are not environmentalists in the mold of the Sierra Club or National Wildlife Federation. These groups typically began with homeowners affected directly by a local hazard—classic not-in-my-backyard (NIMBY) dynamics—but more than a few have endured beyond the original dispute to address the far broader issues relating to justice for those affected most directly by pollution and poverty. They are being joined increasingly by others with roots in civil rights or feminist causes, for example, out of a spreading recognition that environmental justice is tied inextricably to broader economic and social values.

The "new" environmentalists are as multihued as the mainstream groups are accused of being monochromatic, and they generally share a set of beliefs that sets them further apart from the old-line groups. There is, above all, an emphasis on citizen empowerment, beginning with the simple right to know about the potential hazards in one's community. In this vein, perhaps no other single action taken by government has fueled the current surge at the grass roots more than the 1986 Emergency Planning and Community Right to Know Act, requiring manufacturers to report the total amount of hundreds of different chemicals released into the water and air.[39] These data are made public and evaluated by experts in such organizations as CCHW, NRDC, and Greenpeace—analyses that, in turn, enable local groups to act when necessary to make polluters accountable.

These activists are thus motivated less by the traditional conservation ethic and more by concerns about human health. They are generally convinced that the mainstream groups are focused on problems too far removed from the lives of average people and are curiously myopic about issues that may not energize their more affluent suburban contributors. For these activists environmentalism is a direct, personal matter: "The other groups are working toward things that are much more abstract," says Lois Gibbs, the Love Canal housewife-turned-national activist. "They don't know what it's like to live in a community and have everything you've ever worked for—your home—become worthless overnight. It's a different emotional sense that drives people like me. For people like me, the environmental movement is about survival."[40] That perspective, spiced by a lingering suspicion that they are pitted against institutions and forces mostly beyond their control, makes these activists particularly wary of government and industry experts and skeptical about science and technology generally. As a result, argue Freudenberg and Steinsapir, they "resist attempts to define environmental problems as purely technical ones because they would prefer to confront their adversaries on political terrain, where their skills and strengths can be used to maximum advantage."[41] Like the 1960s activists, whose language and methods they have adopted, the new environmental grass roots are not in the mood to compromise.

The new environmentalism is not simply unchecked or hysterical NIMBYism. These groups have not only forced the cleanup of existing hazards and prevented new ones but also, when taken together, begun to influence consumer (and thus business) habits, to create pressures for more preventive approaches to pollution, to expand opportunities for citizen participation, and finally, to extend environmentalism to sectors of the society traditionally unused to thinking ecologically. "By raising health concerns and by linking environmental issues to struggles for social justice and equality," argue Freudenberg and Steinsapir, "the grassroots environmental movement has created the potential for a cross-class movement with a broader agenda, more diverse constituencies, and a more radical critique of contemporary society than that of the national environmental organizations."[42]

That last point remains an essential dividing line. If those in the more mainstream national organizations still tend to believe in working within the system—although that faith may be eroding—those at the grass roots are likelier to believe the system is part of the problem regardless of who controls the White House or any congressional committee. After all, "the system" produced the contaminated weapons plants and the toxic waste dumps, and "the system" has been demonstrably slow to respond to constituencies with little economic or political clout. Relations between the national groups and the new grass roots are more symbiotic than is supposed. Yet the grass roots clearly profess distinct values and, more important, no longer necessarily look to the big national groups for leadership. The environmental movement, if one still wishes to use that term, has in many ways outgrown its vanguard.

The Coming of the Greens?

Finally, there is a stream of environmentalism that is even more socially, conceptually, and philosophically distinct. The "greens" or "deep ecologists" occupy an unimaginably big tent but are bound together generally by a belief that environmentalism is a profound choice, not about issues or interests, but about core values. They include technophobes for whom modern life has destroyed the primal link between humanity and nature, and technophiles with an unalloyed faith in the solutions to be found in science and technology. They include "direct action" groups like Earth First!, whose loosely connected members see "monkey wrenching" as the only way to deal with big government and big business, to reclusive communitarians who reject politics entirely. They include ecofeminists and misanthropes, socialists and libertarians. Many are populists, likely to find a great deal in common with housewives of KFTC, others are unabashed elitists who openly disdain the economic fears and cultural values of the mainstream electorate.[43] The greens sharply disagree with one another about virtually everything, save for the bankruptcy, as they see it, of the strategies and tactics pursued by mainstream environmentalism.

Of particular interest here are the fragmented and frequently internecine efforts to create an effective counterpoise to the two major American political parties. Activists in 1992 placed Green party candidates on the official ballot in several (largely western) states, and individuals have been elected under a green banner of some sort for local offices in New England, the Upper Midwest, the Pacific Northwest, California, and Alaska. By one estimate, there are some 250 green groups nationwide.[44] Yet the obstacles for a truly potent national Green party are many, beginning with the same fundamental disagreements over values and tactics that have plagued Green parties in Europe and Canada.

One major schism is whether greens should have a separate party at all. To many (dubbed "New Agers" or "green-greens"), the political system is a corrosive influence to be avoided, and they want to focus almost purely on promoting cultural change. Others (the "red-greens") remain convinced that only political activism can overcome industry and government resistance to change. Within the latter group are debilitating divisions between those seeking to emulate the structures and tactics of the major parties or the more successful advocacy groups, versus those for whom a true grass-roots movement must be noncentralized and nonhierarchical. Some want a "mainstreaming" party that builds coalitions and seeks electoral victory, others strive to maintain ideological purity.

The stunning demise of Germany's Green party in 1990 only highlighted the pitfalls for its American cousin. The German Greens studiously slighted institution building because of their ideological disdain for structure or hierarchy. They instituted mandatory rotation of party leaders, which served only to confuse voters and eroded the party's parliamentary clout. Incessant internal struggles between pragmatists and ideologues only exacerbated the image of the Greens as unready to govern.[45] Most damaging, Germans who gladly voted Green during the 1980s flocked to a Social Democratic party that over time had adopted many of the Green party's issues and views. Faced with a disorganized, often elitist minor party that opposed German reunification and was ensnared in a nasty dispute over its views on women, voters opted for a major party likelier to weigh in with immediate political clout.

Add to these kinds of generic problems an electoral system dominated by two parties, and prospects for a successful national American Green party are minimal. Yet a Green party is hardly doomed to irrelevance, if the history of third parties in the United States is at all relevant. It is likeliest to have an impact when it promotes core values and gets people to use environmental issues as voting cues. Lacking coherent and cohesive political parties to begin with, Americans usually have to go beyond party label if environmental values are to guide the vote. Here, at least, the greens can break out of their relative isolation by building social and political bridges to other groups, especially those affected most directly by ecological hazards. The Democratic party generally offers more environmentally sensitive candidates and has a "greener" national party platform, yet coalitional politics guarantees that green values will always be balanced against other social and economic concerns. How those trade-offs are defined within the two major parties is where the greens could have considerable influence.

After the Environmental Movement

The environmental movement, as we have seen, is no longer a single, identifiable entity. If, for example, it is defined as comprising all "organizations concerned with the question of human use of nature," then the term no longer has much operational use.[46] Much more than a social force led by a small cadre of true believers, environmentalism increasingly is a social and political ideology whose core values are shared widely by Americans. But, like liberalism and conservatism, its proponents possess real differences over goals, strategies, and tactics. Environmental values have finally moved beyond the activists to the society at large. Had this not happened, the movement would have been relegated to some philosophical and life-style ghetto—interesting, but of little relevance.

As environmentalism becomes a fixture in the national system of beliefs and values, the major environmental groups will have to make tough choices about their size, focus, and overall purpose. For example, it is compelling to ponder just how many large environmental organizations each niche in the overall "market" will bear. The various groups have been very resilient in the face of stiff competition and intraorganizational traumas. Nevertheless, this sector of the advocacy community is due for a serious shakeout. During the 1990s one is likely to see more mergers of groups vying against each other in some of the same issue niches. Is there really a need for both a Wilderness Society and a National Parks and Conservation Association (public lands issues)? For a Natural Resources Defense Council and an Environmental Defense Fund (air and water pollution, energy)? No doubt more than a few national environmental leaders are posing these and other questions. A Clinton administration more hospitable to the environmental agenda ironically exacerbates the problem because scaring contributors into writing checks is going to be a lot harder now that the vice president is an environmental leader. If the Carter years offer any clues, the 1990s may be relatively lean years for many environmental groups.

Another question is one of role. Despite the criticisms leveled against them, the national groups still are environmentalism's flagships. They are the capable quasi parties able to blunt the power of entrenched interests, provide assistance to local and state activists, and, as witnessed during the Reagan and Bush years, generally able to withstand presidential hostility. David Brower may not agree, but somebody in American environmentalism has to play these roles because that is the way the political system works. In this sense the national groups comprise another major national lobby, and thereby face the usual dangers of bureaucratic ossification, staff careerism, routinized advocacy, and passive memberships.[47] What is more (and unlike the big real estate, medical, and senior citizen lobbies), environmental groups represent much more compelling interests. They are thus especially vulnerable to member disenchantment and defection. To balance respectability with zeal will be a feat of legerdemain if the experiences of the groups are any indication.

More intriguing to ponder is the future of the grass roots, the most diverse and vibrant part of environmentalism. In this regard, the "new" environmentalism of citizen empowerment and social justice is especially compelling because, as Mark Sagoff argues, it has "tapped into the artery of mainstream populist sentiment. Environmentalism as a result has begun to fashion itself into a form of patriotism—to express a concern with the continuity of community linked to the integrity of place. To the surprise and chagrin of many political analysts and strategists, environmentalism has thus gained a sizeable constituency who speak the language of American populism."[48]

Indeed, if environmentalists can reach out to the working class, the poor, and to minorities, they can be part of a real democratizing force. How to pursue such a strategy of political empowerment, and at the same time handle such divisive issues as abortion, economic growth, and social justice will be the real trick. In this regard environmentalists do well to heed the lessons of other social movements. As Robert Paehlke argues, "while a successful environmental movement will likely lean to the moderate left of center, it likely cannot lean much further to the left. It will of necessity articulate an imaginative politics that does not continuously affront significant entrenched economic interest."[49]

The "new" environmental movement is thus the future. The most zealous greens, with their biocentric worldviews and startlingly ascetic visions of life, are too culturally and politically unsettling to most Americans. The national groups seem remote, bureaucratic, and too focused on problems distant from the everyday experiences of average citizens. What will matter most are the percolating actions of countless citizens, moderated as always by the coalition-forcing system itself. This process will be messy, incremental, ideologically fractious, often parochial, and always frustrating. But this is the process of new values being expressed and put to everyday use.

The 1990s will be marked by the sharpening of already visible lines between different shades of green, with the 1992 election a more accurate precursor of battles to come than many realize. Everybody professes to be an environmentalist. Yet few agree on what this means, so the notion of a single distinct movement no longer makes operational or philosophical sense. It also is a presumptuous notion, implying that only the anointed can be members of the church. So all of this tumult is probably good, for it is only when environmentalism loses its image as a separate movement and becomes truly part of the American value system that it can be said to succeed. That process may not be complete, but it certainly is under way.

Notes

1. Samuel Hays, *Beauty, Health, and Permanence: Environmental Politics in the United States, 1955-1985* (New York: Oxford University Press, 1987); and Robert C. Paehlke, *Environmentalism and the Future of Progressive Politics* (New Haven, Conn.: Yale University Press, 1990).

2. John Gillroy and Robert Shapiro, "The Polls: Environmental Protection," *Public Opinion Quarterly* 50 (1986): 270.

3. Riley Dunlap and Rik Scarce, "The Polls—Poll Trends: Environmental Problems and Protection," *Public Opinion Quarterly* 55 (1991): 651.

4. "Other Issues on Voters' Minds," *New York Times*, January 27, 1992, A14.

5. "Worldwide Environmental Poll," *Gallup Poll Monthly* (May 1992), 43.

6. Robert Mitchell, "Public Opinion and the Green Lobby: Poised for the 1990s?" in *Environmental Policy in the 1990s*, ed. Norman J. Vig and Michael E. Kraft (Washington, D.C.: CQ Press, 1990), 84.

7. Riley Dunlap, "Public Opinion in the 1980s: Clear Consensus, Ambiguous Commitment," *Environment* 33 (October 1991): 15.

8. National Opinion Research Center, cited in Riley Dunlap, "Trends in Public Opinion Toward Environmental Issues: 1965-1990," *Society and Natural Resources* 4 (1991): 300.

9. Dunlap and Scarce, "Poll Trends," 655-656.

10. Dunlap, "Public Opinion in the 1980s," 33.

11. Timothy Egan, "Effort Under Way in Oregon to Kick Out Governor," *New York Times*, May 8, 1992, A20.

12. Donald Snow, *Inside the Environmental Movement: Meeting the Leadership Challenge* (Washington, D.C.: Island Press, 1992), 5.

13. Robert Mitchell, "From Conservation to Environmental Movement: The Development of the Modern Environmental Lobbies," in *Government and Environmental Politics: Essays on Historical Developments Since World War Two*, ed. Michael J. Lacey (Baltimore: Johns Hopkins University Press, 1991), 83.

14. J. Clarence Davies, Frances H. Irwin, and Barbara K. Rhodes, *Training for Environmental Groups* (Washington, D.C.: Conservation Foundation, 1983).

15. Ronald Shaiko, "More Bang for the Buck: The New Era of Full-Service Public Interest Organizations," in *Interest Group Politics*, 3d ed., ed. Allan Cigler and Burdett Loomis (Washington, D.C.: CQ Press, 1991): 109-130.

16. See Michael T. Hayes, "The New Group Universe," *Interest Group Politics*, 2d ed., ed. Allan Cigler and Burdett Loomis (Washington, D.C.: CQ Press, 1986): 133-145.

17. Tom Arrandale "The Mid-Life Crisis of the Environmental Lobby," *Governing* (April 1992), 32-36; and Sharon Begley, "The War Among the Greens," *Newsweek*, May 4, 1992, 78.

18. Robert Cameron Mitchell, Angela G. Mertig, and Riley E. Dunlap, "Twenty Years of Environmental Mobilization: Trends Among National Environmental Organizations," *Society and Natural Resources* 4 (1991): 224-225.

19. John Lancaster, "War and Recession Taking Toll on National Environmental Organizations," *Washington Post*, February 15, 1991, A3.

20. Ibid.

21. Anne Raver, "Old Environmental Group Seeks Tough New Image," *New York Times*, June 9, 1991, A1; and Roxanne Roberts, "Audubon Fires Editors," *Washington Post*, July 30, 1991, C5.

22. *Chronicle of Philanthropy*, June 28, 1992, 9.

23. John B. Judis, "The Pressure Elite: Inside the Narrow World of Advocacy Group Politics," *American Prospect* 9 (Spring 1992): 22.

24. Keith Schneider, "Natural Foes Bankroll Environmental Group," *New York Times*, December 23, 1991, A12; Jane Hall, "Audubon Specials Are Endangered Species," *Los Angeles Times*, December 17, 1991, F1.

25. Tom Horton, "The Green Giant," *Rolling Stone*, September 5, 1991, 44.

26. Eliza N. Carney and W. John Moore, "From the K Street Corridor," *National Journal*, January 4, 1992, 30.

27. On this notion of policy "niches," see William P. Browne, *Private Interests, Public Policy, and American Agriculture* (Lawrence: University Press of Kansas, 1988).

28. Thomas W. Lippman, "Senate Votes to Abandon Energy Bill," *Washington Post*, November 2, 1991, A1.

29. *Congressional Record*, November 1, 1991, S15755.

30. Michael McCloskey, "Twenty Years of Change in the Environmental Movement: An Insider's View," *Society and Natural Resources* 4 (1991): 274.

31. Keith Schneider, "Fears of Pesticides Threaten American Way of Farming," *New York Times*, May 1, 1989, A14; and Philip Shabecoff, "E.P.A. Proposing Quicker Action Against Suspect Farm Chemicals," *New York Times*, July 20, 1989, A1. On federal pesticides policy, see Christopher J. Bosso, *Pesticides and Politics: The Life Cycle of a Public Issue* (Pittsburgh: University of Pittsburgh Press, 1987); and George Hoberg, *Pluralism by Design: Environmental Policy and the American Regulatory State* (New York: Praeger, 1992).

32. Timothy Egan, "Fund-Raisers Tap Anti-Environmental Sentiment," *New York Times*, December 19, 1991, A18; Keith Schneider, "When the Bad Guy Is Seen as the One in the Green Hat," *New York Times*, February 16, 1992; Denise Goodman, "Land Use Limits Draw Fire," *Boston Globe*, April 19, 1992, 29.

33. Tom Kenworthy and Kirsten Downey, "Court Limits Property 'Takings'," *Boston Globe*, June 30, 1992, 11.

34. For the "manifesto" of the Wise Use movement, see Arnold M. Gottlieb, ed., *The Wise Use Agenda* (Bellevue, Wash.: Merrill, 1989).

35. *National Journal*, February 1, 1992, 281.

36. Lindsy Van Gelder, "Saving the Homeplace," *Audubon* 94 (January-February 1992): 67.

37. Robert Gottlieb and Helen Ingram, "The New Environmentalists," *Progressive* 52 (August 1988): 14.

38. Van Gelder, "Saving the Home Place," 67.

39. Rochelle Stanfield, "Now You Know," *National Journal*, July 9, 1988, 1831; Keith Schneider, "For Communities, Knowledge of Polluters Is Power," *New York Times*, March 24, 1991, E5.

40. Elizabeth Larsen, "Granola Boys, Eco-Dudes, and Me," *Ms.* (July-August 1991), 97.

41. Nicholas Freudenberg and Carol Steinsapir, "Not in Our Backyards: The Grassroots Environmental Movement," *Society and Natural Resources* 4 (1991): 240.

42. Ibid., 242-243.

43. Christopher Manes, *Green Rage: Radical Environmentalism and the Unmaking of Civilization* (Boston: Little, Brown, 1990); and Steven Yearly, *The Green Case: A Sociology of Environmental Issues, Arguments, and Politics* (New York: HarperCollins, 1991).

44. "Let's Party," *Buzzworm* 4 (March-April 1992): 12.

45. "Why Not Here? Prospects for Green Politics in America," *Greenpeace* (July-August 1991), 18-20.

46. Snow, *Inside the Environmental Movement*, 14.

47. Mitchell, "From Conservation to Environmental Movement," 107.

48. Mark Sagoff, "The Great Environmental Awakening," *American Prospect* 9 (Spring 1992): 44.

49. Robert C. Paehlke, "Environmental Values and Democracy: The Challenge of the Next Century," in *Environmental Policy in the 1990s*, ed. Norman J. Vig and Michael E. Kraft (Washington, D.C.: CQ Press, 1990), 357.

3

A New Federalism?
Environmental Policy in the States

James P. Lester

How profoundly state governments have changed. They now are arguably the most responsive, innovative, and effective level of government in the American federal system.

—Carl E. Van Horn
The State of the States (1989)

Some states never make the top ten in any specific policy area.... One cannot assert that the resurgence of the states ... has occurred across the board.

—William R. Lowry
The Dimensions of Federalism (1992)

Opinions differ widely, as we can see from the above remarks, on the effectiveness of state government today. Some argue that because of paltry resources or a lack of political will, state governments are the principal impediment to effective American government. According to these critics, they lack the fiscal resources or technical expertise available to national governments, they suffer from parochialism, they cannot raise revenues to meet service demands, and are dominated by a conservative, business-oriented elite. Others argue that the institutional reforms of the 1970s and the 1980s changed all this. The supporters of state governments argue that, compared with the federal government, the states are more flexible and innovative and, because they are closer to the problems, are better able to fashion appropriate responses.[1]

But what about state environmental policy in the 1990s? Are the states innovative actors, as some suggest, or bastions of resistance? Paying particular attention to environmental pollution issues, this chapter will seek to examine the responses of the fifty states to environmental problems.

This is an especially important time to examine state environmental politics and policy. First, the states are now implementing key environmental laws enacted during the previous three decades. Nearly all major federal environmental statutes call for shared implementation between the federal and state governments. Under the concept of "partial preemption," the federal government sets minimum environmental standards and objectives, but states are given the latitude to design and implement their own laws. Essentially, the procedure allows the federal government to return program responsibility to the states while retaining the authority to judge the acceptability of states' actions. Hence, the role of the states is paramount.[2]

Second, intergovernmental relations (meaning the relations among the federal, state, and local governments) have recently taken on greater significance than ever before. During the 1970s and the 1980s, the doctrine of new federalism stressed the devolution of authority to state and local levels in many areas of public policy. As part of the legacy of the Reagan and Bush presidencies, states and local communities are assuming many responsibilities for protecting the environment that had previously been undertaken by the federal government. Indeed, the head of Vermont's environmental agency, Jonathan Lash, has said that the most important innovations in environmental protection are now occurring at the state level.[3] Many others agree with this assessment.

Finally, the states' institutional capacities have been transformed during the past twenty-five years and constitute a clear break with the past.[4] States are no longer the weak link in the U.S. intergovernmental system. It is therefore necessary here to review these changes in intergovernmental relations since the 1970s and to assess the implications for the future of environmental policy in the states.

Several questions are addressed in this chapter: first, what is the new federalism, and what changes does it entail in federal-state relations? Second, what state-level policy innovations, commitments, and implementation are taking place as a result of the new federalism? Third, why have the states reacted as they have to the new federalism? Finally, what are the prospects for state environmental policy for the rest of the 1990s?

Federal Devolution of Authority and the Resurgence of the States

Two dramatic developments affected the states during the 1970s and the 1980s. First, the Nixon, Reagan, and Bush administrations, under their various programs of new federalism, attempted to return power and authority to the states and cities. New federalism, which began with the State and Local Fiscal Assistance Act of 1972, mandated an expanded role for state and local governments. Among other things, states would become less subject to fiscal control by the federal government. Initially, new federalism involved a number of short-term inducements, such as programmatic flexibility, elimination of de facto dual-planning requirements for categorical grant applications, and increased consultation with state and local decisionmakers prior to the initiation of "direct development" activities.[5]

President Ronald Reagan's new federalism program had two major objectives for environmental policy: to *decentralize* and to *defund* federal environmental protection activities.[6] Proponents of the Reagan program argued that the states, with their greater institutional capacities, were now better able to assume responsibilities. States and cities would make difficult choices about which programs they wanted to retain (and thus replace federal cuts with their own funds) and which ones they wanted to terminate. Public pressure would force state decisionmakers to take actions that reflected localized policy preferences. Critics argued that this devolution of authority was the administration's way to eliminate programs.[7]

During the Reagan and Bush administrations, federal grants to the states were subject to substantial budgetary cuts in a number of environmental program areas, including air pollution control, water pollution control, hazardous waste management, pesticide enforcement, wastewater treatment, and safe drinking water.[8] The significance of the cuts can be seen in the level of state dependency on federal funds for these programs. In the early to mid 1980s, federal grants constituted from 33 to 75 percent of the average state budgets for air and water pollution control and hazardous waste management. Would the states replace the federal cuts with their own funds?

Early assessments have revealed that most of the states did *not* proffer their own funds in the environmental area, at least from 1981 to 1984.[9] States that did had also demonstrated the political will to assume the administration of federal environmental programs under "partial preemption"; they also had an ethos conducive to environmental protection.[10] From 1985 to 1992 many of the states replaced lost federal funds by increasing state and local taxes and user fees.[11] Although we do not have complete evidence on all the states during this period, we can assume that some of the states did *not* replace the federal cuts with their own funds. The states faced a national recession during this time and the fiscal climate was not conducive to raising taxes. Indeed, many states were constrained by an antitaxation ethic regardless of broad public support for environmental protection programs.

The second dramatic development that affected the states during the past two decades was the transformation of their institutional capabilities. The states revised their constitutions, professionalized their legislatures (for example, by increasing salaries and staff support), modernized and strengthened the governor's office, reorganized their executive branches, reformed their courts, increased their revenues through tax diversification, and provided greater opportunities for citizen participation through "open meeting laws" and other reforms.[12] Not all states adopted such reforms, however, nor were all equally able to make these modifications.[13]

Hence, not all of them are able effectively to assume their new environmental responsibilities under the new federalism of the 1990s.

In summary, federal budget cuts and changes in state institutional capacity had serious implications for state environmental policy during the past two decades. Although some of the states replaced the federal cuts with their own funds, other states did not. Similarly, although some of the states reformed their institutions, others did not do so. Therefore, we would expect that states' behavior in environmental protection policy will vary significantly, depending on the extent of their institutional reforms and their commitments to environmental protection.

The States' Response to New Federalism: 1970-1992

So much attention has been focused on activities of the federal government that many important developments at the state level have been overlooked. Some states have been innovative, while others are more conventional. Some of the more impressive state activities are reviewed below.

Environmental Policy Innovations

The Institute for Southern Studies has collected recent information on innovative environmental and natural resource policies. This information, published in the 1991-1992 *Green Index*, began as an assessment of environmental conditions and policies in the fifty states. The Green Policy Initiatives ranking is based on the number of innovative environmental and natural resource policies each state has adopted, in combination with similar indicators of environmental policy in the late 1980s (table 3-1, p. 56).

The ten states with the best records in environmental policy innovation are California, Oregon, New Jersey, Connecticut, Maine, Wisconsin, Minnesota, New York, Massachusetts, and Rhode Island.[14] Innovative state actions include statewide recycling mandates, Proposition 65 in California on toxic use reduction, and source reduction programs that have been adopted in twenty-seven states since 1987.[15] New Jersey has imposed new environmental taxes and fees and established revolving loan funds. In addition, a number of states (New York, Connecticut, New Jersey, Maine, Massachusetts, New Hampshire, Rhode Island, and Vermont) have announced restrictions on the amount of gasoline vapor that may be emitted by automobiles.[16] In another regional effort, Virginia, Maryland, Pennsylvania, and the District of Columbia are cooperating to clean up the badly polluted Chesapeake Bay.[17] Variations in groundwater protection programs suggest some states (Arizona) have been quite innovative while others (Texas) have not.[18]

Recently instituted programs in five states deserve special mention. Massachusetts's Blackstone Project covers industries in the Upper Blackstone Water Pollution Abatement District. It is a joint effort of the Massachusetts Department of Environmental Protection (DEP) and the Office of Technical Assistance (OTA). To make it work, DEP united its separate programs on air, water, and hazardous waste pollution to form a Bureau of Waste Prevention; it then began coordinated inspection visits. The new inspection system took half the time of previous conventional inspections and saved the state considerable money. Initially, regulators found that of the twenty-eight firms inspected in the Blackstone River Valley, twenty were not in compliance. They referred the offending companies to the OTA, which showed the firms how to reduce pollution by reusing materials more effectively or by substituting less toxic chemicals for the hazardous substances they were accustomed to using.[19]

California's "mobile source" (automobile) pollution control policy is a second noteworthy program. Federal policymakers have long acknowledged California's leadership on air quality policy by exempting it from weaker federal standards and allowing other states to follow suit.[20] California's tough tailpipe emissions standards, for example, have led the rest of the country by two to five years. Its standards are even emulated by the federal government. The 1990 revisions to the Clean Air Act incorporated California's existing exhaust emission standards for new cars and light-duty vehicles even as that state began another round of even more stringent controls on air emissions, particularly in the heavily contaminated South Coast Air Quality Management District in Greater Los Angeles.[21]

Another innovative state program is Florida's "Amnesty Days," a free, mobile hazardous waste collection program that visits each county. The program allows each citizen, school, business, or government agency to properly dispose of up to one 55-gallon drum of hazardous waste. One of the first in the nation, this program has been a model for other cities and states as they implement new requirements for small-quantity generators under the Hazardous and Solid Waste Amendments of 1986.

Wisconsin's program to deal with stationary source air pollution deserves special mention. Wisconsin has a strong state implementation plan (SIP) for air pollution. It conducts extensive research on acid rain, has developed a toxics program, and has received very high marks from outside authorities.[22] According to one researcher:

> Wisconsin's regulatory efforts center around permits for polluters. The process works as follows. Rules are proposed by the Department of Natural Resources (DNR) concerning specific areas of pollution, such as sulfur emissions, particulates, and organic compounds. Following public hearings, the rule is subject to approval by the independent DNR board. If [the rule is] approved, the state legislature has thirty days to veto the rule. Without veto, the rules become part of the Wisconsin SIP. The rules define pollutants, specify emission limits for various polluting processes, and explicate compliance schedules and variances. . . . One major attribute of this program is speed, which enables rapid responsiveness by the state to air pollution problems.[23]

Table 3-1   The Best and Worst States in Environmental Policy

State	Green Index[a]	Green Policy Initiatives [b]
Oregon	1	2
Maine	2	5
Vermont	3	12
California	4	1
Minnesota	5	7
Massachusetts	6	9
Rhode Island	7	10
New York	8	8
Washington	9	14
Wisconsin	10	6
Connecticut	11	4
Hawaii	12	24
Maryland	13	15
New Jersey	14	3
New Hampshire	15	20
Colorado	16	26
Michigan	17	11
Florida	18	13
Idaho	19	36
Iowa	20	16
Montana	21	31
Nevada	22	43
North Carolina	23	18
Delaware	24	25
North Dakota	25	37
Pennsylvania	26	21
South Dakota	27	48
New Mexico	28	38
Nebraska	29	30
Missouri	30	23
Illinois	31	17
Virginia	32	22
Utah	33	41
Alaska	34	47
Arizona	35	39
South Carolina	36	32
Ohio	37	19
Wyoming	38	44
Georgia	39	29
Oklahoma	40	42
Kentucky	41	33
Kansas	42	28
Indiana	43	27
West Virginia	44	45
Tennessee	45	40

(Continued on next page)

Table 3-1 *(Continued)*

State	Green Index[a]	Green Policy Initiatives [b]
Texas	46	35
Mississippi	47	46
Arkansas	48	50
Louisiana	49	34
Alabama	50	49

Source: Bob Hall and Mary Lee Kerr, *1991-1992 Green Index: A State-by-State Guide to the Nation's Environmental Health* (Washington, D.C.: Island Press, 1991), 3.

[a] The Green Index used here is a comprehensive measure that incorporates 256 different indicators of a state's environmental health. These measure environmental quality conditions in the state, the nature of state environmental policies, and political leadership on the environment. The states are listed in order of their ranking on this index.

[b] The Green Policy Initiatives ranking reflects a state's position relative to the others based on seventy-seven indicators. Among these are whether or not each state has adopted fifty innovative policies on a broad range of environmental issues, such as recycling, landfills, toxic waste, air and water pollution, energy and transportation, and agriculture; and state ratings compiled by Renew America on seventeen equally diverse environmental policies between 1987 and 1989.

Our fifth example is Delaware's Regulation for the Management of Extremely Hazardous Substances, first implemented in 1989. It helps protect Delaware's population, most of which resides near industrial plants that use, store, transfer, process, or produce hazardous substances. The program mandates that each facility greatly improve its risk management techniques in order to comply with the regulation and to reduce the probability of a catastrophic event. Delaware's program is the first such program to extend beyond the regulation of toxic air contaminants to regulate flammable, combustible, and explosive materials.[24]

During the 1990s the states are likely to formulate equally resourceful programs to deal with problems ranging from high levels of energy use (especially of fossil fuels) to toxic chemical exposure and cleanup of hazardous waste sites. Some states, however, have been far less active in changing their environmental policies during the past decade.

State Commitments and Environmental Policy

Data on the states' overall commitment to the environment reveal that Texas, Mississippi, Arkansas, Louisiana, and Alabama are among the least committed.[25] As mentioned earlier, California, Maine, Massachusetts, Minnesota, Oregon, and Vermont have stellar environmental records (table 3-1).

The Fund for Renewable Energy and the Environment (FREE) also provides data on the states' environmental activities.[26] Since 1987 FREE has conducted an annual nonfiscal study of state activities regarding key environmental issues such as air pollution reduction, soil conservation, solid waste and recycling, hazardous waste management, groundwater protection, and renewable energy and conservation. According to these data, Massachusetts, Wisconsin, California, and New Jersey are the most active or environmentally progressive states; Arkansas, Mississippi, West Virginia, and Wyoming are the least active or progressive. In FREE's most recent study, other states in the top ten are Oregon, Minnesota, Iowa, Florida, Maryland, and Connecticut.[27] Both the *Green Index* and FREE identified essentially the same states as the most "environmentally concerned" over time.

States' institutional capabilities to protect the environment also vary. In 1988, in 1990, and again in 1992, the Council of State Governments studied the fifty states' institutions for environmental management, their expenditures for environmental and natural resource programs, and the numbers of state government employees with environmental or natural resource responsibilities.[28] These data suggest some potential problems in the states' ability to manage the environment, no matter how progressive or innovative they may be. Some environmental problems, such as toxic waste, cannot be effectively managed without enormous sums of money and highly trained staff. Yet states appear to be suffering from inadequate fiscal resources, insufficient and inexperienced staff beset by turnovers, and other problems that affect the states' abilities to respond to environmental problems in the 1990s.[29]

Environmental Policy Implementation

Mere enactment of a policy guarantees little. Effective implementation is essential, and, again, varies considerably from state to state. For example, implementation of federal policies may be achieved by delegation of authority from the federal government to the states after they have met federal guidelines. A number of scholars have studied the extent to which various states have assumed responsibility for environmental programs and thereby stepped up the pace of implementation.[30] Between 1972 and 1988 some states accepted primary responsibility for enforcing national environmental standards within their boundaries. Scoring highest in this regard were California, Michigan, Minnesota, New York, Washington, and Wisconsin.[31]

Environmental policy implementation may also be determined by the amount of money spent on state programs—even though expenditures are an imperfect measure of program effectiveness or a state's commitment. The U.S. Department of Commerce collected data on environmental quality control expenditures from 1969 to 1980,[32] which revealed that

California, Delaware, Maryland, Massachusetts, New Hampshire, Ohio, Rhode Island, and Vermont had the highest per capita expenditures, while Mississippi, Oklahoma, South Carolina, Texas, Utah, and Virginia had the lowest. Budgetary cuts in 1981, however, halted this data collection effort. With no data since 1981, it is difficult to assess the impact of new federalism on state environmental spending, although the data vacuum has been partly filled by the Institute for Southern Studies and the Council of State Governments (table 3-2).

As we can see from the data presented in table 3-2, California, New Jersey, Florida, Illinois, Pennsylvania, Washington, Massachusetts, New York, Michigan, and Louisiana now lead the nation in total environmental expenditures. Note, however, that the top-ten rankings shift significantly when spending per capita is considered or when expenditures are measured as a percentage of the total state budget—perhaps the best indicator of the priority of environmental protection activities within a state.[33] If one accounts for spending as a percentage of a state's total budget, then Wyoming, Alaska, Montana, New Jersey, Oregon, Idaho, Washington, and California lead the nation, while Oklahoma, Ohio, Indiana, and Texas spend the least.

Explaining State Environmental Policy

Political scientists have sought to explain these variations among the states. Such information is useful both for pragmatic and scientific reasons. Understanding *why* states behave as they do gives us a good pragmatic basis for formulating political strategies that might inspire the laggard states to be more responsive. The information is scientifically useful because research findings may be used to suggest policy reforms that might encourage more effective implementation.

Effective policy responses to environmental pollution can be explained in a number of different ways: four are described below.[34]

The "severity" argument.   Rapid and concentrated population growth, extensive industrialization (especially the petrochemical and metallurgical industries), and steady rates of public consumption of goods and services create severe pollution problems that, in turn, bring about strong pressures for environmental protection policies. Thus, one obvious reason for policy differences among the states is the severity of environmental problems themselves.[35] In other words, states with more severe environmental pollution problems, it is assumed, will take the necessary steps to deal with them. Studies suggest, however, that the correlation of severity to protection is not clear, and that more refined indicators of pollution severity and other environmental problems are needed before its effect on state environmental policy can be fully known.[36] Factors other than problem severity (such as politics or economics) appear to be affecting states' behavior in this area.

Table 3-2   State Spending on Environmental and Natural Resource
Programs, 1988

State	Total Expenditures (in thousands of dollars)	Per Capita Expenditures	Percentage of Total State Budget
Alabama	$64,907	$15.73	1.02%
Alaska	131,684	256.69	4.00
Arizona	46,613	13.45	0.96
Arkansas	44,189	8.24	1.15
California	1,486,124	52.76	2.60
Colorado	76,150	23.15	1.65
Connecticut	61,996	19.13	0.77
Delaware	33,170	50.26	1.80
Florida	465,591	37.62	2.51
Georgia	93,344	14.58	1.07
Hawaii	27,832	25.46	0.85
Idaho	61,442	61.50	4.22
Illinois	392,844	34.03	2.26
Indiana	52,776	9.46	0.68
Iowa	88,065	31.07	1.44
Kansas	47,817	19.23	1.23
Kentucky	120,289	32.33	1.64
Louisiana	193,836	43.85	2.64
Maine	39,332	32.61	1.88
Maryland	150,091	32.32	1.60
Massachusetts	237,936	40.53	1.56
Michigan	221,425	23.81	1.42
Minnesota	126,236	29.32	1.46
Mississippi	54,154	20.61	1.40
Missouri	119,907	23.33	1.73
Montana	69,560	86.52	4.29
Nebraska	27,988	17.48	1.29
Nevada	36,487	34.42	2.57
New Hampshire	33,588	30.62	2.41
New Jersey	523,874	67.86	3.61
New Mexico	44,782	29.66	1.48
New York	236,484	13.21	0.59
North Carolina	96,943	14.85	1.00
North Dakota	32,524	49.06	2.32
Ohio	125,669	11.56	0.65
Oklahoma	40,869	12.52	0.79
Oregon	186,438	68.02	3.03
Pennsylvania	288,766	24.01	1.49
Rhode Island	35,879	36.06	1.86
South Carolina	71,124	20.36	1.21
South Dakota	21,264	29.74	1.85
Tennessee	81,180	16.50	1.34
Texas	113,797	6.78	0.60
Utah	51,419	30.41	1.80

(Continued on next page)

Table 3-2   *(Continued)*

State	Total Expenditures (in thousands of dollars)	Per Capita Expenditures	Percentage of Total State Budget
Vermont	20,222	36.37	1.94
Virginia	152,149	25.38	1.47
Washington	246,873	53.45	2.63
West Virginia	56,189	29.82	1.68
Wisconsin	167,779	34.54	1.70
Wyoming	128,051	271.87	7.73

Source: Bob Hall and Mary Lee Kerr, *1991-1992 Green Index: A State-by-State Guide to the Nation's Environmental Health* (Washington, D.C.: Island Press, 1991), 148.

The "wealth" argument.   The socioeconomic resource base of a state is directly related to the level of its commitment to environmental protection.[37] Or so the "wealth" argument asserts. States with greater fiscal resources are assumed to spend more on environmental protection than those with less. Those who assume that the failure of government to act in the environmental area is caused by states' "backwardness" or disregard for the environment often overlook the wealth factor. Wealth accounts for a significant amount of the variation in state efforts to protect the environment.[38]

The "partisanship" argument.   Partisanship is perhaps the most common generalization in the literature: to wit—environmental policy formation can be largely explained by political party (or ideological) differences. Riley Dunlap and Richard Gale argue that there are important reasons to expect significant partisan differences to emerge on environmental issues, with Democrats being more supportive than Republicans. The two major parties differ somewhat in their support for business interests, which tend to balk at policies that regulate their behavior and impose high compliance costs.[39] In a recent review of the literature, Jerry Calvert found that for these reasons Democratic partisanship is strongly related to environmental voting within state legislatures and Congress.[40]

The "organizational capacity" argument.   Administrative and legislative reforms, argue proponents of this theory, are good predictors of environmental policy. For example, when the environmental bureaucracy is reorganized to reduce jurisdictional overlaps and the consequent rivalries and conflicts among the many agencies in this area, environmental protection policy benefits.[41] Moreover, a consolidated environmental bureaucracy increases the governor's control and, with regard to crucial appointments in environmental agencies, improves his or her ability to mobilize the bureaucracy in support of gubernatorial objectives.

In addition, professional legislatures are more effective than their unprofessional counterparts in other states.[42] Professional legislatures are thought to be more responsive to environmental needs, generous in spending and services, and "interventionist" in the sense of having broad powers and responsibilities. Indeed, in some instances it appears that consolidated environmental bureaucracies and professional legislatures do make a positive contribution to the states' efforts to protect the environment.[43]

Although each of these four arguments provides some insight into the determinants of state environmental protection policies, none captures the complexity of the policy process nor sufficiently explains the multiple forces that influence the states' commitment to environmental quality. Each argument simply assumes that conditions within the states themselves are the sole (or even primary) influences on state environmental management. Given the intergovernmental influences on behavior described earlier in the chapter, it seems appropriate to consider external influences on state efforts to protect the environment.[44] The four explanations of state environmental management should be considered in a wider context that includes federal-level, as well as state-level, influences.[45] In other words, the states' actions are shaped within an intergovernmental framework that includes federal-level inducements and constraints, such as environmental aid. Some states (e.g., Rhode Island, Montana, Connecticut, Idaho, Vermont, Nebraska, Arizona, Maine, Missouri, and Alabama) depend heavily on federal aid in the environmental area, while other states (e.g., California, New Jersey, Oregon) are not very dependent at all.[46] When federal aid is reduced, dependent states are even more constrained.

The Future of State Environmental Policies

President Bill Clinton has not yet said what he will do about the devolution of responsibility to the states and cities. Nor has he promised the states more money to fund environmental programs. His appointment of Carol Browner, the head of Florida's Department of Environmental Regulation, to run the EPA is certain to guarantee attention at the highest levels to the problems faced by the fifty states. Nevertheless, the large federal budget deficit, as well as the president's 1992 campaign pledge not to raise taxes on the middle class, leads one to assume that the states will be left largely to their own resources.

The decentralization of federal environmental programs and reduction of federal environmental grants-in-aid are therefore likely to continue into the mid 1990s. If so, state policies will be governed by two considerations that are internal to the states themselves. The first concerns state government institutional capability and the second relates to state commitment to environmental protection. Although federal (and local) influences should be considered in future assessments of state environmental policy, these within-state influences are most useful in predicting how the states will proceed with environmental management in the 1990s.

In the mid 1990s a state's response to the new federalism (as well as action on state and local environmental issues) will depend on two different, but nevertheless complementary, factors: (a) its commitment to environmental protection activities (as measured by the Green Index) and (b) its institutional capabilities.[47] Based on these two qualities, the states can be divided into four groups—progressives, strugglers, delayers, and regressives. For this purpose, the fifty states are ranked and then divided into two groups for each variable: high or low commitment and strong or weak institutional capabilities.

The Progressives

States with a high commitment to environmental protection coupled with strong institutional capabilities fall into the "progressive" group of states. They are California, Florida, Maryland, Massachusetts, Michigan, New Jersey, New York, Oregon, Washington, and Wisconsin (listed alphabetically). They have made substantial improvements in the implementation of federal and state environmental legislation and in the quality of the environment. As their environmental quality gets better, these states may adopt policies independent of federal mandates—as indeed many already have. Environmental conditions will likely get better, not worse.

California, for example, considers environmental protection highly important. For almost three decades "air pollution bills have been winning approval in Sacramento, well ahead of the national government."[48] The state has also been at the leading edge of energy conservation policy, coastal zone protection, and toxic chemical regulation. For states such as California, the major issue will be the extent to which the private and public sectors can reach a consensus on the rather drastic environmental policies being adopted. Significant tensions may arise in the course of these deliberations.

The Strugglers

States with a strong commitment to environmental protection but limited institutional capacities make up the second category. These are Colorado, Connecticut, Delaware, Hawaii, Idaho, Iowa, Maine, Minnesota, Montana, Nevada, New Hampshire, North Carolina, North Dakota, Rhode Island, and Vermont. They have the will but not the resources (fiscally and institutionally) to pursue aggressive environmental protection policies. Progress will probably be made in these states, but it will be slower and possibly less innovative than in the progressive states. The "strugglers" will do the best they can given the constraints imposed on them. The major issues in these states will revolve around finding the means to implement aggressive environmental protection policies. Much of the debate will focus on issues associated with tax increases as these states seek to increase their resource base for environmental protection.

Vermont, for example, is staunchly protective of its environmental assets, but has historically been a "low service, high unemployment, communal" state.[49] That is, it has kept the costs of government low and has preferred a decentralized, "town-meeting" approach to its problems as opposed to the development of strong state-level institutions that are necessary for effective environmental policy.

The Delayers

The "delayers" are states with a strong institutional capacity but a limited commitment to environmental protection. Alabama, Alaska, Arkansas, Georgia, Illinois, Louisiana, Missouri, Ohio, Oklahoma, Pennsylvania, South Carolina, Tennessee, Texas, Virginia, and West Virginia all fall into this third category. They will probably maintain the status quo on the environment and move very slowly in implementing federal legislation. Whatever progress is made will be painstakingly slow.[50]

States dominated by the energy industry, such as Louisiana, Oklahoma, Texas, and West Virginia, are included in this group. West Virginia, for example, has been characterized as "still struggling," which means it has few if any areas of exceptional program management, save for welfare policy.[51] It depends heavily on the federal government for aid and has not been able to build up its political institutions in a way that would sustain innovative environmental policies.[52] Apathetic state bureaucracies are the major concern in this group of states.

The Regressives

The "regressive" states have weak institutional capacities and a limited commitment to environmental protection. They are Arizona, Indiana, Kansas, Kentucky, Mississippi, Nebraska, New Mexico, South Dakota, Utah, and Wyoming. For these states, decentralization of environmental programs will likely be a disaster. They may fail to adequately implement federal laws in this area, and they are unlikely to take independent actions. The quality of life may deteriorate so much that large numbers of the population may move to other states (especially to the more progressive ones). Dirty industries may continue to move into these states, making them even more unattractive to the inhabitants. These states will continue to promote economic development at the expense of environmental quality. At some point a catastrophe may turn the states in this category around, but at present they seem to be captured by an obsessive optimism that prevents their taking necessary precautions against further damage to the environment.

Mississippi, for example, has been described by Neal Peirce and Jerry Hagstrom as a state where federal cutbacks in the early 1980s made the "road ahead bleaker than any time since the Great Depression."[53] Mississippi is frequently singled out as the state that lags behind all the other southern states in the area of environmental protection. The "Mississippi syndrome," as it is called, means a state that cannot, or will not, move ahead in the implementation of its programs to protect the environment.

Conclusions and Implications

In this assessment of state environmental policy under the doctrine of new federalism, I have described changes in federal-state relations and reforms of state institutions. I have also examined environmental policy innovations in the states (including their commitment to and capacity for environmental policymaking). Implementation in the states is discussed, and several explanations are offered for the way states manage their environments. Finally, I have suggested four possible classifications of the states in the 1990s: progressives, strugglers, delayers, and regressives. These scenarios range from extremely optimistic (the progressives) to extremely pessimistic (the regressives). The scenarios assume no major changes in state commitments or institutional capabilities, although public opinion, recent tendencies toward participatory democracy, and media attention could cause some legislators to change if conditions become intolerable.[54]

The policy implications of this discussion are significant. If we find that federal-level factors are crucial influences on state environmental policy, then the argument for centralization of environmental management would once again acquire saliency. That is, if on the one hand federal inducements (such as legislation and aid) are necessary conditions for successful management at the state level, then a policy of decentralization will probably not work effectively for all states. On the other hand, if state-level conditions strongly influence state environmental management, then arguments about a decentralized environmental management would acquire even more credibility. Or decentralization may work well in some states (for example, the innovative ones) but poorly in others. Thus, "selective decentralization," a policy that decentralizes some programs for some states while leaving others alone, may be a more appropriate strategy.[55]

In any case, policymakers need to reconsider the impact of intergovernmental relations on state environmental policy. The federal government should recognize that the fifty states are not equally able to muster the necessary resources to deal with environmental problems in the

1990s. Novel approaches will thus be required and are particularly appropriate in an era of "regulatory federalism," which will likely characterize the 1990s.

Notes

The quotations that open the chapter are from Carl E. Van Horn, "The Quiet Revolution," in *The State of the States*, ed. Carl E. Van Horn (Washington, D.C.: CQ Press, 1989), 1; and William R. Lowry, *The Dimensions of Federalism* (Durham, N.C.: Duke University Press, 1992), 2, 125.

1. Jeffrey Henig, *Public Policy and Federalism* (New York: St. Martin's, 1985); and John T. Scholz, "State Regulatory Reform and Federal Regulation," *Policy Studies Review* 1 (1981): 347-359.

2. Patricia M. Crotty, "The New Federalism Game: Primacy Implementation of Environmental Policy," *Publius* 17 (Spring 1987): 57-63; see also Advisory Commission on Intergovernmental Relations (ACIR), *Regulatory Federalism: Policy, Process, Impact, and Reform* (Washington, D.C.: ACIR, 1984), 19-21.

3. Philip Shabecoff, "The Environment as Local Jurisdiction," *New York Times*, January 22, 1989, E9.

4. Ann O'M. Bowman and Richard C. Kearney, *The Resurgence of the States* (Englewood Cliffs, N.J.: Prentice-Hall, 1986), 1-46.

5. These points are discussed at length in the following texts on intergovernmental relations: Laurence J. O'Toole, Jr., ed., *American Intergovernmental Relations*, 2d ed. (Washington, D.C.: CQ Press, 1993); David C. Nice, *Federalism: The Politics of Intergovernmental Relations* (New York: St. Martin's, 1987); and Thomas J. Anton, *American Federalism and Public Policy* (Philadelphia: Temple University Press, 1989).

6. See, for example, Richard P. Nathan and Fred C. Doolittle, *The Consequences of Cuts: The Effects of the Reagan Domestic Program on State and Local Governments* (Princeton, N.J.: Princeton University Press, 1983); and Richard P. Nathan and Fred C. Doolittle, *Reagan and the States* (Princeton, N.J.: Princeton University Press, 1987). See also James P. Lester, "New Federalism and Environmental Policy," *Publius* 16 (Winter 1986): 149-165; and Michael E. Kraft, Bruce B. Clary, and Richard J. Tobin, "The Impact of New Federalism on State Environmental Policy: The Great Lakes States," in *The Midwest Response to the New Federalism*, ed. Peter K. Eisinger and William Gormley (Madison: University of Wisconsin Press, 1988), 204-233.

7. J. Clarence Davies, "Environmental Institutions and the Reagan Administration," in *Environmental Policy in the 1980s: Reagan's New Agenda*, ed. Norman J. Vig and Michael E. Kraft (Washington, D.C.: CQ Press, 1984), 150.

8. Lester, "New Federalism and Environmental Policy," 152-153.

9. Ibid., 161-164.

10. Charles E. Davis and James P. Lester, "Decentralizing Federal Environmental Policy: A Research Note," *Western Political Quarterly* 40 (September 1987): 555-565.

11. Penelope Lemov, "User Fees, Once the Answer to City Budget Prayers, May Have Reached Their Peak," *Governing* 2 (March 1989): 24.

12. See ACIR, *The Question of State Government Capability;* Advisory Commission on Intergovernmental Relations, *The Transformation in American Politics* (Washington, D.C.: U.S. Government Printing Office, 1986); and Bowman and Kearney, *The Resurgence of the States*, 47-134.

13. Ann O'M. Bowman and Richard C. Kearney, "Dimensions of State Government Capability," *Western Political Quarterly* 41 (June 1988): 341-362.
14. Bob Hall and Mary Lee Kerr, *1991-1992 Green Index: A State-by-State Guide to the Nation's Environmental Health* (Washington, D.C.: Island Press, 1991), 3.
15. U.S. Environmental Protection Agency, *Pollution Prevention News* (Washington, D.C.: Office of Pollution Prevention and Toxics, 1992), 10.
16. Council of State Governments, *Innovations in Environment and Natural Resources* (Lexington, Ky.: Council of State Governments, 1986); Council of State Governments, *Suggested State Legislation* (Lexington, Ky.: Council of State Governments, various years); and U.S. Congress, Office of Technology Assessment, *Serious Reduction of Hazardous Waste* (Washington, D.C.: U.S. Government Printing Office, 1986).
17. Shabecoff, "Environment as Local Jurisdiction," E9.
18. James L. Regens and Margaret A. Reams, "State Strategies for Regulating Groundwater Quality," *Social Science Quarterly* 69 (September 1988): 53-59.
19. Carol Steinbach, *Innovations in State and Local Government: 1991* (New York: Ford Foundation, 1991), 17.
20. William R. Lowry, *The Dimensions of Federalism* (Durham, N.C.: Duke University Press, 1992), 90-97.
21. Ibid., 90.
22. Ibid., 47-55.
23. Ibid., 49.
24. Council of State Governments, *Innovations and Suggested State Legislation in State Environmental Programs, 1990-1992* (Lexington, Ky.: Council of State Governments, 1992), 23.
25. Hall and Kerr, *1991-1992 Green Index*, 3-5.
26. Scott Ridley, *The State of the States: 1987* (Washington, D.C.: Fund for Renewable Energy and the Environment, 1987). Similar reports have also been produced for 1988 and 1989.
27. Mark Obmascik, "Survey Places Colorado 26th in Environmental Efforts," *Denver Post*, March 1, 1989, A1.
28. See R. Steven Brown and L. Edward Garner, *Resource Guide to State Environmental Management* (Lexington, Ky.: Council of State Governments, 1988), 2-96.
29. Interviews with staff at the U.S. Environmental Protection Agency, Office of Solid Waste, State Programs Branch, July 1987.
30. See Pinky S. Wassenberg, "Implementation of Intergovernmental Regulatory Programs: A Cost-Benefit Perspective," in *Intergovernmental Relations and Public Policy*, ed. Edwin Benton and David R. Morgan (Westport, Conn.: Greenwood Press, 1986), 123-137; Patricia M. Crotty, "The New Federalism Game: Primacy Implementation of Environmental Policy," *Publius* 17 (Spring 1987): 57-63; James P. Lester, "Superfund Implementation: Exploring Environmental Gridlock," *Environmental Impact Assessment Review* 8 (June 1988): 159-174; and James P. Lester and Ann O'M. Bowman, "Implementing Environmental Policy in a Federal System: A Test of the Sabatier-Mazmanian Model," *Polity* 21 (Summer 1989): 731-753.
31. Crotty, "New Federalism Game," 57-63; and Deborah H. Jessup, *Guide to State Environmental Programs* (Washington, D.C.: Bureau of National Affairs, 1989).
32. U.S. Department of Commerce, Bureau of the Census, *Environmental Quality Control* (Washington, D.C.: U.S. Government Printing Office, 1982).
33. Hall and Kerr, *1991-1992 Green Index*, 148. The Council of State Governments hopes to continue its data collection effort and eventually to obtain data from 1990 to the present.
34. James P. Lester, James L. Franke, Ann O'M. Bowman, and Kenneth R. Kramer, "Hazardous Wastes, Politics and Public Policy: A Comparative State Analysis,"

Western Political Quarterly 36 (June 1983): 257-285.
35. Lettie M. Wenner, *One Environment Under Law: A Public Policy Dilemma* (Pacific Palisades, Calif.: Goodyear, 1976).
36. Kingsley W. Game, "Controlling Air Pollution: Why Some States Try Harder," *Policy Studies Journal* 7 (Summer 1979): 728-738.
37. James P. Lester and Patrick M. Keptner, "State Budgetary Commitments to Environmental Quality Under Austerity," in *Western Public Lands*, ed. John G. Francis and Richard Ganzel (Totowa, N.J.: Rowman and Allenheld, 1984), 193-214.
38. Ibid.
39. Riley E. Dunlap and Richard P. Gale, "Party Membership and Environmental Politics: A Legislative Roll-Call Analysis," *Social Science Quarterly* 55 (December 1974): 670-690.
40. Jerry W. Calvert, "Party Politics and Environmental Policy," in *Environmental Politics and Policy: Theories and Evidence*, ed. James P. Lester (Durham, N.C.: Duke University Press, 1989), 158-173.
41. James L. Garnett, *Reorganizing State Government: The Executive Branch* (Boulder: Westview, 1980).
42. See *The Sometime Governments: A Critical Study of the Fifty American Legislatures* (Kansas City, Mo.: Citizens Conference on State Legislatures, 1971).
43. Lester and Keptner, "State Budgetary Commitments," 201-207.
44. Douglas Rose, "National and Local Forces in State Politics: The Implications of Multi-level Policy Analysis," *American Political Science Review* 67 (December 1973): 1162-1173.
45. James P. Lester and Emmett N. Lombard, "The Comparative Analysis of State Environmental Policy," *Natural Resources Journal* 30 (Spring 1990): 301-319.
46. Lester, "New Federalism and Environmental Policy," 157.
47. The state rankings on institutional capabilities are drawn from Bowman and Kearney, "Dimensions of State Government Capability."
48. See Neal Peirce and Jerry Hagstrom, *The Book of America: Inside the Fifty States Today* (New York: Warner Books, 1984), 766.
49. Ibid., 199.
50. Donald G. Schueler, "Southern Exposure," *Sierra* (November-December 1992), 44-49.
51. Peirce and Hagstrom, *Book of America*, 345.
52. Ibid., 338-347.
53. Ibid., 456.
54. Raymond L. Goldsteen and John K. Schorr, *Demanding Democracy After Three Mile Island* (Gainesville: University of Florida Press, 1991).
55. Paul E. Peterson, Barry Rabe, and Kenneth Wong, *When Federalism Works* (Washington, D.C.: Brookings, 1986).

II. FEDERAL INSTITUTIONS AND POLICY CHANGE

4

Presidential Leadership and the Environment: From Reagan and Bush to Clinton

Norman J. Vig

I would be a Republican president in the Teddy Roosevelt tradition. A conservationist. An environmentalist.

—Vice President George Bush
August 31, 1988

It's time to put people ahead of owls.

—President George Bush
September 14, 1992

The presidential election of 1992 may be remembered as a watershed election for environmental policy. It appeared that there was a deeper ideological gulf between the two parties on environmental issues than ever before.[1] President George Bush and Vice President Dan Quayle made frequent attacks both on Gov. Bill Clinton's environmental record in Arkansas and on Sen. Al Gore's recently published environmental book, *Earth in the Balance.* Five days before the election President Bush delivered a vitriolic attack on the challengers, ridiculing Mr. Gore as "Ozone Man." "You know why I call him Ozone Man?," the president asked at a rally at Macomb Community College near Detroit. "This guy is so far out in the environmental extreme, we'll be up to our neck in owls and out of work for every American [sic]. He is way out, far out, man."[2]

The president's statement could be written off as mere rhetorical excess in the heat of the battle. In fact, four years before, the Bush-Quayle campaign had made a very different strategic calculation about the costs and benefits of environmentalism. In 1988 Mr. Bush had seized on environmental policy as a way of distancing himself from Ronald Reagan's record and of broadening his appeal to undecided voters in several key states. He promised to be the "environmental president."[3] But in 1992, with the poor state of the economy dominating the election, he opted for a divisive strategy of pitting environmental protection against jobs and economic growth in order to appeal to voters such as loggers and auto workers who felt threatened by environmental restrictions. By contrast, Clinton and Gore called this a "false choice" and argued that new environmental technologies would create jobs and make the U.S. economy more efficient and competitive in the future.

The tension between economic growth and preservation of natural resources has been at the heart of public debate over the environment for much of the past century. But since Teddy Roosevelt, presidents have often used the "bully pulpit" of their office to rally public support for conservation programs that also contribute to the long-term health of the economy. Indeed, the powers of the presidency give the incumbent great opportunities to shape national environmental policies.

First, presidents have a major role in *agenda setting.* They can raise issues to public attention, define the terms of public debate, and mobilize public opinion and constituency support through speeches, press conferences, and other media events. Without presidential endorsement, major policy initiatives are rarely successful. Second, presidents can take the lead in *policy formulation* by devoting presidential staff and other resources to particular issues, by mobilizing expertise inside and outside of government, and by consulting widely with interest groups and members of Congress in designing and proposing legislation. In the field of environmental policy it is especially important that presidents draw on the best science available in formulating proposals. Third, the presidential role has become increasingly important in *policy implementation.* As chief executive, the president makes key appointments to all agencies, determines budget and personnel for particular programs, oversees management and efficiency in the bureaucracy, and sets the tone for administration throughout the government. An increasingly important function is regulatory oversight; that is, how the president influences regulatory policymaking by agencies such as the Environmental Protection Agency (EPA). Finally, presidents have a rapidly growing role in *international leadership* on environmental issues that involve all of these dimensions. As many threats to the environment have been recognized as global problems, the president has had to assume a larger role in international environmental diplomacy.

The following section discusses some precedents for presidential leadership beginning with Theodore Roosevelt. I then focus on how recent presidents (Reagan and Bush) have utilized the White House to reverse or "balance" environmental policies in favor of promoting economic growth. The chapter concludes with a brief assessment of prospects for a much more proenvironmental Clinton-Gore administration.

Presidents and Environmental Eras: From Teddy Roosevelt to Jimmy Carter

Presidents have played an important role in environmental policymaking throughout this century, but they have exerted leadership only sporadically. Environmental activism has gone through three main periods since 1900: first, the Progressive Era, during which President Theodore Roosevelt launched the first major phase of natural resource conservation; second, the New Deal era, when President Franklin D. Roosevelt backed large conservation projects as public works to create jobs and lift the nation out of the Depression; and, third, the contemporary environmental era launched during the presidency of Richard M. Nixon (1969-1974). Only one president, Ronald Reagan, has entered office with a clearly antienvironmental agenda. Most other recent presidents have either supported incremental policy changes or have left definition of the environmental agenda to Congress and interest groups.

The Progressive Era

It is important to note that periods of environmental activism have coincided with times of economic crisis and social change. This is not surprising because environmental issues are deeply embedded in our political economy and way of life. The Progressive Era was a response to the robber baron capitalism of the post-Civil War decades, which were marked by the rise of powerful corporations bent on exploiting resources to the limit. Teddy Roosevelt made the conservation movement an integral part of his presidency (1901-1909). He set aside millions of acres of the remaining public domain as national forests, parks, and wildlife reserves, called a White House conference to proclaim the gospel of conservation, and laid the foundations for modern public land management.[4]

The doctrine of conservationism, as formulated by Roosevelt and his chief forester, Gifford Pinchot, held that natural resources must be held in trust for future generations through careful use and management. Such "stewardship" would allow multiple economic uses of public lands (such as mining, lumbering, grazing, and recreation), while at the same time ensuring that no single use predominated and that overall resource consumption remained within the limits of "sustainable yield." Thus conservationism attempted to reconcile economic growth and environmental preservation; in retrospect, it was a first attempt to define "sustainable development."[5]

The New Deal

Teddy Roosevelt was successful in linking deeper economic and social pressures for reform with an exceptionally able and active use of executive and administrative powers. The same can be said for Franklin Roosevelt. The economic disaster of the 1930s, following another period of rampant economic greed and public neglect, provided an opportunity for both strong leadership and new policies that tied conservation to the war against the Depression. The New Deal administration contained a strong conservationist wing that promoted both huge reclamation projects (such as the Tennessee Valley Authority and the Bonneville Dam) and large investments of human capital to improve national parks, restore wildlife areas, and build other outdoor amenities. Through the Civilian Conservation Corps (CCC), more than 3 million young men were put to work planting 2 billion trees; the Public Works Administration (PWA) launched a sewer construction program to control water pollution. The acreage of the national forests was doubled, and eleven national monuments were set aside by presidential proclamation. For the first time, the unlimited use of the western rangelands by cattle and sheep ranchers was brought under control by the Taylor Grazing Act (1934), and in 1935 the Soil Conservation Service was established to protect agricultural land generally against erosion.[6]

The Contemporary Environmental Era

The quarter-century after World War II was largely a period of incremental progress in environmental policy. Presidents Truman, Eisenhower, Kennedy, and Johnson were preoccupied with the Cold War, economic growth, and social problems such as poverty and civil rights. Federal management of public lands and natural resources gradually advanced but was largely left to lower-level professionals and bureaucrats. Congress predominated on most resource issues, which were usually dealt with in terms of local or regional interests. One landmark piece of national legislation, the Wilderness Act, was passed in 1964 after nearly a decade of debate. President Johnson also launched a campaign to beautify America, and his secretary of the interior, Stewart Udall, helped to restore the earlier conservation ethic to the federal government.

The new national environmental agenda that slowly emerged in the 1950s and 1960s concerned another kind of threat—air and water pollution. As discussed in chapter 1, these problems were largely considered state and local responsibilities until the 1960s, when Rachel Carson's *Silent Spring* and other evidence of extensive chemical contamination triggered the emergence of the contemporary environmental movement.[7] Intense public concern over urban decay, poverty, and the destructiveness of the war in Vietnam added to society's pervasive sense of crisis. The pressure on Congress to act had increased enormously by 1969. One result was passage of the pioneering National Environmental Policy Act (NEPA) late that year, but it was clear that environmental policy would be at the top of the political agenda for the new decade.

President Nixon thus found himself at the center of an entirely new era in environmental politics. But policy on pollution issues was dominated by the U.S. Senate, where powerful Democratic chairmen such as Edmund Muskie (D-Maine) and Henry Jackson (D-Wash.) reigned supreme. Muskie was also the leading contender for the Democratic presidential nomination. Nixon was thus faced with both a massive new popular environmental movement and a formidable rival positioned to champion its cause. In response, he declared himself an environmentalist, proclaimed the "Environmental Decade" on January 1, 1970, and delivered a presidential address to Congress in which he called for far-reaching legislation on air pollution and other environmental problems. Throughout 1970 he attempted to outbid Muskie and others by offering increasingly stringent proposals on the pending Clean Air Act. He not only succeeded in passing the most important pollution control bill in history but also created the Environmental Protection Agency by executive order in late 1970 to implement it.[8]

Although Nixon preempted a potentially damaging issue, his support for tough clean air regulation aroused powerful opposition among traditional Republican constituencies in business and industry. The president soon attempted to mollify them by establishing a business advisory council and opposing a large new program to control water pollution. As the 1972 election approached, he vetoed the Federal Water Pollution Control Act passed by Congress on grounds that it was too expensive, only to have Congress override his veto by a large margin.

Nixon responded to this and other defeats with a vengeance during his second administration. He threatened to veto other environmental legislation and used the energy crisis of 1973-1974 to demand postponement of pollution controls. He impounded sewer construction funds appropriated by Congress, fueling a constitutional conflict over control of the budget. Nixon also sought to impose sweeping controls over the entire regulatory and administrative process from the White House in what presidential scholar Richard Nathan called the first attempt to create an "administrative presidency."[9] Although the Watergate scandal forced Nixon from office before he could fully implement this strategy, it was to provide a model for the Reagan presidency in 1981 (see below).

Power shifted to Congress again in the wake of the Watergate scandal. Economic stagnation, inflation, and soaring energy prices put a damper on new environmental legislation, but a bipartisan congressional coalition passed a series of important laws (app. 1). Presidents Ford and Carter supported many of these initiatives but had limited success in advancing their own legislative proposals.

Carter, a committed environmentalist, did make energy policy a major domestic priority for the first time. He appointed a White House task force on national energy policy and submitted a massive energy bill to Congress early in his administration. But because he failed to consult Congress and to use the bully pulpit effectively, much of his legislation got bogged down on the Hill. He did, however, initiate deregulation of fuel prices; establish extensive programs for energy conservation and development of renewable energy resources; and push through an ill-conceived bill to create a Synthetic Fuels Corporation. Carter also deserves credit for passage in 1980 of the "Superfund" act to clean up toxic waste sites and legislation to preserve much of Alaska as national parks, forests, and wilderness.[10]

The Reagan Revolution

Reagan's Agenda

Ronald Reagan entered office with the most radical political agenda in half a century. Not since the New Deal had any president tried to reorient American government in so fundamental a manner. But in contrast to Franklin D. Roosevelt, Reagan believed government was the problem rather than the solution. And, in contrast to both FDR and Teddy Roosevelt, he thought environmental protection was fundamentally at odds with economic growth and prosperity. He thus defined environmental policy as a hindrance to his economic agenda and attempted to use his executive and administrative powers to reverse or weaken many of the regulatory policies of the previous decade.

The seminal legislative achievement of the Reagan presidency was passage of the Economic Recovery Act of 1981, which provided for a 25 percent cut in personal income taxes over three years and instituted huge tax breaks for business corporations. The expansion of military spending, already begun under President Carter, was greatly accelerated. Cuts in domestic entitlement programs proved much harder to achieve, however, resulting in enormous structural budget deficits that have crippled many federal programs, including those for the environment.

Reagan's environmental policy called for reevaluation of all existing regulations and legislation. But the president faced a dilemma: public opinion polls continued to show solid support for environmental protection and, despite the Republicans' slim majority in the Senate in 1980, a bipartisan coalition in Congress continued to reflect this sentiment. So rather than attacking environmental legislation head-on and risking defeat, Reagan opted for the Nixon-style "administrative presidency"—that is, a presidency that seeks fundamental reorientation of policy through tight control of the bureaucracy and imposition of a political agenda through administrative actions rather than by legislation. This approach had been initiated but not fully implemented during Nixon's disastrous second term, and it was to lead to some of the same difficulties under Reagan.[11]

The Council on Environmental Quality (CEQ), whose staff was nearly eliminated shortly after Reagan took office, outlined the new administration's philosophy in its first report. The principles to guide environmental policy were:

- use of cost-benefit analysis to determine the value of environmental regulations

- reliance as much as possible on the free market to allocate resources
- decentralization of environmental responsibilities to the states
- continuation of cooperation with other nations to solve global environmental problems.[12]

Although the last point remained largely a dead letter until the second term, the administration energetically pursued the first three goals from the outset as part of its deregulation effort.

The Administrative Presidency Rebuffed

One of Reagan's first acts was to create a task force on regulatory relief headed by Vice President George Bush. During its initial two-and-one-half years of existence, the task force reviewed hundreds of new and existing environmental regulations, rescinding some and returning many others to EPA and other agencies for further study and modification.[13] Under Executive Order 12291, issued in February 1981, "regulatory impact analyses" focusing on the costs of proposed regulations were to be prepared by all agencies and submitted to the new Office of Information and Regulatory Affairs (OIRA) within the Office of Management and Budget (OMB). Executive Order 12498 of 1985, which required agencies to submit their regulatory calendars for the coming year to OMB, further strengthened the administration's capacity to impede the flow of new regulations.[14]

In addition to the OMB review process and task force, Reagan attempted to institutionalize his agenda by carefully screening all political appointees to agency positions. He appointed ideological conservatives to head both the Environmental Protection Agency (Anne Gorsuch Burford) and the Interior Department (James Watt), as well as to second- and third-level positions in all of the offices of these and other agencies. Virtually all these appointees came from the business corporations to be regulated or from legal foundations or firms that had fought environmental regulations for years. The result was a highly politicized and ideological form of environmental administration that drove many senior executives and professionals from government service.[15]

Reagan further attempted to tame the regulatory agencies through drastic cuts in their budgets and personnel (chap. 1). He also sought to maintain control and coordination of administrative policymaking through a series of "cabinet councils" consisting of several cabinet secretaries and members of the White House Office of Policy Development, the president's domestic policy staff. James Watt chaired the cabinet council on natural resources and environment, giving it a strongly prodevelopment orientation.

Reagan's effort to achieve radical policy change through policy implementation led to a pitched battle with both environmentalists and Congress during his first term. This opposition blocked many of the proposed changes and culminated in the forced resignations of Reagan's top environmental officials, Watt and Burford, in 1983.

These officials aroused a storm of protest both over their abrasive, confrontational styles and the substance of their decisions. They made it abundantly clear that they intended to use their full administrative powers to reverse the thrust of past environmental policies—which they considered fanatically proenvironmental—to achieve a "balanced approach" that recognized the interests of business and economic development. The prodevelopment shift was manifested in part by the appointment of business and industry executives to key agency positions and by the deliberate exclusion of environmental groups from the policymaking process. Burford announced that EPA would seek to cooperate with regulated industries, leading to frequent informal meetings with their representatives. These closed meetings raised questions about proper administrative procedures and suspicions that sweetheart deals were being signed that violated statutory requirements. But Watt's efforts to promote oil, gas, coal, and mineral development aroused the greatest controversy. His plan for offshore oil drilling would have opened up the entire Outer Continental Shelf to oil and gas exploration, including fragile areas off the coasts of California and Alaska. He also accelerated the leasing of western public lands for coal mining and attempted to open up national wilderness areas to mineral exploration.[16]

These actions provoked the wrath of environmental groups, whose memberships began to grow by leaps and bounds in response to the perceived threat. In March 1982 ten leading environmental organizations issued what they termed an "indictment" of the president, charging that he had "broken faith with the American people" by taking "scores of actions that veered radically away from the sound bipartisan consensus in support of environmental protection that has existed for many years."[17] In another effort, more than a million signatures were collected on a petition calling for Watt's resignation. Numerous lawsuits were also filed against the administration by environmental groups (chap. 7).

Congress also revolted against the Reagan policies. Members of both parties, including leading members of the Republican-controlled Senate Environment and Public Works Committee, fought Watt's unilateral attempts to rewrite regulations to permit exploitation of wilderness areas and other public lands. In the House of Representatives, several riders were attached to appropriation bills to prohibit such actions. A bipartisan majority also opposed weakening the major environmental statutes (chap. 5). Burford was cited for contempt of Congress for refusing to disclose documents regarding Superfund cleanups. She and twenty other top EPA officials were forced to resign over the controversy in March 1983.[18] Watt's political demise came in October, after he made some tactless remarks about the ethnic composition of a commission set up to investigate his coal-leasing policies. By this time, however, it was obvious that his policies had alienated public opinion and that he had become an electoral liability.

The president responded by appointing more moderate environmental officials to defuse the issue before the 1984 election. But the push for deregulation was largely spent before the end of the first term. Reagan's administrative strategy had backfired, fueling a revival of the environmental movement that continued throughout the rest of the 1980s. To many conservatives, Reagan had squandered an opportunity for lasting reform of environmental regulation and statutes.[19]

The Second Term

President Reagan took little interest in environmental issues during his second term. With no mandate for change from his 1984 reelection, he seemed even more detached from the details of domestic policy than in the first term. Congress followed an increasingly independent course on environmental and other matters, revising and strengthening a number of major laws (chap. 5). On one issue the president remained adamant, however: more research was needed before any action could be taken to control acid rain. The Clean Air Act, last revised in 1977, was thus not reauthorized and strengthened until the Bush administration.

EPA regained some funding and political support during Reagan's second term under its new administrator, Lee Thomas. Thomas tightened legal enforcement and inaugurated a necessary review of agency priorities based on scientific risk assessment (chaps. 6 and 10). EPA and the State Department also began to address the global environmental issues that burst into attention in the second half of the decade. The United States took the lead in negotiating the historic Montreal protocol in 1987, by which some thirty nations agreed to reduce chlorofluorocarbon (CFC) production by 50 percent by 1998 to protect the Earth's ozone layer.[20] But in other emerging areas of international diplomacy, such as global warming, ocean pollution, and deforestation, the Reagan administration remained inactive or opposed new treaty commitments (chap. 14).

One area in which the Reagan administration lost a great opportunity was energy policy. From the beginning, the president favored deregulation of fuel prices and reliance on free market incentives to increase supplies and encourage conservation. But as a world oil surplus developed and fuel prices fell, incentives for conserving energy evaporated. By 1986 energy consumption per unit of GNP had leveled off and then began to grow.[21] Oil imports began rising rapidly in the late 1980s, amounting to nearly the same percentage of consumption as before the oil crisis of 1979. Despite these trends the Reagan administration blocked efforts to increase the corporate average fuel economy (CAFE) standards for new automobiles, and the Energy Department provided virtually no support for conservation or the development of renewable energy supplies.

The full impact of Reagan's antienvironmental policies is difficult to measure. Although some of his early actions may have had less of an effect on policy implementation than his rhetoric suggested,[22] the long-term institutional impacts of budget cuts, loss of skilled personnel, and demoralization may be far greater (chaps. 6 and 8). Policy neglect compounded many environmental problems and increased the costs of remedying them. For example, the failure to enforce environmental safeguards led to massive nuclear and chemical contamination at military bases and weapons-manufacturing plants that will take decades and hundreds of billions of dollars to clean up (chap. 15).

Reagan's presidency thus demonstrates the dangers of politicizing environmental administration and the high costs of policy failure. It also illustrates the limits of presidential power in our constitutional system. Congress, the courts, interest groups, and the media all exerted checks and balances that preserved much of the existing policy structure.

The Bush Transition

As suggested by the chapter epigraphs, George Bush started his administration by promising to be an environmental president in the Teddy Roosevelt tradition, yet ended his presidency sounding more like Ronald Reagan. This may appear less surprising if we recall that Teddy Roosevelt's policies were deeply rooted in the reformism of the Progressive Era, while Bush campaigned in 1988 to "stay the course" of the Reagan era. We also need to remember that, as vice president, Bush had played a leading role in weakening environmental regulations early in the Reagan administration and thus inherited many of the resulting problems.

Still, sensing a shift in public sentiment, Bush had promised a "kinder and gentler America" and attempted to distance himself from his predecessor in several areas, including environmental policy. The hot, dry summer of 1988, in which crops dried up, much of Yellowstone Park went up in flames, and global warming suddenly seemed a reality, clearly contributed to this campaign decision. So did focus group research, which showed that Bush's opponent, Gov. Michael Dukakis, was vulnerable on his environmental record in Massachusetts. In fact, it appeared that environmental issues could influence the outcome of the election in half a dozen key states.[23]

Bush's "Environmental Presidency"

In a remarkable speech at Detroit Metropark, near Lake Erie, on August 31, 1988, Bush laid out an ambitious environmental agenda. "The time for study alone has passed," he stated, alluding to Reagan's refusal to address the problem of acid rain and revision of the Clean Air Act. He went on to promise a detailed plan to "cut millions of tons of sulfur dioxide emissions by the year 2000." Bush also promised to end ocean dumping of garbage by 1991 and to prosecute illegal disposers of medical waste; supported a major national effort to reduce waste generation and promote recycling; committed himself to a program of "no net loss" of wetlands; and called for strict enforcement of toxic waste laws. In reference to global warming, Mr. Bush stated: "Those who think we are powerless to do anything about the 'greenhouse effect' are forgetting about the 'White House effect'." "In my first year in office," he said, "I will convene a global conference on the environment at the White House. . . . And we will act."[24] The next day Bush launched his now famous attack on Governor Dukakis for failing to clean up Boston Harbor.

If Bush surprised almost everyone by seizing the initiative on what most assumed was a strong issue for the Democrats, he impressed environmentalists even more by claiming a mandate to act following the election and by actively soliciting their advice. He met with representatives of some thirty environmental organizations who submitted a "blueprint" with more than seven hundred proposals for consideration.[25] Bush also indicated he intended to work closely with the Democratic Congress to pass a new Clean Air Act early in his administration. Perhaps most important, he fulfilled his campaign promise to appoint an environmentalist to head the EPA by selecting William K. Reilly, the highly respected president of the World Wildlife Fund and Conservation Foundation. Several other environmentalists also received high-level appointments, notably Michael R. Deland, former director of EPA's office in Boston, who was brought in to revive the moribund Council on Environmental Quality (CEQ), and Robert E. Grady, who had drafted Bush's environmental campaign speeches and was made associate director of OMB.

Other early actions by the president conveyed more mixed signals, particularly his appointments to other key posts. Bush's nominees to head the public land and natural resource agencies were not much different from those of the Reagan administration. In particular, his choice of Manuel Lujan, Jr., a ten-term retired representative (R-N.M.), to serve as secretary of the interior indicated that no major departures would be made in western land policies.

If the new administration had a "split personality on appointments,"[26] it also displayed deep internal divisions from the outset on the direction of environmental policy. While Reilly pursued more stringent controls on industrial pollution and pushed for strong new clean air legislation, the Interior, Energy, and Agriculture departments continued to encourage greater resource consumption. A third group of policy actors in the White House—centered around chief of staff John H. Sununu, OMB director Richard Darman, and economic adviser Michael Boskin—increasingly gained control over strategic issues such as global-warming policy. Finally, Vice President Dan Quayle turned his Council on Competitiveness into an instrument for weakening environmental regulation in the final two years of the administration.

These internal divisions showed that George Bush approached the presidency quite differently from his predecessor. He did not attempt to reestablish an administrative presidency with a clear sense of mission. The cabinet councils were not revived, and Bush preferred to delegate substantial authority to individual cabinet officers and staff members. A new Domestic Policy Council (DPC) was formed, but it kept a much lower profile than Reagan's early staff. In part this was because Bush had no major domestic policy agenda—at least one comparable to Reagan's. It also reflected Bush's preference for a more collegial, pragmatic style of decisionmaking and his greater respect for professional expertise. Such an approach would give enormous influence to individual advisers such as Sununu.[27]

President Bush faced several constraints in carrying out his environmental agenda. He inherited a substantial budget deficit that would make it difficult to raise spending, and it quickly became clear that only nominal increases in environmental and natural resource programs would be funded. His legislative options would be limited by strong Democratic majorities in both houses of Congress; his party held only 175 seats in the House, the fewest of any twentieth-century president starting his term. At the same time, traditional Republican constituencies in business and industry were certain to oppose major environmental initiatives. Like President Nixon in 1970, he would have to take the lead to overcome this resistance and seek a bipartisan majority for new legislation.

Bush accomplished this in passage of the Clean Air Act, arguably the single most important legislative achievement of his presidency. In line with his campaign promise, he unveiled proposals for far-reaching revision of the flagship environmental law on June 12, 1989. The proposals followed a long and heated struggle among factions within the White House that was largely resolved by the president in favor of EPA's arguments for a strong environmental bill. In retrospect, this was to be one of Reilly's few clear-cut victories over the more conservative forces in the administration.[28]

Bush's draft clean air bill was sent to Congress on July 21, by which time it had already been weakened by industry pressures. Nevertheless, it had three major goals: to control acid rain by reducing sulfur dioxide (SO_2) emissions from coal-burning power plants by 10 million tons (nearly half) and nitrogen oxide (NO_x) emissions by 2 million tons by the year 2000; to reduce air pollution (especially ozone and smog) in some eighty urban areas that still had not met 1977 air quality standards (mainly by reducing auto pollution through use of cleaner fuels and further tightening tailpipe emission standards); and to lower emissions of some two hundred airborne toxic chemicals by 75 to 90 percent by 2000. To achieve the acid precipitation goals—to which the White House devoted most of its attention—Bush proposed an innovative approach advocated by environmental economists that relies on marketable pollution allowances rather than "command and control" regulation to achieve emission reductions more efficiently (chap. 9).

Although Bush later backed away from some of his initial proposals (especially alternative fuels), his staff negotiated with Senate majority leader George Mitchell (D-Maine) and others behind closed doors for ten weeks in early 1990 to reach a bipartisan Senate compromise on the basic outlines of the bill. Many of the technical details were subsequently filled in by the House Energy and Commerce Committee and by a joint conference committee. But the presidential staff was deeply engaged throughout the legislative process; the president was determined to get a bill.[29] Without the president's leadership, it is unlikely that the ten-year stalemate on clean air legislation would have been broken. As Richard Cohen concludes, "Ultimately the Clean Air Act showed that presidents matter. Once Bush was elected and decided to keep his vague clean-air campaign promises, the many constraints of divided government disappeared."[30]

Holding the Line

Unfortunately this was not to set the pattern for Bush in most areas of legislation, including environmental policy. By the time Bush was signing the Clean Air Act, he was deeply enmeshed in negotiations with the Democratic congressional leadership on what became the Budget Reconciliation Act of 1990. Bush was excoriated for violating his "read my lips" pledge against tax increases in this agreement, which in turn soured relations with Congress and led to numerous vetoes during the second half of his term.

This worsening of relations with Congress after 1990 had several other causes, including Bush's limited domestic agenda, preoccupation with foreign policy, the recession, and the need to placate the conservative wing of the Republican party in preparation for the 1992 reelection campaign. The latter two factors were probably most important in explaining Bush's record on environmental policy during the second half of his term. Having delivered a clean air bill that by his own estimates would cost industry some $20 billion a year to implement, Bush felt he had fulfilled his most important environmental pledge and that it was now necessary to hold the line on any further regulation opposed by business and industry.

Indeed, Bush had already drawn a line against any further commitments in another highly contentious area: what to do about global warming, especially pressures for the United States to agree to an international convention to stabilize CO_2 emissions. Although Bush had promised to confront "the greenhouse effect" with "the White House effect," it soon became apparent that strong forces within the administration (as well as from energy industries) opposed any policy that would limit fossil fuel production and consumption. Policy on climate change became closely intertwined with the Bush administration's effort to formulate a new "national energy strategy" (NES), which the president had also promised during the campaign. The Department of Energy, bowing to industry pressures, favored increased oil, gas, coal, and nuclear power development to reduce growing dependence on imported oil. Although public hearings conducted in 1990 by an NES task force indicated strong public preferences for a new strategy favoring energy conservation and efficiency and renewable energy production, most of the proposals of this kind were eliminated from the list of options forwarded to the White House. The remaining proposals were stripped from consideration by Sununu and the OMB.[31]

By early 1990 Sununu had been given the leading role on all matters relating to energy policy and climate change. Along with OMB director Darman, economic adviser Boskin, and science adviser D. Allan Bromley, Sununu assumed an increasingly critical public posture toward any U.S. commitment to a global-warming treaty. This high-powered group (all former university professors!) met frequently to discuss climate policy, which was formally put under control of a DPC committee chaired by Bromley. Sununu, Darman, and Boskin were highly skeptical of existing climate change models and were primarily concerned with the economic costs of limiting fossil fuel consumption. Sununu, who holds a doctorate in mechanical engineering, felt confident in challenging the validity of global-warming models.[32] Other advice, including that from William Reilly, got a hostile reception in the White House.

President Bush, who showed little personal interest in the subject, adopted a policy stance on global climate change similar to Reagan's policy on acid rain: more research was needed. In the meantime, the administration would follow a "no regrets" approach—actions would be taken against the possibility of global warming only if they could be fully justified on other grounds. For example, production of CFCs, which were considered a potent greenhouse gas as well as an ozone-depleting chemical, could be phased out because of their potential impact on the ozone layer. Thus, while the president increased funding substantially for global climate research and development (to a combined total of $1 billion annually), and supported accelerated curtailment of CFCs, he continued to resist all pressures to limit CO_2 emissions.

As negotiations for an international convention on climate change intensified in 1991 in preparation for the 1992 United Nations Conference on Environment and Development, Sununu's outspoken opposition became increasingly controversial. His usefulness as Bush's "lightning rod" on this issue was further undermined by a series of highly publicized embarrassments involving his unauthorized use of government aircraft and vehicles for personal trips. Finally, in a manner reminiscent of James

Watt's resignation eight years earlier, Sununu was replaced as chief of staff in December 1991 by the former secretary of transportation, Samuel K. Skinner. But for two years, from late 1989 to his dismissal, Sununu had played an exceptionally large role in shaping environmental policy. He effectively negated Reilly's influence on many issues during this period.

Consequently, the middle phase of the Bush presidency, although it overlapped with passage of the Clean Air Act, was largely one of holding the line on further environmental initiatives. No major environmental legislation was proposed by the president after the Clean Air Act, nor did he attempt to rally public opinion behind environmental conservation.[33] During the 102d Congress (1991-1992) he opposed action on most of the major environmental statutes up for reauthorization, including the Clean Water Act, the Resource Conservation and Recovery Act, and the Endangered Species Act, effectively delaying consideration of them until after the 1992 election. He did, however, help to martial Republican support for an industry-favored, bipartisan national energy bill that eventually passed at the end of the 1992 session of Congress (chap. 5). He also launched a number of voluntary programs to promote energy efficiency and pollution prevention in industry.[34]

Retreat From Leadership

It can nevertheless be argued that the Bush presidency entered a third and more radical phase of environmental policy during the fifteen months prior to the election. As Sununu's power waned, Vice President Dan Quayle increasingly entered the spotlight as head of the Council on Competitiveness, an obscure White House body that Bush had appointed in 1989. The Quayle Council, which, in addition to the vice president, consisted of the secretaries of treasury and commerce, the attorney general, and Sununu, Darman, and Boskin, assumed a role similar to that of Bush's own Task Force on Regulatory Relief in the early Reagan administration (its powers were justified on the same legal basis, namely Reagan's Executive Order 12291 of 1981). Its function was to invite and respond to industry complaints of excessive regulation, to analyze the costs and benefits of regulation, and to hold up or rewrite any new regulations that were considered unnecessarily burdensome. It operated in secrecy, frequently pressuring EPA and other agencies to ease regulations. During 1991 the council began to intervene actively in regulatory processes to rewrite environmental rules and regulations.[35]

Among the council's most controversial actions were revisions of the manual for defining wetlands, which would have removed as much as half of the lands designated as wetlands from federal protection; regulations for recycling, mixed-waste incineration, and hazardous waste disposal; rules limiting public appeals on timber cutting and other decisions on public lands; regulations for implementing the new Clean Air Act; and opposition to the global biodiversity treaty. These and other actions led to protests from Congress reminiscent of those during the Reagan presidency that the council was acting illegally by violating both statutory intent and rules for open administrative procedures that had been worked out in the 1980s.[36]

Bush carried his regulatory relief policy a step further by declaring a three-month moratorium on new regulations in his 1992 State of the Union address. (He later extended the moratorium through the election.) In fact, the volume of regulation increased at a substantially faster rate during the first three years of the Bush administration than in the Reagan years.[37] No doubt this contributed to Bush's sensitivity to the issue as the election approached. And although the White House held up some of the Quayle Council's proposed orders during the campaign because they were considered too controversial, Bush continued to push for easing regulation.[38] In the final weeks before the election he frequently argued that regulations such as those proposed by Governor Clinton to raise auto mileage efficiency would throw hundreds of thousands of people out of work and destroy the economy.

These obviously political appeals detracted from Bush's credibility on environmental policy as well as from the accomplishments his administration could claim. For example, he had substantially increased funding for EPA research and for the Council on Environmental Quality, and had greatly accelerated efforts to clean up contaminated military bases and production sites. The EPA had also set records for enforcement actions, though the Justice Department remained reluctant to prosecute most environmental crimes. He had proposed raising the EPA to cabinet status but did not reach agreement with Congress on a bill. Initiatives had also been launched to plant a billion trees across America and to clean up the Chesapeake Bay and other major coastal areas, while large areas of the Outer Continental Shelf were declared off-limits for oil development. And, however weak the environmental provisions of the energy bill passed by Congress, Bush at least tried to formulate a national energy policy for the first time since the Carter administration. These actions and others, together with the Clean Air Act, provided sufficient grounds for the president to campaign on a "balanced" environmental record.[39]

However, according to a Gallup poll in June 1992 the public disapproved of Bush's handling of the environment by a two to one majority, and he may have concluded that there was little to gain from this issue.[40] In any event, Bush and Quayle conducted a largely negative campaign against the "environmental extremism" of their Democratic opponents. Perhaps recognizing that this strategy was also failing, during the week prior to the election the president finally attempted to put a more positive face on his record by issuing a series of regulations that had been held up by the Quayle Council.[41]

In retrospect, George Bush's environmental presidency perhaps most closely parallels that of Richard Nixon. Like Nixon, Bush capitalized on a high point in public concern for the environment, but retreated from leadership on environmental legislation after initial success on the Clean Air Act. As business and industry reaction set in, he attempted to balance his record by blocking action on global warming and other issues, much as Nixon had done on water pollution and energy policy. He tried to balance economic and environmental interests, but failed to find compromises on controversial issues such as protection of wetlands and the fate of the spotted owl.

Bush's behavior toward the Earth summit may have defined his place in environmental history. He refused even to attend the historic meeting—the largest diplomatic conference ever held, involving 170 nations and more than 100 heads of state—until he had ensured that the climate change convention to be signed would contain no binding targets for CO_2 reduction. He further alienated much of world opinion as well as the American environmental community by refusing to sign the biodiversity treaty at the conference, despite pleas from his delegation chief, William Reilly, to seek a last-minute compromise. Reilly's cable to the White House was leaked to the press, causing further embarrassment.[42] Although Bush defended his environmental record as "second to none," the United States was isolated in international environmental diplomacy for the first time (chap. 14). Despite his other successes in foreign policy, President Bush failed to make environmental leadership part of his vaunted "new world order."

Prospects for the Clinton Presidency

Environmental issues were clearly overshadowed by the economy and other issues during the 1992 election. According to one exit poll, only 6 percent of voters considered the environment one of the most important issues, ranking it ninth in importance. However, "green" voters reported that they voted for Clinton over Bush by more than a five to one margin (table 4-1). Clinton and Gore also received endorsements from the Sierra Club, the League of Conservation Voters, and other environmental organizations.

It is not surprising that the Clinton ticket won most of the support of environmentalists. Vice presidential candidate Al Gore had been the Senate's leading environmentalist, having published a best-selling book in early 1992 that is widely regarded as among the most impressive environmental statements in print.[43] Gore's environmental credentials were evidently an important factor in his vice presidential nomination, since Clinton's environmental record as governor of Arkansas was mixed at best.[44] Under attack from both the White House and Democratic rival Jerry Brown, Clinton acknowledged his shortcomings in an Earth Day speech but promised strong environmental action as president.[45] The Democratic

Table 4-1   Presidential Election Exit Poll, 1992:
"Issues They Care About"

Issue	All Voters	Clinton	Bush	Perot
Economy, jobs	43%	52%	24%	24%
Deficit	21	36	26	38
Health care	19	67	19	14
Family values	15	23	65	11
Taxes	14	26	57	17
Abortion	13	37	55	8
Education	13	60	25	15
Foreign policy	8	9	86	5
Environment	6	73	14	13

Source: Newsweek, special election issue, November-December 1992, 10. Data are from an election day poll of 15,241 voters conducted by Voter Research & Surveys, an association of ABC News, CNN, CBS News, and NBC News. The margin of error is +/−1.1 percentage points. Voters were allowed to select more than one issue.

platform also took a strong environmental stance.[46]

Clinton's campaign promises included pledges to raise the corporate average fuel economy (CAFE) standard for automobiles from 27.5 miles per gallon to 40 mpg by 2000 and 45 mpg by 2015; to encourage mass transit programs; to increase the use of natural gas and oppose increased reliance on nuclear power; to create a new agency and reorient existing national laboratories to support renewable energy research and development; to create a new solid waste reduction program and provide other incentives for recycling; to pass a new Clean Water Act with standards for nonpoint sources; to reform the Superfund program; to tighten accountability and enforcement of toxic waste laws; to preserve ancient forests; to make "no net loss" of wetlands a reality; to preserve the Arctic National Wildlife Refuge as a wilderness area and halt new offshore oil drilling; to emphasize pollution prevention and use of market forces to reward conservation and penalize polluters; to limit U.S. CO_2 emissions to 1990 levels by the year 2000; to negotiate more debt-for-nature swaps to preserve precious lands such as rain forests in the developing world; and to restore funding to United Nations population programs.[47]

Beyond this impressive list of commitments, Clinton and Gore departed from traditional rhetoric about the relationship between environmental protection and economic growth. For the first time since the New Deal, they argued that the jobs-versus-environment debate presented a false choice because environmental cleanup creates jobs and the future competitiveness of the U.S. economy will depend on developing environmentally clean, energy-efficient technologies. They proposed a variety of investment incentives and infrastructure projects to promote such "green" technologies. Like FDR sixty years earlier, Clinton promised to put people back to work on projects that improve the environment.

Like his predecessors, however, Clinton will be limited to a few key initiatives during the first year of his presidency. He will also have to build bipartisan coalitions in Congress on many controversial policies (chap. 5). Given the problems of the economy and health care, which he promised to address first, the president may have to postpone much of his environmental and energy program to later in his administration. The huge budget deficit inherited from previous administrations will also remain a serious constraint on new policy initiatives. In fact, Clinton's proposed budget calls for only nominal increases in EPA spending for FY 1994 (3.1 percent) and a 5 percent *reduction* in overall funding for environment and natural resources programs.[48]

Nevertheless, it appears that environmental policy will have a strong voice in the White House. Vice President Gore has been given major responsibility for the formulation, coordination, and implementation of environmental policy in the administration. One of Clinton's first acts was to abolish the Quayle Council on Competitiveness.[49] He subsequently announced plans to replace the Council on Environmental Quality (CEQ) with a new Office of Environmental Policy. (Abolishing CEQ will require amendment of the National Environmental Policy Act of 1969, a fact that saved it from Reagan's axe in 1981.) The new office is to coordinate departmental policies on environmental issues and to ensure integration of environmental considerations into the work of other policy bodies such as the Domestic Policy Council, the National Security Council, and the new National Economic Council. Gore is expected to maintain close supervision of the office.[50]

However, Clinton's managerial style, like that of Franklin Roosevelt, appears to favor competition of ideas from rival policy advisers and task forces to allow him to make the final decisions. This "spokes of a wheel" model differs sharply from the more hierarchical organization of the White House under strong chiefs of staff in the Reagan and Bush administrations.[51] The new chief of staff, Thomas F. "Mack" McLarty 3d, is expected to be more of an honest broker than a policy gatekeeper like John Sununu.[52] The Office of Management and Budget is also expected to establish a new regulatory review process to ensure that both the environmental impacts and economic costs of regulations are considered.

Clinton's initial appointments suggest a strongly proenvironmental administration. Carol M. Browner, the new EPA administrator, had served on Gore's Senate staff before becoming head of the Florida Department of Environmental Regulation in 1991.[53] The president will treat her as a member of the cabinet and promises legislation to elevate EPA to permanent cabinet status.[54] Former Arizona governor Bruce Babbitt, the secretary of the interior, is the most prominent environmentalist to hold that position since Stewart Udall in the 1960s. He had most recently served as president of the League of Conservation Voters, a leading national environmental organization, and has appointed many other environmentalists to key positions in his department.[55]

Other presidential staff are also far more sympathetic to the environment than their counterparts in the Bush administration. Physicist John H. Gibbons, the president's science adviser, has devoted much of his life to energy alternatives; and Laura D. Tyson, who heads the Council of Economic Advisers, has expressed strong interest in new environmental technologies. Although regarded as budget "hawks," OMB director Leon E. Panetta and his deputy, Alice M. Rivlin, are also knowledgeable on the environment.[56] Environmentalists were disappointed that retiring Sen. Tim Wirth (D-Colo.) was passed over for secretary of energy in favor of Hazel R. O'Leary, a little-known utility executive from Minnesota.[57] However, O'Leary has promised to shift the priorities of the Energy Department toward renewable and non-nuclear energy technologies, and Wirth was nominated to become special counselor in the State Department for global environmental affairs.

The new cabinet members wasted little time in announcing new approaches to their agency missions. In particular, Secretary Babbitt promised a fundamental change of direction for western land policies.[58] However, Clinton's early decisions indicated that he is willing to listen to all sides and is likely to compromise when necessary on controversial issues. For example, when a group of western senators threatened to vote against his first budget unless proposals to raise grazing, lumbering, and mining fees on public lands were removed, he agreed to take these issues up separately.[59] Clinton also held a "forest summit" with loggers and environmentalists who have been battling for years over cutting the remaining spotted owl habitat in the old-growth forests of the Pacific Northwest, and appointed a task force to draft a compromise proposal within sixty days. White House aides said he was "trying to broker a new approach to environmental policy-making through consensus."[60] Whether this approach is more successful than those of his predecessors remains to be seen.

Nevertheless, after a notable lapse in the Reagan-Bush years, it appears that environmental stewardship has been restored to the executive branch. Indeed, Clinton has assembled the greenest administration ever. Despite budgetary and other constraints, he has the best opportunity since the two Roosevelts to forge a consensus on sustainable economic growth. The domestic policy agenda is formidable, and the global environmental crisis demands a new level of presidential leadership (chap. 17). Clinton's success in meeting these challenges will depend in part on how skillfully he and Gore are in exploiting the full powers of the White House.

Notes

For accounts of President Bush's speeches of August 31, 1988, and September 14, 1992, from which the chapter epigraphs were taken, see the following articles: John Holusha, "Bush Pledges Aid for Environment," *New York Times*, September 1, 1988, 9; Bill Peterson, "Bush Vows to Fight Pollution, Install 'Conservation Ethic'," *Washington Post*, September 1, 1988, A1 and A17; and Michael Wines, "Bush, in Far West, Sides With Loggers," *New York Times*, September 15, 1992, A25. President Bush's statement of August 31, 1988, is reprinted in George Bush, "Promises to Keep," *Sierra*, November-December 1988, 116.

1. Keith Schneider, "Environmental Fight in Prime Time," *New York Times*, August 9, 1992, IV, 1.
2. "Bush, Clinton Clash on State of Economy," *Star Tribune* (Minneapolis), October 30, 1992, 8A.
3. Norman J. Vig, "Presidential Leadership: From the Reagan to the Bush Administration," in *Environmental Policy in the 1990s*, ed. Vig and Kraft (Washington, D.C.: CQ Press, 1990), 44-47.
4. Paul R. Cutright, *Theodore Roosevelt: The Making of a Conservationist* (Urbana: University of Illinois Press, 1985); William H. Harbaugh, *Power and Responsibility: The Life and Times of Theodore Roosevelt* (New York: Octagon, 1975); Donald E. Worster, ed., *American Environmentalism: the Formative Period, 1860-1915* (New York: Wiley, 1973). On Roosevelt's use of administrative powers, see also Robert A. Shanley, *Presidential Influence and Environmental Policy* (Westport, Conn.: Greenwood, 1992), 12-15.
5. See Roderick F. Nash, *American Environmentalism: Readings in Conservation History*, 3d ed. (New York: McGraw-Hill, 1990); Samuel P. Hays, *Conservation and the Gospel of Efficiency* (Cambridge: Harvard University Press, 1959).
6. See Stewart L. Udall, *The Quiet Crisis* (New York: Holt, Rinehart and Winston, 1963), chap. 10; Edgar B. Nixon, ed., *Franklin D. Roosevelt and Conservation, 1911-1945*, 2 vols. (Washington, D.C.: U.S. Government Printing Office, 1957); and Shanley, *Presidential Influence*, 15-17.
7. On postwar environmental politics, see Matthew A. Crenson, *The Un-politics of Air Pollution* (Baltimore: Johns Hopkins University Press, 1971); J. Clarence Davies III and Barbara S. Davies, *The Politics of Pollution*, 2d ed. (Indianapolis: Pegasus, 1975); and James L. Sundquist, *Politics and Policy: The Eisenhower, Kennedy, and Johnson Years* (Washington, D.C.: Brookings, 1968), chap. 8.
8. On Nixon's "policy escalation" on the Clean Air Act, see Charles O. Jones, *Clean Air* (Pittsburgh: University of Pittsburgh Press, 1975). For contrasting views of the Nixon administration, see James Rathlesberger, *Nixon and the Environment: The Politics of Devastation* (New York: Village Voice/Taurus, 1972); and John C. Whitaker, *Striking a Balance: Environment and Natural Resources Policy in the Nixon-Ford Years* (Washington, D.C.: American Enterprise Institute, 1976).
9. Richard P. Nathan, *The Plot That Failed: Nixon and the Administrative Presidency* (New York: Wiley, 1975).
10. Charles O. Jones, *The Trusteeship Presidency: Jimmy Carter and the United States Congress* (Baton Rouge: Louisiana State University Press, 1988); Richard H. K. Vietor, *Energy Policy in America Since 1945* (Cambridge: Cambridge University Press, 1984); and Shanley, *Presidential Influence*, 16-23.
11. Richard P. Nathan, *The Administrative Presidency* (New York: Wiley, 1983).
12. Council on Environmental Quality, *Environmental Quality 1981* (Washington, D.C.: U.S. Government Printing Office, 1981), iii-iv, and chap. 1.
13. Presidential Task Force on Regulatory Relief, *Reagan Administration Regulatory Achievements*, August 11, 1983. See also Richard A. Harris and Sidney M. Milkis,

The Politics of Regulatory Change: A Tale of Two Agencies (New York: Oxford University Press, 1989).

14. See Joseph Cooper and William F. West, "Presidential Power and Republican Government: The Theory and Practice of OMB Review of Agency Rules," *Journal of Politics* 50 (November 1988): 864-892; Harris and Milkis, *Politics of Regulatory Change,* 100-113, 257-265; and V. Kerry Smith, *Environmental Policy Under Reagan's Executive Order: The Role of Cost-Benefit Analysis* (Chapel Hill: University of North Carolina Press, 1984).

15. Chester A. Newland, "The Reagan Presidency: Limited Government and Political Administration," *Public Administration Review* 43 (January-February 1983): 1-21. For critical analyses of Reagan's "administrative presidency," see Michael E. Kraft and Norman J. Vig, "Environmental Policy in the Reagan Presidency," *Political Science Quarterly* 99 (Fall 1984): 414-439; and Shanley, *Presidential Influence.*

16. For a more detailed summary of Watt's policies, see Paul J. Culhane, "Sagebrush Rebels in Office: Jim Watt's Land and Water Policies," in *Environmental Policy in the 1980s,* ed. Vig and Kraft, 293-318; and C. Brant Short, *Ronald Reagan and the Public Lands: America's Conservation Debate* (College Station: Texas A&M University Press, 1989).

17. *Ronald Reagan and the American Environment* (San Francisco: Friends of the Earth, 1982).

18. J. Clarence Davies III, "Environmental Institutions and the Reagan Administration," in *Environmental Policy in the 1980s,* ed. Vig and Kraft, 154-157. Burford tells her side of the story in Anne M. Burford (with John Greenya), *Are You Tough Enough?* (New York: McGraw-Hill, 1986).

19. See, e.g., William A. Niskanen, *Reaganomics* (New York: Oxford University Press, 1988), 125-129; Robert W. Crandall, "What Ever Happened to Deregulation?"; and Fred L. Smith, Jr., "What Environmental Policy?" in *Assessing the Reagan Years,* ed. David Boaz (Washington, D.C.: Cato, 1988).

20. For a fascinating inside account, see Richard E. Benedick, *Ozone Diplomacy* (Cambridge: Harvard University Press, 1991). Some believe that Reagan's support for the Montreal treaty was related to the fact that he had developed a skin cancer.

21. Matthew L. Wald, "U.S. Progress on Energy Efficiency Is Halting," *New York Times,* February 27, 1989.

22. See Paul R. Portney, "Natural Resources and the Environment: More Controversy Than Change," in *The Reagan Record,* ed. John L. Palmer and Isabel V. Sawhill (Cambridge: Ballinger, 1984); B. Dan Wood, "Principal-Agent Models of Political Control of Bureaucracy," *American Political Science Review* 83 (1989): 965-988; and Robert F. Durant, *The Administrative Presidency Revisited* (Albany: SUNY Press, 1992).

23. See Vig, "Presidential Leadership: From the Reagan to the Bush Administration," in *Environmental Policy in the 1990s,* ed. Vig and Kraft (Washington, D.C.: CQ Press, 1990), 45-47.

24. Holusha, "Bush Pledges Aid for Environment," 9; and Peterson, "Bush Vows to Fight Pollution," A1 and A17.

25. Philip Shabecoff, "Bush Lends an Ear to Environmentalists," *New York Times,* December 1, 1988, 13. The "blueprint" presented to Bush was later published as *Blueprint for the Environment: A Plan for Federal Action,* ed. T. Allan Comp (Salt Lake City: Howe Brothers, 1989).

26. Philip Shabecoff, "Environment," *New York Times,* April 11, 1989.

27. On Bush's decisionmaking style, see Michael Duffy and Dan Goodgame, *Marching in Place* (New York: Simon and Schuster, 1992); Colin Campbell and Bert Rockman, eds., *The Bush Presidency: First Appraisals* (Chatham, N.J.: Chatham

House, 1991); and Burt Solomon, "In Bush's Image," *National Journal*, July 7, 1990, 1642-1647.

28. Trip Gabriel, "Greening the White House," *New York Times Magazine*, August 13, 1989, 25; Margaret E. Kriz, "Politics in the Air," *National Journal*, May 6, 1989, 1098-1102; Michael Weisskopf, "Letting Others Take the Wheel," *Washington Post National Weekly Edition*, February 19-25, 1990; Keith Schneider, "Bush Aide Assails U.S. Preparations for Earth Summit," *New York Times*, August 1, 1992, 1.

29. See Richard Cohen, *Washington at Work: Back Rooms and Clean Air* (New York: Macmillan, 1992), which traces congressional negotiations in detail. On the substantive development of clean air policy including the new law, see Gary C. Bryner, *Blue Skies, Green Politics: The Clean Air Act of 1990* (Washington, D.C.: CQ Press, 1993).

30. Cohen, *Washington at Work*, 175.

31. Robert A. Rankin, "Sununu, Aides Oppose Energy-Saving Plan," *St. Paul Pioneer Press*, December 15, 1990; Robert D. Hershey, Jr., "Energy Policy Options Are Submitted to Bush," *New York Times*, December 22, 1990, 36; Phil Kuntz, "Watkins: Energy Glasnost," *Congressional Quarterly Weekly*, February 2, 1991, 297-298; and Keith Schneider, "Bush's Energy Plan Emphasizes Gains in Output Over Efficiency," *New York Times*, February 9, 1991, 1.

32. On the economic approach to environmental policy, see especially *Economic Report of the President* (Washington, D.C.: U.S. Government Printing Office, February 1990), chap. 6. On the role of Sununu and other advisers in the White House, see Fred Barnes, "Raging Bulls," *New Republic*, March 19, 1990, 11-12; Dan Goodgame, "Big Bad John Sununu," *Time*, May 21, 1990, 21-25; David Hoffman and Ann Devroy, "The White House Tough Guy," *Washington Post National Weekly Edition*, February 5-11, 1990; Leslie H. Gelb, "Sununu v. Scientists," *New York Times*, February 19, 1991, 17; and Weisskopf, "Environmental President."

33. Bush did support environmental provisions in the 1990 Farm Bill, as well as an oil spill liability act and a pollution prevention act, included in the 1990 Budget Reconciliation Act at Reilly's request (see app. 1). Bush also proposed legislation in January 1990 to elevate the Environmental Protection Agency to cabinet level, but did not fight for the proposal when jurisdictional disputes emerged in Congress.

34. Council on Environmental Quality, *Environmental Quality 1991* (Washington, D.C.: U.S. Government Printing Office, 1992), 71-80, 151-158.

35. See Kirk Victor, "Quayle's Quiet Coup," *National Journal*, July 6, 1991, 1676-1680; Christine Triano and Nancy Watzman, "Quayle's Hush-Hush Council," *New York Times*, November 20, 1991; Keith Schneider, "Prominence Proves Perilous for Bush's Rule Slayer," *New York Times*, June 30, 1992.

36. Dana Priest, "Competitiveness Council Suspected of Unduly Influencing Regulators," *Washington Post*, January 18, 1991; Ann Devroy and David S. Broder, "Quayle Pressured Agencies to Ease Rules on Business, Groups Say," *Washington Post*, September 6, 1991; Dana Priest, "Competitiveness Council Under Scrutiny," *Washington Post*, November 26, 1991; Philip J. Hilts, "Quayle Council Debate: Issue of Control," *New York Times*, December 17, 1991; and Keith Schneider, "Bush to Relax 1990 Rule on Air Pollution Notices," *New York Times*, May 18, 1992.

37. John H. Cushman, Jr., "Big Growth in Federal Regulation Despite Role of Quayle's Council," *New York Times*, December 24, 1991, 1; Robert D. Hershey, Jr., "Regulations March On, Despite a Moratorium," *New York Times*, September 21, 1992, C1.

38. Robert D. Hershey, Jr., "White House Sees a Mission to Cut Business Regulation," *New York Times,* March 23, 1992, C11; Keith Schneider, "Administration Tries to Limit Rule Used to Halt Logging of National Forests," *New York Times,* April 28, 1992, 7; David E. Rosenbaum, "Bush Is Extending Regulation Freeze With a Fanfare," *New York Times,* April 29, 1992, 1; Schneider, "Environment Laws Are Eased by Bush as Election Nears," *New York Times,* May 20, 1992, 1; Schneider, "White House Drops Plan on Setting Health Risks," *New York Times,* July 28, 1992, 9; Schneider, "Campaign Concerns Prompt White House to Drop Waste Plan," *New York Times,* September 30, 1992, 1.

39. The environmental accomplishments of the Bush administration were summarized in *U.S. Actions for a Better Environment: A Sustained Commitment,* prepared by the White House for the UNCED Conference in Brazil (June 1992); and "The Bush Administration and the Environment: Accomplishments and Initiatives," periodically updated by the Council on Environmental Quality. The Bush campaign belatedly issued a list of this kind, but it got little attention. See Margaret E. Kriz, "The Selling of 'The Green President,' " *National Journal,* September 19, 1992, 2151.

40. The Gallup survey is reported in *National Journal,* July 4, 1992, 1597.

41. John H. Cushman, Jr., "Bush to Announce Environment Plan," *New York Times,* October 24, 1992, 10. Cf. Richard L. Berke, "Bush Criticizes Clinton as Hard on Car Industry," *New York Times,* August 26, 1992, 12; Michael Wines, "Bush, in Far West, Sides With Loggers," *New York Times,* September 15, 1992; Robin Toner, "Quayle and Gore Exchange Sharp Attacks in Debate," *New York Times,* October 14, 1992, 1; Schneider, "For Clinton and Bush, Contradictions in Balancing Jobs and Conservation."

42. Keith Schneider, "White House Snubs U.S. Envoy's Plea to Sign Rio Treaty," *New York Times,* June 5, 1992, 1; Schneider, "Bush Aide Assails U.S. Preparations for Earth Summit."

43. Al Gore, *Earth in the Balance: Ecology and the Human Spirit* (Boston: Houghton Mifflin, 1992). See also Keith Schneider, "Book by Gore Could Become a Campaign Issue, for Both Sides," *New York Times,* July 27, 1992, 11.

44. Keith Schneider, "Clinton Relies on Voluntary Guidelines to Protect Environment in Arkansas," *New York Times,* April 4, 1992, 10; Schneider, "Pollution in Arkansas Area May Be Key Campaign Issue," *New York Times,* April 21, 1992, 8; and Michael Weisskopf and David Maraniss, "When Irresistible Force Met Arkansas' Timber Industry," *Washington Post National Weekly Edition,* June 29-July 5, 1992, 11.

45. Gwen Ifill, "Clinton Links Ecology Plans With Jobs," *New York Times,* April 23, 1992, 10.

46. The Democratic and Republican platforms are reprinted in *Congressional Quarterly Weekly Report,* July 18 and August 22, 1992. Ross Perot's position can be found in *United We Stand: How We Can Take Back Our Country* (New York: Hyperion, 1992).

47. From Gov. Bill Clinton and Sen. Al Gore, *Putting People First* (New York: Times Books, 1992), 89-99.

48. Robert Pear, "Clinton Outlines Spending Package of 1.52 Trillion," *New York Times,* April 9, 1993, 1, 9. Under Clinton's plan, EPA spending would increase 15.4 percent by FY 1998, and total environment and natural resource funding would decrease by 1.4 percent without accounting for inflation.

49. Martin Tolchin, "Last-Minute Bush Proposals Rescinded," *New York Times,* January 23, 1992, 7.

50. Rudy Abramson, "Clinton Creates New Environmental Unit," *Los Angeles Times,* February 9, 1993, 10. The first OEP director, Kathleen McGinty, served as Mr. Gore's top environmental assistant in the Senate.

51. There is a large literature on presidential decisionmaking styles; see, e.g., Colin Campbell, S. J., *Managing the Presidency: Carter, Reagan, and the Search for Executive Harmony* (Pittsburgh: University of Pittsburgh Press, 1988); Richard T. Johnson, "Presidential Style," in *Perspectives on the Presidency*, ed. Aaron Wildavsky (Boston: Little, Brown, 1975), 262-300; Bert A. Rockman, "The Leadership Style of George Bush," in *The Bush Presidency: First Appraisals*, ed. Rockman and Campbell (Chatham, N.J.: Chatham House, 1991).

52. McLarty is former president of Arkla, Inc., one of the largest natural gas companies in the nation, and is likely to support changes in energy policy. See Peter Kerr and Thomas C. Hayes, "Praise for an Arkansan, and Criticism of a Deal," *New York Times*, December 21, 1992, 16; and Keith Schneider, "Gore Making Administration More Environmentally Friendly," *New York Times*, December 15, 1992, 15.

53. Gwen Ifill, "Clinton Turns to Three Women and Adviser for Top Posts in Setting Domestic Policy," *New York Times*, December 12, 1992, 9. See also Keith Schneider, "The Nominee for E.P.A. Sees Industry's Side Too," *New York Times*, December 17, 1992, 13.

54. Laura Michaelis, "Bill Elevating EPA to Cabinet Worries Environmentalists," *Congressional Quarterly Weekly Report*, March 27, 1993, 746.

55. Gregg Easterbrook, "Bruce Babbitt's Interior Motives," *Newsweek*, March 29, 1993, 25; Jon Healey and Phillip A. Davis, "Babbitt Leans on His Actions on Way to Confirmation," *Congressional Quarterly Weekly Report*, January 23, 1993, 176; and "The Sagebrush Set Takes Aim at Clinton," *National Journal*, March 27, 1993, 783.

56. Rivlin served on two blue-ribbon commissions that advocated sustainable development policies; see National Commission on the Environment, *Choosing a Sustainable Future* (Covello, Calif.: Island Press, 1993); and Carnegie Endowment National Commission on America and the New World, *Changing Our Ways: America and the New World* (New York: Carnegie Endowment for International Peace, 1992). Panetta is a former congressman from California who has a solid environmental record.

57. Barnaby J. Feder, "New Energy Chief Has Seen Two Sides of Regulatory Fence," *New York Times*, December 22, 1992, C20; Keith Schneider, "Nominee Is a Veteran of Atomic-Waste Battle," *New York Times*, January 9, 1993, 9.

58. Timothy Egan, "Sweeping Reversal of U.S. Land Policy Sought by Clinton," *New York Times*, February 24, 1993, 1.

59. Richard L. Berke, "Clinton Backs Off From Policy Shift On Federal Lands," *New York Times*, March 31, 1993, 1.

60. Keith Schneider, "Clinton the Conservationist Thinks Twice," *New York Times*, April 4, 1993, E1.

5

Environmental Gridlock:
Searching for Consensus in Congress

Michael E. Kraft

Environmental policy is paralyzed in Congress and mired in the courts. Congress failed to agree on important revisions of the acts governing clean air, clean water, drinking water and abandoned toxic dump sites.

—*New York Times* editorial, November 30, 1984

For the past several years, Congress and the administration have been paralyzed by gridlock, particularly when it comes to environmental policy. . . . Now the American people expect all that to change.

—Max Baucus, D-Mont., chair of the Senate
Environment and Public Works Committee,
January 1993

In vivid contrast to the environmental policy activism and innovation of the 1970s, the 1980s were widely characterized as a period of policy paralysis. As the *New York Times* editorialized in late 1984, Congress seemed unable to advance on virtually any front in furthering America's environmental progress. From community opposition to hazardous waste facilities to congressional immobility on important national policies, the United States seemed afflicted with intractable environmental problems that frustrated all policy actors, governmental and nongovernmental alike.[1] In the mid to late 1980s the tide turned in Congress for some environmental issues. Congress revised and strengthened the Clean Water Act, the Safe Drinking Water Act, and the Superfund program, among other major policies. Most important of all, in 1990, with the active support of the Bush White House, Congress enacted a sweeping revision of the nation's premier environmental statute, the Clean Air Act.

Nevertheless, gridlock has continued into the 1990s, as Senator Baucus stated at the confirmation hearings for Carol Browner, President Bill Clinton's nominee for Environmental Protection Agency (EPA) administrator.[2] Indeed, one could hardly listen to the evening news or a presidential debate in 1992 without hearing the familiar refrain. President Bush railed against "the gridlocked Democratic Congress," and described Congress as a "master of inaction." He was not alone. As a *Washington Post* writer observed, "End-the-gridlock-in-Washington has become a kind of mantra for this year's political candidates."[3]

The sentiment was especially appropriate for Congress, where voter confidence in members sank to new lows in 1992 and term limitation measures attracted widespread support across the nation. That nearly 20 percent of the American public cast ballots for independent presidential candidate Ross Perot in 1992 was a powerful sign of the depth of the public's disaffection with politics as usual, both within and outside of Congress.

Senator Baucus is correct that the American people want gridlock to end. If the polls are any guide, they also tell us that Americans are very concerned about deteriorating environmental quality and therefore strongly support environmental protection policy.[4] With Democratic control of Congress and the White House assured for at least two years, will environmental policymaking in the Clinton administration be free of the gridlock that has plagued government from 1981 to 1993? It may occur less frequently, but gridlock will not disappear.

It is more useful to ask *why* our collective willingness and ability to devise solutions to the nation's environmental ills have varied so much over time. Why did environmental gridlock occur in the early 1980s, and why did it ease somewhat in the mid 1980s and early 1990s? What factors create or end policy stalemate, and what can citizens and political leaders do to affect the outcome?

In this chapter I focus on the U.S. Congress, even though environmental gridlock also occurs in federal bureaucracies, in the states, and in many communities. Congress is given the constitutional authority to enact national environmental policy, and it broadly mirrors the perceptions, attitudes, and policy preferences of the American public. Thus, an examination of Congress affords the opportunity to ask about the robustness of American democracy itself in the face of environmental challenges.

Environmental Gridlock and Its Causes

Policy gridlock refers to an inability to resolve conflicts in a policy-making body such as Congress, which results in governmental inaction in the face of important public problems. There is no consensus on *what* to do and therefore no movement in any direction. Present policies, or slight revisions of them, continue until agreement on change is reached.

Why Gridlock Occurs

Environmental policy stalemate in Congress and elsewhere reflects a fundamental reality of American politics. Policymaking is a complex and convoluted process made especially arduous by peculiar features of the U.S. political system. For decades political commentators have bemoaned the "deadlock of democracy" that derives from the system's highly fragmented authority, weak political parties, and uncertain presidential leadership, especially when control of the White House and Congress is divided between the major parties.[5]

The brunt of the criticism is directed at the constitutionally mandated separation of powers among policymaking institutions and other structural features that make governing difficult. Congressional reforms in the 1970s worsened the fragmentation by dispersing power to more than two hundred subcommittees and creating even more opportunities for small minorities to block action favored by the majority. Along with these changes, legislators have become more independent politically, helping to create a highly individualistic Congress in which members vigorously pursue their narrow district, state, or regional interests, often at the expense of the national welfare.[6]

The institutional argument is persuasive, but only partially so. It implies that gridlock is chiefly caused by structural fragmentation, especially divided government. Fix the structure, for example by centralizing authority, and gridlock is vanquished. Or elect a Congress and a president of the same party (either one will do) and cooperation on policymaking will follow. Institutional structure *is* important, but it is hardly the sole reason for environmental gridlock. Therefore, "fixing" the structure or ending divided government is unlikely to eliminate policy stalemate.[7]

We need to ask about other possible causes of the gridlock over environmental policy. One would seem to be the complexity of environmental problems themselves, compounded by the scientific uncertainty over their scope, causes, and implications. The more complex the issue and the less the consensus among scientists, the more likely gridlock is to occur. Climate change is a good example.

In a representative legislature the degree of public consensus matters a great deal. The greater the public consensus on a particular environmental policy, the easier it is for Congress to reach agreement on that policy. As noted, the general public strongly supports environmental protection. Yet its understanding of the issues (and of Congress) is limited, its views sometimes inconsistent, and its communication with its representatives in government infrequent and often ineffective.

Organized interests willingly enter the political vacuum. Thus, a fourth explanation for gridlock is a variation on the third: disagreement among organized (or "special") interests produces gridlock. The more key interest groups disagree (and are well positioned to act on their beliefs), the greater the probability of gridlock. One common pattern is a standoff between environmental groups and industry, which for years blocked policy action in pesticide policy, clean air legislation, and oil spill prevention and liability.[8] Their disagreement continues to affect renewal of virtually all major environmental policies.

One reason for this phenomenon is the explosive growth during the 1970s and 1980s in the number of Washington-based interest groups. The environmental lobby greatly improved its access to the corridors of power, and its political influence grew appreciably (chap. 2). Its success did not go unnoticed. In response, groups representing industry and resource development interests sharply increased their own presence in Washington.[9] By the late 1970s they were a powerful force often aligned against environmentalists.

In addition, business groups began a multifaceted effort to shift the political climate of the nation to the right, particularly away from increased regulation. They even learned how to give their efforts a grassroots facade through clever public relations campaigns. Sometimes they were blunt about their agenda: "We intend to take the money and the members away from the environmental movement by showing that they are destroying the American economy," said Ron Arnold of the Center for the Defense of Free Enterprise and a leader of the Wise Use movement.[10]

As a fifth explanation, we can say that unlike many other kinds of policy stalemate, environmental gridlock depends on the perceptions that citizens and policymakers alike have of short-term costs and long-term benefits. Action on problems such as climate change, acid rain, or protection of biological diversity—with highly visible short-term costs and uncertain long-term benefits—is difficult in the absence of compelling scientific evidence of the risks to human or ecological health or to economic well-being. Sometimes, however, a well-publicized accident, such as the *Exxon Valdez* oil spill, will shift the balance of forces in favor of environmental protection.

A sixth and final explanation is political leadership. Scholars have argued for years that presidential leadership was one of the most assured ways to overcome the institutional fragmentation of American government, and, conversely, that weak presidents would fare poorly even with a Congress of their own party. More recently, David Mayhew found that strong presidential leadership and a commitment to solving national problems could create the broad bipartisan majorities needed for passage of major bills, even under divided government.[11] Similarly, strong leadership within Congress at either the committee level or among party leaders may help to build the majorities needed for successful policymaking. Passage of the Clean Air Act Amendments of 1990 demonstrated the centrality of both presidential and congressional leadership.[12]

The Consequences of Environmental Gridlock

The consequences of policy gridlock attract more attention than its causes. Concern has focused on what difference it makes to environmental quality and public health when collectively we are unable to make tough decisions in a timely manner. For environmental as well as other issues, the policy dilemma associated with gridlock derives from the tension between two competing expectations for the policy process. One emphasizes prompt and rational problem solving, and the other stresses representation of pertinent interests and policy legitimation.

From the first perspective, gridlock needlessly, and even dangerously, blocks sound policy proposals. Dire consequences are foreseen unless immediate action is taken. But the second perspective advocates improving our understanding of the problems and the costs of action. Then policies are formulated that are broadly acceptable to the diverse interests affected.

For many environmental issues (for example, expansion of wilderness areas or revision of western water policy), short-term legislative delay is not necessarily cause for alarm. A relatively slow movement toward enactment allows time to improve scientific knowledge of environmental and health risks, to compile credible data on the costs and benefits of action, and to analyze and debate policy choices. This process of policy legitimation helps to build the political support so crucial not only to adoption of environmental policies but also to their successful implementation. Poorly designed and hastily approved policies run a significant risk of failure, as Charles Jones argued concerning the Clean Air Act of 1970. Scholars and activists have criticized the environmental and resource policies of the Reagan administration on the same grounds.[13]

Apprehension over environmental gridlock is clearly warranted, however, when long delays may cause severe or irreversible damage to public or ecosystem health. This may be the case for such problems as deterioration of the stratospheric ozone layer, global climate change, loss of biological diversity, and rapid population growth.

These distinctions must be made. Not all environmental threats are equally great, nor do all require "crisis decisionmaking." Where risks are moderate, extended policy legitimation and incremental decisionmaking can be tolerated. Although we may aspire to optimum environmental policymaking in all cases, this may not be possible except where the risks of indecision or ineffective policies are great. In such instances, the need for a high degree of scientific certainty, demonstrably favorable benefit-cost ratios, and agreement among all disputants is not as important as the need to act. John Dryzek, Robert Bartlett, and William Ophuls, among others, have argued that under these conditions we need to think seriously about new criteria for decisionmaking, such as what is ecologically rational and best promotes our long-term, collective well-being.[14] If conventional decisionmaking cannot adequately address the problems likely to be faced in the 1990s and in the twenty-first century, we need to develop a decisionmaking process that can. In the rest of this chapter I try to illuminate some of the key issues surrounding environmental gridlock in Congress and suggest strategies for improving decisionmaking.

Policymaking in the "Environmental Decade"

The 1970s offer abundant examples of both successful and unsuccessful efforts at environmental policymaking, as discussed in chapter 1. The record for this "environmental decade" is nevertheless remarkable, particularly in comparison to most of the 1980s (app. 1). The National Environmental Policy Act, Clean Air Act, Clean Water Act, Endangered Species Act, and Resource Conservation and Recovery Act, among others, were all enacted in the 1970s, demonstrating that despite the much-discussed infirmities of the U.S. political system, major environmental policies can be approved in fairly short order under certain circumstances.[15]

The legislative accomplishments owed much to some basic changes in American society and politics in the 1960s and 1970s. Among the most important of these was rising public concern over environmental threats and the consequent growth in membership and political clout of environmental groups. Public opinion and interest group influence count for much in the U.S. Congress. As these new players entered the political arena, the "scope of conflict" on environmental and natural resource issues was widened, new perspectives on environmental policy received attention, and the older political coalitions were irrevocably altered. The "subgovernments" (alliances of congressional committees, agencies, and interest groups) that once dominated policy areas such as pesticide use, public lands, nuclear power, and water projects were forced to accommodate new and broader issue networks.[16] Congress itself was transformed by a series of internal changes that made it more open to public scrutiny and more responsive to new political forces such as those represented by environmental and other public interest groups.[17]

To these factors we can add the presence in Congress of an extraordinary group of environmental policy entrepreneurs who provided the leadership essential to enactment of the landmark policies of the 1960s and 1970s. They included senators Edmund Muskie (D-Maine), chair of the influential Subcommittee on Air and Water Pollution, and Henry Jackson (D-Wash.), chair of the Committee on Interior and Insular Affairs; and their counterparts in the House, such as representatives Morris Udall (D-Ariz.) and Paul Rodgers (D-Fla.). Along with other key legislators, they used their well-honed political skills to publicize emerging environmental problems and to assemble the necessary legislative coalitions for policy enactment.

These early environmental victories were deceptive in some respects. Congressional support, although broadly based, was thin. As long as the issues were popular and politically safe, members would go along. Most could not imagine what sort of complaints the policies would eventually provoke from the business community, nor anticipate the many technical, administrative, and economic concerns that would arise during implementation.

Congress's enthusiasm for environmental policy gradually gave way to apprehension about its impact on the economy. Hastening this change was the decline in the salience of environmental issues for the American public in the mid to late 1970s. A fortuitous convergence of short-term political forces made the achievements in the 1970s easy victories. The 1980s were different.

Environmental Policymaking in the 1980s

Environmental gridlock became the norm in the early 1980s mostly because the political climate changed with the election of Ronald Reagan as president in 1980. In comparison with the presidential election campaigns of 1988 and 1992, the campaign of 1980 featured little direct discussion of environmental issues. Reagan did target, however, government regulation as a burden on the economy, and he promised relief to the business community.[18] For the first time since 1955, the Republicans captured the Senate, giving conservatives the opportunity to block environmental policy proposals and to roll back some already in existence. The economic recession of 1980-1982 and the high cost of energy also shaped Reagan's decision to subordinate the environment to economic recovery.

These alterations in the political environment in 1981 threw Congress into a defensive posture. It was forced to *react* to the Reagan administration's radical policy shifts, which it did by defending existing policy. Rather than proposing new programs or expanding old ones, it focused its resources on oversight and criticism of the Reagan administration. Between the Ninety-sixth Congress (1979-1980) and the Ninety-seventh Congress (1981-1982), oversight hearings were conducted with far greater frequency by the major environmental committees.[19] Bipartisan leadership on these issues also became more difficult. Thus, for most of Reagan's first term political conditions were ripe for protracted conflict between the president and Congress.

Gridlock: 1981-1984

In assessing environmental policymaking from 1981 to 1984, Mary Etta Cook and Roger Davidson argue that Congress was practicing "deferral politics." As environmental issues became more complex, less salient to the public, and more contentious, there were fewer incentives for policy leadership on Capitol Hill. Members were increasingly cross-pressured by environmental and industry groups, partisanship on these issues increased, and Congress and President Reagan battled over budget and program priorities.[20] Some Democrats also feared that, given the antiregulatory climate, opening existing statutes to amendment might weaken them.

The fragmentation of environmental policy responsibilities added to Congress's inability to respond expeditiously and coherently to the president. Because dozens of committees and subcommittees have jurisdiction over these issues (see table 1-1, p. 6), they often compete with one another. Hearings by different committees are typically uncoordinated, as each seeks attention and political credit for its activities.[21]

The cumulative effect of these conditions in the early 1980s was that Congress adopted a posture of deferring action. It had become impossible to form majority coalitions to act definitively on most of the major environmental statutes coming up for renewal. Thus, members opted to keep programs alive through continuing appropriations and short-term extensions of the existing acts. During the Ninety-seventh Congress, eight comprehensive environmental programs were due for reauthorization; only two were enacted. Although it renewed the Toxic Substances Control Act and the Endangered Species Act in 1982, Congress deferred action on programs for clean air, clean water, pesticide regulation, noise control, safe drinking water, and hazardous waste control.

Moreover, there were virtually no *new* environmental policies proposed in this Congress. With a divided House and Senate and a conservative president, congressional policy initiation was improbable. It was more expedient for Congress to enter a holding pattern and wait for an improved political climate.

Gridlock Eases: 1984-1990

The legislative logjam began breaking up in late 1983, as President Reagan's environmental agenda was repudiated by the American public and as his appointees, Anne Burford and James Watt, were forced from office. These developments altered what John Kingdon has called the "politics stream."[22] Environmental groups took advantage of the favorable political mood to push ahead on their deferred policy agenda. The new pattern was evident in 1984 when, after several years of deliberation, Congress approved major amendments to the 1976 Resource Conservation and Recovery Act that strengthened the program and set tight new deadlines for EPA rule making on control of hazardous chemical wastes. Reauthorization of other major acts followed in the next two years.

Although the Republicans still controlled the Senate, the Ninety-ninth Congress (1985-1986) compiled a record dramatically at odds with the deferral politics of the Ninety-seventh and Ninety-eighth Congresses. Congressional action was spurred by two environmental catastrophes. At Bhopal, India, in December 1984 more than three thousand people were killed and several hundred thousand injured in the world's worst industrial accident. And at Chernobyl in the Soviet Union in April 1986, the worst nuclear power plant accident in history exposed hundreds of people to high levels of radiation and spread radioactive fallout across northern

Europe. The accidents increased the credibility of those arguing for additional environmental protection. They also created windows of opportunity for environmental groups to press their case for renewal of the Superfund program and related policies on toxic chemicals and pollution control. Republican environmental leaders such as John Chafee (R-R.I.) and Robert Stafford (R-Vt.) played important roles as well in building congressional support.

In May 1986 the Safe Drinking Water Act was strengthened and expanded, incorporating a three-year timetable for regulation of eighty-three chemical contaminants. In the fall of 1986, after years of bitter controversy, Congress enacted the Superfund Amendments and Reauthorization Act (SARA), which renewed the program for hazardous waste cleanup for five years at a total budget of $8.5 billion, far greater than the spending level favored by the Reagan administration. As a reflection of public concern following the Bhopal accident, Congress added to SARA a separate Title III, the Emergency Planning and Community Right-to-Know Act. This was an entirely new program mandating nationwide reporting requirements for toxic and hazardous chemicals produced, used, or stored in communities, as well as state and local emergency planning for accidental releases.[23] In addition, in late 1986 Congress reauthorized the Clean Water Act, with a price tag of $18 billion over nine years. President Reagan vetoed the water bill as too expensive, but in February 1987 the One Hundredth Congress (1987-1988) easily passed the same bill (with the authorization raised to $20 billion) and overrode the president's second veto by large margins.

Environmentalists were pleased with these results. At the end of 1986 the Natural Resources Defense Council described the achievements of the Ninety-ninth Congress as "a complete turnaround from recent years," and in early 1987 the Sierra Club congratulated Congress for its "solid record on environmental quality and public lands issues," adding that "bipartisan majorities supported the improvement of key laws despite resistance from President Reagan."[24]

The Democrats regained control of the Senate following the 1986 election, and the newly elected members of both the House and Senate were a more environmentally oriented group. Yet despite what is by any measure a highly productive record, several major environmental policy measures failed not only in the Ninety-ninth Congress but in the One Hundredth Congress as well. These included renewal of the Clean Air Act and the major pesticide control act, the Federal Insecticide, Fungicide, and Rodenticide Act (FIFRA), and new legislation on acid rain and energy.

Cases in Policy Paralysis: Clean Air and Energy

In an assessment of environmental issues at the end of the One Hundredth Congress, one analyst wrote, "Congress stayed largely stalemated on a range of old environmental and energy problems in 1988, even while a generation of new ones clamored for attention."[25] The cases of clean air and energy policy illustrate why environmental gridlock continued in Congress. Perhaps more important, they help to explain how Congress was able to resolve conflicts over air pollution and energy issues and to adopt the Clean Air Act Amendments of 1990 and the Energy Policy Act of 1992.

Air Quality and Acid Rain

For years environmental gridlock was epitomized by Congress's inability to reauthorize the costly and controversial Clean Air Act after its 1977 amendment. By 1981, when funding authorization for the act was to expire, critics had compiled a long list of grievances about air pollution regulation. There was also wide agreement that the 1977 act, itself the product of a fragile coalition, needed at least modest revision.[26] By the 1980s concern over the lack of any national policy to combat acid rain was added to the list. Unfortunately, consensus on the *particulars* of reform proved to be nearly impossible between late 1981 and 1989.

President Reagan was expected to lead a fight to weaken the Clean Air Act in 1981. However, after initial drafts drew sharp criticism and poll results showed broad public support for strong air pollution laws, the administration issued only a vague set of "basic principles" on clean air policy. This action shifted the initiative to Congress.

At center stage on Capitol Hill was a bill sponsored by Rep. John Dingell (D-Mich.), chair of the House Energy and Commerce Committee. Introduced in late 1981 and described as a "moderate compromise," the measure drew its major support from business interests, and won endorsement by the Reagan White House. Environmentalists quickly labeled it the "dirty air" bill and faulted it for omission of acid rain provisions. These first skirmishes in the clean air battles hinted at what lay ahead for the rest of the decade.

Conflicts over clean air policy throughout the 1980s were personified by the incessant wrangling between the powerful Dingell, ever-protective of Michigan's automobile industry, and Rep. Henry Waxman (D-Calif.), chair of the Energy and Commerce Committee's subcommittee on health and the environment, whose district in Los Angeles was one of the smoggiest in the nation. Debate in the Energy Committee was rancorous, and the press described the committee as "polarized and paralyzed." No bill emerged from the committee in 1981 or 1982. After that, Waxman and his subcommittee assumed responsibility, spending the next eight years, in his words, "painting the picture and setting the agenda" for clean air legislation.[27] Policy incubation of this kind was the best Waxman could hope for given the political environment.

In August 1982 the Republican-controlled Environment and Public

Works Committee rejected President Reagan's call for sweeping changes in the act and agreed on a modest revision. The bill never reached the Senate floor. After 1982 the president played no active role on air pollution policymaking, but he made clear to Congress that he would veto any strong clean air bill that placed an economic burden on industry. At the same time, the EPA under Anne Burford pursued an aggressive strategy of undercutting the Clean Air Act's implementation.[28]

Many of the same conflicts were evident in formulating acid rain policy. Acid rain refers to both wet and dry deposition of acids formed by sulfur dioxide (primarily from coal combustion) and nitrogen oxides (primarily from motor vehicle exhaust and electric utilities) emitted into the atmosphere. Although scientific evidence was not conclusive on the severity of all impacts, acid rain was widely believed to adversely affect biological processes in lakes and streams, forests, crops, and buildings, and to threaten human health.[29] The effects were considered particularly serious in the Northeast, and the contributing sources were chiefly in the industrial Midwest, especially areas using older, coal-fired generating facilities.

As concern over the effects of acid rain mounted during the 1980s, repeated attempts were made to formulate policies that would sharply reduce sulfur dioxide and nitrogen oxide emissions. They were opposed by the affected industries and blocked by congressional leaders sympathetic with their plight. The Reagan White House consistently held to the view that further research was needed before any costly regulatory program could be adopted, and thus sided with the opponents. A ten-year federal research program was begun to improve knowledge on the causes and effects of acid rain.[30] Compromise on acid rain policy was made especially difficult because of the intense regional conflicts and the uncompromising positions taken by both environmentalists and industry.

From 1982 to 1988 the politics of clean air remained stalemated. The Senate's Environment and Public Works Committee reported out clean air bills in 1984 and 1987 that failed to receive consideration in the full Senate (although it likely would have approved the measures). The House Energy and Commerce Committee, less proenvironment than the full House, remained mired in controversy over the stringency of air pollution control measures.

In 1988 there was a new atmosphere of moderation in both houses, and Congress came close to breaking the gridlock. For the third time, the Senate Environment and Public Works Committee reported out a comprehensive bill, endorsed by environmentalists, that included sections on ozone, toxic air pollutants, and acid rain control, as well as tougher emission limits on motor vehicles and industry.[31] But Senate majority leader Robert Byrd (D-W.Va.), worried about the impact of the acid rain provisions on his state's coal miners, would not bring it to the floor. Sen. George Mitchell (D-Maine), chair of the Environment and Public Works Committee's subcommittee on environmental protection, hoped the election-year popularity of clean air policy would allow him to piece together a compromise bill, but the coalition fell apart at the end of the session, largely over acid rain measures.

Mitchell had negotiated quietly with Byrd and others to draft broadly acceptable acid rain provisions in the clean air bill. When the bill was derailed at the end of the session in October 1988, Mitchell delivered a blistering twenty-three-page speech on the Senate floor. He blamed both environmentalists and the utilities and coal companies for remaining "rigid and unyielding ... even when faced with the certainty that their rigidity would result in no action this year." In an interview just after his speech, Mitchell described the difficulty of acid rain politics: "The problem remains as it has for over a decade.... It is a complex problem requiring a complex solution affecting virtually every part of the country. The costs can be specifically identified, while the benefits are general in nature. It's very difficult to arouse public support for it, and it is hard to translate public support into legislative support."[32]

In the House an informal caucus of moderate and conservative industrial state Democrats on the Energy and Commerce Committee, known as the "group of nine," made a parallel effort. Saying they were "tired of deadlock," they developed a compromise bill on urban smog that failed to satisfy either side completely.[33] John Dingell continued to oppose proposals to strengthen the Clean Air Act, and, like Waxman in 1982, he made full use of parliamentary rules to delay action in Waxman's subcommittee, for example, by not appearing for quorum calls. The two coalitions of opposing interest groups—the Clean Air Working Group (representing industry) and the National Clean Air Coalition (representing environmental, public health, and consumer groups)—were strong enough to block each other's initiatives.

George Bush's election in 1988, an improved political climate, and several changes in party leadership on Capitol Hill finally offered the promise of a breakthrough on clean air legislation. In one of the key shifts, Senator Mitchell, the chief proponent of clean air laws in the Senate, replaced Robert Byrd as the majority leader, making floor action more likely. Sen. Max Baucus (D-Mont.), the new chair of the subcommittee on environmental protection, reflected this optimistic consensus for passage by citing increasing public support for environmental protection and concomitant legislative backing: "Everyone wants a bill this year—the Speaker, the majority leader, and the president."[34] Reports of worsening ozone levels in urban areas and the release of new data in mid 1989 on toxic air pollutants also improved prospects. Shortly after the new data were released, the Chemical Manufacturers Association said it would support some changes in the Clean Air Act, a significant reversal of its long-standing opposition.[35]

"It's time to break the gridlock on this issue," President Bush said in July 1989 as he sent his clean air bill to Congress. It was the single most important action he would take to fulfill a campaign promise to be the "environmental president." By breaking with his predecessor's implacable opposition to acid rain control measures and other components of clean air policy, the president lent crucial White House backing to congressional efforts to end the stalemate.

Working closely with EPA officials, top White House aides Roger Porter, Robert Grady, and C. Boyden Gray formulated the president's bill over a six-month period. It was directed at the three key problems— urban smog, toxic air pollutants, and acid rain—the latter addressed through innovative trading allowances among utilities that had been pushed by economist Daniel Dudek of the Environmental Defense Fund. In one of the strongest components of his clean air bill, the president supported a 50 percent reduction in sulfur dioxide and nitrogen oxide emissions from utilities.[36] The president's proposal was criticized by environmentalists as too weak and by industry as too demanding, yet White House support virtually guaranteed congressional passage of a clean air bill by 1990.[37]

The bill's success in the Senate was facilitated as well by George Mitchell's election as majority leader. In addition, a decade of policy incubation (which allowed further scientific research and assessment of successful acid rain control programs in several states like Wisconsin and Minnesota) made agreement on some technical and economic issues more likely by 1989. Although regional divisions over the distribution of costs continued, relatively strong and innovative acid rain provisions were incorporated into the bill.[38]

Both the House and Senate committees moved quickly to complete work on the various clean air proposals, with compromises made by both sides. Senate majority leader George Mitchell was instrumental in building consensus on the bill and steering it through the Senate; the active participation in Senate negotiations of Porter, Grady, Gray, and EPA officials was also important. That leadership ensured that the compromise measure would survive a raft of so-called strengthening amendments on the floor that threatened to undermine it. On April 3, 1990, the Senate approved the clean air bill by a vote of 89-11—a margin exceeded later that year in the House.[39]

Energy Policy in the 1990s

Energy policy has rarely occupied a sustained position on the national political agenda, and energy policy initiatives have not fared well in Congress. Despite a succession of presidential proposals in the wake of the Arab oil embargo of 1973, including a major push by President Jimmy Carter in 1977 and 1978, Congress failed to adopt a comprehensive national energy policy. No consensus on energy policy goals existed either among the public or on Capitol Hill, presidential leadership was weak and inconsistent, and intense opposition emerged to the energy proposals by various organized interests. The resulting policy stalemate was a portent of developments in the early 1990s.[40]

After eight years of neglect by President Reagan (and the Congress), energy issues staged a reappearance in the late 1980s. Oil consumption and oil imports were rising rapidly, again putting the United States at risk. More than half the oil consumed in the United States was imported, with serious consequences for both the economy and national security. Moreover, concern over global climate change and the environmental effects of conventional energy use (both fossil fuels and nuclear power) had propelled energy issues to the forefront by 1990.

Well before the Persian Gulf War of early 1991, fought largely because U.S. access to Middle East oil fields was jeopardized, the Bush administration had directed the Department of Energy (DOE) to develop a comprehensive National Energy Strategy (NES). Following eighteen months of nationwide public meetings and internal study, in December 1990 DOE sent its proposals to the Bush White House. The reception was decidedly cool. Between December and early February 1991, conservative White House aides (particularly John Sununu, Michael Boskin, and Richard Darman) and Nicholas Brady, secretary of the treasury, pressed to eliminate virtually all energy conservation measures and pointedly rejected proposed increases in auto and truck fuel efficiency standards. Their ideological objections to a large governmental role in energy policy and fear of economic impacts of higher energy taxes shifted the president's strategy to energy production initiatives. These became the cornerstone of the president's recommendations to Capitol Hill in late February, and the most controversial elements in the NES.

The Senate Energy and Natural Resources Committee, chaired by Sen. J. Bennett Johnston (D-La.), was the chief forum for energy policy decisionmaking and the focus of intense lobbying by all sides. The committee is more conservative on environmental issues than the Senate as a whole and is dominated by members from energy-producing states. Committee members also receive sizable campaign contributions from the oil, natural gas, and nuclear energy industries. Johnston himself, who maintains firm control of the committee, has powerful connections to the same industries and is one of the largest recipients in the Senate of political action committee (PAC) campaign contributions, and the single largest recipient of PAC funds from the nuclear power industry.

Convinced the nation needed a national energy policy, particularly in light of the Gulf War, Johnston strongly backed Bush's NES. Yet he also understood the necessity of adding conservation provisions to sell the measure in the Senate. He incorporated the president's proposals into his own massive energy bill, which he defended as an acceptable balance of energy production and environmental protection. Environmental groups were decidedly unhappy, however, with the tilt of that balance. The Johnston bill was unacceptable to them as long as it included plans for opening the Arctic National Wildlife Refuge (ANWR) to oil and gas exploration and new policies for so-called streamlined licensing of nuclear power plants. Environmentalists also pressed hard for a gradual increase in the corporate average fuel economy (CAFE) standards to 40 mpg (embodied in a bill by Sen. Richard Bryan, D-Nev.) as their chief means to reduce oil imports. Johnston agreed to a lesser increase of 34 mpg, but the oil industry, auto manufacturers, and the Bush White House staunchly opposed any increase at all. Given the committee makeup and the support of the ranking Republican member, Malcolm Wallop of Wyoming, Johnston had little trouble moving his bill quickly through the committee, where it received a 17-3 vote on May 23, 1991.

The extent of opposition to Johnston's bill, however, was evident as it was being moved to the Senate floor. Representing environmental and consumer groups, three junior senators, Bryan, Paul Wellstone (D-Minn.), and Timothy Wirth (D.-Colo.), challenged Johnston with a filibuster. In an unusual coalition, they were joined by conservative Republicans representing electric utilities, Democrats concerned about forcing Detroit to build more fuel-efficient cars or easing the licensing of nuclear power plants, and other senators angered by Johnston's aggressive tactics. In what the press called a stunning victory for environmental groups, Johnston lost the November 1, 1991, cloture vote to end the filibuster by a ten-vote margin. He spoke openly of his admiration for the "political skill" that environmentalists exhibited, saying they "wrote the textbook on how to defeat a bill such as this."

After the vote, Johnston, Wirth, and others agreed to rewrite the bill without either ANWR or the CAFE standards, and to add energy efficiency measures. Bryan agreed not to push his own bill on CAFE standards, for which there was little support in the Senate anyway. Unfortunately, what might have been a significant effort to accommodate environmental concerns fell apart late in the year. The Gulf war receded in memory, energy issues no longer seemed so urgent, and environmentalists lost their momentum. They and their allies in the Senate failed to follow through with the anticipated meetings and bill drafting. As adept as they were at derailing a bill they found wanting, environmental groups could not put together a positive coalition on energy policy. As for the White House, President Bush had threatened to veto any energy bill that didn't open ANWR to oil drilling or raised CAFE standards. By all accounts, however, the Bush White House provided ineffective leadership on the bill. It was not a presidential priority.[41]

Johnston took advantage of the opportunity. By deleting provisions in the bill that offended critical constituencies, skillfully negotiating legislative deals with his colleagues, and helping to coordinate the lobbying by industry groups that would benefit from the energy policy, he regained control of the process. He fashioned a new Senate bill (absent the ANWR provision and increases in CAFE standards), and he and his committee staff aides then engaged in what one journalist described as "four and a half days of whirlwind bargaining in the hallways and cloakrooms off the Senate floor." He won all votes on amendments to the bill, and the Senate approved the new 600-page energy measure on February 19, 1992, by a 94-4 vote.[42] A second round of three days of floor debate followed in July, and on July 30, 1992, the Senate enacted a revised version with additional energy taxes approved by the Senate Finance Committee.

The House began later than the Senate and moved more slowly on its own energy bill. It was formulated chiefly in the Energy and Commerce Committee's Subcommittee on Energy and Power, which held twenty-four days of hearings over a six-month period. Its chairman, Philip R. Sharp (D-Ind.), the leading energy expert in the House, adroitly moved the bill through the hearings and subcommittee markup in 1991, with special attention to coalition building. "We always kept in mind what people wanted, and tried to use that to get them on board," he said of his legislative strategy.[43] The effort paid off when the full Energy and Commerce Committee made few major changes in the four-hundred-page energy bill and approved it on March 11, 1992, by a lopsided vote of 42-1.

The diversity of issues in energy policy required that the Energy and Commerce Committee's action be supplemented by other panels with responsibility for ANWR, tax policy, and other provisions. Fully eight other committees played a role in House action on the bill, a jurisdictional complexity that often dooms controversial legislation. Such an outcome was avoided because Speaker Thomas Foley was determined that the Democratic Congress enact an energy bill before the 1992 election. Foley set deadlines for committee work and steered the bill through the Rules Committee and floor debate. On May 27, 1992, the House voted by a 381-37 margin in favor of the bill.[44]

Political concerns about the impact of such a wide-ranging bill were evident in the unusually large conference committee appointed to settle differences between the House and Senate versions. The Senate named thirty-one of its members to the committee, the House named one hundred, and the conference was under way by early September. Pressed by Senator Johnston to move quickly to settle continuing disagreements on a range of issues, Congress produced a compromise bill by October 1. Along the way, conferees further pruned offensive sections of the bill and altered others to make them acceptable to industries in their states. The Bush administration successfully opposed a provision for a moratorium on offshore oil drilling, and Johnston added a section at the end of the conference to ease construction of the embattled Yucca Mountain, Nevada, nuclear waste repository.[45] By October 8, as Congress was nearing adjournment, the energy bill had passed the House by a 363-60 margin and the Senate by voice vote. It was signed by President Bush on October 24,

1992, although with little of the fanfare or news coverage one might have expected, particularly in an election year.

The lack of celebration fit the modest nature of the final act. Most of the key players acknowledged that it was less of a comprehensive national energy policy than a foundation on which to build future efforts to wean the nation from its appetite for imported oil. As Senator Johnston said at the end of the long process, "Great policy shifts come slowly. . . . They're hard to do, and they're hard to undo."[46] In a television documentary on the energy bill broadcast in the fall of 1992, Johnston blamed the narrowness of the measure on the failure of political will and leadership in America—"from top to bottom, from the president, from Congress, from the media, from the people." He said nothing about the immense lobbying power of the oil, natural gas, and nuclear industries.[47]

As enacted, the Energy Policy Act of 1992 sought to decrease U.S. dependence on imported oil through increased domestic production and conservation. The act mandated greater energy conservation and efficiency in electric appliances and buildings, eased licensing requirements for nuclear power plants, restructured the electric utility industry to create greater competition and efficiency (which should create a larger role for renewable energy sources), encouraged the use of alternative fuels for autos (especially in fleet vehicles used by federal and state governments), and adjusted energy-related sections of the tax code. It also authorized billions of dollars for energy research and development for coal, nuclear power, and renewable fuels.[48]

The act will cap but not reduce U.S. dependence on imported oil, and it will have no immediate effect on CO_2 emissions that contribute to global warming, although they may be reduced over time as the Clean Air Act of 1990 is implemented. Legislators shunned gasoline taxes as politically unacceptable, and they struck the increase in CAFE standards so strongly opposed by the auto industry and the White House. In short, gridlock on energy policy was ended in 1992, but at the price of fairly weak policy that would necessitate further amendment in the years ahead. One sign of the ongoing policy cycle was evident in February 1993 when President Clinton proposed a modest and broad-based energy tax as part of his deficit reduction package. The new tax would increase the cost of gasoline, home heating oil, natural gas, and electricity generated from coal or nuclear power, though it would not affect the price of renewable energy sources such as solar, wind, or geothermal power.[49]

Conclusion

The cases of clean air and energy policy illustrate the many reasons for the gridlock on environmental issues in Congress. No single solution exists to solve the problem. The technical complexity of environmental problems, lack of public or scientific consensus, weak presidential and congressional leadership (or outright opposition), and especially the proficiency with which well-organized groups are able to frustrate coalition building and compromise are all important impediments to policymaking.

Some of these conditions, for example scientific knowledge, leadership, and the political climate, change over time, making gridlock worse in some periods than in others. The institutional characteristics of Congress, however, such as the dispersion of authority, continue unchanged, and the ability of interest groups to thwart one another's proposals seems to have increased of late. All these forces have implications for the environmental gridlock we can expect in the 1990s. They also suggest strategies that can be used by citizens and political leaders eager to improve environmental policymaking.

The Future of Environmental Gridlock

Environmental policymaking in the mid 1990s is likely to resemble the patterns of the past fifteen years in at least some respects. When the major environmental statutes are up for renewal, we can expect significant conflict over expansion of statutory authority, the pace of implementation, and the level of resources to be made available. From endangered species and clean water acts to hazardous waste policies, the potential for deadlock will continue as affected interests seek to reduce their financial and other burdens while environmental groups press for strengthening the acts.

We are also likely to see a continuation of innovative policymaking at the state level over the next decade. During the stalemate in Washington in the 1980s, many states grew tired of waiting for Congress and the White House to act and developed path-breaking policies on their own in areas as diverse as energy conservation, recycling, clean air, and acid rain control. For example, California, the nation's most populous state, developed an energy policy based almost exclusively on conservation and renewable sources that won the support of environmental, utility, and industry groups.[50]

Important contrasts with previous environmental policymaking at the federal level can be expected as well. In 1992, for the first time in sixteen years, the nation elected a president and Congress of the same political party, prompting Majority Leader George Mitchell to announce "The decade of gridlock has ended. . . . The decade of progress now opens before us." As of February 1993 the prospects for a cooperative relationship on environmental policy between the Clinton-Gore administration and Congress did indeed seem promising. One sign could be found in congressional leadership positions. In addition to Mitchell's continuation as Senate majority leader, Max Baucus became chair of the Senate Environment and Public Works Committee. In the House, George Miller (D-Calif.) continued as a strongly proenvironmental chair of the newly renamed Natural Resources Committee, Norman Mineta (D-Calif.) became chair of the Public Works and Transportation Committee, and Gerry Studds (D-Mass.) was made chair of the Merchant Marine and Fisheries Committee. Their average League of Conservation Voters score for 1991-1992 of 83 percent was well above the House Democratic average of 57 percent. Perhaps of greater importance, the 124 newly elected members of Congress held views that were more proenvironment than those of their predecessors, continuing a trend of the past twenty years.[51]

For some environmental issues, the policymaking process may well become more difficult in the years ahead. This is likely to be the case for "third-generation" environmental problems such as global climate change, deforestation, and loss of biological diversity. The most important effects on environmental quality will be felt in the future, which offers few political incentives for policy leadership. Scientists disagree over the causes and appropriate remedies, and responding to these challenges will impose significant economic and social costs. Dealing with global environmental threats also will require unprecedented international cooperation.

For these reasons, several scenarios could unfold in the 1990s. One is protracted political conflict and stalemate. This may be especially likely when the issues are complex, scientific evidence remains inconclusive, economic costs and social impacts are perceived to be great, there are unresolved regional inequities, and public opinion is divided. Alternatively, we might see a much-reduced level of political conflict if consensus among the public on environmental policy goals increases and creates a durable political constituency for environmental protection, and if Congress and the White House heed such public sentiment.

What might political leaders and citizens do to forestall gridlock and improve the chances of enacting policy that is responsive to public concerns about the world's deteriorating environment? Several strategies come to mind.

Congress could do a great deal to reduce jurisdictional overlap and conflicts among committees responsible for environmental policy. It could also improve the flow of policy advice from congressional advisory bodies such as the Office of Technology Assessment and the General Accounting Office.[52] In recent years Congress has used a variety of informal mechanisms to build consensus on environmental policy among its members.[53] These could be supplemented by formal changes in rules and procedures in order to facilitate majority governance, lessening the opportunity for minorities to block legislation. Another much-discussed need is campaign finance reform. Some form of public financing of congressional elections and sharp limits on political action committee contributions might reduce the inordinate power of special interests so evident in energy and environmental policy.

Political leadership at all levels is crucial in defining the environmental agenda, articulating policy needs, and arguing persuasively for government action. Such leadership depends critically on the public's attitudes and political behavior. Citizens will need to become more alert to environmental problems and to cooperate in the search for effective solutions, from local communities to the nation as a whole. They also need to encourage elected officials to move boldly ahead where the pathway may be obstructed by narrow economic, regional, and other interests. Public opinion remains a powerful force in environmental policymaking. But as decisions about environmental policy become increasingly contentious, concerned citizens will have to improve their ability to translate diffuse support for environmental protection into effective political influence.

Notes

The chapter epigraph quoting Sen. Max Baucus (D-Mont.) is from Phillip A. Davis, "Browner Short on Specifics in Confirmation Hearing," *Congressional Quarterly Weekly Report*, January 16, 1993, 127.

1. See, for example, Daniel A. Mazmanian, Michael Stanley-Jones, and Miriam J. Green, *Breaking Political Gridlock: California's Experiment in Public-Private Cooperation for Hazardous Waste Policy* (Claremont, Calif.: California Institute of Public Affairs, 1988); and Mary Etta Cook and Roger H. Davidson, "Deferral Politics: Congressional Decision Making on Environmental Issues in the 1980s," in *Public Policy and the Natural Environment*, ed. Helen M. Ingram and R. Kenneth Godwin (Greenwich, Conn.: JAI, 1985).
2. Davis, "Browner Short on Specifics," 127.
3. Helen Dewar, "The Politics of Gridlock," *Washington Post National Weekly Edition*, August 10-16, 1992, 6-7.
4. Riley E. Dunlap, "Public Opinion in the 1980s: Clear Consensus, Ambiguous Commitment," *Environment* 33 (October 1991): 9-15, 32-37; Riley E. Dunlap and Rik Scarce, "Environmental Problems and Protection," *Public Opinion Quarterly* 55 (Winter 1991): 651-672.
5. See James McGregor Burns, *The Deadlock of Democracy* (Englewood Cliffs, N.J.: Prentice-Hall, 1963); and James A. Thurber, ed., *Divided Democracy: Cooperation and Conflict Between the President and Congress* (Washington, D.C.: CQ Press, 1991).
6. Roger H. Davidson, ed., *The Postreform Congress* (New York: St. Martin's, 1992); Morris P. Fiorina, *Congress: Keystone of the Washington Establishment*, 2d ed. (New Haven, Conn.: Yale University Press, 1989).
7. David R. Mayhew, *Divided We Govern* (New Haven, Conn.: Yale University Press, 1991). Mayhew studied 267 major laws enacted between 1947 and 1990 and found that divided partisan control of Congress and the White House made little difference in legislative output (i.e., the number of laws passed). Of course, output is only a crude measure of policymaking, and divided government may make a great difference in the specific provisions of laws enacted.
8. Christopher J. Bosso, *Pesticides and Politics: The Life Cycle of a Public Issue* (Pittsburgh: University of Pittsburgh Press, 1987); Gary C. Bryner, *Blue Skies, Green Politics: The Clean Air Act of 1990* (Washington, D.C.: CQ Press, 1993); and Phil Kuntz, "Long-Delayed Oil-Spill Measure Closer to Reaching President," *Congressional Quarterly Weekly Report*, July 28, 1990, 2401-2403.
9. See Jeffrey M. Berry, *The Interest Group Society*, 2d ed. (Glenview, Ill.: Scott, Foresman/Little, Brown, 1989), 16-43; and Kay Lehman Schlozman and John T.

Tierney, *Organized Interests and American Democracy* (New York: Harper and Row, 1986), 58-87.

10. Eliza Newlin Carney, "Industry Plays the Grass-Roots Card," *National Journal*, February 1, 1992, 281-282. See also Chip Berlet and William K. Burke, "Corporate Fronts: Inside the Anti-Environmental Movement," *Greenpeace* (Jan.-Feb.-Mar. 1991), 9-12; and William Poole, "Neither Wise Nor Well," *Sierra* (November-December 1992), 59-61, 88-93.

11. Mayhew, *Divided We Govern.*

12. See Richard E. Cohen, *Washington at Work: Back Rooms and Clean Air* (New York: Macmillan, 1992); and Bryner, *Blue Skies, Green Politics.*

13. Charles O. Jones, *Clean Air: The Policies and Politics of Pollution Control* (Pittsburgh: University of Pittsburgh Press, 1975). On Reagan's policies see Norman J. Vig and Michael E. Kraft, eds., *Environmental Policy in the 1980s: Reagan's New Agenda* (Washington, D.C.: CQ Press, 1984); and chap. 4 in this volume.

14. John Dryzek, *Rational Ecology: Environment and Political Economy* (New York: Basil Blackwell, 1987), esp. chap. 3; Robert V. Bartlett, "Ecological Rationality: Reason and Environmental Policy," *Environmental Ethics* 8 (Fall 1986): 221-239; and William Ophuls and A. Stephen Boyan, Jr., *Ecology and the Politics of Scarcity Revisited* (San Francisco: W. H. Freeman, 1992). For a more mainstream view of the same argument, see National Commission on the Environment, *Choosing a Sustainable Future* (Washington, D.C.: Island Press, 1993), esp. chap. 5.

15. A useful summary of key legislative actions can be found in the reference work *Congress and the Nation* (Washington, D.C.: Congressional Quarterly Inc., various dates), vol. 3, 1969-1972, 745-849; vol. 4, 1973-1976, 201-320; and vol. 5, 1977-1980, 451-597.

16. See, for example, Bosso, *Pesticides and Politics*, chaps. 6 and 7.

17. Davidson, *Postreform Congress.*

18. Michael E. Kraft, "A New Environmental Policy Agenda: The 1980 Presidential Election and Its Aftermath," in *Environmental Policy in the 1980s.*

19. Cook and Davidson, "Deferral Politics"; Gary C. Bryner, "Science, Law, and Politics in Environmental Policy" (Paper presented at the annual meeting of the American Political Science Association, Chicago, September 2-6, 1987); and Henry Kenski and Margaret Corgan Kenski, "Congress Against the President: The Struggle Over the Environment," in *Environmental Policy in the 1980s.*

20. Cook and Davidson, "Deferral Politics"; and Kenski and Kenski, "Congress Against the President."

21. For example, Gary Bryner reported in 1987 that fourteen committees and twenty subcommittees in the Senate and eighteen committees and thirty-eight subcommittees in the House had at least some jurisdiction over EPA. See Bryner, "Science, Law, and Politics in Environmental Policy."

22. John W. Kingdon, *Agendas, Alternatives, and Public Policies* (Boston: Little, Brown, 1984).

23. Susan G. Hadden, *A Citizen's Right to Know: Risk Communication and Public Policy* (Boulder: Westview, 1989), esp. chap. 2.

24. Sierra Club, "Scorecard," *Sierra* 72 (January-February 1987): 16-17; and Natural Resources Defense Council, "The 99th Congress—A Strong Voice for the Environment," *NRDC Newsline* 4 (November-December 1986): 1-3.

25. Joseph A. Davis, "Environment/Energy," *1988 Congressional Quarterly Almanac* (Washington, D.C.: Congressional Quarterly Inc., 1989), 137.

26. Richard J. Tobin, "Revising the Clean Air Act: Legislative Failure and Administrative Success," in *Environmental Policy in the 1980s.* See also Michael Weisskopf, "A Qualified Failure: The Clean Air Act Hasn't Done the Job," *Washington Post National Weekly Edition*, June 19-25, 1989, 10-11.

27. Josh Getlin, "Mr. Clean's Air Act," *Sierra* 74 (November-December 1989): 77-81.

28. For details, see Tobin, "Revising the Clean Air Act."

29. See James L. Regens and Robert W. Rycroft, *The Acid Rain Controversy* (Pittsburgh: University of Pittsburgh Press, 1988), chap. 2.

30. See Tobin, "Revising the Clean Air Act," 242-246; and Regens and Rycroft, *Acid Rain Controversy*, chaps. 3 and 5. The research program appears to have had relatively little effect on congressional decisionmaking on the Clean Air Act. See, for example, Keith Schneider, "State Without Acid Rain Is Dealt Another Problem," *New York Times*, March 22, 1993, C8.

31. Rochelle L. Stanfield, "Punching at the Smog," *National Journal*, March 5, 1988, 600-602.

32. Rochelle L. Stanfield, "For Acid Rain, 'Wait Till Next Year,' " *National Journal*, October 15, 1988, 2606.

33. Joseph A. Davis, " 'Group of Nine' Determined to Break Clean-Air Deadlock," *Congressional Quarterly Weekly Report*, April 16, 1988, 984-990.

34. Personal interview, Washington, D.C., July 14, 1989.

35. Margaret E. Kriz, "Politics in the Air," *National Journal*, May 6, 1989, 1098-1102.

36. See Philip Shabecoff, "An Emergence of Political Will on Acid Rain," *New York Times*, February 19, 1989, E5; and George Hager, "Acid-Rain Controls Advance on Both Sides of Aisle," *Congressional Quarterly Weekly Report*, April 1, 1989, 688-691.

37. Philip Shabecoff, "President's Plan for Cleaning Air Goes to Congress," *New York Times*, July 22, 1989, 1, 7; and George Hager, "Critics Disappointed by Details of Bush Clean-Air Measure," *Congressional Quarterly Weekly Report*, July 22, 1989, 1852-1853.

38. Bryner, *Blue Skies, Green Politics;* and Cohen, *Washington at Work.*

39. Cohen, *Washington at Work.*

40. Michael E. Kraft, "Congress and National Energy Policy: Assessing the Policymaking Process," in *Environment, Energy, Public Policy: Toward a Rational Future,* ed. Regina S. Axelrod (Lexington, Mass.: Lexington, 1981).

41. Margaret E. Kriz, "Omnibus Opposition," *National Journal*, November 9, 1991, 2767; Holly Idelson, "Lingering Controversies Stall Rewrite of Energy Bill," *Congressional Quarterly Weekly Report*, November 9, 1991, 3274-3275.

42. Clifford Krauss, "Senate Votes Energy Bill, 94 to 4, Without Allowing Arctic Drilling," *New York Times*, February 20, 1992, 1, C10; Holly Idelson, "Senate Passes Energy Bill, 94-4; Arctic Refuge Issue Dropped," *Congressional Quarterly Weekly Report*, February 22, 1992, 397-399; Margaret E. Kriz, "The Power Broker," *National Journal*, February 29, 1992, 494-499.

43. Martin Tolchin, "Victory and Compromises for Shaper of Energy Bill," *New York Times*, May 30, 1992, 30.

44. Holly Idelson, "House Gives Energy Bill Big Win; Lengthy Conference Expected," *Congressional Quarterly Weekly Report*, May 30, 1992.

45. Holly Idelson, "Rifts Remain on National Policy as Huge Conference Races On," *Congressional Quarterly Weekly Report*, September 26, 1992, 2927-2929; Idelson, "Conferees at Last Find Harmony on National Energy Strategy," *Congressional Quarterly Weekly Report*, October 3, 1992, 3030-3033; and Clifford Krauss, "Energy Bill Cleared for Final Votes," *New York Times*, October 2, 1992, C2.

46. Holly Idelson, "After Two-Year Odyssey, Energy Strategy Clears," *Congressional Quarterly Weekly Report*, October 10, 1992, 3141-3146; and Clifford Krauss, "Energy Bill Is Limited but Offers a Beginning," *New York Times*, October 9, 1992, A11.

47. "The Politics of Power," on "Frontline," PBS, October 1992. The program reported that between 1985 and 1992 the nuclear industry contributed $16 million

in congressional campaign contributions, the oil industry $18 million, and the automobile industry $11 million.

48. For a detailed summary of the act's provisions, see "National Energy Strategy Provisions," *Congressional Quarterly Weekly Report,* November 28, 1992, 3722-3730.

49. Steven Greenhouse, "Fuels Tax: Spreading the Pain," *New York Times,* February 18, 1993, A12.

50. Dan Mazmanian, "Toward a New Energy Paradigm," in *California Policy Choices,* ed. John J. Kirlin, vol. 8 (Los Angeles: University of Southern California School of Public Administration, 1992); and DeWitt John, *Civic Environmentalism: Alternatives to Regulation in States and Communities* (Washington, D.C.: CQ Press, forthcoming).

51. Jon Healey, "From Conflict to Coexistence: New Politics of Environment," *Congressional Quarterly Weekly Report,* February 13, 1993, 309-313.

52. See Gary C. Bryner, ed., *Science, Technology, and Politics: Policy Analysis in Congress* (Boulder: Westview, 1992).

53. Cohen, *Washington at Work.*

6

The Clenched Fist and the Open Hand: Into the 1990s at EPA

Walter A. Rosenbaum

My vision of EPA in the closing years of the twentieth century consists of two related images—a clenched fist, representing our continued emphasis on controlling pollution and vigorously enforcing our nation's environmental laws, and an open hand, symbolizing our receptivity to new ideas [and] our desire to work with the public . . . to develop new and better ways of reducing environmental risk.

—former EPA administrator William K. Reilly

On Friday, July 3, 1992, the *New York Times* carried a front-page story that seemed like a scene from Washington's theater of the absurd. A federal district court, the article reported, had instructed the U.S. Environmental Protection Agency (EPA) that it could not wait until January 1993 to publish regulations that the states were expected to implement two months earlier. Complying with the rules before they were written, the judge observed, "would be difficult without time travel or clairvoyance."[1]

At issue were several hundred pages of regulations, required by 1990 amendments to the Clean Air Act, instructing the states on how to comply with new, stricter requirements for auto emission inspections in seventy-five of the nation's largest metropolitan areas. The court ordered EPA to publish its regulations by November 6, leaving the states exactly nine days to comply with the law. Even then, the EPA would be a year late in publishing the required regulations that were mandated in the law by November 15, 1991.

Nonetheless, the agency defended itself. EPA's highest-ranking attorney argued that the agency's apparent negligence was almost predestined by Congress. "If you look at the Clean Air Act, there are literally hundreds of deadlines in the first year and a half," he told the court. "You try as hard as you can to make as much progress as you can. You try to push the most important regulations up, but sometimes you have slippage." Another EPA spokesperson asserted that EPA had finished writing the regulations only three months behind the deadline but the White

House Office of Management and Budget had further delayed the work by slow review and requests for revision.

A spokesman for state and local government officials dismissed these explanations as the equivalent of "the dog ate my homework." Environmentalists were also offended by EPA's behavior. The Natural Resources Defense Council had initiated the suit against the agency and remained aggrieved. "One hundred million people live in areas of unhealthy air," it complained. "For EPA to hold up this rule . . . seems unjustifiable." The battle, in any case, was not over. EPA and the states did not agree on the details of what must be done by November 15, 1992. Further litigation and contention were certain.

The Struggle for Environmental Regulation

The EPA's predicament was not so unusual, nor its proposal as peculiar, as might have seemed. To the EPA officials compelled by legislation to be the unwilling principals in this bureaucratic comedy, it was merely another extremity in a continuing series of difficulties created by legislatively mandated deadlines. They had found an impossible solution to an insoluble problem.

The substance and style of conflict, the character of the participants, the kind of administrative choices, and the economic implications all make the case a virtual microcosm of contemporary environmental regulation, almost a snapshot of business as usual at EPA. During a typical year, for example, the agency can expect to be sued by public or private interests about a hundred times. At least half these actions will be initiated by environmental interests or the states.[2] More than 80 percent of EPA's major regulatory decisions were challenged in courts by environmental organizations or industry during the 1970s, and such challenges, while decreasing, continued through the 1980s to impede the agency's rule making. Relentless litigation is one inevitable result of the adversarial political milieu in which the EPA operates.[3]

In this case, EPA's response to the statutory deadlines imposed on it by the Clean Air Act was one solution to an inherently irreconcilable conflict among legislatively mandated regulatory deadlines, White House insistence on regulatory review, and the administrative complexity of the task itself. There were no satisfactory solutions. Writing the auto emission regulations under these circumstances is only one among a multitude of complex, confounding, often infeasible regulatory tasks assigned to EPA—tasks that make regulatory policymaking technically and administratively difficult, and repeated failure inevitable.

The EPA in the 1990s: The Problem of Institutional Capability

The auto inspection controversy is a warning that EPA's regulatory tasks are becoming increasingly intractable, if not impossible. Can the

Environmental Protection Agency, now beginning its third decade, carry out its essential environmental mission in this difficult, often hostile political milieu? This is the most compelling and transcendent issue in U.S. environmental politics in the early 1990s. To fulfill this difficult and imperative mission, EPA must present—in former EPA administrator William K. Reilly's apt language—both the "clenched fist" (symbolizing regulatory enforcement) and the "open hand" (public concern and policy innovation). Today it offers neither.

Many observers believe, like legal scholar Richard Lazarus, that EPA is locked into "a pathological cycle of regulatory failure."[4] Others assert that, although making limited progress, the EPA is so crippled by institutional and policy deficiencies that major reform is imperative. Almost nobody believes EPA has been a substantial success. Institutional restructuring and policy redesign dominate all discussions of EPA's future among both its partisans and critics. Such reform will be a compelling priority and standard of judgment on every EPA administrator in the 1990s.

Evaluating EPA's Performance

Evaluating EPA's performance and prescribing reform imply a standard of judgment. Assessing EPA's role in the 1990s requires some paradigm of administrative competence that serves as a measure of performance and a criterion for reform. What must EPA be, what must it achieve, if it is to be an effective environmental regulator? Although many standards have been proposed, five of the most commonly cited are especially practical for a comprehensive evaluation of EPA's performance and prospects.

A clear and coherent mission. Public agencies need a statutory charter that explicitly declares their primary policy objectives and establishes priorities among them. Such institutional definition is essential for establishing politically and judicially defensible program priorities and for deciding how limited resources must be administratively allocated. Moreover, the American political system is dominated by shifting and often highly transient policy coalitions. Shifting legislative and presidential majorities, highly pluralistic, competitive, and aggressive organized interests, and public institutions acutely sensitive to public opinion nurture a volatile policy milieu. Agencies with policy agendas and associated programs unprotected by the stabilizing, conservative influence of charters or other organic laws are especially vulnerable to the disruption of planning, the sudden shifts of political pressure and discontinuity of policy priorities created by short-term changes in public opinion, legislative majorities, or presidential agendas.

Feasible policies. Successful environmental regulation requires that those who make policy and those who implement it "must discern and respect the limits on policy choice imposed by available engineering, scientific and managerial understanding."[5] In short, policies should be technically, administratively, and politically feasible. The policy instruments to which this applies include not only the legislative enactments whose implementation is the agency's responsibility—the Clean Air or Toxic Substances Control acts, for instance—but also the regulations, guidelines, and other discretionary policies created by the agency to interpret, implement, or enforce its legislative mandates.

Sufficient resources. No domain of federal policymaking requires a greater diversity of technical information and professional skills than environmental regulation. Environmental policymaking, in particular, requires a great deal of scientific and administrative support.[6] Among the most crucial scientific resources are technical information together with a continuing research and development program that is responsive to the scientific demands of policymaking. Administrative staff must be adequate in number and professional skills. The administrative budget must be allocated appropriately for the agency's mission. The administrators must also be flexible and innovative in carrying out mandated agency objectives. Additionally, continued monitoring and enforcement are essential if regulatory standards are to be credible.

Policy effectiveness. Environmental policies should produce measurable results and demonstrate substantial attainment of objectives. Both the economic and environmental impacts need to be accounted for in determining the effectiveness of environmental regulations. Ideally, environmental regulations should achieve their purpose at the lowest cost and least expenditure of limited resources. In reality, governmental policies almost always involve a trade-off between economic efficiency and such other considerations as fairness, public health and safety, or timely response to problems. Economic efficiency cannot be the sole criterion for policy selection; nevertheless, agencies should strive to make cost reduction a continuing criterion for policy implementation. Although environmental results would seem an obvious standard for policy effectiveness, agencies often prefer to measure effectiveness by the amount of administrative activity or the size of their budgets—to count the number of permits issued, for example, or abatement actions initiated against polluters—instead of determining improvements in air or water quality (if any).

Political resources. The real world of environmental regulation is intensely political and partisan. Environmental laws are constantly embroiled in partisan and ideological conflicts; they are always disagreeable to one or another politically aggressive private interest. Environmental agencies must therefore possess the skill and resources to defend themselves *through* politics and *from* politics. Political strategies are essential if an agency is to defend its mission, promote its institutional interests, and mobilize support, publicly and bureaucratically, in the inevitable struggles that attend environmental regulation. This means, among other things, developing a politically articulate and active constituency of organized interests ready to defend the agency and its mission. Agencies must also cultivate political allies in Congress, the White House, and the bureaucracy. They should also be able to protect their programs and personnel from political forces that subvert the agency's mission or corrupt staff, professional standards, or policy. Regulatory agencies, in particular, need considerable autonomy in their fact-finding and rule-making processes.[7] Striking the proper balance between political activism and political disengagement is difficult and no agency will be continually successful at it. But agencies incapable of effective political offense or defense are almost predestined to large programmatic failures and policy subversion.

Measured against these standards, the EPA begins its third decade with much still to accomplish. Its achievements, modest in light of its mission, are nonetheless significant, if often unacknowledged by its critics. There are still many agency deficiencies and failures. Many of these problems originate in the agency's initial conception and design. Some result from institutional rivalries deeply embedded in the U.S. constitutional system. Other problems arise because the EPA has launched government into a new domain of regulation with which policymakers have had no experience. And some problems are EPA's own responsibility. EPA's first twenty years could define the trajectory of what might become an institutional learning curve. Some deficiencies can be corrected, or remedies attempted, with the benefit of this experience. The EPA's first administrator in the 1990s, William Reilly, who began his term in 1989, acknowledged this with a rhetoric of reform that called for "new budget priorities," a "fresh perspective," and a "willingness to break out of traditional constraints." Reilly's reform agenda was the first major test in the 1990s of EPA's ability to improve its regulatory capabilities.[8]

To understand EPA's agenda for the 1990s and its implications, and to comprehend other aspects of EPA's performance and future prospects, it is essential to examine its organizational design, its statutory mandates and rule-making process, and its bureaucratic culture.

The EPA at Work

EPA's policymaking style, political environment, and regulatory effectiveness have been greatly affected by its origins. No organic act or legislative charter clearly defines the agency's mission or helps to set its policy priorities. Created in 1970 through an executive reorganization, the agency's mission is the sum of all the individual laws it administers—a conglomeration of legislative acts written at different times and for different purposes and bereft of overall coherence.

The EPA was designed to be chiefly a pollution control agency rather than a comprehensive department of natural resources. With oversight of natural resources staying with the existing departments of Interior and

Agriculture, the EPA was given no jurisdiction over public lands and natural resource activities that contribute to environmental degradation. This also precluded comprehensive environmental planning. The media specific orientation of the agency's program offices (air, water, solid waste, toxics) further limits the agency's ability to offer comprehensive environmental analysis and management. All these characteristics have important implications for the EPA's work.

The EPA is by far the biggest federal regulatory agency; indeed, it is the largest in the world. In 1992 the agency employed more than eighteen thousand individuals; two of three work in one of its ten regional offices. In FY 1992, the agency's budget exceeded $6.5 billion. $2.1 billion of this budget, however, is distributed to the states under a continuing construction grants program for waste treatment facilities and underwrites no regulatory, research, monitoring, or enforcement activities.[9] An additional $1.6 billion is mandated to the Superfund Trust to pay for cleanups of hazardous waste sites. Thus, the agency's daily administrative activities are underwritten by an actual budget of approximately $2.8 billion.

The agency is wholly or largely responsible for the implementation of the ten major statutes (see list below; for a description of these laws see app. 1). These statutory activities cover an enormous range of ecological problems, technical or scientific expertise, regulatory activity, and geographic space. Still, they greatly understate the actual scope of EPA activities because they do not include major amendments to these statutes, which created significant new programs requiring yet additional resources. The Clean Air Act Amendments of 1990, for example, consisted of eight hundred pages of fine statutory print (the original act was only fifty pages long) that required the agency to hire an additional two hundred employees and write fifty-five major new regulations within the first two years of its passage.[10] Nor does the list below hint at the multitudinous laws administered by other agencies, yet requiring EPA participation. The Federal Food, Drug and Cosmetics Act, for instance, is administered by the Food and Drug Administration (FDA) but authorizes EPA to establish tolerance levels for pesticide residues on food and food products.

Ten major statutes form the legal basis for the EPA's programs:

- *Clean Air Act (CAA):* requires EPA to set mobile source limits, ambient air quality standards, hazardous air pollutant emission standards, standards for new sources, significant deterioration requirements, and to focus on areas that do not attain standards.
- *Clean Water Act (CWA):* establishes the sewage treatment construction grants program, and a regulatory and enforcement program for discharges into U.S. waters.

- *Ocean Dumping Act (ODA):* regulates the intentional disposing of materials into ocean waters and establishes research on effects of, and alternatives to, ocean disposal.
- *Safe Drinking Water Act (SDWA):* establishes primary drinking-water standards, regulates underground injection practices, and establishes a groundwater control program.
- *Resource Conservation and Recovery Act (RCRA):* provides cradle-to-grave regulation for hazardous substances and waste.
- *Comprehensive Environmental Response, Compensation, and Liability Act (CERCLA),* or Superfund: establishes a fee-maintained fund to clean up abandoned hazardous waste sites.
- *Federal Insecticide, Fungicide, and Rodenticide Act (FIFRA):* governs pesticide products.
- *Toxic Substances Control Act (TOSCA):* requires the testing of chemicals and regulates their use.
- *Environmental Research and Development Demonstration Act (ERDDA):* provides authority for all EPA research programs.
- *National Environmental Policy Act (NEPA):* requires EPA to review environmental impact statements.[11]

The Organizational Culture: "Bureaucratic Pluralism"

Regulatory rule making. EPA's most important policy process, like other modes of agency decisionmaking, involves what Thomas McGarity has called "bureaucratic pluralism."[12] A multitude of different bureaucratic, professional, geographic, and political interests must be included in agency decisionmaking. Thus, competition for power, conflicts of professional values and interest, and diverse statutory responsibilities must be routinely accommodated. A team ("workgroup") approach to writing program regulations and guidelines ordinarily prevails in a complex and time-consuming process. Major decisions can be exquisitely complicated. "It is settled EPA lore that internal agency meetings typically include fifty to one hundred of the agency's employees most expert on an issue to be debated," writes Richard Lazarus. "Not only are there multiple representatives from both the functional and media-specific offices but also individuals from the relevant regional and enforcement offices and from the General Counsel's office."[13] Veteran EPA employees would consider this but slight exaggeration.

Program offices and functional offices. The EPA's most important operational units are the program offices (sometimes called "media offices"), each headed by an assistant administrator (fig. 6-1). Each program office lives with its own statutory programs, deadlines, criteria for decisions, and, usually, possesses a steel grip on large portions of its office budget, to which it is entitled by the laws it enforces. Thus, the Office of Toxic Substances (OTS) administers the massive Comprehensive Environmen-

Figure 6-1 Organizational Chart of the U.S. Environmental Protection Agency

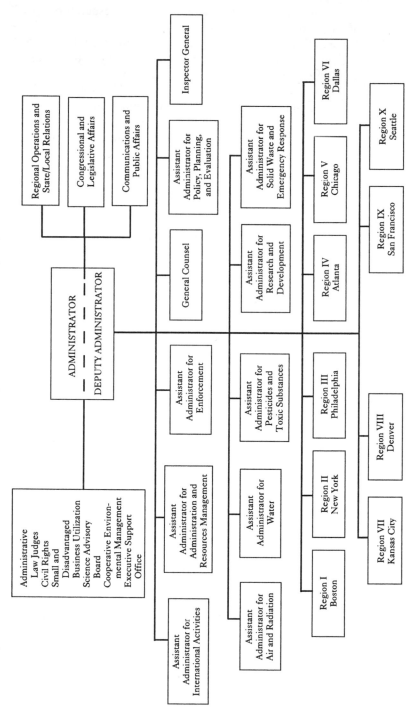

Source: U.S. Environmental Protection Agency, 1993.

tal Response, Compensation and Liability Act of 1980 (Superfund) program, intended to clean up the nation's abandoned hazardous waste sites, follows the mandated statutory procedures and deadlines of the law, and claims $1.6 billion of EPA's budget earmarked in FY 1992 specifically for waste site cleanup.

Program offices work continually and closely with Congress, often looking to it for guidance and support. Often, not only the members but also the staff of major committees with jurisdiction over EPA exert considerable influence and acquire enormous expertise about the agency's programs, because they are so continually involved in its work. A recent assistant administrator observed that congressional committee staff often have their own agenda, which may not reflect the concerns of the congressional members they ostensibly serve. During his tenure at EPA, he was "surprised at the extent to which an aggressive staff can dominate an issue," a situation that further fragments congressional control over the agency.[14]

Program offices, in turn, are populated by a variety of professionals: engineers, scientists, statisticians, economists, professional planners, and managers—perhaps also lawyers and mathematicians. Each group brings to rule making, observes McGarity, "more than just pure expertise. . . . Along with the expertise comes an entire professional [worldview] that incorporates attitudes and biases ranging far beyond the specialized knowledge of particular facts."[15] These differing professional perspectives often breed disagreement and conflict, as Marc Landy and his associates observed in their penetrating study of EPA decisionmaking:

> Engineers are trained to solve problems, not resolve them. The formulae and rules on which they base calculations are often arbitrary. Nonetheless, they have been trained to use them to provide numerical solutions. They come to believe that there are right answers to problems. . . . Unlike lawyers or engineers, economists are trained to regard all variables as continuous . . . choices are not "yes" or "no," but matters of degree. Thus, economists instinctively see all issues as arenas for trade-offs, and outcomes that produce "a little of this and that" are judged desirable.[16]

The functional offices, such as Enforcement, General Counsel, or Policy, Planning, and Evaluation, are also headed by assistant administrators. These offices are concerned with internal management, with activities common to all program offices (such as enforcement), and policy evaluation. Functional offices are often more attuned to the White House and the administrator's office, often more "political" than program offices (although all assistant administrators are officially classified as "political appointees" because they must be presidentially nominated and congressionally approved). The functional offices also have distinctive bureaucratic and professional interests. Unlike the other offices, however, their budgets and activities are not usually driven by statutory mandates and deadlines.

Regional offices and the states. The administration of most laws implemented by EPA is highly federalized: the states undertake the actual implementation under the guidance of EPA's headquarters and regional offices. The agency's regional offices, each embracing a multistate area, are intermediaries between the states and EPA headquarters. Regional offices are intimately involved in state regulatory activities, knowledgeable about state concerns and viewpoints, and attuned to events and moods at the state level.

EPA's regional administrators (RAs) and regional offices constitute another bureaucratic-political tier within EPA, and the states yet another. Together, they add to the agency's pluralistic decisionmaking process. Regional offices and regional administrators often represent state viewpoints and defend state interests in negotiations or conflicts over agency rules and other policies. The states themselves are a potent force within EPA because, among other reasons, each has a congressional delegation to which it can appeal in efforts to influence the agency. For example, when EPA announced in 1976 that it was considering a requirement that states develop transportation control plans in order to meet air quality standards required by the Clean Air Act, ". . . members of Congress held oversight hearings and made statements on the floors of their respective chambers in which they uniformly denounced EPA's intrusion into matters of traditionally state and local concern."[17] EPA subsequently rejected the notion.

The EPA and Congress

Defying a biblical admonition, the EPA serves two masters. The agency is responsible to Congress for implementing environmental legislation and managing its budget as Congress intends. Congress and its committees also exercise continuing legislative oversight of EPA's activities within their jurisdiction. As an executive agency, it must also implement the president's management directives and his policy agenda insofar as these coincide with its legislatively mandated activities. EPA's relations with both Congress and the White House are typically adversarial, with occasional lapses into uneasy cooperation.

Oversight or "EPA bashing"? From the EPA's inception, its activities have been a matter of intense congressional concern, scrutiny, and criticism. EPA's programs fall under the jurisdiction of at least eleven Senate standing committees, nine House standing committees, and nearly one hundred subcommittees in both chambers.[18] Probably no other federal agency is exposed to such sustained and critical oversight. So regularly is EPA a subject of congressional investigation that Congress's own watchdog agency, the General Accounting Office (GAO), has a large, permanent branch office at EPA headquarters.

The EPA's relationship with Congress has been almost continually adversarial. A major reason was cited by former EPA administrator Lee

Thomas: The administrator rarely goes to Capitol Hill with good news.[19] However essential Congress may consider them, EPA's regulatory activities are extremely costly and the benefits often unclear. Regulatory programs customarily require years or even decades to implement. It may be equally long before results appear. Environmental regulations frequently require far-reaching economic and political change sure to antagonize powerful economic and political interests. Further, the scientific basis of many expensive programs is uncertain and the environmental impacts difficult to measure. During a national economic recession, environmental regulations are especially suspect as an impediment to recovery. Thus, EPA provides continual opportunities for criticism—so much that former administrator William Ruckelshaus recently complained that the agency has become Congress's "designated whipping boy."[20]

Overload: The toll of pen and "hammer." Congressional distrust of the EPA, greatly fueled by frequent and sharp confrontations with Reagan administration appointees at the agency, has bred a legislative style that frequently confounds the agency's efforts to comply with an avalanche of legislative responsibilities. The agency can claim conspicuous success for a few programs, especially its national reduction of sulfur dioxide, particulates, and lead in ambient air, and its stabilization of several major surface-water pollutants. But by the mid 1980s it was already obvious, as the Council on Environmental Quality (CEQ) noted, that "the Environmental Protection Agency cannot possibly do all the things its various mandates tell it to do."[21] Conditions have not improved and are not likely to improve.

EPA is decades behind in complying with major requirements in virtually all its ten major statutory programs. The EPA's air program, for example, has issued emission standards on fewer than ten of approximately fifteen hundred reportedly hazardous air pollutants requiring regulation under the Clean Air Act. The Federal Insecticide, Fungicide and Rodenticide Act (FIFRA) has been amended to require EPA to evaluate more than fifty thousand individual pesticide products containing more than six hundred active ingredients and nine hundred inert ingredients. "If EPA has to prepare interim registration standards for all 600 ingredients," concluded a GAO study, "then the Agency may finish the first round reviews in about 2004."[22] Enforcement of the Toxic Substances Control Act of 1976 (TSCA), the Resource Conservation and Recovery Act (RCRA) of 1976, and the Superfund program has been especially difficult. TSCA, for instance, authorized EPA to require manufacturers to test potentially harmful chemicals among the sixty thousand to which Americans are exposed. In mid 1991 the GAO reported:

EPA has made little progress in developing information on the safety of the thousands of chemicals that affect our daily lives and has not taken action to regulate, or warn the public, about chemicals found to be harmful. Since TSCA was enacted in 1976, EPA has received health and environmental assessments on only 22 chemicals and assessed the test results for 13 of these.[23]

The EPA's compliance headaches are, for the most part, caused by Congress's habit of packing legislation with a number of demanding deadlines, inflexibly detailed management instructions, and "hammer" clauses that threaten dire consequences should the agency fail to comply with various statutory directives. All are evidence of deep legislative distrust and a resulting resolve to control EPA's behavior by leaving it little discretion in implementing the law. By 1988 EPA had already inherited eight hundred statutory deadlines.[24]

Deadline writing continues to be a legislative growth industry. The Clean Air Act Amendments of 1990 require EPA to write 55 major new rules within two years, list 189 toxic air pollutants for which the agency must write standards for all major sources, and specify a schedule for writing each standard. The EPA is left with little flexibility in implementing the law, virtually guaranteeing failures to meet often arbitrary deadlines. Former EPA administrator William Reilly estimates that EPA had been able to meet less than 20 percent of congressionally imposed deadlines.[25]

As noted in chapter 1, EPA's budget has failed to keep pace with its staff and resource needs. Employees in Research and Development (R&D), whose work is essential to creating an adequate science base for rule making, decreased from 2,300 to 1,800 between 1981 and 1992. Other vital support services have been similarly underfunded. The development of environmental indicators and environmental monitoring to measure regulatory success, for instance, is poorly supported in good part because its lacks political "sex appeal." In mid 1991 only three of EPA's twenty-three major programs were appropriately monitored with adequate indicators.[26] Although the agency itself bears responsibility for some delays and failures in program implementation, considerable responsibilities rest with Congress and, as we shall observe, other aspects of the governmental setting.

The EPA and the White House

The political and economic importance of EPA's work assures wary White House attention and daily involvement in its activities. One significant source of presidential influence in the agency arises from the president's authority to appoint its administrator, assistant administrators, and other upper management. The political appointees are expected to work closely and cooperatively with the White House in implementing the president's policy agenda.

A more potent source of White House influence in agency decision-making is the president's Office of Management and Budget (OMB), which reviews and evaluates the agency's annual budget. Also influential are two Executive Orders (EOs) signed by President Ronald Reagan to strengthen "executive oversight" of regulatory policies. EO 12291 requires EPA and all other federal agencies to prepare a cost-benefit analysis, or "regulatory impact analysis" (RIA), for all proposed major regulations and authorizes OMB to enforce the requirement and to review the resulting RIAs. EO 12498 requires EPA and all other federal agencies to give a yearly agenda to OMB and to indicate how the proposed policies are consistent with the president's own agenda.[27] Additionally, President George Bush created within his office the president's Council on Competitiveness, headed by the vice president, to apply cost-benefit analysis to existing rules.

OMB review of proposed EPA rules has slowed the rule-making process and compelled EPA to withdraw, or make substantial changes in, many proposed rules. From 1981 to 1989 the average review time for major and minor EPA rules was sixty-four days, longer than for other federal agencies. Moreover, "EPA is one of the agencies whose regulations are most frequently modified during the review process," notes Robert Percival. "Less than half of the EPA regulations reviewed in 1989 were approved without change. . . . Only the Departments of Housing and Urban Development and Labor . . . had smaller percentages of regulations approved without change in 1989."[28] Of greater importance, OMB's reviews of policy and RIAs for newly proposed regulations have undoubtedly inhibited the proposal of many regulations to which the Bush and Reagan administrations were hostile, and prevented the enactment of others.

The Fragmentation of Environmental Regulation

There are other important influences in the agency's working life. The EPA's mission, its regulatory effectiveness and its resources are also affected by the fragmentation of authority for environmental management and regulation among a multitude of federal agencies—a reminder that EPA lacks a unitary environmental charter. At least twenty-seven other federal agencies and bureaus share regulatory authority over the environment and occupational health (fig. 1-1, p. 8).

This fragmentation of authority denies EPA the resources needed to fulfill its regulatory responsibilities. For example, the agency is required by the Clean Water Act to control the discharge of harmful pollutants in navigable waterways of the United States. But the most common source of surface-water contamination is "nonpoint" pollution (sedimentation, pesticides, and other chemicals from agriculture, forestry, and other activities), whose control requires land use management. Federal authority for this purpose is vested in the departments of Agriculture and Interior and several other smaller bureaucracies. More than twenty-five different federal laws concern some aspect of toxic and hazardous waste management, involving not only EPA but the Food and Drug Administration, the Department of Transportation, the Consumer Product Safety Commission, and many others. Although EPA is made responsible for some aspect of groundwater protection by six of the ten major laws it administers, it must share regulatory authority over groundwater with seven other departments and agencies, including seven agencies within the Department of the Interior and five in Agriculture.[29]

EPA's difficulties with nonpoint pollution illuminate perhaps the single greatest deficiency in its regulatory powers arising from fragmented authority. The EPA has no authority over land use and no prospects for soon acquiring it. It can use whatever influence, or authority, it may obtain from its existing programs to coax and prod the states—where land use authority resides—into some forms of land use planning. But the states, and most of Congress, have resolutely refused to cede to EPA any significant, direct authority over land use, which is a traditional, ferociously defended state and local prerogative. So politically charged is the issue that land use has become the "L-word" of agency politics. EPA's leadership, always extraordinarily circumspect in discussing land use controls, must continually strive to avoid the appearance of contemplating, or promoting, land use powers for the agency.

Fragmented authority renders truly coordinated pollution management impossible and creates a multitude of aggressive competitors with EPA for money, personnel, and authority. Moreover, bureaucracies are loath to surrender their existing jurisdictions and authority. Even the EPA's statistical activities can provoke a turf battle. When congressional legislation was recently introduced to expand EPA's existing statistical services into a national center for environmental statistics, twelve other federal statistical agencies, including offices in the Department of Commerce, the Council for Environmental Quality, and the Department of the Interior, stifled the proposal.

Agency Morale

Despite its political and administrative difficulties, the EPA has generally enjoyed strong public approval. In late 1981, for instance, a national poll indicated that 77 percent of the public "trusted" the agency at a time when Ronald Reagan had just been elected on a platform strongly critical of environmental regulation. In mid 1991 a Roper poll reported that 54 percent of the public believed environmental regulation had "not gone far enough," and 67 percent rated EPA's performance favorably.[30]

EPA's staff, however, has worked in a political and physical setting that squelches high morale. The agency is headquartered in two converted apartment towers in Southwest Washington, wholly unsuited to a large bureaucratic workforce, and in several floors of the aging Waterside Mall shopping center, which the EPA has slowly cannibalized. Far from the other major agencies ringing the Washington Mall and consigned to a marginal sector of the city, EPA headquarters seems to symbolize the agency's continual struggle for status and respect. The offices themselves, commonly cramped and uncomfortable, have a decided Third World ambience, while the agency's antiquated, overcrowded elevators cause legendary tribulations and present a serious impediment to staff efficiency. Largely unresponsive to the EPA's requests for major workplace improvements, Congress has refused employees even the feeble pleasures of a federal cafeteria commonly found at other major agencies. In recent years agency employees have been disappointed by Congress's repeated failure to agree on the details of legislation elevating EPA to cabinet rank, despite White House assurances of promotion, and by the uncertain prospects of a large, new headquarters in downtown Washington that Congress had promised by 1996.

Reform in the 1990s

If the past is indeed prelude, what does the EPA's experience during its first twenty years promise for the 1990s? As the EPA begins its third decade, there is a clear need for major changes in the agency's policy designs, a sizable increase in the amount and quality of its resources, and a transformation of its institutional relations with other agencies and branches of government. Without these improvements, the EPA will not have the regulatory capabilities expected of it.

William Reilly's term as administrator brought some immediately important improvements to EPA. Reilly's stature among both environmentalists and the business community, together with his appealing public style and forceful advocacy, raised staff morale considerably. As one high-level EPA career professional put it, "Reilly is a class act and he makes EPA look good and sound relevant to the 1990s." The high priority he assigned to getting EPA involved in global environmental issues was also welcomed by most agency professionals. However, the agency's authority, resources, and scientific base—the foundations of its regulatory abilities—are the issues to which he repeatedly turned during his term.[31] The administrator's reform agenda constitutes a short list of problems that must be solved if EPA's regulatory abilities are to be improved significantly in the 1990s.

Regulatory Capability

Judged by the standards of capability discussed earlier, EPA's achievements at the end of its first twenty years are disappointing. Without a legislative charter and yet responsible for implementing at least ten major statutes with differing, inconsistent, and competitive goals, the EPA cannot yet claim to have a clear and coherent mission. Ultimately, the agency might be able to achieve a number of its major policy objectives if their statutory designs were more practical. Congressional renunciation of "hammer clauses," impossible administrative deadlines, and legislative micromanagement would also be especially helpful.

In addition, the agency's resources—technical, administrative, and political—have never been equal to its responsibilities. Not only does the EPA require more personnel and managerial discretion in administering its programs, it needs very substantial increases in support for the unglamorous and politically dull, but essential, technical work of environmental monitoring, research and development, environmental data collection, and development of better indicators of environmental quality, among many other tasks.

In light of EPA's regulatory difficulties, Reilly's term as administrator and the reforms he aggressively promoted came at an auspicious time. His ideas were a constructive response to needed improvements in EPA's regulatory capabilities and are the most important among the major EPA reforms still being debated. The administrator's outspoken advocacy was a catalyst for debate, within and without EPA, over the agency's priorities in the 1990s. Although few of these proposals have yet been tested, there is reason to believe that the agency's regulatory abilities and program accomplishments would substantially improve if the proposals were adopted.

Clarifying Priorities Through Risk-Based Regulation

"We have developed our environmental policies piecemeal," Reilly observed in mid 1991, "with each problem addressed separately and without sufficient reference to other problems or to overall effects, risks and costs." A better approach, he argued, was to set EPA's priorities on a more scientifically defensible basis: "To the extent allowed by the law, sound science can help us establish priorities and allocate resources on the basis of risk—risk to human health and welfare." Relative risk as the standard for EPA's program priorities, a concept first explored by EPA administrator Lee Thomas in the mid 1980s, became leadership gospel after Reilly's arrival at EPA in 1989. The scripture was *Reducing Risk: Setting Priorities for Environmental Protection*, a report published and widely distributed by EPA's Science Advisory Board (SAB) with Reilly's encouragement, which contains many other tenets of the Reilly reform agenda.[32]

The evolving interest in relative risk as a management strategy, together with the scientific and administrative controversies entailed, is fully discussed in chapter 10. Suffice it to say that the approach has several attractions. First, it could provide a scientifically defensible order-

ing principle for EPA's programs, encouraging priorities within and between programs where today there are none. Moreover, it could provide
Congress and EPA with a defensible alternative to the public's sometimes
inaccurate perceptions of environmental risk as a basis for future environmental regulation. Congress's environmental agenda has largely been determined by public perceptions of risk that often do not correspond with
those considered most serious by scientific professionals. For instance,
comparisons of expert and public evaluations of human health risks from
various environmental pollutants show that the experts, unlike the public,
consider radon and other indoor air pollutants a significant public health
risk. Conversely, the public perceives hazardous waste sites and oil spills
to be far greater health risks than do the risk technicians.[33]

Finally, comparative risk could be used in EPA's strategic planning,
budgeting, and other long-range administrative management activities.
EPA's long-term planning and resource allocations today are based largely
on congressionally dictated budget priorities and program deadlines.
Greater use of risk-based criteria for future budgeting and strategic planning would appear to encourage more efficient use of scarce resources and
more critical appraisal of alternative planning strategies.

Greater Use of Market-Oriented Regulatory Strategies

One long-advocated major reform, already under way at EPA, promises potentially great economic and environmental benefits. The agency is
implementing the first significant "market oriented" regulatory strategy
mandated by Congress in the 1990 Clean Air Act Amendments. Market
approaches to regulation, long advocated by many economists and other
regulatory experts, were endorsed and promoted by Reilly and his leadership staff at EPA. The initiation of a market-oriented strategy in a major
EPA media program is perhaps the most sweeping and potentially important agency reform in the early 1990s.

EPA's approach to regulation has been almost exclusively based on
the command-and-control strategies dictated by Congress and embodied
in the original Clean Air Act and the current Clean Water Act. This
approach, further examined in chapter 9, involves four phases: (1) Congress mandates that EPA, perhaps in cooperation with the states,
achieve stated regulatory goals, such as protecting public health and
safety from air pollution, or making navigable waters "fishable and
swimmable" by regulating water pollutants; (2) Congress designates the
pollutants to be regulated or invests EPA with the responsibility; (3)
EPA, perhaps in cooperation with the states, decides the limits of permissible pollution, specifies what pollution sources are to be controlled
and how controls will be applied; and (4) a permit system is created to
control pollution together with an enforcement structure to assure compliance.

Many regulatory experts attribute the EPA's difficulties with regulatory enforcement and compliance to this command-and-control approach. Thus, Title IV of the 1990 Clean Air Amendments permitting the states and EPA to establish a system of "marketable emissions allowances," or emissions trading, has been welcomed as an overdue, constructive experiment that may well lead to more ambitious market-oriented regulatory approaches in other major legislation. It will be several years before marketable emissions trading will be fully implemented and several years thereafter before the arrangement can be appropriately evaluated. Nonetheless, it appears to be among the most constructive EPA reforms promoted by Reilly and enacted by Congress in the early 1990s.

Greater Administrative Discretion in Program Management

EPA's administrative planning is today primarily driven by congressionally determined budgets and program deadlines, by "hammer" clauses, and other arrangements inhibiting discretionary administrative decisions. For example, EPA has estimated that the cost of preventing groundwater contamination by protecting wellheads might be as little as 10 percent of the cost of cleaning up a contaminated well. "Though EPA acknowledges the benefits of prevention," reported the GAO, "its allocation of resources between programs has consistently been weighed heavily toward remediation."[34] Congressionally mandated expenditures on groundwater management compelled EPA to spend almost 80 percent of all its groundwater budget on cleanup rather than prevention strategies in the late 1980s. Greater discretionary authority in budgeting could have given EPA water program managers the freedom to invest more money in the apparently more cost-effective strategy of pollution prevention. In a related example, in FY 1990 more than 90 percent of EPA's water quality funding was legislatively mandated for point source control although, as we have observed, nonpoint pollution is a major problem also.[35]

Immutable budgets and inflexible program deadlines also set severe limits on how much EPA can improve its strategic planning through risk-based approaches or other innovative approaches. Program offices, preoccupied with deadlines and other mandated activities, may also resist major changes in administrative procedures that could obstruct or delay compliance with actions for which Congress will hold them accountable. Environmental groups, the states, regulated industries—any interests whose purpose or planning is tied to some specifically required program goal or expenditure in current law—may also prefer the existing management style with its fixed budgets and mandated procedures instead of untested new procedures that make EPA's actions less predictable and judicially enforceable. In short, administrative discretion will not be easily or cheaply achieved.

More Attention to Waste Reduction: The Pollution Prevention Act

Virtually all EPA administrators have argued that more importance be given in law to eliminating pollutants before they enter the environment—usually called "source reduction"—because it is cheaper and more effective than end-of-the-pipe pollution controls. In 1990 Congress contributed significantly to clarifying EPA's program priorities by enacting the Pollution Prevention Act. The act created, for the first time, a hierarchy of waste management activities; source reduction was assigned priority. EPA is also required to prevent industrial pollution through a variety of procedures, including development of measurable goals, improved data collection, grants to the states, and assessment of existing public and private programs.

In addition to creating a new pollution prevention division within EPA, the agency has initiated two prevention programs with considerable potential. The Green Lights Program encourages energy-efficient lighting by both government and the private sector. By mid 1992 more than four hundred companies, nine states, and many private groups and other institutions had joined the program, and EPA has estimated that if all eligible facilities were to join, national electric power used from lighting could be reduced by half. The 33/50 Project has invited more than six thousand companies to join with EPA in reducing emissions of seventeen high-priority toxic chemicals by 33 percent at the end of 1992 and 50 percent by 1995. In early 1992, about seven hundred companies had voluntarily joined.[36]

Although the preliminary results of these two programs are promising, EPA's implementation of the Pollution Prevention Act is barely under way and problems have cropped up in organizing the division. Still, the act gives EPA both an explicit mandate and better resources for preventing pollution, thereby focusing on the most desirable strategy for environmental protection. There is reason for at least cautious optimism that pollution prevention will become one of the agency's more important accomplishments.

Improving the EPA's Science Base

In *Reducing Risk*, the agency's Science Advisory Board urged that the EPA "improve the data and analytical methodologies that support the assessment, comparison, and reduction of different environmental risks."[37] Reilly and his staff launched a number of administrative initiatives in response to SAB's recommendation. More resources were invested in the development of environmental indicators and statistical capabilities, and greater emphasis was given to improving environmental monitoring and developing an environmental forecasting capability. Efforts are under way to reverse the long decline of support for agency R&D

activities. Initiatives of this sort are inherently problematic, however, because they involve activities seldom prized by Congress or the public and unlikely to produce easily understood, interesting "results." EPA's increased attention to its science base, however, is for the moment another contribution to increased regulatory capability.

Conclusion: The EPA At Risk

During its first two decades, the EPA has been an experiment in regulatory innovation. No national government institution resembling the EPA, or its policy mission, existed in the United States or in any other country prior to 1970. In the two decades since its creation, the EPA has been continually testing the institutional, political, and economic principles on which the nation's unprecedented approach to environmental regulation have rested. The cumulative result of this experience can be, in the best perspective, a progressive learning curve through which constructive institutional change evolves in response to the success, failures, and surprises of institutional history. If the EPA fails to confront the problems of the past, the agency's history will be but a descending spiral of institutional incapability and rigidity.

Learning curve or trajectory to failure—what will the EPA's history become? The answer will likely be found in the 1990s, the most crucial decade in EPA's brief history. If the reforms proposed by William Reilly, or other initiatives intended to improve the agency's regulatory achievements on the basis of its twenty years' experience, do not produce a substantial success, EPA will find it increasingly difficult to resist sweeping changes in its structure and mission that may result in radical transformation or its abolition. If the economic recession of the early 1990s continues, or deepens, attacks on EPA based on the economic cost of its regulatory programs may be especially intense and effective. The passage of the long-delayed congressional legislation elevating EPA to cabinet status might bring the prestige and visibility EPA has so long sought, but it will produce only cosmetic enhancements unless EPA also gets the administrative resources it needs to do its job properly. Even with successful reform, EPA also needs some conspicuous success, and a more supportive White House, if it is to survive politically in the 1990s.

Notes

William K. Reilly's remarks, quoted in the chapter epigraph, were taken from his article, "The Greening of EPA," EPA Journal 15, no. 4 (July-August 1989): 9-10.

1. New York Times, July 3, 1992.
2. Richard J. Lazarus, "The Tragedy of Distrust in the Implementation of Federal Environmental Law," Law and Contemporary Problems 54 (Autumn 1991): 334;

see also Gary C. Bryner, *Bureaucratic Discretion* (New York: Pergamon, 1987), 115-118.

3. On the impact of litigation at EPA generally, see Robert Glicksman and Christopher H. Schroeder, "EPA and the Courts: Twenty Years of Law and Politics," *Law and Contemporary Problems* 54 (Autumn 1991): 249-309.

4. Lazarus, "Tragedy of Distrust," 363. For other critical evaluations of EPA's performance, see also Marc K. Landy, Marc J. Roberts, and Stephen R. Thomas, *The Environmental Protection Agency: Asking the Wrong Questions* (New York: Oxford University Press, 1990); Alfred A. Marcus, *Promise and Performance: Choosing and Implementing Environmental Policy* (Westport, Conn.: Greenwood, 1980); John Quarles, *Cleaning Up America: An Insider's View of the Environmental Protection Agency* (Boston: Houghton Mifflin, 1976); Richard A. Harris and Sidney M. Milkis, *The Politics of Regulatory Change* (New York: Oxford University Press, 1989); Bruce Yandle, *The Political Limits of Environmental Regulation* (New York: Quorum Books, 1989); and Paul R. Portney, ed., *Public Policies for Environmental Protection* (Washington, D.C.: Resources for the Future, 1990).

5. Landy, Roberts, and Thomas, *Environmental Protection Agency*, 6; see also Ralph A. Luken, "How Efficient Are EPA's Regulations?" *Environmental Law Reporter* 20 (October 1990): 10419-10424; Eugene Bardach and Robert A. Kagan, *Going by the Book* (Philadelphia: Temple University Press, 1982); and John S. Dryzek and James P. Lester, "Evaluating Environmental Policy: Alternative Views on the Environmental Problematique," in *Environmental Politics and Policy: Theories and Evidence*, ed. James P. Lester (Durham, N.C.: Duke University Press, 1989), 314-330.

6. On the problems of information integration in environmental policymaking, see Gary C. Bryner, *Bureaucratic Discretion*, chap. 3; Committee on the Institutional Means for Assessment of Risks to Public Health, Commission on the Life Sciences, National Research Council, *Risk Assessment in the Federal Government* (Washington, D.C.: National Academy Press, 1983); Milton Russell and Michael Gruber, "Risk Assessment in Environmental Policy-Making," *Science* 236 (April 17, 1987): 286-290; Robert Formaini, *The Myth of Scientific Public Policy* (New Brunswick, N.J.: Transaction, 1990); John M. Mendeloff, *The Dilemma of Toxic Substance Regulation* (Cambridge: MIT Press, 1989); and Daniel Mazmanian and David Morell, *Beyond Superfailure* (Boulder: Westview, 1992).

7. On the problem of agency autonomy and its implications, see Douglas Yates, *Bureaucratic Democracy* (Cambridge: Harvard University Press, 1982); George C. Eads and Michael Fix, *Relief or Reform? Reagan's Regulatory Dilemma* (Washington, D.C.: Urban Institute Press, 1984); Kenneth C. Davis, *Discretionary Justice* (Urbana-Champaign: University of Illinois Press, 1971); and Stephen Breyer, *Regulation and Its Reform* (Cambridge: Harvard University Press, 1982).

8. William Reilly's reform agenda is discussed in "An Interview With William K. Reilly," *EPA Journal* 15 (March-April 1989): 2-8.

9. EPA employment information is found in Office of the Federal Registrar, National Archives and Records Administration, *The United States Government Manual, 1991-1992* (Lanham, Md.: Bernan Press, 1992); budget figures are found in Executive Office of the President, Office of Management and Budget, *The Budget of the United States Government, FY 1992;* see also app. 3, "Budgets of Selected Environmental and Natural Resource Agencies."

10. William K. Reilly, "The New Clean Air Act: An Environmental Milestone," *EPA Journal* 17 (January-February 1991): 3.

11. U.S. Congress, Congressional Research Service, Environmental Protection Section, Environment and Natural Resource Policy Division, *Summaries of Environmental Laws Administered by the Environmental Protection Agency*, March 27, 1989, 2.

12. Thomas O. McGarity, "The Internal Structure of EPA Rulemaking," *Law and*

Contemporary Problems 54 (Autumn 1991): 59. A more extensive discussion of EPA's internal structure and its decisionmaking implications is found in McGarity, *Restoring Rationality* (New York: Cambridge University Press, 1991).

13. Lazarus, "Tragedy of Distrust," 362.

14. J. Clarence (Terry) Davies III, former assistant administrator for policy, planning, and evaluation. Quoted in *Inside EPA*, March 1, 1991, 5.

15. McGarity, "EPA Rulemaking," 61; see also Brian J. Cook, *Bureaucratic Politics and Regulatory Reform* (New York: Greenwood, 1988).

16. Landy, Roberts, and Thomas, *Environmental Protection Agency*, 11.

17. Richard J. Lazarus, "The Neglected Question of Congressional Oversight of EPA," *Law and Contemporary Problems* 54 (Autumn 1991): 216.

18. Ibid., 211.

19. Quoted in John H. Trattner, *The Prune Book: The 100 Toughest Management and Policy-Making Jobs in Washington* (Lanham, Md.: Madison Books, 1988), 249.

20. William Ruckelshaus, "EPA," *EPA Journal* 16 (January–February 1991): 14; see also James J. Florio, "Congress as Reluctant Regulator," *Yale Journal on Regulation* 3 (Spring 1986): 351–382; and Michael E. Kraft, "Congress and Environmental Policy," in *Environmental Politics and Policy*, ed. Lester, 179–211.

21. Executive Office of the President, Council on Environmental Quality, *Environmental Quality, 1985: Sixteenth Annual Report* (Washington, D.C.: Government Printing Office, 1987), 14.

22. U.S. General Accounting Office, "Pesticides: EPA's Formidable Task to Assess and Regulate Their Risks," Report no. GAO/RCED-86-125 (April 1986), 35.

23. U.S. General Accounting Office, "EPA's Chemical Testing Program Has Not Resolved Safety Concerns," Report no. GAO/RCED-91-136 (June 1991), 2.

24. Lazarus, "Tragedy of Distrust," 323.

25. Ibid.

26. U.S. Environmental Protection Agency, Environmental Indicators and Forecasting Branch, *Managing for Environmental Results: A Status Report on EPA's Environmental Indicator Program* (Washington, D.C.: Environmental Indicators and Forecasting Branch, 1991).

27. The history of these Executive Orders and the ensuing controversies is described in V. Kerry Smith, ed., *Environmental Policy Under Reagan's Executive Order* (Chapel Hill, N.C.: University of North Carolina Press, 1984); Richard A. Liroff, "Cost-Benefit Analysis in Federal Environmental Programs," in *Cost-Benefit Analysis and Environmental Regulations*, ed. Daniel Swartzman, Richard A. Liroff, and Kevin G. Croke (Washington, D.C.: Conservation Foundation, 1982); U.S. General Accounting Office, "Cost-Benefit Analysis Can Be Useful in Assessing Environmental Regulations Despite Limitations," Report no. GAO/RCED-84-62 (April 1984).

28. Robert Percival, "Checks Without Balances," *Law and Contemporary Problems* 54 (Autumn 1991): 163.

29. Problems of fragmented environmental management are discussed in Advisory Commission on Intergovernmental Relations, *Regulatory Federalism: Policy, Impact, Process and Reform* (Washington, D.C.: U.S. Government Printing Office, 1984); Barry G. Rabe, *Fragmentation and Integration in State Environmental Management* (Washington, D.C.: Conservation Foundation, 1986); see also Charles E. Davis and James P. Lester, "Federalism and Environmental Policy," in *Environmental Politics and Policy;* the specific problems of groundwater protection are discussed in U.S. General Accounting Office, "More Emphasis Needed on Prevention in EPA's Efforts to Protect Groundwater," Report no. GAO/RCED-92-47 (December 1991).

30. The 1981 poll was taken by the National Opinion Research Corporation and reported in *Public Opinion* 4, no. 6 (February–March 1982): 37. The Roper poll

was cited in "Environmental Protection in the 1990s: What the Public Wants," a presentation to the U.S. Environmental Protection Agency, June 1991.

31. See U.S. Environmental Protection Agency, Science Advisory Board, *Reducing Risk: Setting Priorities and Strategies for Environmental Protection* (Washington, D.C.: U.S. Environmental Protection Agency, September 1990).

32. Ibid.

33. Comparisons between public and scientific rankings of risk were first reported in U.S. Environmental Protection Agency, Office of Policy Analysis, Office of Policy, Planning, and Evaluation, *Unfinished Business: A Comparative Assessment of Environmental Problems* (Washington, D.C.: Environmental Protection Agency, 1987), chap. 4. These were subsequently reported in *EPA Journal* 13 (November 1987): 11.

34. U.S. General Accounting Office, "More Emphasis Needed on Prevention," 28-29.

35. Ibid., 31.

36. U.S. Environmental Protection Agency, Office of Communications, Education, and Public Affairs, *Securing Our Legacy: An EPA Progress Report, 1989-1991* (April 1992), 20-25.

37. EPA, SAB, *Reducing Risk,* 6.

7

Environmental Policy in the Courts
Lettie M. Wenner

The logical method and form flatter that longing for certainty and for repose which is in every human mind. But certainty generally is illusion, and repose is not the destiny of man.

—Oliver Wendell Holmes
Harvard Law Review 39 (1897)

The Role of the Courts in Environmental Policy

In 1803 John Marshall, then chief justice of the United States, established the power of courts to oversee the constitutionality of actions by other branches of government when he declared that it is "the duty of the judicial department to say what the law is."[1] Even before Marshall made this famous pronouncement, state and federal courts were helping to formulate and implement public policy through their powers to interpret and enforce laws, and they continue to do so to this day. Judicial decisions in public policies as diverse as abortion rights and desegregating public schools have been celebrated or deplored by commentators for the last thirty years. Less well publicized, but just as important, has been their participation over the past two decades in shaping environmental policies from water pollution control to preservation of endangered species. Were it not for court injunctions, even fewer ancient trees would be surviving in the United States. Were it not for enforcement actions brought by citizen activists, our waters would be more choked by industrial wastes than they are.

Critics of judicial activism bemoan these developments; yet they are as much a part of the public policy process as congressional debates and executive management of the budget. Nevertheless, some analysts argue that judges are singularly unsuited to make policy decisions in technical areas such as pollution control because they must respond to individual demands for justice.[2] Other scholars caution against the dominance of technical experts and urge the continued use of lay judges to counterbalance inequities that arise when an unrestrained technocracy controls policy.[3] There is a tension between Americans' desire on the one hand for substantively "correct" decisions reached by experts and, on the other, for democratic decisions made through public participation and facilitated by the courts' insistence on due process. Like other government institutions, courts are caught between these two equally important values in the American polity, and they continue to struggle to reconcile them.

In the first section of this chapter I look at how regulatory law has come to involve courts heavily in environmental policy. Next, I consider two approaches—procedural and substantive—used by judges to enforce new laws. Also investigated are the interest groups' use of courts, and the courts' response. Originally, environmental groups regarded federal courts as sympathetic forums; more recently, business groups have developed their own creativity with the law. I also describe some cases that have been decided in trial and appellate courts. The Supreme Court's conservative orientation toward environmental issues is analyzed. Finally, I speculate about issues, such as the concept of standing to sue and property rights claims, that are likely to be seen in environmental cases in the 1990s.

The Common Law: Compensation After Injury

Before environmental legislation exploded in the 1970s, common law concepts such as trespass, personal injury, and liability for damages provided the only legal recourse when people or organizations imposed the costs of their economic activities on others. Parties injured by polluted air, water, toxic wastes, or other hazards may still ask the courts for compensation for the harm imposed on them as a result of a degraded environment. In such cases, however, the burden of proof customarily falls on the plaintiff, who must show that each injury is the fault of a particular polluter. This is extremely difficult to prove, as can be demonstrated by the experiences of thousands of Vietnam veterans who argued that they were damaged by exposure to Agent Orange in the 1970s. Too many other variables may have contributed to the victims' problems for most judges or juries to assign fault for the injuries.

The relatively few victims who successfully prove that the manufacturer of a product, or the operator of a plant that dumps toxic materials into the air, water, or soil, is at fault are often dissatisfied by the outcome. From their perspective, the greatest drawback to the judicial remedy of damages is that nothing is done to change the situation in which the injury occurred. It is often cheaper for the industry to pay damages and continue the harmful behavior. Theoretically, the fear of having to pay damages for injuries done to customers, workers, and innocent bystanders will affect the behavior of firms that manufacture products and dispose of wastes without concern for the consequences. The uncertainty of being sued, however, and the difficulty of establishing proof often diminish the impact of this fear.[4]

The equity suit is an alternative common law remedy to damage judgments. It gives courts the power to issue an injunction forcing the party causing the harm to cease doing so. Judges are loath, however, to order organizations performing essential services for a community, such as operating a hazardous waste landfill, to halt operations. The damage done to third parties is balanced against the economic good that the polluter provides; it is extremely difficult to shut down a business that is providing hundreds of jobs, especially when many different polluters have contributed to a cumulative problem. Just as courts are reluctant to compensate for injuries, so too do they find it difficult to balance interests and restore equity.

Public Law: The Goal of Prevention

The common law of nuisance, trespass, and injury has proved a weak and inconsistent remedy for many problems of environmental degradation, and most proponents of resource conservation and pollution control have turned to public law as an alternative. Rather than depending on the fear of a potential lawsuit after harm has been done, statutory law attempts to prevent the harm from occurring. By proscribing certain actions (for example, dumping crude oil into waterways) and prescribing others (for example, treating sewage before release into waterways), lawmakers hope to prevent many injuries to public health and the natural environment. By shifting legal recourse out of the realm of private law (suits between individuals and groups) and into that of public law (with the government as a prominent actor) policymakers hope to redress the imbalance between the two parties in traditional common law cases. Prevention, rather than remediation, is the goal of public law.[5]

The number of statutory environmental laws intended to regulate behavior grew in the 1970s, but this did not reduce the courts' role. Rather, the courts' workload increased greatly, as some of the burden of resolving uncertainty was passed to the courts. The proliferation of new statutory laws not only creates the need for an administrative state to enforce them but also increases the need for courts to interpret them. Regulatory law forces courts to make prospective decisions about the potential for harm rather than retrospective judgments about the causes of demonstrated injuries. It casts judges in entirely new roles as quasi legislators and quasi administrators.[6]

Court Oversight of Administrative Discretion

Federal judges are aware of the new role they are being asked to play in the field of public law and the more specific policy area of environmental law. In their traditional role as neutral arbiter of individual disputes, judges have finished their work once a verdict has been rendered; but as makers of public policy judges must now also oversee how well the responsible agency carries out the court's order. In many cases a judge will order an agency to comply with the letter of the law passed by Congress by writing regulations by a certain date, issuing a permit, or even rethinking the grounds for its previous decision. Sometimes a judge must continue to exercise managerial control over the same case for years.

For the period preceding the court's verdict as well, the judge's role has greatly expanded. Judges today often act as intermediaries, bringing opposing parties into their chambers to work out a compromise before the case reaches trial. In so doing, judges' discretion and influence over policy are broadened greatly. The judge's informal role of mediator has meant that the number of cases going to trial has declined. Many cases are settled by the parties and their attorneys, often with judicial encouragement. Indeed, some adversaries in environmental disputes are now able to negotiate their differences without resort to the court system at all through a process called environmental dispute resolution (EDR). This method was pioneered by the Conservation Foundation in the 1980s, and its former president, William Reilly, urged business and environmental groups to use EDR when he was appointed administrator of the Environmental Protection Agency (EPA) in the Bush administration.[7]

Judges have disagreed among themselves about their role in overseeing administrative agency decisions. Judge Harold Leventhal, who in the 1970s sat on the U.S. Court of Appeals for the District of Columbia Circuit, argued that it is the courts' responsibility to guarantee that agencies take a "hard look" at all factors when making their decisions.[8] Judge Leventhal also argued that judges need access to court-appointed scientific experts to help them understand the conflicting testimony of adversarial expert witnesses.

Others have argued that, on these knotty technical issues, the United States needs a "science court" composed of natural scientists to define the common ground among experts over controversies involving scientific phenomena. These panels of expert judges would not be asked to make value judgments but would rule only on the scientific aspects of the policy.[9] Skeptics doubt, however, that it would be possible to distinguish between issues of scientific fact and value judgments. They also fear that definitive statements from a science court would stifle future debate over the same issues.[10] Judge Leventhal himself was skeptical of separate specialized courts to try environmental cases. He believed that the selection of judges for such a court would become a political issue within the administration making the appointments.

One of Judge Leventhal's colleagues on the D.C. Circuit in the 1970s, judge David Bazelon, was even skeptical of the suggestion that experts be assigned to the courts. Instead, Bazelon proposed that all opinions about an issue be incorporated into the agency's decisionmaking process. Although he did not dispute the complexity of the technical problems facing the courts, Bazelon believed that science and technology are not the exclusive domain of scientists and engineers. Many cases before the courts, he argued, involve major value choices that may be cloaked in technical questions but should be open to public scrutiny and participation. Rather than cure the problem with separate expert advisers for judges, he preferred that all contending groups have an opportunity to have their rival experts heard before administrative agencies and in court as well.[11]

Interest Groups and the Federal Courts

Judge Bazelon's affinity for a pluralist competition of ideas in the judicial process has been adopted by many interest groups concerned with environmental policy. The same groups that try to influence Congress to pass and modify environmental laws are usually active in tracking the way agencies carry out these laws. Not surprisingly, environmental groups that urged Congress to pass legislation also come before the courts to have the law enforced. Industries and others who were disappointed in the outcomes at either the legislative or executive level also have another chance to influence policy in court. Given the ambiguity of many of the policies made by both legislative and administrative actors, the shift to the courts for further debate is the obvious next step.

Most environmental litigation is initiated by one of three actors. The best known are groups like the National Audubon Society and Sierra Club, which worked to get environmental protection and natural resource legislation passed and reformed in the 1970s. Subsequently, these groups and newer organizations (such as the Natural Resources Defense Council and the Environmental Defense Fund) sued government agencies to carry out their congressional mandates. During the early 1970s they went to the federal courts to get the new laws enforced, where they often succeeded in having their strict interpretations of the laws accepted.

Initially caught off guard by environmental litigation, business and property interests are now responding with increasing confidence and stridency. With their superior legal and economic resources, major corporations and trade associations have asked the courts to reinterpret environmental laws in a more probusiness light. It is common, for example, for both industry and environmental groups to simultaneously sue EPA over the same regulation; one litigant claims the regulation is too strict, the other that it is too lenient. In addition, industry and private property owners are making intense demands on federal courts (outstripping the environmental groups), arguing that the laws themselves should be declared unconstitutional and unenforceable.

Government is the third major actor in environmental law, and it participates on both sides of the issues. When challenged by environmental groups, it often represents an economic or development interest normally associated with major corporations. When challenged by industry, it must defend the law and the environmental point of view. In addition, government agencies have a sizable agenda of their own. After all, their official role is to enforce statutory laws, ensure the conditions of permits, and halt violations of regulations by industry and private property owners.

Most environmental cases can be classified into one of three modal types—environmental groups vs. government, industry vs. government, and government vs. industry. There are additional cases in which government appeals an environmental victory at the trial level, and these have become more common as the Justice Department has grown more defensive about environmental regulation. There is also a fifth type of case between different agencies and levels of government. In such cases one government body accuses the other of polluting the environment. Reacting against the emphasis in the Reagan and Bush administrations on deregulation, state authorities have increasingly assumed a regulatory stance against such federal agencies as the Department of Defense.

Litigants and Their Changes in Strategy

The traditional approach of environmental groups has been to sue government for regulating too loosely. But in recent years these groups have confronted business corporations directly in court rather than suing the government as a surrogate. Congress facilitated this type of suit by writing into several of the environmental laws provisions for private attorneys general to enforce them. This power enables a private citizen or group to take legal action against a polluter when a government agency does not.

Disappointed by EPA's unwillingness to undertake enforcement actions, environmental groups have sued to force individual industries and plants to conform to the limits written into water pollution discharge permits. In this way environmental groups have been able to pursue their disagreements directly with their chief rival, industry, even when the responsible agencies are unwilling to play their proenvironmental role.

Calling these cases "judicial activism," conservative critics argue that the litigants do not deserve standing before the courts. Implementation of the laws should be left, they contend, to technical experts in the administrative agencies; environmental groups should not be allowed to involve the courts. This argument has received a sympathetic hearing in some courts, especially the Supreme Court, and is being pursued not only by business defendants but also by government defendants against environmental initiatives. As long as Congress continues to provide authority for private attorneys general in pollution control laws, however, environmental groups will use this power in the face of what they see as benign neglect by the executive branch. Congress is so convinced of the need for these citizen suits that in 1990 it amended the Clean Air Act to require permits for plant emissions similar to those issued to industries that discharge into waterways.[12] The primary complaint brought by citizens groups against industry has been violation of permits because this constitutes a legal requirement for which there is a clear paper trail.

In addition to objecting to environmental groups' standing in court, business has found a new theme around which to focus its arguments against government regulation. Developers and other landowners argue that almost any government regulation, federal or state, constitutes an unconstitutional violation of their property rights if it diminishes the value of their land. These litigants use the Fifth Amendment language (". . . nor be deprived of life, liberty, or property without due process of law; nor shall private property be taken for public use without just compensation") to attack such federal laws as wilderness preservation and endangered species acts and the language of the Fourteenth Amendment's due process clause to challenge state police powers such as zoning laws. Moreover, even if the court strikes down the law, the litigants believe they are entitled to compensation from the government for any property loss suffered in the interim.[13] These arguments have been upheld often by the U.S. Court of Claims, which hears suits against the U.S. government for monetary damages, and to some degree by the U.S. Supreme Court. (I discuss this below in the section on court outcomes.) This development has sent a chill through federal and state policymakers, who may relax their regulations rather than face large damage judgments.

Types of Issues in Federal Courts

Most federal cases about the environment fall into three major categories: (1) National Environmental Policy Act (NEPA) cases, in which public interest groups challenge government projects because of their adverse environmental effects; (2) public health threats, from air and water pollution as well as from toxic materials such as pesticides and hazardous wastes; and (3) natural resource management issues, including disputes over energy development, the use of public lands, and wildlife and wilderness protection.

The Rise and Fall of NEPA

During the "environmental decade" of the 1970s, many cases concerned NEPA, which requires the federal government to write an environmental impact statement (EIS) before undertaking a government-funded or regulated project, such as highway or dam construction, or permitting the operation of a nuclear reactor. Federal courts started by treating such questions substantively, insisting that agencies should prove that they had indeed taken Leventhal's "hard look" at all such projects.[14] District and circuit court judges also fashioned stringent procedural requirements for federal agencies to ensure that all interested parties have an opportunity to enter the process, in accordance with Judge Bazelon's desire for complete procedural protection.

By the end of the 1970s, however, the Supreme Court had narrowed the scope of NEPA by overturning many of these cases. In *Vermont Yankee* v. *NRDC* (1978), the Supreme Court reversed two District of Columbia Circuit Court decisions remanding Nuclear Regulatory Commission (NRC) decisions for inadequate treatment of environmental issues, including conservation of energy and disposal of nuclear wastes, before issuing permits for nuclear plants.[15] Writing for a unanimous Supreme Court, Justice William H. Rehnquist chastised the D.C. Circuit for interfering with NRC discretion and inserting its own policy preferences for that of an expert commission. After having their decisions overturned by the Supreme Court repeatedly in the 1970s, the federal courts came to treat the writing of environmental impact statements as a paper exercise. They generally ruled in favor of government projects as long as the EIS requirement had been observed. As a consequence, the number of NEPA cases declined dramatically in the 1980s as environmental groups turned their resources to pollution control and natural resource management issues.

Public Health Threats

Air and water pollution cases have been the most persistent topic in the federal courts' workload. Although air pollution cases constitute a modest percentage of environmental cases, there are many water pollution cases chiefly because permits are required for every point source, which opens the door to enforcement actions. Recently, government enforcement actions have declined substantially, but environmental groups replaced many government actions with their own private attorneys general cases. During the Carter administration, environmental groups initiated only 20 percent of water pollution control cases at the trial level, but in the Reagan years they initiated nearly 50 percent of them, and this trend continued in the Bush administration.

Courts have been somewhat receptive to the claim of environmental groups that they are appropriate private attorneys general to enforce pollution control statutes. When the state starts a public enforcement action in response to the citizen action, or when the pollution stops, environmental groups are unlikely to win their cases, but they have achieved their desired end. When pollution continues and enforcement at either the state or federal level is not forthcoming, the courts are willing to give private attorneys general standing and likely to decide these cases substantively for the environmental groups, even awarding them attorney's fees afterward. With the renewed attack on environmental groups' standing in courts, however, this type of victory may become less common.

Toxic substances and solid waste problems have resulted in a steep increase in cases. In 1976 Congress passed the Resource Conservation and Recovery Act to control the disposal of solid wastes, including hazardous wastes, and in 1980, the Comprehensive Environmental Response, Compensation, and Liability Act (Superfund) to clean up abandoned waste dumps. Whenever a law is first implemented, courts have numerous opportunities to interpret it, given the key actors' uncertainty about what the new law means. After the law becomes routinized, there are fewer reasons to test it in court.

Many of the initial Superfund cases concerned procedural questions: Were defendants entitled to a jury trial? How much notice must the government give before initiating proceedings against a violation? And what are the statutory limitations for recovery of costs?[16] Superfund provides for recovery of costs from owners and former users of abandoned waste sites, and many cases have concerned the division of liability among different responsible parties. Courts have been willing to assess liability quite broadly on former and present operators, haulers, and users of sites in the 1980s. One corporation often sues another to accept responsibility for its share of the damage, and federal courts have generally agreed that other liable parties should share the cleanup costs, except when the owner is a government entity, in which case sovereign immunity has frequently been invoked. Some companies have gone bankrupt, and courts have differed over the question of whether costs of cleaning up such sites should take precedence over other debts owed by the same corporation.

Natural Resources Cases

Energy issues were rarely contested in the courts until the energy crisis in the mid 1970s. Related to energy issues are cases that concern publicly owned land and other natural resources located primarily in the western United States. Although the number of cases declined somewhat in the early 1980s, energy-public land issues now constitute an important subject for environmental cases. The March 1989 *Exxon Valdez* disaster in Prince William Sound, which spilled 11 million gallons of oil, generated one criminal conviction that was eventually overturned and innumerable civil actions about liability that will take years to adjudicate. Resulting arguments about opening up additional Alaskan wilderness areas to oil exploration are likely to involve the courts again in balancing risks to the environment against benefits to the economy from developing energy resources. Conflicts over the exploitation of the country's natural resources are thus likely to constitute an even larger portion of environmental confrontations in the future.

Timber and ranching interests are as eager as the oil and gas industry for rapid development of all public lands, and conservation groups are continually seeking to slow this process. One such natural resource conflict that reached the federal courts in the early 1990s was the dispute in the Pacific Northwest over proposals to harvest the last large remaining stands of old-growth timber not protected by wilderness or park status. Conservationists argue that further loss of virgin forests will reduce biodiversity and set a negative example for developing nations that are rapidly depleting their own forests. The timber industry responds that preserving old growth will throw loggers and mill workers out of work in a time of economic depression in the Northwest. Environmentalists counter that the industry's automation and its trade in raw logs to Japan have eliminated more jobs than conservation ever could. Nevertheless, loggers regard the last stands of ancient forest as a means of staving off the inevitable time when they will become entirely dependent on second-growth trees.

In court the controversy centered around the Endangered Species Act (ESA), which prohibits destroying the habitat of endangered plants and animals. Although the northern spotted owl, which lives in the Northwest forests, had been in decline for years, the Fish and Wildlife Service would not label the species as threatened—much less endangered—until a federal judge in Washington State, responding to a suit from the Sierra Club, ordered it to reconsider.[17] Once Fish and Wildlife had labeled the owl threatened, ESA's unambiguous language forced judges to issue injunctions that halted logging in several national forests. At the urging of Washington and Oregon representatives and senators, Congress took the unusual step of stripping the federal courts of jurisdiction over these cases in 1989 and again in 1990. Environmentalists challenged the constitutionality of these acts, but the U.S. Supreme Court eventually upheld the Congress.[18]

After Congress failed to pass similar laws in 1991, trial judges renewed their injunctions against logging areas where the spotted owl lives. Faced with ESA's unequivocal language, the Bush administration argued the law should be amended. At the same time environmentally oriented members of Congress drafted new bills that would afford protection for old-growth forests for the sake of biodiversity per se, rather than relying on finding endangered species that depend on them for habitat. However the issue may ultimately be resolved between Congress and the executive branch, the courts will be called on to interpret any new or amended law and to redress the grievances of whoever loses the political battle.

Patterns in Court Outcomes

Given the Reagan and Bush administrations' opposition to governmental regulation, especially for the sake of environmental and conservation causes, federal court decisions in this policy area were expected to change in the 1980s. When William French Smith and later Edwin Meese headed the Justice Department, candidates for the federal bench were carefully screened for ideological purity. This presumably meant conforming not only with the administration's social policies regarding abortion and church-state relations but also with its philosophy of increasing business discretion in the marketplace and reducing government control over economic behavior. One would have expected that as the decade wore on and more Reagan-Bush appointees were available to make judicial decisions, fewer environmental victories would be recorded in federal courts. That was the case. Moreover, it is the impression of all but the most developmentally oriented observers that environmental causes are continuing to lose ground in the courts in the 1990s.[19]

The Lower Federal Courts

Because courts tend to favor official government actors in all areas of litigation, government agencies win more often than either their industrial or environmental opponents. This did not change from 1970 into the 1990s, but individual case outcomes belie the overall pattern. The EPA lost many major legal battles at the beginning of the 1990s. In October 1991 the Fifth Circuit in New Orleans overruled EPA on banning asbestos, a regulation the agency had spent ten years perfecting. The court ruled that the agency had not considered the costs to industry for finding substitutes, and the benefits to be gained were insufficient.[20] An extreme example of judicial intervention into administrative decisionmaking, this case contradicts the assertion often made by presidents Reagan and Bush that they chose federal judges who would refrain from inserting their own values into their decisions. In December 1991 a panel of the D.C. Circuit consisting of two Reagan judges and Clarence Thomas, who was subsequently appointed to the Supreme Court by President Bush, threw out EPA's twelve-year-old definition of hazardous wastes that included certain wastes from the petroleum industry.[21]

Specific examples, no matter how important the cases, do not tell the whole story. It is important to look at overall trends. How federal judges ruled for business, environmental groups, and government agencies in the Ninth Circuit Court of Appeals (the West Coast) from 1970 to 1991 is represented in table 7-1. Judges appointed by Democratic presidents (including Jimmy Carter) tend to favor environmental litigants more than Republican appointees do. Republican appointees, however, do not favor business litigants in a similar systematic way. And Reagan-Bush appointees, who now dominate the federal courts, seem to prefer the government perspective regardless of who the opposing party is. Perhaps this is because Reagan-Bush appointees have faced only executive decisions made by their fellow partisans. Perhaps they feel confident in deferring to Republican administrators even when business interests oppose them. Only when these judges have an opportunity to rule on decisions made by Democratic administrators will we be able to discern whether Reagan-Bush appointees exhibit a true pattern favoring government regardless of who runs it.

Table 7-1   Judges' Support for Businesses, Environmental Groups, and Government Agencies, by Appointing President, in Cases Before the Ninth Circuit Court of Appeals, 1970-1991

Judges Appointed by	Litigants					
	Businesses		Environmental Groups		Government Agencies	
	Votes	% Votes in Favor	Votes	% Votes in Favor	Votes	% Votes in Favor
Reagan/Bush	42	20	44	41	80	73
Other Republican presidents	171	31	212	44	358	66
Carter	125	25	180	53	289	63
Other Democratic presidents	66	33	64	56	124	59

Sources: Environmental Reporter Cases (Washington, D.C.: Bureau of National Affairs, 1970-1991) and *Federal Reporter—2d Series* (St. Paul, Minn.: West, 1970-1991).

Note: Data are from 399 environmental cases. Since three judges usually voted in each case, more than 399 votes were cast. Votes cast vary across columns because not all three litigants were involved in any one case. Most cases involved a government agency and either a business or an environmental group. In cases in which businesses were litigants, for example, judges appointed by Reagan or Bush cast 42 votes; 20% of the votes favored businesses. Voting patterns on the Ninth Circuit are similar to those on the D.C. Circuit.

There is no mistaking the fact, however, that Reagan-Bush appointees look with disfavor on most demands made by environmental litigants. In the 1980s Reagan policymakers reduced the severity of many of the regulations originally drafted by regulatory agencies. Many of these new regulations have now been appealed to the courts, and there have been few victories for environmental groups. In 1988 EPA promulgated new rules to enforce the amendments to the Resource Conservation and Recovery Act (RCRA), which control the injection of wastes into wells. The Natural Resources Defense Council claimed that rules controlling migration of hazardous wastes were too lenient, and the chemical disposal industry countersued that they were too severe. The D.C. Circuit Court of Appeals found for EPA against both litigants. But Judge Patricia Wald, a Carter appointee, objected, arguing that her colleagues were misinterpreting Congress's intention to instruct EPA to be conservative in deciding what types of wastes could move off site.[22] NRDC also challenged new EPA-set ambient air quality standards. Judge Wald led another panel of three judges to a compromise decision whereby EPA was asked to give better justification for its decision not to set a secondary standard to reduce acid rain. One Carter holdover judge argued for remanding more of the standards to EPA for review, while a new Reagan appointee dissented in favor of supporting the government's revisions completely.[23]

Regional patterns in federal court decisions have proved important in the United States. The Northeast, Midwest, West Coast, and D.C. circuits have been favorably disposed toward environmental litigants since the 1970s.[24] Judges in the Southeast, Southwest, and Rocky Mountain states have tended to favor development and economic growth. Interest groups, whether economic or environmental, are aware of the forums that are most favorably disposed toward their cause. Whenever they have a choice about where to raise an issue, they take their case to the court most likely to agree with them, which may have contributed to the decision by industry to appeal the asbestos case to the Fifth Circuit in New Orleans.

Court of Claims

One forum in which the new property rights movement has received a warm reception is the U.S. Court of Claims, where landowners take their allegations that the government must compensate them for any diminution in value of their property because of regulations. Two cases involving the filling of wetlands exemplify the court's generosity. In one case the Corps of Engineers, the agency that regulates wetlands, refused to permit a New Jersey developer to build a subdivision on 12.5 acres of wetlands. Although the Corps had authority to deny the permit, the Court of Claims found that the owner had lost all economic use of the wetlands and was entitled to $2.6 million in compensation.[25] The judge accepted the developer's argument that the best use for the land was residential development despite the clear objective of preserving wetlands found in the Clean Water Act. In a second case, the Corps refused a permit to quarry limestone in an area where the aquifer was rapidly becoming polluted by such strip-mining operations. The judge awarded the company $1 million for the loss of all use of its property despite evidence that the land could be sold for about $4,000 an acre.[26]

In both cases the judges rejected the government's argument that the parcels of land were small parts of larger holdings, and their owners had already reaped large profits from the larger portion of the parcel. The proposed housing development in New Jersey was part of 250 acres, bought for $300,000, most of which had already been developed. The Florida quarry was 98 acres out of 1,560 acres of wetland, most of which had already been mined. The land in both cases had escalated in value, and the court ruled the owners were entitled to the present-day fair market value of the land because they had expected to gain from their initial investment.[27] In both cases the judges also found that the burden on the private property owners outweighed any public benefit from preserving wetlands or preventing the contamination of groundwater.

In addition to private land use cases, the Court of Claims has responded positively to numerous complaints from timber, mining, and ranching interests, as well as inholders of private lands inside public parks, that the government's efforts to control uses and preserve the ecology of public lands interferes with their property rights. These decisions are supported by the property rights philosophy increasingly espoused by conservative judges and law professors in recent years. They have also been supported by recent decisions in the Supreme Court, which has looked favorably on private landowners' claims against state land use regulations.

The Supreme Court's Treatment of Environmental Issues

The Supreme Court in the 1970s was less receptive to environmental claims than were the lower federal courts, overturning almost all proenvironmental cases brought to it. Today the Supreme Court is an even more business-oriented institution. It became increasingly conservative during the early 1980s under the leadership of Chief Justice Warren Burger, and since 1986, when William Rehnquist became chief justice, it has become still more probusiness. It was also a severely divided court in the 1980s, with some justices vigorously opposed to their colleagues' desire to reduce government regulation. Since President Bush had the opportunity to replace the last two remaining liberal judges with solid conservatives, there is less resistance to the majority's views.

One major issue that the Supreme Court took up in the 1980s, which is likely to be reconsidered often in the 1990s, is the need for agencies to strike a balance between the costs of keeping contaminants out of the environment and the benefits obtained by avoiding risks to human health. A closely divided Court came to opposite conclusions in two similar industry challenges to regulations set by the Occupational Safety and Health Administration (OSHA) to protect workers' health.

The first came from the U.S. Court of Appeals for the Fifth Circuit in New Orleans, known for its probusiness point of view. That court agreed with the American Petroleum Institute that estimated risks to workers from exposure to benzene were not worth the costs to industry to avoid them. In 1980 the Supreme Court upheld this ruling in a 5-4 decision. But in the same year the D.C. Circuit upheld a cotton dust standard set by OSHA, and the Supreme Court upheld the agency's decision on the grounds that the same law as in the benzene case did not mandate cost-benefit justification.[28] In this case, three of the majority justices in the benzene standard case became dissenters. One changed his position and voted in favor of the cotton dust standard because the agency had shown that 25 percent of all workers in the industry suffered from a disease caused by inhalation of cotton fibers.

Since these two cases were decided by the Supreme Court, cost-benefit analysis and its companion concept, risk assessment, have become even more important in the public discussion of health and environmental issues. The Council on Competitiveness, appointed by President Bush (and disbanded by President Bill Clinton), and the Office of Management and Budget together tried to halt any further regulation of business. Five of the justices who made the two OSHA decisions have been replaced, among them the most health-conscious of the original Burger Court: justices William Brennan and Thurgood Marshall. The newest justices—David Souter and Clarence Thomas—have impeccable probusiness Republican credentials, and it seemed at the end of 1992 that the Court was due to become more protective of business interests. Well aware of the Supreme Court's attitude, environmental litigants long ago ceased taking appeals there. With the November 1992 election of Bill Clinton and the resignation of Justice Byron White in early 1993, it appears that the Supreme Court's long drift toward a probusiness bias has been arrested. There remains, however, a conservative majority on the Court and a considerable legacy of antienvironmental decisions.

Justice Scalia, who leads the most conservative wing of the Court, has responded favorably to business's attacks on the constitutionality of government regulation of property on the grounds that overregulation amounts to taking property without due process. In one case, Justice Scalia, writing for the Court majority, agreed with landowners that the California Coastal Zone Commission attempted to take their property without due process when it tried to force them to provide public access to the ocean in exchange for a permit to rebuild their beachfront house.[29] In another case, Chief Justice Rehnquist addressed an additional question that the Court had avoided until then. Instead of restricting the remedy for any regulatory taking of property to striking down the unconstitutional regulation, he stated that landowners are entitled to be compensated by the state for any loss of value from the property that occurred between the time the regulation was put in place and its invalidation.[30]

Finally in 1992 *Lucas* v. *South Carolina Coastal Council* was decided in favor of a South Carolina landowner who had invested in property before the state passed a law prohibiting developers from building on erodible beach land. Although the Court did not determine whether Lucas had lost all economic use of the land itself, it sent the case back to state court to determine this fact. Justice Antonin Scalia's decision said that the state's only rationale for justifying its regulation would be through the common law of nuisance, which normally requires proof that harm would be done to adjacent property.[31] This ruling effectively extends the taking doctrine to restrict the state's regulatory powers to those it would have under the nuisance doctrine in common law. Taken to an extreme, this interpretation could reduce the police powers of the states to prevent property owners from imposing externalities on the larger society only when the state can prove individual harm to specific individuals.

Standing to Sue

For environmental litigants, however, another development is more ominous. This stems from several recent Supreme Court decisions that threaten to remove environmentalists' access to all federal courts. In 1972 a far different Supreme Court from the current Rehnquist Court signaled its willingness to look sympathetically on nontraditional litigants who hoped to raise ecological and even esthetic issues in court. Earlier courts had created a barrier for noneconomic grievances through the concept of "standing to sue," which holds that only persons or groups with a particular injury can present their arguments in court. Although the Court did not give the Sierra Club standing in this landmark case, it laid out how this status could be achieved by claiming specific injury to individual club members on the grounds that they used the area in question.[32]

Other environmental groups were quick to take the Court up on this suggestion, and lower federal courts followed precedent by opening their doors to these kinds of suits. This movement quickly reached its peak, however, when a group of law students got into court by alleging they hiked in open space that might be reduced if railroad rates on recycled materials were higher than those on virgin materials.[33] The Burger Court throughout the remainder of the 1970s refused to open the door to the federal courts further. Since then the Rehnquist Court has been gradually narrowing the opening that many on the Court, including Justice Scalia, believe was wrongly initiated.[34]

This latest trend was demonstrated when the Court refused to allow the National Wildlife Federation to protest a Bureau of Land Management decision to open up some public land to development. Justice Scalia wrote the majority decision that denied standing on the ground that the federation had not demonstrated any specific injury it had suffered aside from asserting that its members use the public land under consideration for recreation.[35]

This case was closely followed by another decision against the Defenders of Wildlife, which wanted the courts to force the Department of the Interior to challenge overseas projects funded by the State Department that endangered the survival of rare species. Justice Scalia opined again that because the Defenders had suffered no particularized injury (despite language in the Endangered Species Act that permits citizen suits), they had no right to sue.[36]

Both these cases came to the Supreme Court only because the executive branch was willing to make the argument that public interest groups should have no standing to sue. But once the argument about standing was made, the present Supreme Court seemed eager to accept it. This precedent goes beyond those that simply find against the merits of environmental arguments. It implies that the groups with the most effective arguments are not eligible to make them in any federal court. Many critics of the courts agree with Justice Scalia that judges, because of their focus on individual rights, are unsuited to make decisions that can influence broad social policy. They believe technical decisions are better left to administrators with appropriate expertise who can determine priorities for agencies that are pressed to respond to multiple legislated requirements.[37]

Opponents of this restrictive view of the courts' role argue that executive agencies are no more democratically elected than judges and that Congress would not have provided the mechanism of citizen suits if it trusted administrators to render unerringly proper decisions. Judges admittedly do not have the agencies' concerns for efficient use of resources foremost in mind. But other values, such as individual justice, should outweigh these considerations. Experts do disagree about many technical issues regarding pollution and resource management. Eliminating standing for one group of experts will mean that much information and even some issues, such as the spotted owl's status as a threatened species, may be precluded from discussion at any level in the federal court system.

Projections for the 1990s

The presidential election in November 1992 created an opportunity to begin the slow evolution of the Supreme Court back to a moderate position on the environment, as President Clinton is likely to appoint justices more favorably disposed toward the environment than any on the Court in the October 1992-July 1993 term. It should be noted, however, that it takes considerable time to change the ideology of the Supreme Court as its members have life tenure and Clinton's opportunities will be limited to voluntary resignations and deaths of sitting justices. The most recent Bush appointees are among the youngest and most conservative. It seems likely that justices Harry Blackmun and John Paul Stevens, both moderate Republicans, will follow the example of Justice White, the only remaining Democrat, who resigned in March 1993.

This will afford President Clinton the opportunity to make three appointments early in his administration. While these new justices will probably be selected for their attitudes on civil liberties rather than on the environment, it is likely they will be more favorably disposed toward the environment. Three votes do not make a majority on a nine-justice court, however, and they will have to modify their stands considerably if they are to pick up two more votes from the most moderate of the conservative Republicans remaining on the High Court. The same logic applies to the lower federal courts, where more than half the judges have been appointed by either President Reagan or Bush.

Through the remainder of the 1990s it seems likely that most federal courts will view skeptically any regulation of economic behavior whether at the state or federal level. This is likely to take three forms: an increased use of cost-benefit analysis, continued favorable reception to arguments about taking property without due process, and reduced standing for public interest organizations.

The conservative judiciary could be offset by countertrends in other branches of government. Congress could restrict, or at least clarify, the use of cost-benefit and risk-benefit standards in specific pollution control laws, such as the Clean Air Act. It could choose to explain whether its intention was to require that benefits from risk reduction equal the costs to industry, or whether it wanted to give EPA the discretion to set minimum pollutant levels based on public health goals without regard to cost. Also the regulatory agencies could become more tough-minded in their dealings with industry, in which case the Reagan-Bush judges will have to decide if they should continue to defer to the executive branch.

Two other issues are more difficult for Congress or the executive branch to address, as they depend on constitutional interpretation—a judicial function. If laws and/or administrators become more restrictive, it is likely that arguments about taking private property without due process of law will become more common in the courts. In such an event, the United States could experience a conflict between the judiciary and the elected branches of government over the appropriate role for the government to play in the economy—a conflict reminiscent of the New Deal, when the Supreme Court overturned much new legislation.

Because it is easier to show a specific monetary loss than any other kind, the Supreme Court's standing-to-sue rulings favor economic interests over ecological ones. Industry by definition has a material interest in its cases, and this may mean that only one side of some controversial cases will be allowed to take its grievances to court. Although the new administration could choose not to make standing arguments against allowing environmental interest groups into court, it is still possible for business litigants to initiate such claims. Congress could increase the citizen suit provisions in its laws, stating explicitly what zone of interest the legislation is designed to protect. But if the courts decide that the litigant making the claim has experienced no particular injury, they may still find no grounds for standing to sue. Even though environmental groups are less likely to win the cases they bring, this reduction in their ability to sue is even more important because it prevents them from ever making their arguments.

In addition to the three patterns in Supreme Court decisions, there is a more general societal trend toward negotiated rule making and alternative forms of dispute resolution. Many environmental disputes are now settled out of court, with or without judicial supervision. This trend is likely to continue given the high costs of litigation and the increased reluctance of industry and environmental groups to prolong cleanup controversies.

A final complicating factor is the internationalization of environmental disputes. As policies such as protecting the Earth's ozone layer are adopted by international treaties and protocols, the role of U.S. courts in interpreting and administering environmental standards could diminish. Given the lack of enforcement power by international bodies, however, American courts could face an increasing volume of cases brought by foreign parties who seek to challenge U.S. policies that affect their territory. How the courts will respond to such challenges remains to be seen.

Notes

1. *Marbury* v. *Madison*, 5 U.S. (1 Cranch) 137; 2 L.Ed. 60 (1803).
2. Donald L. Horowitz, *The Courts and Social Policy* (Washington, D.C.: Brookings, 1977); and R. Shep Melnick, *Regulation and the Courts* (Washington, D.C.: Brookings, 1983).
3. Lawrence Tribe, "Policy Science: Analysis or Ideology? " *Philosophy and Public Affairs* 2 (1972): 56; and Joel Yellin, "High Technology and the Courts: Nuclear Power and the Need for Institution Reform," *Harvard Law Review* 94 (1981): 489.
4. Lettie M. Wenner, *One Environment Under Law* (Pacific Palisades, Calif.: Goodyear, 1976), 7-9.
5. James Willard Hurst traced the law's development from common law in the nineteenth century through the development of public laws to regulate individual behavior for the common good. See Hurst, *Law and Social Order in the United States* (Ithaca, N.Y.: Cornell University Press, 1977). Also see Norman Vig and Patrick Bruer, "The Courts and Risk Assessment," *Policy Studies Review* 1 (May 1982): 716-727.
6. Among those who applaud this development are Hurst, *Law and Social Order;* and Abram Chayes, "The Role of Judges in Public Law Litigation," *Harvard Law Review* 89 (1976): 1281-1316. Among those who criticize it are Nathan Glazer, "Toward an Imperial Judiciary?" *Public Interest* 41 (1975): 104-123; and Horowitz, *Courts and Social Policy.*
7. Douglas J. Amy, "Environmental Dispute Resolution: The Promise and the Pitfalls," chap. 10 in *Environmental Policy in the 1990s*, 1st ed., ed. Norman J. Vig and Michael E. Kraft.
8. Harold Leventhal, "Environmental Decisionmaking and the Role of the Courts," *University of Pennsylvania Law Review* 122 (1974): 509-555.
9. The science court's primary spokesperson is Arthur Kantrowitz, chairman of Avco Everett Research. See Arthur Kantrowitz, "Controlling Technology Democratically," *American Scientist* (1975), 505; and Arthur Kantrowitz, "Science Court Experiment," *Trial* 13 (March 1977): 48-49.
10. James A. Martin, "The Proposed 'Science Court'," *Michigan Law Review* 75 (April-May 1977): 1058-1091; and A. D. Sofaer, "Science Court: Unscientific and Unsound," *Environmental Law* 9 (Fall 1978): 1-27.
11. David L. Bazelon, "Coping with Technology Through the Legal Process," *Cornell Law Review* 62 (1977): 817-832.
12. Pub.L. 101-549, Title V, Section 501, 104 Stat. 2635 28.
13. Richard A. Epstein, *Takings, Private Property, and the Power of Eminent Domain* (Cambridge: Harvard University Press, 1985).
14. The high point of the Supreme Court's acceptance of this doctrine came in *Citizens to Preserve Overton Park* v. *Volpe*, 401 U.S. 402 (1971). The Supreme Court in this decision agreed with the lower federal court that the Department of Trans-

portation had exercised too much discretion in deciding to take a public park in order to build a highway under the Federal Aid Highway Act of 1968.

15. James F. Raymond, "A *Vermont Yankee* in King Burger's Court: Constraints on Judicial Review Under NEPA," *Boston College Environmental Affairs Law Review* 7 (1979): 629-664; Richard Stewart, "*Vermont Yankee* and the Evolution of Administrative Procedure," *Harvard Law Review* 91 (1978): 1805-1845; and Katherine B. Edwards, "NRC Regulations," *Texas Law Review* 58 (1980): 355-391.

16. *U.S.* v. *Charles George Trucking Company,* 24 ERC 1812 (1986); *U.S.* v. *Carolina Transformer Company,* 25 ERC 1644 (1987); and *U.S.* v. *Dickerson,* 24 ERC 1875 (1986).

17. *Northern Spotted Owl* v. *Hodel,* 716 F. Supp. 479 (1988).

18. *Robertson* v. *Seattle Audubon,* 112 S.Ct. 1407 SC (1992).

19. "Courthouse No Longer Environmentalists' Citadel" *New York Times,* March 23, 1992, p. 1.

20. *Corrosion Proof Fittings* v. *EPA,* 33 ERC 1961 (1991).

21. *Shell Oil* v. *EPA,* 34 ERC 1049 (1991).

22. *NRDC* v. *EPA,* 31 ERC 1697 (1990).

23. *NRDC* v. *EPA,* 31 ERC 1233 (1990).

24. Lettie M. Wenner, "Contextual Influences on Judicial Decision Making," *Western Political Quarterly* 41 (March 1988): 115-134.

25. *Loveladies Harbor* v. *United States,* 21 Cl Ct. 153 (1990).

26. *Florida Rock Industries* v. *United States,* 21 Cl. Ct. 161 (1990).

27. Lee R. Epstein, "Takings and Wetlands in the Claims Court: *Florida Rock* and *Loveladies Harbor,*" *Environmental Law Reporter* 10 (1990): 10517-10521. Thomas Hanley, "A Developer's Dream: the U.S. Claims Court's New Analysis of Section 404 Takings Challenges," *Environmental Affairs* 19 (1991): 317-353.

28. *Industrial Union Department AFL-CIO* v. *American Petroleum Institute,* 100 S.C. 244 (1980); *Textile Manufacturers Institute, Inc.* v. *Donovan,* 425 U.S. 490 (1981). See William H. Rodgers, Jr., "Judicial Review of Risk Assessments: The Role of Decision Theory in Unscrambling the Benzene Decision," *Environmental Law* 11 (1981): 301-320.

29. *Nollan* v. *California Coastal Zone Commission,* 107 S.C. 3141 (1987).

30. *First English Evangelical Lutheran Church* v. *Los Angeles,* 107 S. Ct. 2378 (1987).

31. *Lucas* v. *South Carolina Coastal Council,* 112 S. Ct. 2886 (1992).

32. *Sierra Club* v. *Morton,* 405 U.S. 727 (1972).

33. *U.S.* v. *Students Challenging Regulatory Agency Procedures* 412 U.S. 669 (1973).

34. Antonin Scalia, "The Doctrine of Standing as an Essential Element of the Separation of Powers," *Suffolk University Law Review* 17 (1983): 881-899.

35. *Lujan* v. *National Wildlife Federation,* 110 S. Ct. 3177 (1990).

36. *Lujan* v. *Defenders of Wildlife,* 112 S. Ct. 2130 (1992).

37. In *Sierra Club* v. *Gorsuch,* 18 ERC 1549 (1982), a federal district court in California forced EPA to set radioactive nuclides standards, which may have taken attention away from other types of priorities EPA had under the Clean Air Act. See Melnick, *Regulation and the Courts.*

III. PUBLIC POLICY DILEMMAS

8

Evaluating Environmental Policy
Success and Failure

Robert V. Bartlett

*All you need in this life is ignorance and confidence; then success
is sure.*

—Mark Twain

A quarter of a century ago, in great ignorance yet with considerable confidence, governments worldwide began responding to the concerns raised by the then-coalescing environmental movement. The result has been an outpouring of environmental policy declarations, legislation, programs, regulations, and reorganizations. But has all this activity and investment been worth it? Has environmental policy as a whole succeeded? Have individual environmental policies, programs, or efforts failed?

Success for environmental policy has been much less sure than Mark Twain cynically suggested was the case for ignorant but confident individuals. All of these new, sometimes bold, environmental policies were implemented in an era when general confidence in government as problem solver was declining, such that by the 1980s policy failure had become conventional wisdom among voters, journalists, and politicians.[1] Particularly in the United States, where the dominant public ideology has always been pragmatism, demand for evidence of success has become increasingly insistent, impatient, and narrowly focused. Environmentalists have found failure because policy initiatives so far have been inadequate to the challenges raised by the environmental *problematique*, but others have been quick to allege more thoroughgoing policy failure.

For example, the Comprehensive Environmental Response, Compensation, and Liability Act, known as CERCLA or Superfund, which was passed with high hopes in 1980, has been judged a "superfailure."[2] Analysts have found that U.S. hazardous and toxic waste policies have cleaned up few dump sites, prevented few spills and accidents, and led to the expenditure (waste) of billions of dollars on litigation and administration.[3]

Another example might be the Endangered Species Act, labeled a failure by some because the protection procedures it establishes have been cumbersome and susceptible to politically influenced delay, resulting in few species being listed and inadequate steps being taken to protect those so designated. For others, the act is a failure because it does not permit, except as an extraordinary last resort, explicit consideration of costs, benefits, or other compelling social values. Like CERCLA, the few concrete achievements of the Endangered Species Act are accomplished inefficiently and ineffectively, and the act is unreasonably costly in its effect on the efficiency of the overall economy.[4]

Even the environment's Magna Carta,[5] the National Environmental Policy Act of 1969 (NEPA)—which established the Council on Environmental Quality (CEQ), declared a national policy for the environment, revised the missions of all federal agencies, and originated the environmental impact assessment process—has been labeled ineffective. According to one evaluation, its "significance is hollow and ephemeral, of a figurehead quality."[6] Another judged it to be a "disaster in the environmental movement."[7]

Damning evaluations are not limited to these three illustrative, but hardly representative, environmental policies. A. Myrick Freeman, for example, finds policy failure in estimates that federal water pollution control policy costs in excess of $30 billion per year (if estimated in 1992 dollars), costs that exceed estimated benefits. Paul Portney argues that the annual costs of complying with the Clean Air Act may be in excess of $50 billion and that those costs could be substantially reduced.[8] (Other negative assessments of environmental policies are discussed in chaps. 1 and 9.)

These negative evaluations pose a vexing problem for analysts making them: "How can a program that is inefficient and inequitable survive and even thrive in lean budgetary times?" The cynical answers proffered are several. Such programs continue to have "strong public support—particularly from wealthy and well-educated communities that are more likely to vote and contribute money."[9] Fingers are pointed at lawyers and the news media, and allusions are made to fashion, irrationality, selfishness, ignorance, and unholy political alliances.[10] But there may be deeper reasons that point to problems with the findings of policy failure themselves.

Not all evaluators agree that these and other programs and policies have indeed failed, or mostly failed. For example, some other analysts have found that CERCLA provides "strong incentives to mitigate the effects of past contamination and to prevent future contamination."[11] Similarly, the Endangered Species Act has been found to have "worked rather well" as developers "by and large, have found mitigating strategies to protect species their projects might otherwise eradicate."[12] As for the National Environmental Policy Act, many have pronounced it to have been a profoundly influential piece of legislation. For example, Russell Train, who in the 1970s served first as chairman of CEQ and later as administrator of EPA, has declared, "I can think of no other initiative in our history that had such a broad outreach, that cut across so many functions of government, and that had such a fundamental impact on the way government does business."[13]

Can we make sense of such widely and wildly divergent evaluations? The answer is yes—but it does require some skill and insight. What we need is appreciation for how, in the rush to judgment, the slippery concepts of success and failure may be used in ways, to paraphrase George Orwell, that give the appearance of solidity to pure wind.[14] Both success and failure are variably defined, often implicitly. Claims are often consciously crafted to be consistent with some ideological standpoint and perspective or to support or attack some a priori political position. Such claims, forcefully advanced, may be persuasive in environmental policy debates if definitions of failure are not questioned, criteria of success are not articulated, and the process of evaluation is conceived as a narrow, technical one reserved to experts of one particular stripe.

Yet even evaluations that are intended to be careful, thorough, serious efforts frequently conceptualize and define success simplistically. Thus, claims made by persons with impressive analytic and scholarly credentials are nevertheless often based on a single narrow criterion, limited measures, a short-term perspective, and a social scientific and cultural bias toward findings of no effect. It is *not* a firm scientific conclusion of no effect if careful investigation is unable to link outcomes to a policy—yet it is often interpreted as a finding of policy failure. Obsession with fitting everything into the categories of "success" and "failure" blinds us to the richer, more fruitful possibilities of environmental policy evaluation. In short, the question being answered may have only a slight connection with the simple but broad and demanding question being asked: what is the merit or worth of a policy?

The challenge of identifying environmental policy success and failure has been insufficiently recognized. The problems are partly political, partly theoretical, and partly methodological. Some difficulties are inherent in the business of policy, others in the task of evaluation. Still others stem from a lack of understanding and lack of a broader vision—whether a vision of politics and policy, of the "transdiscipline" of evaluation, or of the environmental *problematique* itself and the ecological complexity of the cumulative, interactive, sleeper, and threshold effects with which environmental policy must contend. Some problems could be overcome with better design of policy research and the allocation of greater resources to evaluation, whereas others demand a reorientation of social expectations regarding policy success and failure. What we need is to cultivate a broader appreciation of how reality is defined by the questions we ask. If nothing succeeds like immediate, unqualified, obvious success, can anything at all succeed? If the kind of evaluation of environmental policy we undertake largely determines our judgments, then indeed we have no choice but to learn to ask better questions.

Kinds and Levels of Evaluation: Structuring the Questions

Evaluation is, simply, "the process of determining the merit, worth and value of things, and evaluations are products of that process."[15] Michael Scriven points out that the intellectual process of evaluation is ubiquitous, permeating all areas of thought and practice. We may say, then, that the evaluation of environmental policy is routinely engaged in by politicians, bureaucrats, journalists, environmentalists, students, and other ordinary citizens. But systematic, disciplined evaluation, or evaluation based on a body of theory, methodology, and analytical skills, is more rare and is typically undertaken by professional analysts who may be employed in academia, bureaucratic agencies, legislatures, lobbying organizations, or consulting firms.

There is a tendency to think of evaluations as an assessment of merit or worth after the fact, soon after a project has been completed, a program executed, a policy implemented. But frequently proposals, plans, and alternatives—mere ideas with no tangible manifestations beyond paper—are also the subjects of anticipatory evaluation at all levels. Evaluation may also be conducted while a project is under way, with an intent to improve it or stop it, or it may be done by historians long after completion.

At least three general categories of systematic environmental policy evaluation can be identified: (1) outcomes, (2) process, and (3) institutional. Each encompasses an enormous variety of evaluation criteria, methods, and practices. But the fundamental differences among the categories hobble discourse about evaluation itself, leading ultimately to arrogant claims about values and flawed arguments about the merit of environmental policies.

Outcomes Evaluation

Traditionally, outcomes evaluation is seen as performing a small number of functions, the most important of which is assessing "the extent to which needs, values, and opportunities have been realized through public action" and making "practical inferences about the degree to which policy problems have been resolved."[16] Outcomes evaluation is based on the seemingly unassailable assumption that policy is purely instrumental, comprising means for producing results or effects—e.g., improved water quality, preserved habitats, reduced waste generation. One difficulty, however, is that outcomes may not be directly or reliably measured, or even measurable. Worse, we often have little understanding of how outcomes are caused. These can be particularly intractable problems for environmental policy where there is little meaningful agreement on what constitutes environmental quality and only spotty monitoring of environmental variables (chap. 6). For example, as Walter Rosenbaum points out, EPA cannot adequately measure the impact of many, if not most, of its programs:

A recent internal agency document asserts that among the twenty-three environmental problem areas for which EPA has some program responsibility, only three appear to be currently monitored with technically appropriate indicators for measuring change. A large segment of [the] Agency's technical staff and scientific advisors believe that many traditional indicators now used to measure environmental quality are unreliable or inappropriate.[17]

In the absence of good evidence about substantive policy consequences, outcomes evaluation must rely on counts or measures of outputs, or immediate administrative actions—such as hazardous waste sites inspections, habitat protection actions, approved species recovery plans, or environmental impact statements. Sometimes even output information is not available and evaluation must be even more tenuously based on quantity and quality of resources used, assuming a definite relation between inputs and outcomes.

The practice of outcomes evaluation is usually directed at one of three levels: (1) the project, (2) the program, or (3) some broader, more encompassing aspect of policy. Much of the literature on outcomes evaluation is directed at only one or another of these levels, although they share theoretical frameworks, analytic tools, and methods and may in fact overlap in practice.

Project evaluation. A project is a time-bound effort that may be a component of a more general continuing program. A great deal of environmental policy evaluation occurs at the project level, where the analytic tools of evaluation are most fully developed, conceptual complications are fewest, and the relationship between systematic evaluation and political action is most apparent. Evaluations of projects are undertaken by virtually all government agencies, by organized private proponents and opponents of projects, and, less often, by dispassionate independent analysts such as academic researchers. Indeed, much project evaluation is mandated and institutionalized, and thus is done routinely in accordance with legal requirements for planning, monitoring, and auditing government projects.

Project evaluations of CERCLA, for example, have focused on the identification, designation, and cleanup of particular hazardous waste sites (projects).[18] These evaluations may address the effectiveness of EPA's management of the investigation and cleanup of an individual site, pointing out deficiencies in site studies, selection of remedies, determination of cleanup levels, imposition of monitoring requirements, and determination of financial responsibilities of remediation. A project evaluation under the Endangered Species Act might assess, say, the Fish and Wildlife Service's project of translocating southern sea otters from the California coast to

San Nicolas island.[19] An environmental impact assessment, mandated by NEPA, is an evaluation of a possible set of actions, usually a project, and is one of several project appraisal techniques used in project planning and decisionmaking. And a particular environmental impact assessment effort might itself be a project subjected to evaluation.

Program evaluation. Evaluation of a project is most often aimed at assessing the merit or worth of that project only, but in many cases it may be a research strategy for evaluating a whole program. In this case the claim is made, explicitly or implicitly, that the project being evaluated represents a class of projects that collectively constitute a government program. Programs usually have official titles or labels and readily identifiable boundaries; typically they are formally created by executives or legislators, have (often poorly) defined goals, and are administered by a single agency or a relatively small, designated group of agencies. Program evaluation, then, refers to either the process or the result of evaluating programs or subprograms, for example, the EPA program for identifying and cleaning up hazardous waste sites.

Program evaluation has a long history, but it only began to be recognized as a field in the 1960s, its growth stimulated by government funding of large-scale evaluations of social programs. The field of program evaluation research expanded further in the 1970s such that it came to be identified, or misidentified, as synonymous with evaluation generally.

Because the doctrine of value-free science was dominant in the social sciences in the 1960s and 1970s, social scientists coming to program evaluation brought this intellectual heritage with them.[20] The result is a dominant model of program evaluation that accepts only the specified a priori goals of a program as legitimate criteria for assessing that program. Identifying program goals is presumed, therefore, to be the first step of any evaluation. Data collection and analysis is then planned to produce empirical evidence of "whether or not programs or policies are achieving their goals and purposes," with effectiveness defined accordingly.[21]

Thus, if the "worthwhile" and "highly laudable goal" of CERCLA is the cleanup of the most dangerous toxic waste sites, then CERCLA is properly evaluated according to how thoroughly, accurately, and rapidly dangerous sites are identified and by the number of such sites actually cleaned up. Numerous evaluations of CERCLA of these sorts have been produced by EPA itself, the General Accounting Office, the Office of Technology Assessment, and nongovernmental consultants and think tanks.[22] Likewise, in a recent scholarly evaluation of the Endangered Species Act, Richard Tobin begins with identifying the "clear and unambiguous" ultimate goal of the legislation—the recovery of all species threatened with extinction.[23] Similarly, a goals-based evaluation of NEPA would begin with the goals apparent in the wording of the act (possibly also considering goals articulated during the legislative history) and then seek empirical evidence bearing on their accomplishment.

Beginning with identifiable goals seems to many professional evaluators and consumers of evaluation to be an obvious and necessary first step. The necessity of basing evaluation on achievement of goals is seldom questioned in published evaluations, and may even be stated baldly as a truism; for example: "The first step in any evaluation involves a determination of goals or objectives."[24]

Yet basing an evaluation primarily on goal accomplishment may make it unnecessarily limited, biased, and narrow. A goals-based evaluation may also look at goals critically, undertake comparisons, analyze unexpected and unintended consequences, and explore ethical dimensions of program activities. But if the evaluation turns on measuring goal achievement, then all of these are likely to be examined only in connection with the accomplishment of identified program goals. The evaluation will still be afflicted with "serious problems such as identifying these goals, handling inconsistencies in them or false assumptions underlying them and changes in them over time, dealing with outcomes that represent shortfall and overrun on the goals, and avoiding the perceptual bias of knowing about them."[25]

Programs seldom have clear, consistent, and realistic goals that are explicitly stated, and programs are rarely able to achieve whatever vague, contradictory, and idealistic goals that can be identified. Statutory goals often express wishes at variance with the inevitable. Consequently, a goal-based approach to evaluation is almost always biased toward a conclusion of policy failure. The conclusions of Tobin regarding the U.S. endangered species program, for example, are typical:

> The program can point to few successes, at least when measured against its statutory goal. Only a handful of listed species have been recovered after more than two decades of effort and expenditure. Of these successes, few are due to program-related activities. During the program's life, in contrast, a larger number of species [have] become extinct.[26]

The state of the art in program evaluation, however, has progressed far beyond this simplistic goal-achievement approach.[27] The outcomes of programs can be evaluated according to independently determined needs or validated standards, the sources of which might be legal, moral and ethical, esthetic, economic, logical, political, scientific, managerial, technical, social, or ecological. Evaluation standards might be derived from intrinsic values (integrity, sustainability, creativity, autonomy, dignity, distribution), professional standards, or the value of something to an institution or collective.[28]

Perhaps most common non-goal-based evaluations are by economists, who assess programs using such values as efficiency, cost-effectiveness, and cost minimization—all criteria promoted by the evaluators independently of the explicit goals of the program being evaluated. Such evaluations frequently find environmental programs to be failures. Economic-based evaluations, for example, have tended to find policy failure built into CERCLA, which provides few incentives to minimize costs or to relate marginal expenditure of dollars to marginal benefits. Overall costs of cleaning up toxic waste sites are high and the benefits low as compared with other programs for reducing environmental risk. NEPA has been assessed according to the transaction costs of producing and circulating environmental impact statements versus the benefits of risk reduction. Endangered species preservation has been evaluated by economists using innovative methods to determine the value in economic terms of species preservation and ecological diversity compared with the costs of doing so. Not surprisingly, the costs have often been found to far exceed the economically measurable benefits.

Alternatively, endangered species preservation might be evaluated according to ethical commitments and moral obligations that a program seeks to honor, evaluations that find achievements in entirely different outcomes evidence. NEPA might be assessed in light of the organizational and managerial changes it stimulated in bureaucratic agencies. The scientific foundation of hazardous waste site cleanup might be evaluated.

Of course, nothing prevents the use of multiple values and criteria in evaluations, in which "identifiable goals" are only one source of values and "goal achievement" just one of many valid criteria. This is an approach recommended by many evaluation theorists. Even the General Accounting Office, which has become the major evaluation agency of the U.S. government, uses a checklist for program evaluation that lists ten criteria, of which only one is goal achievement.[29]

Still, however broadly evaluation is conceived, program evaluation is circumscribed by its focus on programs. The usefulness of program evaluation is thus limited to management issues and other immediate concerns rather than broader concerns of how a political system can take action to address social issues. Quite often the desired subject of evaluation is considerably broader than, or just different from, a formally bounded government program, requiring a broader level of evaluation.

Policy performance evaluation. Project evaluation, program evaluation, and policy performance evaluation (usually just called "policy analysis") overlap considerably in practice and in the literature on each, as they share a number of theoretical and methodological concerns. Project evaluation and program evaluation are in fact kinds of policy analysis. But policies or potential policies are often more than mere collections of projects or coordinated programs, and policy analysis may need to be more encompassing.

Policy performance evaluation tends to be conceptually organized around problem analysis and problem solving and is not necessarily bounded by formal program descriptions. If public policy is understood as an intended and actual course of action by government, then a policy might entail multiple whole programs or parts of many programs, or the interaction of rules and programs. It might have a substantial symbolic component. Policy analysis then usefully addresses strategies, issues, or problems.

For example, unlike program evaluation that would focus on evaluating CERCLA or some part of CERCLA, a policy analysis might address the problem of hazardous wastes and the interrelated policies for addressing that problem, which would include among others CERCLA, the Resource Conservation and Recovery Act, the Safe Drinking Water Act, and the Nuclear Waste Policy Act.[30] Or, alternatively, a policy analysis might address some feature that characterizes several related policies or programs, such as the provisions for criminal penalties found in CERCLA, the Clean Air Act, the Clean Water Act, the Safe Drinking Water Act, the Toxic Substances Control Act, and the Federal Insecticide, Fungicide, and Rodenticide Act.[31] Likewise, rather than a focus on NEPA per se, a policy analyst might examine environmental impact assessment as a particular policy innovation; rather than evaluate the Endangered Species Act alone, a policy analyst might consider it as one component of a larger policy to protect wildlife.[32]

Much policy performance evaluation, like project and program evaluation, is dominated by what Giandomenico Majone calls the "received view" of policy analysis or what Allen Schick and William Dunn call an "analycentric perspective."[33] Underlying this approach to evaluation are several assumptions, among others, that: (1) politics and policy are primarily about problem solving, (2) policymaking is synonymous with decisionmaking, (3) optimal policy is achieved only through application of rationality, which is purely intellectual, utilitarian, and instrumentalist, and (4) policymaking is instrumentalist, concerned primarily with outcomes or end results.

Evaluation of policy for cleanup of hazardous waste sites would then assume that hazardous waste sites can be objectively defined as a "real" problem, that policy consists of "big" decisions about how the problem should be solved or addressed, that any policy must have as its sole aim cleaning up waste sites to an optimal level at an optimal speed and cost, and that the only way to arrive at policies producing the best outcomes is through rational analysis of means.

Not surprisingly, evaluations of CERCLA using any of these assumptions find current policy to be a near-complete failure. But each of these assumptions is problematic—politics and policy may only secondarily be concerned with problem solving, policymaking entails a great deal more than decisions, policymaking is partly nonrational and also involves multiple rationalities, and policymaking is concerned with a great deal more than substantive outcomes. The validity and applicability of policy evaluation based on such a model are more limited than is commonly appreciated.

As a consequence, not all evaluations by policy analysts focus on policy performance alone. Policy analyses also frequently attempt to contribute to the clarification and critique of values that underlie policy design and implementation itself, as well as to offer arguments for redefining and restructuring problems. For example, EPA's own analyses of efforts to clean up hazardous waste sites have contributed to the agency's attempts to reorder its strategies and priorities in implementing CERCLA and with respect to environmental policy generally.[34]

But to go beyond a problem-solving conception of policy evaluation, and to forgo insistence on tangible, measurable outcomes as the sole basis for assessing the merit or worth of environmental policy, requires a whole reorientation of evaluative framework. Policy process evaluation offers a framework quite different from those of outcomes evaluation.

Policy Process Evaluation

Simply assessing whether outcomes, or often inputs and outputs, are satisfactory does not always tell very much about what ought to be done (chap. 11). Majone notes that "in many situations this type of evaluation gives policymakers, program managers, and interested citizens very little information upon which to act." What is missing in this "black box" approach to evaluation is information about what produced the observed outcomes, and how.[35]

Policy process evaluations are assessments of the merit or worth of policy processes themselves. The instrumental, utilitarian purposes and accomplishments of policy are incidental values in process evaluation. What is central, in this view, are the values of the processes used to define problems, set agendas, formulate alternatives, select actions, and govern implementation. The merit or worth of policy processes may be judged according to many criteria, such as responsiveness, coordination, legitimacy, leadership, participation, efficiency, representation, fairness, integration, practicality, and pluralism.

Because evaluation is itself a political activity and part of any policy process, evaluation of policy processes may focus on claims made regarding the role of evaluation in policymaking. A number of scholars have offered cogent critiques of the idea that rational analysis should determine how policy is made. Most influential, perhaps, has been Charles Lindblom, who has argued in several books and articles that real world public decisions cannot be made purely by rational analysis and evaluation and moreover that this would be undesirable even if it were possible.[36]

Lindblom's criticisms call into question the basic assumptions and promises of the analycentric approach, arguing that the policy process is essentially one of political and social interaction, to which formal analyses and evaluations may contribute but for which they cannot substitute. In the policy process, with its diversity of interests, it is not possible for goals to be clear, precise, and agreed on in advance. To strive unnecessarily for clarity, specificity, and agreement with regard to goals is in fact to invite unresolvable conflict, limit opportunities, and risk paralysis. In the real political world, means-ends analysis always gets turned on its head as means and ends are closely intertwined—objectives evolve as agreement is sought on means.[37]

Even the orientation of policy analysis toward finding solutions to problems does not fit the real political world terribly well. Policy does not always, or even usually, begin with a problem. Much policymaking is not problem directed. In fact, policy entrepreneurs, like citizens, often have solutions in mind as they look for problems to which they may be applied. An example of this was the initial drafting of CERCLA by EPA, when the public controversy over the Love Canal site from 1978 through 1980 was seized as an opportunity for EPA to implement a "public health" strategy for strengthening its legislative base. According to Landy, Roberts, and Thomas:

> Comparing the chronology of Love Canal with that of the Superfund legislation makes it clear that the former did not cause the latter. . . . Except for the very first national attention it received in the summer of 1978, each subsequent wave of publicity appeared to serve less as the source of new initiatives than as the occasion for mobilizing support for those already underway. To find the source of Superfund, one must look within EPA itself.[38]

If, as Deborah Stone contends, the essence of policymaking is not the production of problem-solving policies per se but instead a struggle over ideas, then evaluation of processes—processes that give rise to a policy and then to new processes created by the policy—may provide the kind of information most needed by citizens and policymakers as they "struggle over the criteria for classification, the boundaries of categories, and the definition of ideals that guide the way people behave."[39]

Similarly, Majone argues for a dialectic conception of policy analysis that has less to do with problem solving than with the process of argument and the aim of persuasion: "Professional evaluation is only a small part of the general process of criticism and appraisal of public policies to which all politically active members of a democratic community contribute in different but equally useful ways." From this perspective, because of inescapable disagreement about the meaningfulness, fairness, or acceptability of evaluative criteria, "much evaluation analysis is really concerned with the merits of various standard-setting proposals rather than with the application of particular standards of merit to a given program."[40] All environmental policies, de facto, are about determining and expressing values, setting norms, and problem definition, as are all environmental policy evaluations.

For example, NEPA explicitly seeks to change the substantive values by which all agency decisions would henceforth be made, by declaring norms and precepts that are binding on all the policies, regulations, and public laws of the United States. NEPA further mandates certain processes that must be followed in making decisions (e.g., "utilize a systematic, interdisciplinary approach which will insure the integrated use of the natural and social sciences and the environmental design arts in planning and in decisionmaking"), thereby fundamentally changing procedural norms of policymaking. Much of what passes for evaluation of NEPA is really a contribution to a policy debate about the merits of these policy standards.

Likewise, the Endangered Species Act is a product of a decades-old debate about nature and wild animals that has progressed from ideas to organizations to public policy.[41] Bureaucratic actions under this legislation provide a catalyst and forum for further evaluative debate.

Process evaluation is crucial to assessing CERCLA as well. CERCLA profoundly restructured hazardous waste policy processes around liability determination and right-to-know rules. The liability for the costs of hazardous waste site cleanups can no longer be easily evaded by corporate restructuring, poor record keeping, a legal necessity to prove harm, or even bankruptcy or foreclosure. Certain kinds of information about potentially hazardous substances must now be made available by governments and businesses. Whole new political, financial, legal, and managerial incentives—and processes—have been created, thus recasting both the debate *within* hazardous waste policy and *about* hazardous waste policy.

Moreover, public policy processes "have an intrinsic moral element which exists apart from their instrumental value."[42] The Endangered Species Act, for example, can be said to be good because it codifies a collective ethical judgment and declares a responsibility, and because in doing so it creates a cognitive dissonance between moral commitment and political action that forces perpetual reconsideration of both ethics and action.

Dialogue is an end in itself, as is public participation. Yet environmental policy cannot ever be only about debate, participation, and problem definition. For one thing, process evaluation does not replace the purposes served by outcomes evaluation. Substantive values ought not be neglected. As William Gormley points out, "If we confine our attention to such values as democracy, accountability, coordination and administrative efficiency, we forfeit the opportunity to design institutions that promote other important goals."[43] Moreover, both process evaluation and outcomes evaluation may direct attention away from evaluation of the institutional contexts of public policy. But it is only in relation to institutional transformation that any lasting merit or worth of environmental policies can be ascertained, and it is the transformation of institutions to be ecologically rational and sustainable that poses the ultimate test for environmental policy.

Institutional Evaluation

Institutional evaluation assesses how processes work and outcomes are produced within a larger institutional framework created in part by policies and within which policies are made and remade. In short, what is evaluated is "political architecture,"[44] architecture that influences outcomes, structures processes, and constructs and elaborates meaning. Institutional analysis, according to March and Olsen, sees policy as "conspicuously influenced by the institutional structure within which politics occurs."[45] Without denying the importance of both the social context of politics and the motives of individual actors, institutional analysis posits a more independent role for political institutions as they define the framework within which politics takes place. Thus, institutional evaluation uses a broad range of procedural criteria and substantive criteria, but must also wrestle with assessing the social creation of reality. Institutional evaluation requires an appreciation for the ways that political action is governed primarily by rules rather than by rational calculation and for how policy-making constructs meaning through institutions.

March and Olsen argue that much of the behavior observable in political institutions is rule based. By rules they mean routines, procedures, conventions, roles, strategies, and organizational forms, as well as "the beliefs, paradigms, codes, cultures, and knowledge that surround, support, elaborate, and contradict those roles and routines."[46] Rules are independent of individual actors and are capable of surviving considerable turnover of individuals. Rules are followed even when it is not obviously in the narrow self-interest of the person doing so. Most choices of action are governed by identifying a normatively appropriate behavior, rather than by utilitarian, instrumental, rational calculation of values, alternatives, and anticipated consequences as assumed by the decisionist model of politics and policy analysis.

Institutions shape politics not only by reducing chaos and bringing order through rules but also through the construction and elaboration of meaning. Political values and preferences are not independent of political institutions. We construct our political expectations, preferences, policy experience, and interpretations of actions *within* political institutions. Through institution-based politics, individuals also develop their identities and their sense of purpose, direction, and belonging. Meanwhile, institutions in part create their own environments, as the actions of each political actor become part of the environments of others and each reacts to the others.

Any policy change that is more than superficial, then, entails institutional change. Even though transformations cannot be controlled with any great precision, change in a desired direction can be initiated intentionally by exploiting processes for mundane adaptiveness, by exploiting the incompleteness of rules and routines, and, less predictably, by administering some kind of radical shock to an institution or political system.

What are the implications of this institutional perspective for evaluating environmental policy? For the most part, environmental policy analysts have been unimaginative in analyzing the institutional frameworks that are created by environmental policies and within which policies are made as they are implemented. A blindered focus on action and outcomes, or for that matter on process, leads policy evaluators to find policy failure everywhere, without any careful analysis of the appropriate criteria for evaluating institutions, much less integrative institutions.

If, for example, CERCLA is analyzed in terms of changes it has wrought in rules, routines, and roles, as well as the beliefs, cultures, and knowledge that surround and support those roles and routines, then (in conjunction with the Safe Drinking Water Act, the Toxic Substances Control Act, and the Resource Conservation and Recovery Act) it can be seen to have been immensely consequential and likely to become more so. Although not mentioned in the legislation, CERCLA can be credited with causing the following institutional transformations, among others, over a very short time: establishment of extensive separation, collection, and recycling programs by state and local governments across the United States; profound changes in commercial lending practices and norms; reversal of longstanding packaging policies by McDonald's and other marketers of fast food; and growth in environmental auditing as an accepted good business practice.

These profound transformations were not specified as program goals by drafters of the original legislation, nor do they solve "the" problem of cleaning up existing environmental degradation. But waste reduction, hazardous waste disposal, landfills, and recycling all mean something different now throughout American society, and different rules for handling wastes have been quickly entrenched. Indeed, this set of legislation has begun a wide-ranging and complex process of institutional change that extends beyond the borders of the United States. These kinds of consequences of policy are overlooked by traditional outcomes or process evaluation, whatever the valuation criteria used.

Likewise, only institutional evaluation can do justice to assessing the merit or worth of NEPA. Outcomes assessment of a law that makes a broad policy declaration and mandates a planning and decision process is an extraordinarily difficult task, one unlikely to produce any unambiguous evidence. Given our inability to say what would have been if not for NEPA, outcomes evaluations could tell us little after the first few years of its implementation. Most evaluations instead focus on process, namely the environmental impact assessment process mandated by NEPA, seen purely as a set of mandated procedures unconnected with substantive purposes and institutional transformations. To do so, however, is to evaluate an eviscerated, truncated requirement that has only the obvious purpose of improving decisionmaking by increasing the information available.

Such evaluations are certain to miss the most important consequences of institutionalized environmental impact assessment, seriously misunderstanding how such a policy works or does not work.

In fact, environmental impact assessment systems do not work merely or even primarily by changing informational inputs to political decisionmaking. NEPA shapes bureaucratic politics and economic development politics through the construction and elaboration of meaning and the establishment of new policy rules. Comprehending the significance of NEPA and environmental impact assessment requires appreciation for the complexity of the ways that choices are shaped, channeled, learned, reasoned, and structured before they are officially made:

> [NEPA] requires consideration of particular sets of factual premises (ecological especially) and otherwise precarious values, and it demands the kinds of reasoning associated with those values and factual premises. It changes patterns of relationships among organizations and among individuals inside and outside of organizations. It creates powerful incentives, formal and informal, that thereafter force a great deal of learning and self-regulation upon individual and organizational actors. And it provides opportunities for individuals to develop and affirm environmental values and to press for innovative adaptation of structures and processes to a changing political world.[47]

The analyst who looks only for dramatic direct effects is likely to be disappointed. NEPA must be understood as meta-policy, or a policy on policymaking, and as such must be understood and evaluated on an institutional level. NEPA imbeds ecological rationality—a way of thinking about actions, organizations, and ultimate ends and values—in political institutions, and its worth or merit must be evaluated with regard to that institutional transformation.[48]

Opportunities for useful institutional evaluation in environmental policy extend well beyond analysis of existing policies; they exist in policy design as well. Institutional evaluation is based on analysis of how institutions can produce outcomes indirectly. It requires insight into and appreciation for how changes in rules can in turn force further changes—which can be only imperfectly anticipated—in other rules and the interpretation of reality, thus fundamentally transforming an institution. It also demands considerable sophistication from the users and consumers of evaluation. In public policy debates in which glibness, simple intuitive appeal, and brevity make an argument more persuasive, institutional evaluation is inherently disadvantaged.

Evaluating Environmental Policy Evaluation

There is no need to argue that one level or kind of evaluation is superior to the others. Nor does it make sense to think of combining them into one grand, all-purpose evaluation model. Each is appropriate to different kinds of questions, and each may be more or less appropriate for different kinds of policies. But there is a serious imbalance in the kinds of evaluations of environmental policy that we have sought and done over the past quarter-century. If current environmental policies are our response to the thoroughgoing, fundamental challenge that the environmental *problematique* poses for the institutions of modern society, then finding out if objective outcome indicators have changed or whether our processes have become more participatory can only tell a part of what we really want to know. Only institutional evaluation looks at the change in the system that environmental policy may have effected and attempts to appraise its merit. Yet institutional evaluation may be critically dependent on outcomes and process evaluations that provide indispensable insights and through which invaluable evidence is generated.

The outcomes evaluations most needed, however, are those based on complex and expensive monitoring systems that will require considerable, repeated, stable investment of resources over long periods of time. This kind of investment has not been politically attractive to either politicians or a public eager to find new problems, make quick judgments, and apply easy solutions. Unfortunately, easy evaluations are likely to be about as useful to us in the long run as easy policy answers to what are patently tangled, wicked environmental policy problems. Because of their strong bias toward findings of no impact, simple outcomes evaluations almost always play into the hands of the do-nothing crowd and the undo-what-we've-done-right wingers. The political effect is to retard environmental policy progress by arming critics with *apparently* rigorous ammunition.

What can we learn from our experience in evaluating environmental policies that could help us to do better? That is, to help us to do better evaluations and, informed by these evaluations, to design better policies? There is no reason to believe that we are necessarily condemned to failure, either of policies or evaluations, although we may yet prove to be damned by our unrealistic expectations for policy success, especially in the extraordinarily complex and still young field of environmental policy. Unadulterated environmental policy failure is actually quite rare, in spite of the impression offered by the popular press and the cautious, dismal conclusions of untold numbers of policy evaluators. We must begin to appreciate that unambiguous policy failure is, like unalloyed success, a rare phenomenon, leaving us most of the time trying to make sense of a very mixed and muddy picture of the policy world. To make sense of this world often means assessing the merit or worth of arbitrarily sectioned pieces of it, but it is not desirable that we always go one step further and force our assessments into simplistic categories such as "success" and "failure."

The difficulties of good evaluation, however, are not an excuse for living with bad or mediocre policy without attempting to judge it or improve it. Clearly desirable are multiple evaluations, done with a keen appreciation of the strengths and limitations of each approach and a frank recognition of the advantages of others. As Majone argues, a shared level of understanding and appreciation of multiple perspectives that is more than the sum of separate evaluations ought to be possible. There is "no reason why the larger understanding of public policy to which these separate perspectives are contributing should remain forever invisible to the different evaluators, as the coral atoll is to the polyp."[49]

At every level, then, we must somehow overcome the widespread and dangerous affection for quick and simple judgments. Evaluation, particularly environmental policy evaluation, is a difficult and challenging business, and we must begin to take it more seriously than we do. Politics, including environmental politics, is truly messy, which is perhaps an unfortunate virtue but, nevertheless, a given. There is little point to bemoaning the failure of politicians to provide clear, precise, and easily evaluated goals for programs and policies. Aside from the debatable point of whether such goals are desirable, they are seldom possible even with the best of intentions. Programs, policies, processes, and institutions, particularly environmental ones, are messy things, and environmental policy evaluation must develop richer theories, concepts, and methodologies to provide useful information for further policymaking in spite of that messiness.

Our addiction to simple judgments will be no easier to shake than our compulsive affection for simple, complete answers to complex sets of policy problems. Environmental policy, whether dealing with hazardous wastes, endangered species, or the impacts of government actions, addresses policy problems and issues with which government does not have long experience. We ought, for example, to have some sympathy for a remark of an EPA official responsible for implementing CERCLA: "It took forty years to build an interstate highway system, but we are expected in only four years to clean up hazardous waste sites that were 100 years in the making."[50] Because our current policies have not yet solved our environmental problems, and no true solution is in sight, does not necessarily mean that doing nothing would be a better choice.

In conclusion, then, the implications are not that we can learn how to engineer real solutions to our policy problems, or that we can learn to create policy processes that engage us in some ideal way in search and interaction. Nor is good environmental policy, or governance generally, impossible. But we have become accustomed to thinking about policy as a problem of engineering or production on the one hand, and policymaking as a game or drama on the other, and we have sought to understand and direct it accordingly. These are all inappropriate metaphors, and the models we base on them are all fatally flawed. Policy, especially environmental policy, is more a matter of gardening than engineering or building; of cultivating than participating or acting.

Like gardening, policymaking involves neither playing nor controlling but rather the constant discovery and shaping of potential. Environmental policy cannot be constructed in a mechanistic way to precise specifications, and certainly more is at stake than how the game is played or whether a particular policy contest is won or lost. Policy is a result of organic interactive processes that can be partially understood and directed, processes that ultimately are dependent on an institutional environment being changed by policy. Old policies contribute to the soil in which new policies are sown and nurtured. Even outcomes and process evaluation of environmental policy, both badly needed, should be seen as aids in starting, pruning, and weeding policies given the existing political landscape, not as means to solve problems once and for all or as ways to devise a utopian policy system.

Accordingly, success and failure, as traditionally understood in policy evaluation, are concepts of very limited applicability or usefulness. They are wholly dependent on their terms of reference for meaning, and dangerous in their potential for abuse. At best, they allow us to think too simplistically about the value, merit, or worth of our environmental policies, indeed all our public policies, and what they accomplish. It makes little sense to call NEPA, CERCLA, or the Endangered Species Act—or environmental policy generally since 1968—a failure, although disappointments abound and should be recognized. But success is a term few should be comfortable with either. Both success and failure suggest a level of ignorance and confidence that is unjustified. Richer yet more modest judgments, and more of them, are needed and need to be used if we are to cultivate more reliably fruitful environmental policy in the 1990s and beyond. In this sense, success can have a more organic meaning, as "a process, a quality of mind and way of being, an outgoing affirmation of life."[51] The challenge of environmental policy in the 1990s is to secure the continuity of this kind of success.

Notes

For helpful criticisms and suggestions I thank Michael E. Kraft, Norman J. Vig, Walter F. Baber, Priya Kurian, Ian McChesney, Ton Bührs, and Bronwyn Hayward. The epigraph is taken from Caroline Thomas Harnsberger, ed., *Mark Twain at Your Fingertips* (New York: Beechhurst, 1948), 459.

1. Helen M. Ingram and Dean E. Mann, "Policy Failure: An Issue Deserving Analysis," in *Why Policies Succeed or Fail*, ed. Helen M. Ingram and Dean E. Mann (Beverly Hills: Sage, 1980).
2. Daniel Mazmanian and David Morell, *Beyond Superfailure: America's Toxics Policy for the 1990s* (Boulder: Westview, 1992).
3. Roger C. Dower, "Hazardous Wastes," in *Public Policies for Environmental Protection*, ed. Paul R. Portney (Washington, D.C.: Resources for the Future, 1990), 151-194; Bruce Yandle, *The Political Limits of Environmental Regulation: Tracking the Unicorn* (Westport, Conn.: Quorum Books, 1989); Daniel E. Koshland, Jr.,

"Toxic Chemicals and Toxic Laws," *Science* 253 (August 30, 1991): 949; John A. Hird, "Environmental Policy and Equity: The Case of Superfund" (Paper delivered at the annual meeting of the Midwest Political Science Association, Chicago, April 9, 1992).

4. These kinds of arguments are summarized in Richard J. Tobin, *The Expendable Future: U.S. Politics and the Protection of Biological Diversity* (Durham, N.C.: Duke University Press, 1990); Steven Lewis Yaffee, *Prohibitive Policy: Implementing the Federal Endangered Species Act* (Cambridge: MIT Press, 1982).

5. M. C. Blum, "The National Environmental Policy Act at Twenty: A Preface," *Environmental Law* 20 (1990): 477-483.

6. William Renwick, "The Eclipse of NEPA as Environmental Policy," *Environmental Management* 12, no. 3 (1988): 267-272.

7. Sally K. Fairfax, "A Disaster in the Environmental Movement," *Science* 199 (February 17, 1978): 743-748.

8. A. Myrick Freeman III, "Water Pollution Policy," and Paul R. Portney, "Air Pollution Policy," in *Public Policies for Environmental Protection*, ed. Paul R. Portney (Washington, D.C.: Resources for the Future, 1990), 27-149.

9. Both quotes are from Hird, "Environmental Policy and Equity," 15, 17.

10. For example, Yandle, *Political Limits;* Koshland, "Toxic Chemicals"; Mark Trumball, "Costs of Superfund Lawsuits Stir Up Calls for Change," *Christian Science Monitor*, May 11, 1992, 7.

11. Terry Dinan and F. Reed Johnson, "Effects of Hazardous Waste Risks on Property Transfers: Legal Liability vs. Direct Regulation," *Natural Resources Journal* 30 (Summer 1990): 527.

12. Mark Sagoff, *The Economy of the Earth: Philosophy, Law, and the Environment* (New York: Cambridge University Press, 1988), 76.

13. Robert V. Bartlett, "Impact Assessment as a Policy Strategy," in *Policy Through Impact Assessment: Institutionalized Analysis as a Policy Strategy*, ed. Robert V. Bartlett (Westport, Conn.: Greenwood, 1989), 2.

14. George Orwell, "Politics and the English Language," *Horizon* 13 (April 1946): 252-265.

15. Michael Scriven, *Evaluation Thesaurus*, 4th ed. (Newbury Park, Calif.: Sage, 1991), 1, 139.

16. William N. Dunn, *Public Policy Analysis: An Introduction* (Englewood Cliffs, N.J.: Prentice-Hall, 1981), 341.

17. Walter A. Rosenbaum, "Curing Regulatory Incapacity at EPA: What Can Policy Studies Add to Reilly's Rosary?" (Paper delivered at a workshop on environmental politics and policy at the annual meeting of the American Political Science Association, Washington, D.C., August 28, 1991), 4.

18. For example, Environmental Protection Agency, *Case Studies—Remedial Response at Hazardous Waste Sites*, EPA-540-540/2-84-002 (Washington, D.C.: Office of Emergency and Remedial Response, Environmental Protection Agency, 1984).

19. William Booth, "Reintroducing a Political Animal," *Science* 241 (July 8, 1988): 156-158.

20. Scriven, *Evaluation Thesaurus*, 27-32.

21. Richard A. Berk and Peter H. Rossi, *Thinking About Program Evaluation* (Newbury Park, Calif.: Sage, 1990), 15. See also Peter H. Rossi and Howard E. Freeman, *Evaluation: A Systematic Approach*, 4th ed. (Newbury Park, Calif.: Sage, 1989).

22. For example, General Accounting Office, *Superfund: Extent of Nation's Potential Hazardous Waste Problem Still Unknown*, GAO/RCED-88-44 (Washington, D.C.: General Accounting Office, 1987); Office of Technology Assessment, *Coming Clean: Superfund Problems Can Be Solved* (Washington, D.C.: U.S. Government Printing Office, 1989); Environmental Protection Agency, *Superfund Advisory* (Washington, D.C.: Environmental Protection Agency, 1989); Jan Paul Acton and

Lloyd S. Dixon, *Superfund and Transaction Costs: The Experiences of Insurers and Very Large Industrial Firms* (Santa Monica, Calif.: RAND, Institute for Civil Justice, 1992).

23. Tobin, *Expendable Future.*
24. Ibid., 27.
25. Scriven, *Evaluation Thesaurus,* 179.
26. Tobin, *Expendable Future,* 257.
27. Scriven, *Evaluation Thesaurus,* 41.
28. Ibid., 179-182, 207.; Michael Quinn Patton, *Practical Evaluation* (Beverly Hills, Calif.: Sage, 1982), 44-47.
29. Scriven, *Evaluation Thesaurus,* 174.
30. Mazmanian and Morell, *Beyond Superfailure.*
31. T. H. Tietenberg, ed., *Innovation in Environmental Policy: Economic and Legal Aspects of Recent Developments in Environmental Enforcement and Liability* (Aldershot, Eng.: Edward Elgar, 1992).
32. Peter Wathern, ed., *Environmental Impact Assessment: Theory and Practice* (London: Unwin Hyman, 1988); Robert V. Bartlett, ed., *Policy Through Impact Assessment: Institutionalized Analysis as a Policy Strategy* (Westport, Conn.: Greenwood, 1989); William R. Mangun, ed., symposium on Wildlife Conservation and Public Policy, *Policy Studies Journal* 19, nos. 3-4 (1991).
33. Giandomenico Majone, "Analyzing the Public Sector: Shortcomings of Current Approaches—Part A. Policy Science," in *Guidance, Control, and Evaluation in the Public Sector,* ed. Franz-Xaver Kaufman, Giandomenico Majone, and Vincent Ostrom (New York: Walter de Gruyter, 1986), 61-70; Dunn, *Public Policy Analysis,* 21-31; Allen Schick, "Beyond Analysis," *Public Administration Review* 37 (1977): 258-263.
34. U.S. Environmental Protection Agency, *Unfinished Business: A Comparative Assessment of Environmental Problems* (Washington, D.C.: Environmental Protection Agency, 1987); U.S. Environmental Protection Agency, Science Advisory Board, *Reducing Risk: Setting Priorities and Strategies for Environmental Protection* (Washington, D.C.: Environmental Protection Agency, 1990).
35. Giandomenico Majone, *Evidence, Argument, and Persuasion in the Policy Process* (New Haven: Yale University Press, 1989), 173; see also Michael Quinn Patton, *Utilization-Focused Evaluation,* 2d ed. (Newbury Park, Calif.: Sage, 1986), 129-131.
36. Charles E. Lindblom, "The Science of Muddling Through," *Public Administration Review* 19 (1959): 79-88; David Braybrooke and Charles E. Lindblom, *A Strategy of Decision: Policy Evaluation as a Social Process* (New York: Free Press, 1963); Charles E. Lindblom, "Still Muddling, Not Yet Through," *Public Administration Review* 39 (November-December 1979): 517-526; Charles E. Lindblom, *Inquiry and Change* (New Haven: Yale University Press, 1990).
37. Robert Gregory, "Political Rationality or 'Incrementalism'? Charles E. Lindblom's Enduring Contribution to Public Policy Making Theory," *Policy and Politics* 17 (1989): 139-153.
38. Marc K. Landy, Marc J. Roberts, and Stephen R. Thomas, *The Environmental Protection Agency: Asking the Wrong Questions* (New York: Oxford University Press, 1990), 140.
39. Deborah A. Stone, *Policy Paradox and Political Reason* (Glenview, Ill.: Scott Foresman, 1988), 7.
40. Majone, *Evidence, Argument, and Persuasion in the Policy Process,* 168-169.
41. Thomas R. Dunlap, *Saving America's Wildlife* (Princeton, N.J.: Princeton University Press, 1988).
42. Richard I. Hofferbert, *The Reach and Grasp of Policy Analysis: Comparative Views of the Craft* (Tuscaloosa: University of Alabama Press, 1990), 156.

43. William T. Gormley, Jr., "Institutional Policy Analysis: A Critical Review," *Journal of Policy Analysis and Management* 6 (Winter 1987): 156-157.
44. Charles Anderson, *Statecraft: An Introduction to Political Choice and Judgment* (New York: John Wiley, 1977).
45. March and Olsen, *Rediscovering Institutions: The Organizational Basis of Politics* (New York: Free Press, 1989), 16. Most of the next four paragraphs draw heavily from March and Olsen, 17-18, 39, 46-48, 58-65.
46. Ibid., 22.
47. Robert V. Bartlett, "Ecological Reason in Administration: Environmental Impact Assessment and Administrative Theory," in *Managing Leviathan: Environmental Politics and the Administrative State* (Peterborough [Ont.]: Broadview, 1990), 92; see also Robert V. Bartlett, "Rationality and the Logic of the National Environmental Policy Act," *Environmental Professional* 8 (1986): 105-111.
48. Robert V. Bartlett, "Ecological Rationality: Reason and Environmental Policy," *Environmental Ethics* 8 (Fall 1986): 221-239; James P. Boggs, "Procedural vs. Substantive in NEPA Law: Cutting the Gordian Knot," *Environmental Professional* 15 (1993): 25-33.
49. Majone, *Evidence, Argument, and Persuasion*, 9.
50. Not an exact quote; remark reported on "Morning Edition," National Public Radio, September 25, 1991.
51. Alex Noble, "In Touch With the Present," *Christian Science Monitor*, March 6, 1979.

9

Economics, Incentives, and Environmental Regulation

A. Myrick Freeman III

The environment is a scarce resource that contributes to human welfare in a variety of ways. It is the source of the basic means of life support—clean air and clean water. It provides the means for growing food. It is the source of minerals and other raw materials that go into the production of the goods and services that support modern society's standard of living. The environment can be used for a variety of recreational activities such as hiking, fishing, and observing wildlife. And it is the source of amenities and esthetic experiences, including scenic beauty that elicits our awe at the wonder of nature. Finally, and unfortunately in some respects, the environment can be used as a place to deposit the wastes from the production and consumption activities of the modern-day economy. It is this latter use, along with conversion of natural environments to more intensely managed agricultural ecosystems or to residential and commercial development, that gives rise to today's environmental problems.

To say that the environment is a scarce resource means that it cannot provide all of the desired quantities of all of its services at the same time. Greater use of one type of environmental service usually means that less of some other type of service is available. Thus, the use of the environment involves trade-offs. Increasing the life-sustaining or amenity-yielding services it provides may require reducing the use of the waste-receiving capacities of the environment or cutting back on development, and vice versa.

Economics is about how to manage the activities of people, including the way they use the environment, to meet their material needs and wants in the face of scarcity. Environmental protection and the control of pollution are costly activities. Society wishes to protect the environment and reduce pollution presumably because the value it places on the environment's life-sustaining and -enhancing services is greater than the value it places on what it has to give up. Devoting more of society's scarce resources of labor, capital, and administrative and technical skills to controlling pollution necessarily means that fewer of these resources are available to do other things that are also valued by society.

The protection of a particular environmental resource to preserve amenities or wildlife habitat typically precludes other uses of that resource, such as mining of minerals and production of forest products. The costs of environmental protection are the value of these alternative uses that are forgone and the labor, capital, materials, and energy that are used up in controlling the flow of wastes to the environment. Because pollution control and environmental protection are costly in this sense, it is in society's best interest to be economical in its decisions in these areas.

There are two senses in which this is true. First, society needs to be economical about its environmental objectives. If Americans are to make the most of their endowment of scarce resources, they should compare what they receive from devoting resources to pollution control and environmental protection with what they give up by taking resources from other uses. They should undertake more pollution control activities only if the results are worth more in some sense than the values they forgo by diverting resources from other uses such as producing food, shelter, and comfort. This is basically what benefit-cost analysis is about.

Second, whatever pollution control targets are chosen, the means of achieving them should minimize the costs of meeting these targets. Using more resources than are absolutely necessary to achieve pollution control objectives is wasteful. Yet many environmental protection and pollution control policies are wasteful in just this sense. One of the major contributions of economic analysis to environmental policy is that it reveals when and how these policies can be made more cost-effective.

In the next section of this chapter, I will describe how benefit-cost analysis can be used to decide how far to go in the direction of environmental protection. Also discussed are recent applications of benefit-cost analysis to environmental policy decisions and contributions that this economic approach to environmental policymaking might make in the future.

In the third section I will briefly describe the basic approach to achieving pollution control objectives that is embodied in the major federal statutes—the Clean Air Act of 1970 and the Federal Water Pollution Control Act of 1972. The fourth section is devoted to the concept of cost-effectiveness.

Then in the last three sections I describe and evaluate a variety of economics-based incentive devices (such as pollution taxes, deposit-refund systems, and tradable pollution discharge permits) that encourage pollution-control activities by firms and individuals and reduce the overall costs of achieving environmental protection targets. I also discuss the possibility of increasing the use of economic incentives in environmental policy in the 1990s.

Benefit-Cost Analysis and Environmental Policy

Two basic premises underlie benefit-cost analysis. First, the purpose of economic activity is to increase the well-being of the individuals who make up the society. Second, each individual is the best judge of how well off he or she is in a given situation. If society is to make the most of its scarce resources, it should compare what it receives from pollution control and environmental protection activities with what it gives up by taking resources from other uses. It should measure the values of what it gains (the benefits) and what it loses (the costs) in terms of the preferences of those who experience these gains and losses. Society should undertake environmental protection and pollution control only if the results are worth more in terms of individuals' values than what is given up by diverting resources from other uses. This is the underlying principle of the economic approach to environmental policy. Benefit-cost analysis is a set of analytical tools designed to measure the net contribution of any public policy to the economic well-being of the members of society.

Although in some respects benefit-cost analysis is nothing more than organized common sense, the term is usually used to describe a more narrowly defined, technical economic calculation that attempts to reduce all benefits and costs to a common monetary measure (that is, dollars). It seeks to determine if the aggregate of the gains that accrue to those made better off is greater than the aggregate of losses to those made worse off by the policy choice, where gains and losses are both measured in dollars. If the gains exceed the losses, the policy should be accepted according to the logic of benefit-cost analysis. The gains and losses are to be measured in terms of each individual's willingness to pay to receive the gain or to prevent the policy-imposed losses.

Policies where the aggregate gains outweigh the aggregate costs can be justified on ethical grounds because the gainers could fully compensate the losers with monetary payments and still themselves be better off with the policy. Thus, if the compensation were actually made, there would be no losers, only gainers.[1]

Setting Environmental Standards

Selection of environmental quality standards illustrates some of the issues involved in using benefit-cost analysis for environmental policy-making. An *environmental quality standard* is a legally established minimum level of cleanliness or maximum level of pollution in some part of the environment. For example, the U.S. Environmental Protection Agency (EPA) is required by law to establish maximum allowable levels (ambient air quality standards) for major air pollutants such as sulfur dioxide and ozone. Once established, a standard can form the basis for enforcement actions against a polluter whose discharges cause the standard to be violated. Benefit-cost analysis provides a basis for determining that standard. In general, economic principles require that each good be provided at the level for which the marginal willingness to pay for it (the maximum amount that an individual would be willing to give up to get one more unit of the good) is just equal to the cost of providing one more unit of the good (its marginal cost).

Consider, for example, an environment badly polluted by industrial activity. Suppose that successive one-unit improvements are made in some measure of environmental quality. For the first unit, individuals' marginal willingness to pay for a small improvement is likely to be high. The cost of the first unit of cleanup is likely to be low. The difference between them is a net benefit. Further increases in cleanliness bring further net benefits as long as the aggregate marginal willingness to pay is greater than the marginal cost. But as the environment gets cleaner, the willingness to pay for additional units of cleanliness typically decreases, at least beyond some point, while the additional cost of further cleanliness rises. At that point where the marginal willingness to pay equals the marginal cost, the net benefit of further cleanliness is zero, and the total benefits of environmental improvement are at a maximum. This is the point at which the environmental quality standard should be set, if economic reasoning is followed.[2]

An environmental quality standard set by this rule will almost never call for complete elimination of pollution. As the worst of the pollution is cleaned up, the willingness to pay for additional cleanliness will decrease, while the cost of further cleanup will increase. The extra cost of going from 95 percent cleanup to 100 percent cleanup may be several times larger than the total cost of obtaining the first 95 percent cleanup. Society is rarely willing to pay such costs.

The logic of benefit-cost analysis does not require that those who benefit pay for those benefits or that those who ultimately bear the cost of meeting a standard be compensated for those costs. Whether compensation should be paid is considered to be a question of equity. Benefit-cost analysis is concerned exclusively with economic efficiency as represented by the aggregate of benefits and costs. If standards are set to maximize the net benefits, then the gainers could fully compensate the losers and still come out ahead. But when beneficiaries do not compensate losers, there is political asymmetry. Those who benefit call for ever-stricter standards and more cleanup because they obtain the benefits and bear none of the costs, while those who must control pollution call for laxer standards.

The Uses of Benefit-Cost Analysis

One possible use of benefit-cost analysis is retrospective (that is, to evaluate existing policies by estimating the benefits actually realized and comparing them with the costs of the policies). In an early effort to evaluate federal legislation on air and water pollution, I found that policies to control air pollution from stationary sources had probably yielded benefits (primarily in the form of improved human health) substantially greater than the economic costs of the control, while the opposite was true of the control of automotive air pollution and industrial and municipal sources of water pollution.[3] Where retrospective analysis shows that costs have exceeded benefits, it may be possible to find ways to reduce the costs through adopting more cost-effective policies. But excessive costs may also indicate that the targets or environmental standards need to be reconsidered.

Benefit-cost analysis can also be used to evaluate proposed regulations and new environmental policies. A major stimulus to this use of benefit-cost analysis in the federal government is Executive Order 12291, issued by President Ronald Reagan in February 1981. This order mandates that major federal regulations be subject to an economic analysis of benefits and costs.[4] The EPA has prepared benefit-cost analyses for several new regulatory initiatives and for revisions of existing air quality standards. In some cases the results of these "regulatory impact analyses" have supported new regulations or tightening of existing air quality standards.

Is Benefit-Cost Analysis Biased?

The typical textbook discussions of the use of benefit-cost analysis implicitly assume a disinterested decisionmaker who has access to all of the relevant information on the positive and negative effects of a policy and who makes choices based on this information so as to maximize social welfare. The real world, however, seldom corresponds to the textbook model. First, decisionmakers seldom have perfect information on benefits and costs. Also, the physical and biological mechanisms by which environmental changes affect people may not be well understood. And the economic values people place on environmental changes can seldom be measured with precision. But even more important, environmental policy decisions are usually made in a highly political setting in which the potential gainers and losers attempt to influence the decision.

Some contend that in such a setting the benefits of environmental regulation tend to be underestimated and the costs of regulation overestimated. Consequently, benefit-cost analysis will appear to justify less environmental protection and pollution control than is really desirable. There are three responses to this argument.

First, this is not so much an argument for rejecting the benefit-cost criterion for decisionmaking as it is for electing and appointing decisionmakers who are more capable and for trying to achieve greater objectivity and balance of conflicting views. To be sure, proindustry groups will present information that minimizes estimates of benefits and maximizes estimates of costs. But there is room in the process for the presentation of alternative estimates and points of view.

Second, the argument is based on an, at best, oversimplified view of process. Policy analysts within government seldom accept industry estimates at face value and, for major regulations, often prepare their own estimates of benefits and costs or have them prepared by consultants. Some agencies have adopted procedures that systematically overestimate the risks of chemicals to human health and therefore the benefits of controlling chemical exposures.[5] In addition, in some important cases, an agency's careful analysis of the benefits and costs of a regulation has led to the adoption of stricter environmental protection. An example of this is the EPA's 1985 decision to reduce the maximum allowable lead in gasoline from 1.1 grams per gallon to 0.1 grams per gallon. Controlling lead in the environment means reduced incidence of adverse health and cognitive effects in children, fewer blood-pressure-related effects in adult males, and lower automotive maintenance expenditures. Not all of the benefits can be easily measured in monetary terms, but counting only measurable benefits resulted in a benefit-cost ratio in excess of 10:1.[6] Consequently, the regulation was adopted.

The third response is to point to areas of environmental policy in which greater reliance on benefit-cost analysis would clearly lead to decisions that are more economically sound as well as more protective of environmental values. One such area is federally financed water resources development. For many years decisions on funding for specific development projects for water resources were based nominally on benefit-cost analyses. But these analyses used techniques that systematically overstated the benefits of development, understated the economic costs, and ignored environmental costs. As a consequence, a number of economically wasteful and environmentally damaging projects were undertaken. Indeed, serious consideration was given to building a dam in the Grand Canyon and other misguided proposals.[7] Competent and objective benefit-cost analyses clearly demonstrate that many of these projects are uneconomical even without taking into account their environmental costs.

Individuals opposed to environmentally destructive water resource developments have found benefit-cost analysis to be a useful weapon. For example, a study showing that economic costs exceeded benefits helped to weaken congressional support for the Dickey-Lincoln School hydroelectric power project on the St. John River in Maine. The Army Corps of Engineers estimated the benefit-cost ratio to be about 2.1:1 in 1976, but a more reasonable accounting showed the ratio to be much less favorable—between 0.8 and 0.9:1. This estimate was made without placing a price tag on the cost of destroying a free-flowing wild river.[8] Congress eventually deauthorized this project.

The Future of Benefit-Cost Analysis

The United States has made substantial progress in controlling some forms of pollution over the past twenty years. Examples include emissions of soot and dust from coal-burning power plants and municipal trash incinerators and the discharge of sewage and other organic wastes into rivers. In part, this is because these problems were highly visible and the costs of cleaning them up were relatively low. But the pollution problems of the present and future are likely to be much more costly to deal with. Thus, it will be important to try to estimate what the benefits of cleanup will be.

For example, consider the question of how much further the United States should go in controlling emissions of the substances that form atmospheric ozone or smog. This is just the kind of question that benefit-cost analysis is best suited to answer. The authorities in the South Coast Air Basin, of which smog-ridden Los Angeles is a part, recently approved a new air quality management plan to impose additional strict controls on a number of the sources of ozone pollution. This plan specifies three tiers of control measures, each tier increasing in stringency. The total cost may exceed $13 billion per year. To put this whopping sum in perspective, consider the cost in 1988 of all federal policies on air pollution control in the United States: about $30 billion. Does it make sense to have all three tiers? Paul Portney and his colleagues at Resources for the Future in Washington, D.C., have estimated that the benefits of implementing all three tiers together would be around $4 billion per year.[9] This casts some doubt on the wisdom of going all the way. But undertaking the first and second tiers might be justified. What is required is a comparison of the incremental benefits and costs for each tier. Questions of this sort will become increasingly important in the 1990s, and economists will become increasingly busy seeking the information needed to answer them.

For some kinds of problems, analysis of the benefits and costs is complicated by the scientific uncertainties about the physical and ecological consequences of policies. Examples include protecting the stratospheric ozone layer and preventing greenhouse-induced global climate change. Nevertheless, some effort to describe and quantify benefits and costs may provide useful information to decisionmakers. For example, William Cline has attempted to estimate the benefits of controlling emissions of CO_2 and to compare them with estimates of the costs of controlling emissions provided by other authors. Although he finds the benefit-cost ratio to be somewhat less than 1, his estimates contain great uncertainties. He concludes that if society is prudent and wishes to avoid unnecessary risks, "it appears sensible on economic grounds to undertake aggressive abatement to sharply curtail the greenhouse effect."[10]

Direct Regulation in Federal Environmental Policy

The major provisions of the federal laws controlling air and water pollution embody what is often termed a *direct regulation* (or *command and control*) approach to achieve the established pollution control targets. This direct regulation approach is based on specific limitations on the allowable discharges of polluting substances from each source, coupled with an administrative and legal system to monitor compliance with these limitations and to impose sanctions or penalties for violations.

In this approach the pollution control authority must carry out a series of four steps:

1. Determine the rules and regulations for each source that will achieve the given pollution control targets. These regulations might include the installation of certain types of pollution control equipment, restrictions on activities, or control of inputs, such as limiting the sulfur content in fuels. The regulations typically establish maximum allowable discharges of polluting substances from each source.
2. Establish penalties or sanctions for noncompliance.
3. Monitor sources so that incidents of noncompliance can be detected. Alternatively, the authorities might establish a system of self-reporting with periodic checks and audits of performance.
4. Punish violations. If violations of the regulations are detected, the authorities must use the administrative and legal mechanisms spelled out in the relevant laws to impose penalties or to require changes in the behavior of the sources.[11]

Economists have criticized the direct regulation approach on two grounds. First, the regulations require a pattern of pollution control activities that tend to be excessively costly—in other words, not cost-effective. Second, the incentive structure created for firms and individuals is inappropriate. Because compliance is so costly, there is no positive incentive to control pollution, although there is the negative incentive to avoid penalties. Not only is there no incentive to do better than the regulations require, but also the incentives to comply with the regulations themselves may be too weak to overcome the disincentive of bearing the costs of compliance.

Efficiency and Cost-Effectiveness

Even if one objects, for either philosophical or pragmatic reasons, to basing environmental policy on benefit-cost analysis, it still makes good sense to favor cost-effective environmental policies. Cost-effectiveness means the stated environmental quality standards are achieved at the lowest possible total cost. The importance of achieving cost-effective pollution control policies should be self-evident: cost savings free resources that can be used to produce other goods and services of value to people.

When several sources of pollution exist in the same area, a pollution control policy must include some mechanism for dividing the responsibility for cleanup among the several sources. The direct regulation form of policy typically does this by requiring all sources to clean up by the same percentage. But such a policy will rarely be cost-effective. A pollution control policy is cost-effective only if it allocates the responsibility for cleanup among sources so that the incremental or marginal cost of achieving a one-unit improvement in environmental quality at any location is the same for all sources of pollution. Differences in the marginal costs of improving environmental quality can arise from differences in the marginal cost of treatment or waste reduction across sources; also, discharges from sources at different locations can have different effects on environmental quality.

Suppose that targets for air pollution control have been established by setting an ambient air quality standard for sulfur dioxide. To illustrate the importance of differences in marginal costs of control, suppose that two adjacent factories are both emitting sulfur dioxide. A one-ton decrease in emissions gives the same incremental benefit to air quality whether it is achieved by factory A or factory B. Now suppose that to achieve the ambient air quality standard, emissions must be reduced by fifty tons per day. One way to achieve the target is to require each factory to clean up twenty-five tons per day. But suppose that with this allocation of cleanup responsibility, factory A's marginal cost of cleanup is $10 per ton per day, while at factory B, the marginal cost is only $5 per ton per day. Allowing factory A to reduce its cleanup by one ton per day saves it $10. If factory B is required to clean up an extra ton, total cleanup is the same, and the air quality standard is met. And the total cost of pollution control is reduced by $5 per day. Additional savings are possible by continuing to shift cleanup responsibility to B (raising B's marginal cost) and away from A (reducing A's marginal cost). This should continue until B's rising marginal cost of control is made equal to A's now lower marginal cost. Emissions of a pollutant may have different impacts on air quality depending on the location of the source. This must also be taken into account in finding the least-cost or cost-minimizing pattern of emissions reductions.[12]

Nothing in the logic or the procedures for setting pollution control requirements for sources ensures that the conditions for cost minimization will be satisfied. In setting discharge limits, agencies do not systematically take into account the marginal cost of control, at least in part because of the difficulties they would have in getting the data. Thus, discharge limits are not likely to result in equal marginal costs of reducing discharges across different sources of the same pollutant. One analysis of the marginal cost of removing oxygen-demanding organic material under existing federal water pollution standards found a thirtyfold range of marginal costs within the six industries examined.[13]

Another way to look at the question of cost-effectiveness is to ask how to get the greatest environmental improvement for a given total budget or total expenditure on pollution control. The answer is to spend that money on those pollution control activities with the highest level of pollution control benefit per dollar spent (the biggest "bang for the buck"). For example, if society decides for whatever reason to spend $1 million to control organic forms of water pollution, it should require that the money be spent on industries with the highest pollutant removal per dollar, which is to say, the lowest cost per pound of removal. The study cited in the preceding paragraph shows that spending an extra dollar for controlling organic pollution in a low-cost industry will buy thirty times more pollution removal than spending the same dollar in an industry with high marginal costs.

A number of environmental protection and public health policies are cost-ineffective because of large differences across activities in the marginal cost of control or the benefit of dollars spent. For example, a study of the costs of regulating different chemicals in the environment and the expected reductions in the incidence of cancer found that the costs per cancer death avoided varied widely.[14] In one case, the use of the pesticide chlorobenzilate on noncitrus fruits has been regulated at a cost of $4 to $14 million per cancer death avoided. But its use in citrus fruit has gone unregulated, even though substantially more cancer deaths could be avoided at costs perhaps as low as $38,000 each. Similarly, some sources of benzene emissions have been regulated at a high cost per death avoided while other sources have gone unregulated even though their control costs are lower by a factor of ten.

Probably the greatest opportunities for more cost-effective pollution control are in the realm of the conventional pollutants of air and water. The problem of cost-effectiveness has stimulated many empirical studies comparing the costs of direct regulation policies (under provisions of the Clean Air Act and Federal Water Pollution Control Act) with cost-effective alternatives based on equalizing the marginal costs of meeting environmental quality standards across all sources of pollution. In his review of these studies, Tom Tietenberg found that least-cost pollution control planning could generate cost savings of 30 to 40 percent, and in some cases more than 90 percent.[15] This means that in some instances pollution control costs are *ten times* higher than they need to be.

How can cost savings of this magnitude be realized? Can pollution control policies be made more cost-effective without causing further environmental degradation? The answer lies in changing the incentives that face polluters.

Incentives vs. Direct Regulation

In an unregulated market economy pollution arises because of the way individuals and firms respond to market forces and incentives. Safe and nonpolluting methods of disposing of wastes are usually more costly for firms than dumping them into the environment, even though such disposal harms others. Because polluters are generally not required to compensate those who are harmed, they have no incentive to alter their waste disposal practices.

Incentives Under Direct Regulation

In deciding how to respond to a system of regulations and enforcement, polluters will compare the costs of compliance with the likely costs and penalties associated with noncompliance. The costs of compliance may be substantial, but the costs of noncompliance are likely to be uncertain. Incidents of noncompliance might not be detected. Minor violations, even if detected, might be ignored by the authorities. Rather than commit itself to the uncertain legal processes involved in imposing significant fees and penalties, the overburdened enforcement arm of the pollution control agency might negotiate an agreement with the polluter to obtain compliance at some future date. And even if cases are brought to court, the court might be more lenient than the pollution control agency would wish. All of these problems of monitoring and enforcement of regulations add up to a weak incentive for polluters to comply with the regulations.

One of the consequences of these weak incentives has been high rates of violations of existing standards. For example, for an eighteen-month period in 1981 and 1982, the U.S. General Accounting Office compared the actual discharges of a sample of water polluters with the permissible discharges under the terms of their discharge permits. They found a major noncompliance problem. Eighty-two percent of the sources studied had at least one month of noncompliance during the study period. Twenty-four percent of this sample was in "significant noncompliance," with at least four consecutive months during which discharges exceeded permitted levels by at least 50 percent.[16]

Improving the Incentives

Economists have long argued for an alternative approach to pollution control policy; it is based on the creation of strong positive incentives for firms to control pollution.[17] One form that the incentive could take is a charge or tax on each unit of pollution discharged. The tax would be equal to the monetary value of the damage that pollution caused to others. Each discharger wishing to minimize its total cost (cleanup cost plus tax bill) would compare the tax cost of discharging a unit of pollution with the cost of controlling or preventing the discharge. As long as the cost of control was lower than the tax or charge, the firm would want to prevent the discharge. In fact, it would reduce pollution to the point where its marginal cost of control was just equal to the tax and, indirectly, equal to the marginal damage caused by the pollution. The properly set tax would cause the firm to undertake on its own accord the optimum amount of pollution control.

The pollution tax or charge strategy has long appealed to economists because it provides a sure and graduated incentive to firms by making pollution itself a cost of production. And it provides an incentive for innovation and technological change in pollution control. Also, since the polluters are not likely to reduce their discharges to zero, the government would collect revenues.

A system of marketable or tradable discharge permits (TDPs) has essentially the same incentive effects as a tax on pollution. The government would issue a limited number of pollution permits or "tickets." Each ticket would entitle its owner to discharge one unit of pollution during a specific time period. The government could either distribute the tickets free of charge to polluters on some basis or auction them off to the highest bidders. Dischargers could also buy and sell permits among themselves. The cost of purchasing a ticket or of forgoing the revenue from selling the ticket to someone else has the same incentive effects as a tax on pollution of the same amount.

Polluters can respond to the higher cost of pollution that a tax or TDP system imposes in a variety of ways. Polluters could install some form of conventional treatment system if the cost of treatment were less than the tax or permit price. But more important technical options also exist. Polluters can consider changing to processes that are inherently less polluting. They can recover and recycle materials that otherwise would remain in the waste stream. They can change to inputs that produce less pollution. For example, a paper mill's response to a tax on dioxin in its effluent might be to stop using chlorine as a bleaching agent. Finally, since the firm would have to pay for whatever pollution it did not bring under control, this cost would result in higher prices for its products and fewer units of its products being purchased by consumers. The effects of higher prices and lower quantities demanded would be to reduce the production level of the firm and, other things being equal, to further reduce the amount of pollution being generated.

A system of pollution taxes or TDPs can make a major contribution to achieving cost-effectiveness. If several sources are discharging into the environment, they will be induced to minimize the total cost of achieving any given reduction in pollution. This is because each discharger will control discharges up to the point where its marginal or incremental cost of control is equated to the tax or permit price. If all dischargers face the same tax or price, their marginal costs of pollution control will be equal. This is the condition for cost-effectiveness. Low-cost sources will control relatively more, thus leading to a cost-effective allocation of cleanup responsibilities. There is no reallocation of responsibilities for reducing discharges that will achieve the same total reduction at a lower total cost.

One difficulty with implementing a pollution charge system is knowing what the charge should be. In some cases enough is already known about the costs of control for average polluters so that the appropriate charge could be calculated. The charge can be adjusted, too, if experience reveals that it was initially set too high or too low.

One advantage of the TDP system is that the pollution control agency does not have to determine the level of the tax. Once the agency determines the number of permits, the market determines the permit price. Another advantage of a system of TDPs in comparison with effluent charges is that it represents a less radical departure from the existing system. Since all sources are presently required to obtain permits specifying the maximum allowable discharges, it would be relatively easy to rewrite them in a divisible format and to allow sources to buy or sell them. A source with low marginal costs of control should be willing to clean up more and sell the unused permits as long as the price of a permit was greater than the marginal cost of control. And a source with high pollution control costs would find it cheaper to buy permits than to clean itself up.[18]

A marketable permit program of this sort is a key component of the recently adopted federal program to reduce acid deposition resulting from emissions of sulfur dioxide. The Clean Air Act Amendments of 1990 established a two-phase reduction of sulfur dioxide emissions of 10 million tons per year (to about 50 percent of 1980 levels) by the year 2000. Major sources of these emissions (primarily coal-burning electric power plants) will receive permits for emissions (called allowances) based on, but less than, historic emissions levels. The numbers of permits will be reduced over time until the goal is achieved. Trading of allowances for 1995 emissions has already begun. Agreements on proposed trades are already being announced. The cost savings relative to direct regulation will be in the billions of dollars per year.

In other developments, a TDP system has been implemented by EPA for emissions of chlorofluorocarbons, the chemicals which cause depletion of stratospheric ozone. And the Air Quality Management District in Los Angeles is planning the details of a marketable pollution permit system for reactive organic gases, one of the major sources of smog in Southern California.

More Modest Reforms

The EPA has also found several ways to use economic incentives in a more limited way to introduce greater flexibility into the existing legal framework and to foster cost-effectiveness in meeting existing targets. Two of the most interesting of these are the creation of "bubbles" and pollution control "offsets."

The bubble concept was first applied to multiple-stack sources of air pollution. It was given this name because it treats a collection of smokestacks or sources within a large factory as if it were encased in a bubble. Pollution control requirements are applied to the aggregate of emissions leaving the bubble rather than to each individual stack or source. EPA has also begun to apply the concept to the control of water pollution.

A major industrial facility (such as an integrated steel mill or petro-chemical plant) may contain several separate activities or processes, each of which is subject to a different pollution limit or standard. Many of these activities discharge the same substances, yet the incremental costs of pollution control may vary a great deal across activities. As a result, the total cost of controlling the aggregate discharge from the plant is often higher than necessary. The bubble concept allows plant managers to adjust the levels of control at different activities if they can lower total control costs. But the total amount of a pollutant discharged from the plant must not exceed the aggregate of the effluent limitations for individual processes. Aggregate savings have probably amounted to several billion dollars.[19] Because EPA regulations sometimes require a net reduction in emissions from the "bubble," the net effect on air quality has probably been positive.

The so-called offset policy was created in the mid 1970s to re-solve a potential conflict between meeting federal air quality standards and allowing economic growth and development. The Clean Air Act of 1970 prohibited the licensing of new air pollution sources if they would interfere with the attainment of federal air quality standards. Taken literally, this would prohibit any new industrial facilities with air pollu-tion emissions in those parts of the country not in compliance with exist-ing air quality standards. In response to this dilemma, EPA issued a set of rules that would allow new sources to be licensed in nonat-tainment areas provided they could show that there would be no net increase in pollution. The offsetting reduction in polluted air would come from reducing emissions from existing sources of pollution in the nonattainment area above and beyond what had already been required —either by installing additional controls on these sources or by shutting them down.

For firms desiring to expand or to enter a region, the offset rules provide an incentive to reduce emissions from existing sources in the region. The offsets need not be limited to reductions at other sources owned by the firm planning a new source investment. Firms are free to seek offsets from other firms as well. Since EPA rules require that offsets be executed on a greater than one-for-one basis, the net impact on air quality has probably been positive. The policy also encourages technologi-cal innovation to find means of creating offsets and probably encourages older, dirty facilities to shut down sooner than they otherwise would in order to sell offsets.

Economic Incentives and Environmental Policy in the 1990s

Interest in the use of economic incentives appears to be growing in Congress as well as at the EPA. Evidence of this can be found in two reports released in 1989 and 1991 under the banner of *Project 88*. These reports were cosponsored by former Sen. Tim Wirth (D-Colo.) and the late Sen. John Heinz (R-Pa.). The first report, *Project 88, Harnessing Market Forces to Protect Our Environment: Initiatives for the New President*, contends that "conventional regulatory policies need to be supplemented by market-based strategies which can foster major improvements in environmental quality by enlisting the innovative capacity of our economy in the development of efficient and equitable solutions."[20] The report urges much greater use of incentive-based systems such as TDPs and pollution taxes. It also suggests how these systems can be applied to many different environmental problems.

The second report, *Project 88—Round II, Incentives for Action: Designing Market-Based Environmental Strategies*, provides more detailed proposals for using incentive-based policies to deal with global climate change, energy conservation, solid and hazardous waste management, the supposed scarcity of water in the arid West, and the management of our timber and other resources of the National Forest System.

I will briefly discuss several possible applications of economic incentive strategies. They include using taxes or tradable permits to reduce carbon dioxide emissions and excessive applications of pesticides, using deposit-refund systems to prevent improper disposal of hazardous wastes, and "getting the prices right" to prevent excessive use of scarce resources.

Reducing CO_2 Emissions: Taxes or TDPs?

If present trends in emissions and atmospheric concentrations of CO_2 continue, average temperatures worldwide could increase by several degrees Celsius over the next fifty years. If this global warming is to be avoided or at least retarded, global emissions of CO_2 must be held steady if not substantially reduced. A major policy question facing all nations is how to slow, if not reverse, the rising trend in CO_2 emissions. One possibility is to implement an economic incentive system such as a tax or TDP program.[21]

Given a policy decision to seek a reduction in CO_2 emissions, the case for preferring an incentive-based system over direct regulation is strong. In terms of incentives, enforcement, cost-effectiveness, and administrative ease, both the tax and TDP system come out ahead of direct regulation. The most important consideration in choosing between a tax and TDP system is the different ways in which the consequences of uncertainty are felt. With a tax, there is uncertainty about the degree to which emissions will be reduced. With a TDP system, the reduction in emissions is determined by the number of permits the government chooses to issue. But there is uncertainty about the price of permits. The greater certainty about emissions reductions under a TDP system is not a great advantage because at this time a specific target for emissions reductions does not seem to be essential. And because very little is known about the economic costs of controlling CO_2 emissions, the uncertainty of the costs and economic impact of a TDP is a significant disadvantage.

This suggests that, at least in the near term, a tax on CO_2 emissions is preferable to a TDP system. Many authors have proposed taxes at various rates. Most of the proposals fall in the range of $10-100 per ton of carbon content of the fuel. To put these numbers in perspective, a tax of $75 per ton of carbon is equivalent to an increase in the gasoline tax of about twenty cents per gallon.

Pesticides

Heavy use of chemical pesticides in agriculture has resulted in two kinds of environmental problems. First, pesticide residues can adhere to soil particles that erode from the land, causing ecological problems in downstream lakes and rivers. Second, these residues can leach directly into aquifers and contaminate water supplies to households.

EPA currently has the power to ban specific pesticides entirely or to ban or otherwise regulate applications on particular crops. The degree of erosion and the potential for pesticide residues to leach into groundwater vary widely across different regions of the country. Also the value of pesticide use varies widely by crop and region. Thus, any system of direct regulation is likely to be very cost-ineffective in protecting surface and groundwater quality. The first *Project 88* report suggests placing a tax on the use of certain pesticides both to discourage their use and to encourage the development and utilization of environmentally sound agricultural practices. In the absence of specific knowledge about the costs to farmers of reducing their applications of pesticides, it is difficult to know at what level to set a tax for each pesticide in question.

A better alternative might be a regionally based system of marketable pesticide application permits (PAPs). Local officials could estimate the maximum allowable applications of each pesticide in the region that are consistent with protecting surface and groundwater quality. Farmers could then bid for PAPs in an auction. Some farmers would find that the auction price was greater than the value to them of using the pesticide, so they would seek out other ways to deal with pest problems. Assuming adequate monitoring and enforcement, the maximum safe levels of pesticide application would not be exceeded.

Soda Cans and Hazardous Wastes

Federal policy on hazardous wastes focuses on regulating disposal practices. The effectiveness of this policy is highly dependent on the government's ability to monitor and enforce these disposal regulations and to detect and penalize illegal practices. Both industry and government have recognized that the problem of safe disposal can be made more manageable by reducing the quantities of hazardous wastes being generated. The high cost of complying with disposal regulations is itself an incentive for industry to engage in source reduction, but it is also an incentive to violate the regulations on safe disposal, the so-called midnight-dumping problem.

For some types of wastes, a deposit-refund system could provide better incentives to reduce hazardous wastes at their source as well as to dispose of them safely. The system would resemble the deposits on returnable soda and beer cans and bottles established in some states. For example, the manufacturer of a solvent that would become a hazardous waste after it is used could be required to pay EPA a deposit of so many dollars per gallon of solvent produced. The amount of the deposit would have to be at least as high as the cost of recycling the solvent or disposing of it safely. Because paying the deposit becomes, in effect, part of the cost of producing the solvent, the manufacturer would have to raise its price. This would discourage the use of the solvent and encourage source reduction. The deposit would be refunded to whoever returned one gallon of the solvent to a certified safe disposal facility or recycler. Thus, the user of the solvent would find it more profitable to return the solvent than to dispose of it illegally. In this way private incentives and the search for profit are harnessed to the task of environmental protection.[22]

Getting the Prices Right

A surprising number of environmental problems are caused, at least in part, by inappropriate prices for some of the goods and services that people buy and by barriers to the effective functioning of markets. A basic economic principle is that if the price of a good is increased, the quantity purchased decreases, while the quantity that producers are willing to sell increases. Many environmental problems are linked to government policies that keep the prices of some things artificially low. For example, the federal government sells water to farmers in the West at prices that are far below the government's cost of supplying the water. And most states in the arid West either prohibit or place substantial restrictions on the ability of private owners of water rights to sell their water to others who might be able to make better use of it. As a consequence, vast quantities of water are wasted in inefficient irrigation practices while some urban areas face water shortages. This increases the political pressure to build more dams and to divert larger quantities of water from rivers already under ecological stress from inadequate water flows.[23]

The U.S. Forest Service often sells rights to harvest its timber at prices that do not cover the government's own cost of supervising the harvest and constructing access roads. Not only do taxpayers bear the direct financial cost, but there is an indirect cost in that too much forest land is subject to cutting with the attendant loss of wildlife habitat and recreation opportunities.[24]

Free access to public facilities is a special case of a low price. In many urban areas, access to the public highway system is free. Even where tolls are charged, these do not always cover the cost of constructing and maintaining the highways. And, more important, the tolls do not reflect the costs that each driver imposes on others when he or she enters an already congested highway and slows traffic even further. If each driver were charged a toll that reflected his or her marginal contribution to congestion, this would reduce the incentives drivers have to use the highway during peak traffic hours. Average speeds would be higher with more efficient use of fuel and less air pollution. This would diminish the pressure to build more roads with their impacts on land use, and so forth.[25]

In some cases, prices are too high. The government supports the prices of some agricultural products at artificially high levels. This gives farmers incentives to plant more of these crops on less productive lands and to apply excessive quantities of pesticides and fertilizers. The result can be excess soil erosion and pollution of streams and rivers in rural areas as runoff carries sediments, pesticides, and nutrients into adjacent waters.

Conclusion

Economic analysis is likely to be increasingly useful in grappling with the environmental problems of the 1990s for at least four reasons. First, as policymakers address the more complex and deeply rooted national and global environmental problems, they are finding that solutions are more and more costly. Thus, it is increasingly important for the public to get its "money's worth" from these policies. This means looking at benefits and comparing them with costs. Therefore, some form of benefit-cost analysis, such as that required by President Reagan's Executive Order 12291, will play a larger role in policy debates and decisions in the future.

Second, the slow progress over the past twenty years in dealing with conventional air and water pollution problems shows the need to use private initiative more effectively through altering the incentive structure. This means placing greater reliance on pollution charges, tradable discharge permits, and deposit-refund systems. I have suggested three possible applications of incentive-based mechanisms to emerging problems, but the list of potential applications is much longer, as is made clear in the *Project 88* reports.

Third, the high aggregate cost of controlling various pollutants and environmental threats makes it imperative to design policies that are cost-effective. Incentive-based mechanisms can play a very important role in achieving pollution control targets at something approaching the minimum possible social cost. Finally, economic analysis can help us to identify those cases where government policies result in prices that send the wrong signals to consumers and producers and fail to provide the right incentives to make wise use of scarce resources and the environment.

Notes

1. For introductions to the principles of benefit-cost analysis and applications in the realm of environmental policy, see Tom Tietenberg, *Environmental and Natural Resource Economics,* 3d ed. (Glenview, Ill.: Scott, Foresman, 1992); and Daniel Swartzman, Richard A. Liroff, and Kevin G. Croke, *Cost-Benefit Analysis and Environmental Regulations: Politics, Ethics, and Methods* (Washington, D.C.: Conservation Foundation, 1982).
2. See, for example, Tietenberg, *Environmental and Natural Resource Economics,* chap. 14.
3. A. Myrick Freeman III, *Air and Water Pollution Control: A Benefit-Cost Assessment* (New York: Wiley, 1982).
4. For a discussion of some of the economic implications of Executive Order 12291, see V. Kerry Smith, ed., *Environmental Policy Under Reagan's Executive Order: The Role of Benefit-Cost Analysis* (Chapel Hill: University of North Carolina Press, 1984).
5. Albert L. Nichols and Richard J. Zeckhauser, "The Perils of Prudence," *Regulation* (November-December 1986), 13-24.
6. U.S. Environmental Protection Agency, *Costs and Benefits of Reducing Lead in Gasoline: Final Regulatory Impact Analysis* (Washington, D.C.: U.S. Environmental Protection Agency, 1985).
7. For a description of how bad economic analysis is used to justify proposals of this sort, see Alan Carlin, "The Grand Canyon Controversy: Or, How Reclamation Justifies the Unjustifiable," in *Pollution, Resources, and the Environment,* ed. Alain C. Enthoven and A. Myrick Freeman III (New York: Norton, 1973).
8. See A. Myrick Freeman III, "The Benefits and Costs of the Dickey-Lincoln Project: A Preliminary Report" (Unpublished paper, Bowdoin College, Brunswick, Maine, 1974); and A. Myrick Freeman III, "The Benefits and Costs of the Dickey-Lincoln Project: An Interim Update" (Unpublished paper, Bowdoin College, Brunswick, Maine, 1978).
9. See Paul R. Portney et al., "L. A. Law: Regulating Air Quality in California's South Coast," *Issues in Science and Technology* 13, no. 4 (1989): 68-73.
10. William R. Cline, *The Economics of Global Warming* (Washington, D.C.: Institute for International Economics, 1992), 9.
11. For more detailed discussions of the major provisions of federal air and water pollution law, see Paul R. Portney "Air Pollution Policy," and A. Myrick Freeman III, "Water Pollution Policy," in *Public Policies for Environmental Protection,* ed. Paul R. Portney (Washington, D.C.: Resources for the Future, 1990).
12. See Tietenberg, *Environmental and Natural Resource Economics,* chap. 14.

13. Wesley A. Magat, Alan J. Krupnick, and Winston Harrington, *Rules in the Making: A Statistical Analysis of Regulatory Agency Behavior* (Washington, D.C.: Resources for the Future, 1986), table 6-1.

14. See Curtis C. Travis, S. Richter Pack, and Ann Fisher, "Cost-Effectiveness as a Factor in Cancer Risk Management," *Environment International* 13 (1987): 469-474.

15. T. H. Tietenberg, *Emissions Trading: An Exercise in Reforming Pollution Policy* (Washington, D.C.: Resources for the Future, 1985), 38-47.

16. See U.S. General Accounting Office, *Waste Water Dischargers Are Not Complying with EPA Pollution Control Permits* (Washington, D.C.: U.S. General Accounting Office, 1983). This study and other evidence are discussed by Clifford S. Russell in "Monitoring and Enforcement," in *Public Policies for Environmental Protection*, ed. Paul R. Portney.

17. The idea can be traced back to A. C. Pigou, *The Economics of Welfare* (London: Macmillan, 1932).

18. A more modest step would be to allow two (or more) sources to propose a reallocation of cleanup requirements between them if they found it to their mutual advantage and if there were no degradation of environmental quality.

19. Robert W. Hahn and Gordon L. Hester, "Marketable Permits: Lessons from Theory and Practice," *Ecology Law Quarterly* 16, no. 2 (1989): 361-406.

20. *Project 88, Harnessing Market Forces to Protect Our Environment: Initiatives for the New President*, a public policy study sponsored by Sen. Tim Wirth (D-Colo.) and Sen. John Heinz (R-Pa.) (Washington, D.C.: Project 88, December 1988). See also Bruce A. Ackerman and Richard B. Stewart, "Reforming Environmental Law: The Democratic Case for Market Incentives," *Columbia Journal of Environmental Law* 13 (1988): 171-199; and Richard B. Stewart, "Controlling Environmental Risks Through Economic Incentives," *Columbia Journal of Environmental Law* 13 (1988): 153-169.

21. See Roger C. Dower and Mary Beth Zimmerman, *The Right Climate for Carbon Taxes: Creating Economic Incentives to Protect the Atmosphere* (Washington, D.C.: World Resources Institute, 1992).

22. See *Project 88*, chap. 7; and Clifford S. Russell, "Economic Incentives in the Management of Hazardous Waste," *Columbia Journal of Environmental Law* 13 (1988): 1101-1119.

23. See *Project 88—Round II, Incentives for Action: Designing Market-Based Environmental Strategies*, a public policy study sponsored by Sen. Tim Wirth (D-Colo.) and Sen. John Heinz (R-Pa.) (Washington, D.C.: Project 88, May 1991), chap. 4.

24. Ibid.

25. Kenneth A. Small, Clifford Winston, and Carol A. Evans, *Road Work: A New Highway Pricing and Investment Strategy* (Washington, D.C.: Brookings, 1989); and James J. MacKenzie, Roger C. Dower, and Donald D. T. Chen, *The Going Rate: What It Really Costs to Drive* (Washington, D.C.: World Resources Institute, 1992).

10

Risk-Based Decisionmaking

Richard N. L. Andrews

Environmental regulation in the 1980s was pervaded by the concept of risk, and environmental policy analysis by the concepts and methods of quantitative risk assessment (QRA). Between 1976 and 1980 QRAs were performed on only eight chemicals proposed for regulation; between 1981 and 1985, on fifty-five. By the end of the 1980s the idea of risk-based decisionmaking had become the framework for environmental policy in the Environmental Protection Agency (EPA), and to varying degrees in other agencies as well.[1] In 1984 EPA administrator William Ruckelshaus officially endorsed "risk assessment and risk management" as the primary framework for EPA decisionmaking. In 1987 a major agency report stated flatly that "the fundamental mission of the Environmental Protection Agency is to reduce risks"; and another influential report, issued in 1990, recommended that EPA "target its environmental protection efforts on the basis of opportunities for the greatest risk reduction."[2]

The adoption of this risk-based framework has important implications for the course of U.S. environmental policy. Risk assessment remains controversial, both among scientists and policymakers and in general political debate; even many of its advocates are uneasy that it is often oversold or abused. Originally developed as a technical procedure for evaluating the health risks of toxic chemicals, the risk-based approach is now used to justify and set priorities for the whole range of environmental policy decisions made by the EPA—and the agency is now promoting its use by other federal agencies, state and local governments, and other countries. Although risk-based decisionmaking is an important and still-evolving approach to making environmental policy, it may still not be farsighted enough to deal with the most important policy issues of the 1990s and beyond. To appraise its significance, one must first understand how it has come to be so widely used; what it is, and why it is controversial; and how it is now being applied to the environmental issues of the 1990s.

The Regulatory Legacy

U.S. environmental policy up to 1970 included more than seven decades' experience in managing the environment as a natural resource base—lands and forests, minerals, water, fish and wildlife—but almost none in regulating environmental quality. Beginning in 1970, however, U.S. policy shifted dramatically from managing the environment to regulating it, and from state and local to national primacy. EPA was created by reorganizing many of the existing regulatory programs into one agency. And Congress embarked on a decade of unprecedented expansion of federal regulatory mandates, enacting more than a dozen major new statutes, each requiring many individual regulatory actions governing particular substances, technologies, and practices.

Risk-Based Regulation

Initially these laws emphasized the use of known technologies and clear statutory directives to reduce the most obvious problems: urban sewage, automotive air pollution, and the half-dozen or so major industrial pollutants of air and water. The Clean Air Act of 1970, for instance, established explicit national ambient air quality standards for six major pollutants, based on health criteria, and set deliberately "technology forcing" statutory timetables for meeting them. The Federal Water Pollution Control Act Amendments of 1972 similarly required federal permits for all new water pollution sources, again using technology-based standards—"best practicable" and "best available" technologies—to force improved pollution control throughout each industrial process.

As these measures took effect, however, environmental politics became increasingly intertwined with the fear of cancer, and specifically with the possibility that pesticides and other manufactured chemicals might be important environmental causes of it.[3] The environmental control agenda was broadened and redirected, therefore, to address the far larger domain of chemical hazards as a whole: toxic air and water pollutants, production of toxic substances, pesticides, drinking water contaminants, hazardous wastes, and others. This domain included thousands of compounds, far too many to address explicitly in statutes—most not yet even well studied, and many that had important economic uses despite (or, for pesticides, even because of) their toxicity.[4]

To deal with toxic chemicals, therefore, Congress enacted "risk-based" and "risk-balancing" statutes that required the EPA to assess the risks of each substance it proposed to regulate, and then either to protect the public with "margins of safety" against "unreasonable risks" or to make choices that would balance those risks against the substance's economic benefits. In turn, EPA and other agencies (such as the Occupational Safety and Health Administration and the Consumer Product Safety Commission) had to develop methods for *setting risk priorities* among many possible candidates for regulation; for *justifying particular regulatory decisions*, balancing risks against benefits; and for *approving site decisions,* based on an "acceptable risk" for certifying a cleaned-up hazardous waste site or permitting construction of a new facility.[5]

The Politics of Accountability

By the late 1970s EPA and other regulatory agencies faced calls for closer political oversight and greater accountability. From one side, these pressures came from environmental groups frustrated by the agency's slow implementation of regulatory mandates. Congress responded by setting deadlines (with "hammer clauses" for implementation of each new regulatory mandate); organizations filed lawsuits to compel EPA regulation of high-priority substances by agreed deadlines.

Business interests, meanwhile, pressed for closer oversight to restrain the scope and pace of regulation. By increasing the agency's burden of analytical requirements before the promulgation of each regulation, business interests were able both to slow the process of issuing each regulation and to reduce the number of regulations the EPA could develop. Two important examples were President Ronald Reagan's Executive Order 12291, which required "regulatory impact assessments" and review by the Office of Management and Budget (OMB) for all proposed regulations; and a Supreme Court decision in 1980 that held, in effect, that many proposed environmental health standards for chemicals could be invalidated if the agency did not justify them by quantitative risk assessments.[6] These pressures spurred the growth of quantitative risk assessment as an analytical framework for policymaking.

Risk Assessment and Risk Management

Quantitative risk assessment has been defined as "the process of obtaining quantitative measures of risk levels, where risk refers to the possibility of uncertain, adverse consequences."[7] To EPA, "risk" is normally assumed to mean "the probability of injury, disease, or death under specific circumstances," and risk assessment means "the characterization of the potential adverse health effects of human exposure to environmental hazards."[8] Note that these definitions combine two separate concepts, that of hazard (adverse consequence, usually assumed to be a health hazard) and that of probability (quantitative measures of possibility or uncertainty). This mixing of two concepts is one cause of the confusion and controversy that surrounds risk assessment. Other approaches are sometimes discussed, but it is the concepts and methods of QRA that have come to dominate environmental regulatory practice.

One fundamental doctrine of this approach was that risk assessment should be clearly distinguished from risk management. Risk assessment, in this view, was a purely scientific activity based on expert analysis of facts. Risk management was the ensuing decision process in which the scientific conclusions were considered along with other elements (such as statutory requirements, costs, public values, and politics). William Lowrance advocated this distinction in an influential book on risk in 1976. A National Research Council report endorsed it in 1983, and it was adopted as EPA policy by Administrator William Ruckelshaus. It remains a basic tenet in the literature on risk assessment, though Ruckelshaus himself subsequently acknowledged the difficulty of maintaining such a clear distinction in practice.[9]

Risk Assessment

Quantitative risk assessment has now been refined into a detailed analytical procedure that includes four elements:

- *hazard identification*, in which the analyst gathers information on whether a substance may be a health hazard;
- *dose-response assessment*, in which the analyst attempts to describe quantitatively the relationship between the amount of exposure to the substance and the degree of toxic effect;
- *exposure assessment*, in which the analyst estimates how many people may actually be exposed to the substance and under what conditions (how much of it, how often, for how long, from what sources); and
- *risk characterization*, in which the analyst combines information from the previous steps into an assessment of overall health risk: for example, an added risk that one person in a thousand (or a hundred, or a million) will develop cancer after exposure at the expected levels over a lifetime.

Suppose, for instance, that the EPA decides to assess the health risks of an organic solvent used to degrease metal parts: a liquid, moderately volatile, that is somewhat soluble in water and degrades slowly in it.[10] The hazard identification step uncovers several experimental animal studies between 1940 and 1960, all showing lethal toxicity to the liver at high doses but no toxic effects below an identifiable "threshold" dose; cancer was not studied. One more recent study, however, appears to show that lifetime exposure to much lower doses causes significant increases in liver cancers in both mice and rats. The only human data are on exposed workers, too few to draw statistically valid conclusions (two cases of cancer diagnosed in fewer than two hundred workers, when one case might have been expected). From these data, EPA decides that the solvent is a "possible" (as opposed to probable or definite) human carcinogen.

In dose-response assessment, the analyst then uses a mathematical model to predict a plausible "upper-bound" estimate of human cancer risk by extrapolating from the animal studies: from high to low doses, and from laboratory species (rats and mice) to humans. Applying these models to the measured animal data, EPA estimates a "unit cancer risk" (risk for an average lifetime exposure to 1 milligram per kilogram [mg/kg] of body weight per day) of about two in one hundred for lung cancer from inhalation, based on studies of male rats, and about five in one hundred for liver cancer from ingestion, based on studies of male mice.

In exposure assessment, the analyst then uses monitoring data and dispersion models to calculate that approximately 80 neighbors may be exposed to about eight ten-thousandths mg/kg of body weight per day, and 150 workers to about one thousandth mg/kg per day; and through gradual groundwater contamination, about 50,000 people may be exposed to one to two thousandths mg/kg per day in their drinking water after about twenty years.

Finally, the risk characterization combines these calculations into numerical upper-bound estimates of excess lifetime human cancer risk. In this hypothetical case, the result might be eight in one hundred thousand of the general population, one in one thousand nearby residents, and three in a thousand workers (note from the previous paragraph that the actual numbers—of neighbors and workers, at least—are far smaller, but risk assessments are normally expressed in numbers per thousand for consistency's sake). These estimates are then to be used by the EPA's "risk managers"—that is, the officials responsible for its regulatory decisions—to decide what risks are the highest priority for regulation and what regulatory action (if any) is justified.

Risk Management

In current EPA practice, risk management primarily means choosing and justifying regulatory initiatives. EPA does not have an "organic act," a single broad statutory mandate for environmental management. It administers a complex patchwork of separate statutes, each of which addresses a particular set of problems, establishes its own range of authorized management actions (usually regulations), and specifies its own criteria for making such decisions. Some of the laws direct that health risks be minimized regardless of costs; others that the risks be balanced against costs; and still others that the best available technology be used to minimize risks (allowing some judgment about what technologies are economically "available"), or that new technology be developed to meet a standard.[11]

In practice EPA and other regulatory agencies actually apply their own rules of thumb, based on risk and cost, to manage health risks. In one study that examined 132 federal regulatory decisions on environmental carcinogens from 1976 through 1985, two clear patterns emerged. Every chemical with an individual cancer risk greater than four chances in one thousand was regulated; and with only one exception, no action was taken to regulate any chemical with an individual risk less than one chance in one million. In the risk range between these two levels, cost-effectiveness was the primary criterion. That is to say, risks were regulated if the cost per life saved was less than $2 million, but not if the cost was higher.[12]

These findings strongly suggest that risk managers use their own norms to distinguish among *de manifestis* risks (risks so high that agencies will almost always act to reduce them, regardless of cost), *de minimis* risks (risks judged too small to deserve consideration, even though highly exposed or susceptible individuals in the population may be at serious risk), and a gray area in between where cost-effectiveness is the primary criterion.

Science and Values

QRA has now been adopted in varying degrees by all the federal environmental and health regulatory agencies. It has also been institutionalized in a professional society (the Society for Risk Analysis), a journal, and a growing professional community of practitioners in government agencies, chemical producer and user industries, consulting firms, universities and research institutes, and advocacy organizations.

Despite its widespread use, however, serious dispute remains as to whether risk assessment is really scientific or merely a recasting of value judgments into scientific jargon. The language of risk assessment is less accessible to the general public and their elected representatives; does it nonetheless provide a more scientifically objective basis for public policy decisions?

Risk Assessment Policy

Risk assessment in practice is permeated by value judgments. One such judgment governs the selection of substances for risk assessment in the first place. In practice, these value judgments are based not only on preliminary evidence of risk but also on publicity, lawsuits, and other political pressures. Another judgment concerns what effects, or "end points," are considered: most focus on cancer, with less attention as yet to other health hazards, other species, ecosystems, or other environmental values.

In conducting each risk assessment, the analysts' own value judgments come into play whenever they must make assumptions or draw inferences in the absence of objective facts. Such judgments are identified collectively as "risk assessment policy." Hazard identification, for example, relies on evidence from epidemiological studies of human effects, from animal bioassays, from short-term laboratory tests *(in vitro)*, or simply from comparison of the compound's molecular structure with other known hazards. In practice, these data are usually few and fragmentary, often collected for different purposes, and of varied quality; the analyst must make numerous judgments about their applicability.

For both dose-response and exposure assessment, analysts must routinely use mathematical models to generate risk estimates. Even the best dose-response models, however, are based on simplified biology and fragmentary data. Scientists must interpolate the dose-response relationship between a small number of observations, extrapolate it to lower doses often far beyond the observed range, and adjust for the many possible differences between species and conditions of exposure. Similarly, in exposure assessment, analysts must make many assumptions about variability in natural dispersion patterns and population movements, about other sources of exposure, and about the susceptibility of those exposed (for instance, healthy adults compared with children or chemically sensitive persons).

Finally, the analyst must synthesize a characterization of overall risk out of the diverse, uncertain, and sometimes conflicting estimates derived from the previous three steps. Such choices include weighing the quality, persuasiveness, and applicability of differing bodies of evidence; deciding how to estimate and adjust for statistical uncertainties; and even choosing which of various possible estimates to present ("best estimate" or "upper bound," for instance).

Inference Guidelines

Given these many unavoidable judgments, the conclusions of health risk assessments are inevitably shaped far more by their assumptions than by objective "facts." Both the EPA and other agencies have therefore developed guidance documents called "inference guidelines," which specify what assumptions and rules of thumb are to be used in calculating risks. Such guidelines cannot be scientifically definitive because the underlying science contains fundamental uncertainties. They are, rather, policy directives based on a mixture of scientific consensus and political choices about the appropriate level of prudence. The rationale for inference guidelines is that even if absolute risk levels are unknown, better comparative decisions can still be made if all risk assessments use a consistent set of methods and assumptions.

The EPA published its first interim guidelines for cancer risk assessment in 1976.[13] More detailed guidance was published in 1986 for health risk assessment of chemical mixtures and suspect developmental toxicants (including guidelines for carcinogenicity and mutagenicity risk assessment) and for estimating exposures; proposed guidelines for assessing reproductive risks were published in 1988.[14] Other agencies also proposed guidelines for cancer risk assessment during this period: the National Cancer Advisory Board in 1976; the Interagency Regulatory Liaison Group, the Regulatory Council, and the president's Office of Science and Technology Policy (OSTP) in 1979; the Occupational Safety and Health Administration in 1980; and OSTP again in the 1980s.[15]

These guidelines differed in important respects. The 1982 OSTP draft, for instance, recommended more skeptical evaluation of extrapolation from high to low dosages, reasoning that high dosages introduce artificially toxic effects of their own that would not occur at lower dosages. This position represented one view within the scientific community, but it differed from the EPA's and was consistent with the Reagan administration's goal of less regulation.

A Conservative Bias?

A major reason for differences among the guidelines is an intense and continuing debate—both scientific and political—over whether the regulatory agencies' risk estimates are systematically biased in favor of excessive caution. If each assumption includes some intuitive "safety factor" favoring health protection, for instance, and these factors are then multiplied (as they often must be), the overall safety factor may be far greater than any of them individually. A conventional wisdom has developed among many risk analysts, especially in the business community but also at the EPA, that these practices have rendered the agency's risk assessments excessively cautious and that they should be revised to reflect only best estimates of risk rather than large margins of safety. In September 1988 EPA decided to rewrite its inference guidelines once again, possibly because of pressure to incorporate less conservative assumptions.[16]

Other risk experts argue, however, that many of these assumptions may not be excessively cautious at all. Human susceptibility and exposure levels can both be as easily underestimated as overestimated, as can the toxicity of a substance itself. A distinguished risk research group in 1988 identified plausible biological reasons showing that existing risk assessment methods—despite all their "safety factors"—may in fact underestimate some risks of low-level exposure. Given scientific uncertainty, moreover, "best estimate" methods cannot themselves avoid value judgments, errors, and biases: they may simply substitute different ones, favoring less prudence toward health protection.[17]

Multiple Risks and Risk Management

The unavoidability of value judgments pervades risk assessment even in its simplest forms, applied as above to the risk of a single result (cancer) from a single substance. Beyond these simplest cases, however, lies the far greater complexity of the decisions that EPA and other agencies must actually make, and the multiplicity of risks involved in such "risk management" decisions.

Imagine, for instance, a relatively common issue: EPA must establish requirements for air and water emissions and hazardous waste storage permits at a new facility for chemical reprocessing and incineration. Many risks must be considered in setting such standards: cancer, respiratory ailments, fish mortality, stream eutrophication, crop damage, diminished visibility, and economic hardship to the surrounding community, to list just a few. There may be many beneficial effects as well: reduced damage to health and ecosystems because of improved waste disposal practices, economic benefits to the surrounding community, and others.

In principle, risk assessment can estimate the probability of each of these effects individually. It does not specify, however, which should be considered, nor make them commensurable, nor provide weights specifying their relative importance. In practice, risk assessment has dealt with these issues by oversimplifying them, focusing on only a few human health effects. This simplification may, however, obscure the more diverse considerations required by more complex decisions.

Risk Assessment and Environmental Decisions

By the end of the 1980s risk assessment was established as the primary language of analysis and management at the EPA. The agency's statutes did not contain this consistency of discourse, but virtually every EPA administrative decision was couched in terms of how much risk it would reduce: allocating budget priorities among programs, justifying individual regulatory proposals, even framing EPA's proposed research program for the 1990s. Why?

Management Tool

From the perspective of senior EPA administrators such as Ruckelshaus and his successors, formal risk assessment offered a powerful new management tool. One of the most intractable problems facing every EPA administrator is the proliferation of uncoordinated statutes, programs, and regulatory mandates, each advocated (and opposed) by powerful constituencies in the glare of the mass media. This fragmentation is exacerbated by innumerable ad hoc restrictions—statutory deadlines and "hammer clauses," court orders and consent decrees, and others—by which these constituencies have sought to force EPA's priorities and decisions in one or another direction.[18]

Risk assessment provided a common denominator—human health risk—by which the administrator could rationalize and defend the administrative decisions he or she must ultimately make across these many mandates and constituencies. Lacking any unified framework or criteria in statutes, the administrator in effect used risk assessment to *create* such a framework, justified by the common-sense virtues of reasonableness, consistency, and scientific objectivity.

Assistant Administrator Milton Russell argued in a 1987 article, for instance, that risk balancing was the only alternative to a much cruder and more fragmented approach, in which priorities were set mainly by historical accident and political influence, and regulatory remedies were limited to requiring specific technologies to clean up individual media (ignoring, for example, the risks that might be increased by moving pollutants from water to land or land to air).[19]

A Political Tool

At least as important as its managerial value, however, was its political value: it gave the EPA administrator a powerful new way to control the agenda of regulatory debates.

An important antecedent to EPA's risk assessment requirements was set by the Office of Management and Budget (OMB), which required cost-benefit analysis as a framework for evaluating proposed regulations. By the early 1980s OMB had obtained vastly broadened authority to impose cost-benefit requirements—"regulatory impact assessments"—on environmental (and other) regulatory proposals. These requirements shifted the terms of debate from health and environmental quality to economics and thus significantly expanded OMB's influence on the environmental regulatory agenda—and that of the regulated businesses—at the EPA's expense.

Risk assessment, however, made risk rather than dollars the new focus for policy analysis, and provided a criterion by which to compare programs and proposals on terms relevant to EPA's mission and expertise. To be sure, risk assessment was also being used by practitioners in the business community as a weapon *against* aggressive regulation, by lobbying for less cautious inference guidelines.[20] But at least the debate was defined in terms of scientific issues, about which EPA's scientists could argue from strength, and on which the EPA administrator's decisions were normally accorded greater deference than in the broader domains of economics and politics.[21] Whatever its imperfections, therefore, risk assessment allowed EPA to wrap its decisions in the legitimacy and apparent objectivity of science, and in the language of health effects rather than merely economic benefits.

Risk Perception and Communication

While the use of risk assessment strengthened EPA's hand in dealing with OMB, it tended to exacerbate conflict between EPA and the general public. First, most controversies over environmental hazards turned on the question of how much evidence was needed before regulating. Public advocacy groups tended to take the stand, "If in doubt, regulate to protect health," whereas businesses' attitude was, "If in doubt, don't regulate until you have proof." From the perspective of the public, quantitative risk assessment tipped such controversies in favor of business, both by implicitly accepting the view that proof rather than prudence was required to justify regulations and by promoting "paralysis by analysis" in the regulatory process.

Second, the professionalization of risk assessment created a new commonality of perspective among risk "experts," who shared a technical view of risks and disdained the broader concerns of the general public as ignorant, irrational, or self-interested. Expert risk analysts frequently held strong prejudices that their relatively narrow and specialized methods were not merely one source of relevant information, but the *only* proper basis for risk management decisions; and these value judgments themselves exacerbated public distrust of risk analysis.[22] Why are technical estimates of hypothetical cancer risks any more "real," or any more exclusively the proper basis for policy decisions, than public concerns about unanticipated leaks, spills, or plant malfunctions, about risks to their economic well-being, or about harm to their community because of industrial waste disposal? Indeed, what if the estimates made by today's risk analysts turn out to be wrong?

Most risk experts, moreover, were employed either by businesses or by the regulatory agencies themselves; and while they might disagree about technical details, most shared the attitude that as professionals they understood the issues better than the lay public. The result was therefore to create an alliance between experts in the agencies and those in the regulated industries and to redefine the issues as matters of expert reason versus the lay public's irrationality. Perhaps understandably, the public responded with distrust, suspecting both the experts' jargon and their value judgments.[23]

Risk analysts reacted by advocating better "risk communication." Most such efforts, however, were essentially one-way attempts to convince the public that the technical understanding of risks was the correct one. Risk communication seems unlikely to succeed until the experts accept the legitimacy of public perceptions and begin to deal with them. Quantitative risk assessment is a useful tool, but not the only basis, for making environmental decisions.[24]

The 1980s in Retrospect

Risk assessment was an effective response to the environmental agenda of the 1980s, an agenda dominated by the EPA's need to set regulatory priorities among large numbers of toxic chemicals and to justify regulatory decisions. It has also been useful in other settings: examples include regulation of drugs, cosmetics, and food additives; other consumer products; occupational health hazards; siting of industrial facilities; and the design and management of hazardous technologies. EPA optimists envision a trend toward the substitution of real data, backed by scientific consensus, for the cautious assumptions and safety factors that have so far dominated the process.[25]

Most observers, however, and even many practitioners, are more skeptical. Beyond a few well-studied substances and health effects, data remain scarce and expensive, basic mechanisms (let alone magnitudes) of toxicity remain uncertain, and exposure patterns and confounding factors will always be too complex to identify with certainty. Interestingly, a study of EPA risk-assessment personnel found that although most of those trained in the physical or social sciences, engineering, and law favored the use of risk assessment in policymaking, two-thirds of those trained in biomedical and environmental sciences—presumably those most familiar with its substance—opposed it.[26]

The political limits of risk assessment were also illustrated by the new provisions for regulating hazardous air pollutants under the Clean Air Act Amendments of 1990. In this statute the Congress, frustrated by the appearance of "paralysis by analysis" in the slow pace of risk assessment, directed EPA to set technology-based standards within two years regardless of risk for some 189 substances listed as high-priority hazardous air pollutants, and then to reconsider any remaining risks eight years later. It is not clear that this approach will prove to be more effective, given the need for EPA to make determinations of the "maximum achievable control technology" for each substance in each regulated industry, but the decision clearly showed Congress's impatience with the expensive and time-consuming levels of proof demanded by risk assessment as it has come to be practiced.

The politics of environmental decisionmaking is unlikely to yield to a new era of expert authority in any case. Political pluralism is deeply rooted in the statutes and procedures of U.S. environmental management, and these procedures are moving toward more explicit negotiation processes that involve all affected parties rather than relying only on expert authority.[27] A more likely result is that risk assessment will continue to be routinized, refined, and elaborated to incorporate additional health risks. As with cost-benefit analysis before it, however, arguments about the assumptions and inferences in risk assessment will continue to be used as surrogates for arguments about the real issues: whether particular substances or sites will be more tightly regulated, who will bear the risks and costs, and whether such decisions should be made by consensus among experts or through political negotiation.

The 1990s: Comparing Risks and Tools

Risk-based decisionmaking is now a centerpiece of EPA policy, but it has nevertheless undergone an important shift in meaning, reflecting changes both in the environmental policy agenda and in the use of risk assessment to address that agenda. These include changes in policy concerns (from toxic chemicals and hazardous wastes to other sources of exposure, from health risks to ecological damage, and from specific sites and substances to global hazards); in the use of risk assessment itself, from quantitative analysis of particular substances to comparative analysis of risk priorities; and in policy responses to these new priorities, from pollution control to pollution prevention and from "command-and-control regulation" to a broader range of "risk reduction tools."

Changing Issues, Changing Risks

Environmental policy in the 1980s emphasized the regulation of hazardous wastes and toxic chemicals, for which QRA provided a useful analytical framework, but most of these substances ultimately involved relatively low levels of risk. The agenda of the 1990s, however, has moved toward other issues for which the established risk assessment and management procedures are less suited. As the big industrial sources began to control emissions, the most serious domestic pollution problems that remained came from more ubiquitous sources that were harder to assess in isolation or to control by regulation: some examples were surface water runoff, indoor air pollution, and stubborn multicausal problems such as urban smog.

Even more important, the agenda of the 1990s shifted to broader international and global issues for which a domestic regulatory approach by itself was no longer adequate: for example, transboundary pollution, the environmental impacts of international trade arrangements, and larger global problems requiring international solutions, such as stratospheric ozone depletion, maintenance of ocean fisheries, mitigation of global warming, and sustainable development initiatives to accommodate the material needs and aspirations of the world's population without destroying the environmental conditions and natural processes on which they depend.

Are these problems amenable to quantitative risk assessment? In principle, yes, perhaps, but in practice, the costs and complexity of such assessments themselves may often outweigh their value: prudence in action is ultimately more important than proof in analysis. One can describe many patterns of global environmental degradation as serious risks in reasoned though intuitive terms, for instance, and it is hard to say what the formalized language and procedures of risk assessment would add. The causes are often reasonably clear; the magnitudes and probabilities are imperfectly understood but serious enough to command attention; and the goal is not a finely tuned regulation, but changes in the directions of very gross trends. If we defer action until EPA can develop detailed quantitative risk estimates, these trends may progress far beyond our control, if they have not already. Instead of waiting for more quantitative risk assessment, therefore, one can seek at least to slow the trends while continuing to monitor the results.

Comparative Risk Analysis

QRA was developed to estimate health risks associated with specific chemicals and exposures and therefore to permit comparisons among the health hazards they posed. It was not originally designed for setting priorities among diverse *kinds* of environmental problems, such as between a chemical threatening health and a development project threatening a wetland. Beginning in the mid 1980s, however, EPA administrators undertook a broader and more ambitious initiative: to use the language of risk as an agencywide framework for setting priorities among all its programs and issues. Within the constraints of statutory authorities and budget procedures, the EPA's top management advocated a strategic planning process based on relative risk criteria as a primary process for setting priorities, across and beyond its established regulatory programs as well as within them.

A pioneering study by EPA in 1987, entitled *Unfinished Business,* compared the relative risks of some thirty-one environmental problems spanning the full range of EPA's responsibilities. The study considered four different kinds of risk: cancer, noncancer health risks, ecological effects, and other effects on human welfare (such as pollution damage to historic structures). It found that the information available to assess risks for virtually any of these problems was surprisingly poor: best for cancer (though even that was spotty) but seriously inadequate for hazardous waste sites, biotechnology, new chemicals, pesticides, ecosystems, and others. It also found that the agency's actual risk management priorities were more consistent with public opinion than with the problems EPA managers thought most serious (for example, the agency was devoting more resources to the problem of chemical waste disposal than to indoor air pollution and radon). Third, it found that in all programs except surface water quality, the EPA had been more concerned with pollution that affected public health than with the protection of natural habitats and ecosystems. Finally, it found that even with respect to public health hazards, localized hazards caused much higher risks to individuals than overall risk estimates revealed.[28]

This study was a remarkably candid step on the EPA's part to take stock of its diverse responsibilities and to lay the groundwork for setting conscious priorities among them. Significantly, it was *not* a formal quantitative risk assessment, because both data and methodology were lacking for most noncancer risks. Rather, it was based on the consensus of perceptions of relative risk offered by some seventy-five EPA senior managers, and on comparisons of those perceptions with opinion poll data on perceptions held by the general public. These perceived risks were then compared with the amount of effort the agency was devoting to each problem.

The study showed both the opportunities and the difficulties of using risk as a common denominator for all these concerns. On the one hand, it used the idea of relative risk to build consensus about priorities across the patchwork of statutes and programs that EPA must administer. At the same time, however, it accepted the necessity of using subjective managerial judgments, rather than quantitative methodology, as the basis for these priorities. By doing so, it implicitly redefined risk to include not only quantifiable health hazards but also all environmental concerns—and reaffirmed the need for reasoned judgments about values, rather than quantitative formulas and technical procedures, as the ultimate basis for policy decisions. The result was to make risk assessment a more general language of political debate about environmental priorities, but at the same time to blur its image as a precise technical procedure for health risk estimation.

In 1989 EPA administrator William Reilly asked the agency's Science Advisory Board to sponsor a thorough review of the *Unfinished Business* report by a committee of outside scientists and policy experts and to make recommendations on further use of the relative risk approach. The committee's report endorsed the EPA's further development of this approach, recommended its use in setting budget priorities, and made substantive recommendations for addressing several high-priority environmental threats.[29] It recommended increased emphasis, for instance, on reducing human destruction of natural habitats and species, and on slowing stratospheric ozone depletion and global warming, and correspondingly less emphasis on more localized concerns such as oil spills and groundwater contamination. Among health risks, it recommended high-risk emphasis on pollution of air and drinking water and on occupational and indoor exposures. Like *Unfinished Business* itself, this report too was based on expert consensus rather than on quantitative risk assessment procedures.

Administrator Reilly publicly endorsed the report and its recommendations and made its implementation a personal priority. All EPA regions were now required to use comparative risk studies to justify their annual budget requests; perhaps even more significant, the EPA was reportedly using relative risk estimates to guide its enforcement priorities. It also encouraged states to conduct similar studies; as incentives, it provided funding for pilot projects and offered modest increases in state authority to reallocate funds from low-risk to higher-risk problems. EPA also sponsored comparative risk studies in several of the newly democratic countries of eastern Europe, which faced severe environmental problems with equally severe shortages of money to correct them. Even the OMB embraced the idea, advocating pilot projects to set budget priorities among environmental programs within the departments of Defense and Energy;

ultimately, it would like to use comparative risk analysis to set priorities for environmental programs across government.

A key issue for the future of comparative risk assessment is how it should be done: by experts using technical procedures (as in traditional QRA), by consensus of expert judgments, or by a broader public involvement process. EPA's own pilot projects reveal examples of each approach and unresolved debate about which should be used. To the extent that comparative risk assessment is modeled on the technocratic procedures of QRA—the "hard" version—it implies several fundamental premises that are at least debatable. One is that "risks" of different sorts can be reduced to simple measures and that these measures can be compared. Ecosystems, for example, may be too complex to be measured by any single "sentinel species" or common denominator of risk, and some human impacts may simply make them different rather than better or worse. A second assumption is that priorities should be based only on the highest overall risks, rather than on risks to the most exposed populations or ecosystems (in fact, *both* may legitimately be important). Another is that experts' perceptions of risks are more accurate than laymen's (in reality most risks are both too diverse and too uncertain to permit "scientific" conclusions about them, so that experts too are ultimately making personal value judgments—and many experts themselves disagree). Finally, comparative risk assessment may set up false choices by defining only a fixed set of problems and solutions for comparison—comparing environmental risks only with each other rather than with alternative possibilities, and by implication ruling out tradeoffs with other sectors—and thus introducing a hidden bias against more fundamental reforms.[30]

In many of the state pilot projects, however, comparative risk assessment has been introduced in a variety of "soft" versions: that is, broader political processes for developing consensus about values and priorities. These processes typically use technical information and expert judgments to the extent that they are available, but they also use information about public concerns, whether or not they are well-documented technically; and they ultimately recommend priorities based on public consensus rather than on technical or administrative judgments alone. These "soft" versions carry their own possible pitfalls, such as intensely held misconceptions or self-interested agendas on the part of participants. But these hazards can in principle be checked by the necessity of explicit and persuasive reasoning, and they offer at least the potential for developing greater consensus about environmental priorities through an open democratic process.[31]

Pollution Prevention and Life-Cycle Risks

A third major policy change in the 1990s has been the shift from correction and mitigation of pollution to reducing risks through pollution prevention. Historically, U.S. environmental policy relied primarily on dilution of wastes in the environment, on isolation of materials in shallow landfills, and since 1970 on waste treatment, requiring businesses to install costly technologies to remove or neutralize wastes at the "end of the pipe" before discharging them into the environment. By the 1980s all these practices had become both costly and substantially discredited. They had not reduced pollution but had simply spread it around differently—from water to land (sludge), land to air (incineration), air to land (incinerator ash), and so forth—and their expense was becoming a significant and rising cost of production. Leading businesses recognized this problem as early as the late 1970s and initiated campaigns to reduce pollution and simultaneously save money: "Pollution Prevention Pays" (3M), "Waste Reduction Always Pays" (Dow), and others. Additional firms began to pay attention after 1986, when the Superfund Amendments and Reauthorization Act (SARA) began to require them to report their total annual emissions of several hundred toxic chemicals: both the adverse publicity and the costs of these losses got the attention of many chief executives.

In 1989, in the midst of its shift toward risk-based priorities, EPA adopted a new policy statement emphasizing pollution prevention over treatment and safe disposal and established the Office of Pollution Prevention to guide its implementation.[32] This policy was given legislative support in the Pollution Prevention Act of 1990 (though it is not yet systematically reflected in the EPA's many regulatory statutes, some of which—by mandating specific control approaches and investments—are serious barriers to prevention incentives). Beginning in 1990 EPA initiated two widely publicized pollution prevention projects, both relying on voluntary cooperation by businesses. One was the Industrial Toxics Project ("33/50" program), under which businesses agree to reduce emissions of seventeen targeted toxic chemicals, from a 1988 baseline, by 33 percent by the end of 1992 and by 50 percent by 1995. The Green Lights Program was the other project, under which participating organizations agree to switch to long-lasting, low-energy lightbulbs: the goal is to reduce national electricity demand (and associated air pollution emissions) by 10 percent. As of February 1992, 734 companies had committed to the 33/50 program, and 40 corporations had signed up for Green Lights. Some companies reported major reductions already achieved: AT&T reported a 66 percent reduction of the seventeen priority toxins, and BF Goodrich a 32 percent reduction; Dow reported reducing releases of all reportable toxic chemicals by 30 percent. Under Green Lights, forty-nine buildings have already been upgraded, reducing electricity usage for lighting by 40 percent to 70 percent—equivalent to avoiding emissions of 224 tons of sulfur dioxide, 97 tons of nitrogen oxides, and 26,400 tons of carbon dioxide.

Pollution prevention has provided a valuable step forward in the debate about risks, demonstrating in case after case that preventing environmental risks often costs far less—and provides greater benefits—than capital-intensive treatment facilities. Two important issues remain for the 1990s. One is to assure that pollution prevention initiatives really do reduce pollution and its related risks, and do not just create different risks that may be no better. This requires a new form of comparative risk study, called "life-cycle analysis," in which products are compared with their substitutes throughout their whole life-cycles—from resource extraction through production, consumption, reuse, and recycling to ultimate disposal. Interesting life-cycle studies have now begun to appear—comparing paper versus plastic bags and cloth versus disposable diapers, for instance—and such studies are already shedding valuable new light on the interrelationships among risks and the real choices that are necessary to reduce them (for instance, phasing out the whole cycles of extraction and use of some high-risk materials, such as chlorofluorocarbons [CFCs], rather than merely reducing their use in particular products or processes).

The second issue is to decide how much pollution prevention should be required. Most pollution prevention actions so far have been voluntary, reflecting circumstances in which reducing risks serves the economic self-interest of the polluter as well as the social goal: the only reasons they were not done years before were that no one stopped to think about them, or that changes in costs—caused by rising energy prices or waste disposal charges, for instance—have now made pollution prevention preferable. But what about preventing pollution when it really does cost the polluter more to do so than to throw it away? In principle, the answer is that everyone who causes pollution should be charged its real costs, and these payments should actually be used to prevent the risk, restore the damage, and compensate the victims. In practice, however, it is hard to calculate the "correct" levels of such charges, and there is no single institutional mechanism for imposing and collecting them. The focus of this debate, therefore, has shifted to the issue of what policy "tools" are most effective in promoting reduction of environmental risks.

Risk Reduction Tools

The *Reducing Risk* report not only recommended priorities among risks but also urged the EPA to use a broader range of policy tools to reduce them. EPA's tools have historically been the powers to regulate the facilities, technologies, and substances that cause pollution, to enforce these regulations, to subsidize wastewater treatment plants and hazardous waste site cleanups, and to sponsor applied research and development related to these activities. These tools have been effective in many ways, particularly in reducing the emissions of well-known pollutants from many industries. As early as the mid 1970s, however, both the EPA and other agencies and governments began experimenting with other approaches. One reason was the practical limits of regulatory approaches:

whatever the law said, the EPA could not simply prohibit all new pollution in areas such as the Los Angeles Basin, so it needed to create mechanisms for trading pollution between old and new sources (with at least some net improvement on each trade). A second reason was that risk priorities were shifting toward more ubiquitous problems that were less amenable to traditional regulatory solutions. For these latter types of problems in particular, different policy tools were necessary.

In fact, governments have many tools besides regulation and subsidies for reducing environmental risks. A first group of such tools includes market-oriented economic incentives. Tradable permits, for instance, allow businesses to buy and sell their permitted amounts of emissions so that pollution standards can be achieved at the least cost. Another example is pollution charges, which can be used both to pay for environmental services and as an economic incentive to reduce emissions. Deposit refund programs can be used to encourage recycling of containers and toxic or bulky products. Still other economic tools include strict liability requirements for high-risk substances (such as hazardous wastes), which significantly increase the incentives to reduce unnecessary use, substitute less toxic alternatives, and manage the remainder carefully; and procurement specifications, which use the power of government purchasing to expand markets for recycled materials and other "environmentally friendly" products. These approaches are discussed in chapter 11.

A second group of tools includes information disclosure mandates, such as toxics-labeling and emissions-reporting requirements. The federal Superfund Amendments of 1986 required annual public reporting of all significant use and emissions of some four hundred toxic chemicals; both the unwelcome publicity and the new awareness of the costs of these emissions provided powerful new incentives for businesses to reduce them and to substitute less risky chemicals. By negotiating with local businesses, some communities have found ways to reduce the use of toxic chemicals.[33] California's Proposition 65 went even further, requiring businesses to put warning labels on all products that contain significant levels (1 additional cancer per 100,000 people) of substances that can cause cancer or birth defects. In effect, Proposition 65 linked risk assessment to mainstream economic ideology—let the marketplace decide, but with full information. By 1989 some 250 chemicals had been listed, and allowable doses were being set for the 50 most widely used ones.[34]

Perhaps most effective of all could be increased policy coordination with other agencies, whose policies often influence environmental problems and risks more strongly than the EPA's (for instance in agriculture, energy, transportation, military spending, and other sectors). Many federal policies continue to promote environmental risks even while the EPA is trying to prevent them, often for reasons that are no longer economically justified—rather like pressing the accelerator and the brake at the same time. Changing the policies that promote the problems might be far more effective than simply trying to add environmental regulations at the same time.

EPA has therefore begun to promote this broader range of policy tools. Voluntary programs, such as 33/50 and Green Lights (mentioned above), are one example. Marketable permits and pollution trading are another: both lead in auto fuels and chlorofluorocarbons are now being phased out through market trading, sulfur emissions futures are being traded on commodity markets, industries can reduce emissions by buying up and retiring old cars if that is cheaper than putting expensive controls on their smokestacks, and some municipalities may soon reduce water pollution by paying for runoff control by farmers. Others have developed alternative tools (such as environmental taxes and charges) further and faster than the EPA has (for example, some state and local governments as well as other nations), although President Bill Clinton has proposed a national tax on energy as a tool to slow global warming. Finally, the EPA has sought to work more actively with other federal agencies to reduce risks in each of the sectors for which they are responsible, such as agricultural crop support programs, national energy policies, and military procurement practices.

As in the case of the EPA's risk-based priorities policy, however, the use of alternative tools remains so far mainly an administrative initiative, using both the statutory and the persuasive powers of the agency as creatively as possible to address what seem to be the most important problems. Its statutes, in contrast, remain a vast patchwork of uncoordinated mandates, deadlines, and procedural and reporting requirements, some of which are even obstacles to effective risk reduction. It has no single "organic act" authorizing it to set priorities among its responsibilities, or to use nonregulatory tools as substitutes or complements to its regulatory mandates; and beyond the EPA's persuasiveness there is no national environmental strategy or other effective institutional mechanism for integrating environmental risk reduction into the priorities of other agencies. The EPA's initiatives have provided a good model and set a valuable agenda for risk-based decisionmaking, but a crucial question for the 1990s remains how consistently these initiatives will be sustained, followed through, and institutionalized in statutes and budgets.

From Risk Reduction to Sustainable Development

Ultimately, environmental management cannot be *only* a matter of "reducing risks." To sustain human civilizations we must sustain the environmental conditions and ecosystems that make them possible. As René Dubos has so articulately noted, however, we humans and our environment constantly shape each another, in beneficial and beautiful ways as well as in damaging and ugly ones.[35] To sustain environmental quality therefore requires positive action and creative vision, not merely control of risks. Where in the language of risk would one find the creative vision of environmental design? Or even the stewardship perspective of environmental conservation? On a more concrete level, where would one place the idea of rehabilitating degraded ecosystems? The vocabulary of risk-based decisionmaking is a valuable step forward from the patchwork of disparate and sometimes conflicting laws that preceded it (many of which are still in force), but it is ultimately too narrowly oriented toward adverse outcomes to provide an adequate framework for these more complex and creative tasks of environmental management.

These questions require a broader understanding of the interactions between human societies and their environments, and a more systematic and positive vision of their future, than is provided by the concept of risk. A framework for such a vision was proposed in 1987 by the United Nations' World Commission on Environment and Development in the concept of "sustainable development." This idea was further developed by the U.N. Conference on Environment and Development (the Earth summit) in Brazil in 1992; but as yet it remains more an idealized concept than a specific program of actions. Perhaps the highest-priority task for environmental policy in the 1990s is to spell out its details and work toward its implementation.[36]

Notes

1. Curtis C. Travis, Samantha A. Richter, Edmund A. C. Crouch, Richard Wilson, and Ernest D. Klema, "Cancer Risk Management: A Review of 132 Federal Regulatory Decisions," *Environmental Science and Technology* 21 (1987): 415-420.
2. Environmental Protection Agency, *Risk Assessment and Risk Management: Framework for Decisionmaking* (Washington, D.C.: EPA, 1984); *Unfinished Business: A Comparative Assessment of Environmental Problems* (Washington, D.C.: EPA, 1987), 1; EPA, *Reducing Risk: Setting Priorities and Strategies for Environmental Protection* (Washington, D.C.: Environmental Protection Agency, 1990), 16.
3. Mark E. Rushefsky, *Making Cancer Policy* (Albany: State University of New York Press, 1986), 74-80.
4. Ibid., 59-84.
5. Milton Russell and Michael Gruber, "Risk Assessment in Environmental Policy-Making," *Science* 236 (April 17, 1987): 286-290.
6. Executive Order No. 12291, February 17, 1981; and *Industrial Union Department, AFL-CIO* v. *American Petroleum Institute*, 448 U.S. 607 (1980). As a legal matter, the extent to which quantitative risk assessment (QRA) is required must be decided on a statute-by-statute basis; while this decision actually involved a proposed standard by the Occupational Safety and Health Administration for occupational exposure to benzene, it influenced all the regulatory agencies to put increased emphasis on QRA.
7. Vincent Covello and Joshua Menkes, *Risk Assessment and Risk Assessment Methods: The State of the Art* (Washington, D.C.: Division of Policy Research and Analysis, National Science Foundation, 1985), xxiii.
8. ENVIRON Corp., *Elements of Toxicology and Chemical Risk Assessment*, rev. ed. (Washington, D.C.: ENVIRON, July 1988), 9; National Research Council, *Risk*

Assessment in the Federal Government: Managing the Process (Washington, D.C.: National Academy Press, 1983), 18.

9. William Lowrance, *Of Acceptable Risk: Science and the Determination of Safety* (Los Altos, Calif.: William Kaufman, 1976); National Research Council, *Risk Assessment in the Federal Government,* 1983; William D. Ruckelshaus, "Science, Risk, and Public Policy," *Science* 221 (September 9, 1983): 1027-1028; ENVIRON, *Elements of Toxicology;* William D. Ruckelshaus, "Risk in a Free Society," *Risk Analysis* 4 (1984): 157-162.

10. Example adapted from EPA, "Workshop on Risk and Decision Making" (Materials prepared for EPA by Temple, Barker, and Sloane Inc. and ENVIRON Corp., 1986).

11. For a list see Rushefsky, *Making Cancer Policy,* 68-70.

12. Travis et al., "Cancer Risk Management."

13. Environmental Protection Agency, "Health Risk and Economic Impact Assessments of Suspected Carcinogens: Interim Procedures and Guidelines," *Federal Register* 41, May 25, 1976, 21402-21405.

14. *Federal Register* 51, September 24, 1986, 33992-34054; *Federal Register* 53, June 30, 1988, 24836-24869.

15. See Rushefsky, *Making Cancer Policy,* chaps. 3-6.

16. See, for instance, Adam M. Finkel, "Has Risk Assessment Become Too 'Conservative'?" *Resources* (Summer 1989): 11-13; and Terry F. Yosie, "Science and Sociology: The Transition to a Post-Conservative Risk Assessment Era" (Plenary address to the 1987 annual meeting of the Society for Risk Analysis, Houston, November 2, 1987). Dr. Yosie was then director of the EPA Science Advisory Board.

17. Finkel, "Risk Assessment?"; John C. Bailar III, Edmund A. C. Crouch, Rashid Shaikh, and Donna Speigelman, "One-Hit Models of Carcinogenesis: Conservative or Not?" *Risk Analysis* 8 (1988): 485-497.

18. See Bruce A. Ackerman and William T. Hassler, *Clean Coal/Dirty Air* (New Haven, Conn.: Yale University Press, 1981), for a fuller discussion of the politics of administrative decisionmaking processes for environmental protection.

19. Russell and Gruber, "Risk Assessment," 286-290.

20. Rushefsky, *Making Cancer Policy,* 92-94; see also *AIHC Recommended Alternatives to OSHA's Generic Carcinogen Proposal* (Scarsdale, N.Y.: American Industrial Health Council, 1978); and Edith Efron, *The Apocalyptics: Cancer and the Big Lie; How Environmental Politics Controls What We Know About Cancer* (New York: Simon and Schuster, 1984).

21. Yosie, "Science and Sociology."

22. Sheldon Krimsky and Alonzo Plough, *Environmental Hazards: Communicating Risks as a Social Process* (Dover, Mass.: Auburn House, 1989).

23. Ibid.; see also K. S. Shrader-Frechette, *Risk and Rationality: Philosophical Foundations for Populist Reforms* (Berkeley: University of California Press, 1991); Hugh Heclo, "Issue Networks and the Executive Establishment," in *The New American Political System,* ed. Anthony King (Washington, D.C.: American Enterprise Institute, 1978); and EPA, *Unfinished Business.*

24. Krimsky and Plough, *Environmental Hazards.* The "tool versus rule" issue has also been discussed in relation to cost-benefit analysis of regulatory proposals; see Richard N. L. Andrews, "Cost-Benefit Analysis as Regulatory Reform," in *Cost-Benefit Analysis and Environmental Regulations: Politics, Ethics, and Methods,* ed. Daniel Swartzman, Richard A. Liroff, and Kevin G. Croke (Washington, D.C.: Conservation Foundation, 1982).

25. Yosie, "Science and Sociology."

26. Robert W. Rycroft, James L. Regens, and Thomas Dietz, "Incorporating Risk Assessment and Benefit-Cost Analysis in Environmental Management," *Risk Analysis* 8 (1988): 415-420.

27. Michael P. Elliott, "The Effect of Differing Assessments of Risk in Hazardous Waste Siting Negotiations," in *Negotiating Hazardous Waste Facility Siting and Permitting Agreements*, ed. Gail Bingham and Timothy Mealey (Washington, D.C.: Conservation Foundation, 1988).

28. EPA, *Unfinished Business.*

29. EPA, *Reducing Risk.*

30. Donald T. Hornstein, "Reclaiming Environmental Law: A Normative Critique of Comparative Risk Analysis," *Columbia Law Review* 92 (1992): 562-633.

31. *Comparative Risk Bulletin* 2, no. 9 (September 1992): 1-4. The *Bulletin* is published by the Northeast Center for Comparative Risk, Vermont Law School.

32. EPA, "Pollution Prevention Policy Statement," *Federal Register* 54, January 26, 1989, 3845-3847.

33. Frances M. Lynn, "Citizen Involvement in Using Right-to-Know Information for Emergency Planning and Source Reduction" (Paper presented at the annual meeting of the Air and Waste Management Association, Anaheim, California, June 25-30, 1989), paper no. 89-44.4.

34. Leslie Roberts, "A Corrosive Fight Over California's Toxics Law," *Science* 243 (January 20, 1989): 306-309.

35. René Dubos, *The Wooing of Earth* (New York: Scribner's, 1980).

36. World Commission on Environment and Development, *Our Common Future* (New York: Oxford University Press, 1987); see also chapter 13 by Richard Tobin in this volume.

11

The "NIMBY" Syndrome: Facility Siting and the Failure of Democratic Discourse

Daniel A. Mazmanian and David Morell

NIMBYs are noisy. NIMBYs are powerful. NIMBYs are everywhere. NIMBYs live near enough to corporate or government projects—and are upset enough about them—to work to stop, stall, or shrink them. NIMBYs organize, march, sue and petition to block the developers they think are threatening them.

—William Glaberson
New York Times, June 19, 1988

The democratic process as we know it today—the institutions of liberal, representative democracy—seem incapable of achieving democratic control of the "crucially important and inordinately complex" issues of modern technological society.

—H. D. Forbes (1988)

Reaching America's goals for cleaning up the nation's polluted air, water, and land will require industry to introduce safer and more efficient facilities and to dramatically alter its hazardous materials management practices. The ability of business to carry out these tasks is stymied in part by the equally compelling effort of local citizens and communities to protect themselves from the degradation that might result from having even a state-of-the-art facility built in their midst. When faced with a siting proposal, local residents often "just say no."[1] They need only demonstrate an ability to use the legal and political systems to cause interminable delays that, in turn, force many project developers to retreat and inhibit many other proposals entirely. Major energy, industrial, and waste management projects once accepted as vital to the nation's growth and well-being are now routinely opposed because of their perceived adverse impacts. The clamor of "not in my backyard" (NIMBY) is heard across the land.

What are the causes of this NIMBY syndrome? Does it help or hinder in achieving the nation's environmental agenda? How does it fit in the broader context of modern participatory democracy? These questions are addressed in this chapter.

The good news for many, especially those living near a proposed site, is that most projects can today be stopped through concerted action by local citizens working with environmental and health advocates from within or outside the community. The bad news is that society often pays a high price for such local vetoes, harming the economic viability of these communities and eventually weakening the nation's economy.[2] A confounding factor is that neither project opponents nor proponents are always able to distinguish between unsafe and unneeded facilities and those that are truly necessary for society and can be expected to operate safely. When "needed" facilities are rejected, nevertheless, there are serious consequences. When modern facilities for hazardous waste treatment, for example, are successfully opposed, all of us are left dependent on the leaky landfills of the past (or on export to places that manage wastes even less soundly than the United States), despite federal and state laws mandating that these wastes undergo treatment.

One of today's most important questions is how to move beyond the current gridlock created by NIMBYism in siting power plants, major industrial facilities, and hazardous waste facilities in ways that make sense ecologically, technologically, politically, and economically. Workable answers are central to realizing the nation's environmental and economic agendas.

Causes of the NIMBY Syndrome

In one sense, the NIMBY syndrome is a response to an inherent imbalance in the distribution of any project's benefits and costs. The costs in human health risks and environmental and esthetic decay are concentrated in one locale; benefits accrue across a much broader area.

NIMBYism goes beyond narrow self-interest, however. It springs from an awareness in our nuclear age that science and technology have the ability not only to improve the human condition but also to change it for the worse. The widely shared sympathy with project opponents ("it could have been my town") reveals an underlying sense of guilt about shifting too many health and environmental costs onto others, especially when this intrusion is done explicitly—as is always the case with facility siting. The modern paradox is that the industrial system that spawns America's material affluence is simultaneously the source of enormous pollution loads for the air, water, and land.

In recent years, the most strident environmental opposition has been aimed at projects designed to handle hazardous wastes and materials—toxins, petroleum, chemicals, and industrial by-products. This experience forms the backdrop of the discussion. NIMBYism is exacerbated by a widespread fear of hazardous substances from asbestos, food preservatives, and pesticides to PCBs (polychlorinated biphenyls), and a growing "chemophobia."[3] This fear often comes out as outrage when citizens suspect that someone, knowingly or otherwise, has placed, or proposes to place, the lives of their family, friends, and community in jeopardy by exposing them to toxic and hazardous materials.[4] Outrage then clouds the community's ability to consider a project on its merits. How can one expect otherwise? A disposal facility for hazardous chemical wastes is seen as no more desirable than a nuclear power plant in the eyes of the public: few people want either one located within one hundred miles of where they live.[5]

Fear and outrage over toxics surfaced at the very moment when the public's overall confidence in business and government leaders to make well-informed, impartial, safe, and prudent decisions had severely diminished.[6] This created a profound crisis of legitimacy in American politics. The conventional public policy process, from the smallest community up through the states and federal government, has been rendered incapable of effectively balancing the country's needs for growth, development, and facility siting with those of health and environmental protection for current and future generations. Not even the courts, the traditional forum for those who believe they stand to suffer personal harm, have provided the needed leverage for the opponents of unwanted facilities.[7]

The year 1970 is a key date in these developments, for it ushered in the environmental movement as a social and political force to be reckoned with in the United States. Earth Day, the signing of the National Environmental Policy Act (NEPA), and the creation of the president's Council on Environmental Quality and the Environmental Protection Agency were followed quickly by dramatic revisions to the nation's air and water pollution laws. Decisions about major infrastructure projects, industrial facilities, and waste management have never been the same.

Solutions to NIMBYism

In view of these changes in the political landscape, to respond appropriately to the NIMBY syndrome presents a serious challenge to conventional thinking and to the practices of business, government, and individual citizens. Several promising approaches have surfaced. Each one balances the need for siting economically and socially critical facilities with the needs of the host communities to preserve their basic political rights and have their health and safety concerns taken seriously. The goal is to achieve a process whereby "good" facilities are sited in a timely manner in "good" locations. At the same time, the process would not site "good" facilities in "bad" locations, and would not approve siting of "bad" facilities anywhere.

Although disagreements persist over criteria for "good" and "bad," attention must be paid both to facility characteristics and locational quality. Facility proponents will need to reassess their designs and site preferences, while adversaries review their reasons for opposition. Both groups will need to approach the whole siting dilemma anew. As such, the methods most successful in responding to the NIMBY syndrome hold profound implications not only for accelerating the cause of environmental protection but also for stimulating the United States' economic growth and ensuring a more democratic society.[8]

The Crucial Questions of Siting

To understand how projects are stymied today, and how this might change in the future, it is important to recognize how the answers to a few key questions about the siting of any major new facility have evolved over the course of two decades in response to the environmental movement.

1. Who takes the initiative in defining the need for a facility? As the United States underwent industrialization and grew virtually unchecked from the end of the Civil War up through the 1960s, manufacturing plants, energy facilities, and petrochemical factories were built whenever and wherever business deemed it profitable. Air and water were treated as free goods, land for expansion was relatively cheap, and wastes were easily disposed of. Scant attention was paid to the irreplaceability of the energy and material feedstocks that fueled the industrial order. Faith was placed instead in technological innovation and substitution. When oil ran low, it would be replaced by nuclear energy (wood by plastics, rubber by synthetics, and so on.) Technological optimism remained paramount until the dawn of the environmental age.

The pollution caused by any one business was seldom significant enough or scientifically (or legally) documentable enough to cause alarm and provoke action. The consequence by midcentury was that many of America's streams and rivers became open sewers; the air over major cities was polluted; and liquid and solid industrial wastes were routinely poured on the land to evaporate and percolate away, dumped into landfills, or pumped deep into the earth.

Contemporary pollution control laws and regulations empowered those who opposed these practices. Although some controls were placed on existing polluters, the opportunity to raise more extreme concerns emerged with particular clarity when any new projects were proposed. The initiative for project siting remained with business and government; but federal and state laws now require project proponents to notify communities of their intentions, meet stringent, new source pollution control standards, and produce extensive environmental impact reports. These reports are to disclose the proposed new facility's pollution potential and present information on feasible, less-polluting alternatives. Although an environmental impact report alone cannot kill a project, it can provide the opportunity to tie it up for years in administrative procedures and in the courts. The time so gained can be used to rally further political opposition. When the moment comes for the local land-use decision, often city hall is no longer ready to "just say yes." The potential "need" for the facility gets lost in the NIMBY furor.

Another major change today is that opponents are usually able to recruit their own environmentally oriented scientists and technical experts to counter claims by business and government that a project's health and environmental impact will be insignificant. Meanwhile, the Clean Air Act, Clean Water Act, Resource Conservation and Recovery Act, and Superfund laws have begun compelling industry to include in their business planning the cost of reducing or recapturing their wastes, and more safely disposing of that which remains.[9] Some hazardous substances used in business and commerce, such as DDT (dichlorodiphenyltrichloroethane), asbestos, and lead in gasoline and paints, have been banned outright because of their extreme threat to human health and the environment.[10]

Especially hard hit have been proposals for newer, more effective waste-management facilities designed to treat hazardous wastes that have traditionally been sent to landfills or injected underground. The resulting paralysis is a profound threat to the needed upgrading of U.S. industry.

2. *What are the economic/technical characteristics of the proposed project, and of its location?* Traditionally, just as the demand for a new facility was market-driven, so too were decisions about its technical configuration, location, emissions, and method of waste disposal. Local governments might use zoning to direct facilities to industrial areas and away from residences, and they usually required the facilities to meet health and safety codes. Waste disposal was handled in out-of-sight locations to avoid nuisance complaints from neighbors. Little attention was given by anyone to the potential it had for despoiling the ground or contaminating aquifers. Since 1980 the legacy of the United States' poor waste management practices has been exposed at the more than ten thousand potential Superfund sites, which the nation will be cleaning up over the next fifty or more years.[11]

At the onset of the environmental era, the predisposition of policymakers and the public was to set broad guidelines for pollution reduction, leaving the needed actions up to business. This approach produced several desired changes: in some areas of the country, less-polluting natural gas became favored over coal for powering major utilities; the combination of energy conservation with cogeneration and small-scale hydroelectric power helped meet the nation's electric energy needs; the catalytic converter was added to automobiles to reduce air emissions nationwide; and a massive campaign was undertaken to clean up the nation's waterways. In one area, however, there was little change. Most new industrial facilities received land-use approvals and permits, even in the face of NIMBY opposition.

By the 1980s fear over pollution and the health threats posed by industrial facilities had increased substantially.[12] Seemingly unaware of what this implied, industry continued to pursue its traditional ways in siting new facilities. Proponents, slow to realize that the ground rules of siting had altered radically, continued their efforts to convince local communities and state policymakers to site these facilities according to conventional technical and economic guidelines. For example, they continued to think of a facility's pollution potential as a technical problem, not understanding the intense fears that local communities harbored about their own health and economic well-being.[13]

Only recently have businesses begun to design facilities that anticipate environmental needs, thus making environmental protection an integral business consideration. This strategy is epitomized in the emergent pollution prevention campaign. "Pollution prevention pays," the motto of the 3M Company for more than a decade, went unheard until the mid 1980s, but now has become the rallying cry around which all parties can agree. Dow, Union Carbide, and General Dynamics, for example, have all set significant targets for dramatically reducing their waste flow and for achieving total management of those wastes that remain.

Germane to the siting dilemma, the potential now arises for compromise to emerge as an important prerequisite to successful siting. Facility proponents might commit to more source reduction measures than originally planned. In return, the NIMBY groups would drop their opposition to that facility-siting proposal. Each party would profit from such a solution.

Even the best source reduction technologies cannot eliminate hazardous wastes from the U.S. economy, however. A significant number of incinerators, hazardous waste collection stations and treatment facilities, and long-term storage and repositories will still be required. Yet no one wants these facilities in their backyards.

3. *What standards of fairness are applied—substantively and procedurally—when dealing with competing interests in a siting controversy?* Public confidence in the fairness of public decisionmaking—in the way decisions are made, and in their outcome—is vital to the success of the democratic political process. Although people in a local community may never be pleased that a facility is being sited in their midst, they may come to accept the process by which the decision is made. The public's definition of what is fair can change over time, of course, and this is precisely what is occurring with the siting of major facilities.

Conventionally, a project was justified if it could satisfy the utilitarian test of the greatest good for the greatest number, as understood within the context of the host community. In practice, this meant that siting approval would be granted by local leaders if the project would produce new jobs, pay local property taxes, and contribute to local economic development. The second criterion was that "might [i.e., money] makes right." Americans extend a great deal of deference to wealth, and it was expected and considered legitimate that money would be used to influence the public policy process. Dependence on developers was (and, in many places, still is) the lifeblood of local politics, where most land use and siting decisions are made.

Ideas are changing about what is just in siting. The principles of individual property rights and utilitarian economics must now compete with new definitions of individual, ecological, and community political rights, and considerations of equal treatment for minorities and women.[14] Consequently, projects that might serve powerful economic interests are challenged in light of these newer interests—one's home, one's local environment, one's personal health, one's minority group— as never before possible. Local leaders can no longer approve facilities on their own.

Legally and politically, the burden of proof that harm will or will not occur has shifted to those who would generate potentially harmful materials. This trend can be seen in the new stringent liability provisions of pollution laws, such as the "strict, joint, and several liability" proviso of the federal Superfund law that holds the producers and handlers of hazardous waste fully responsible for its safe disposal. At the state level, California's Proposition 65 makes users of a long list of substances known to cause cancer or birth defects liable if these chemicals are not managed and disposed of safely. Legal protection is now even accorded to a growing range of nonhuman species and even inanimate objects.[15]

Misperceptions, failed communications, and conflicts over values are at the base of much of today's NIMBYism.[16] Proponents of state-of-the-art toxics incinerators, for example, claim that their minimal level of pollution would cause far less harm overall than continuing disposal of hazardous wastes in landfills and through other traditional methods. From this perspective, incinerators are the most cost-effective waste management alternative. Conventional thinking encourages these proponents to expect that they can proceed with their projects. Yet opponents argue that these incinerators pose unacceptable health risks to nearby residents and should therefore not be sited. They may well be right, too. Although those on each side believe they are speaking the same language, they are not. This is the failure of democratic discourse in the United States today.

The result is public confusion and a sense that no consistent rationale exists to judge either the process or the outcome of a siting decision. Chided for whichever side they take, makers of public policy find themselves in a no-win situation.

4. Who makes the siting decision, and through what process? Traditionally, siting decisions have been made by the facility developer, community officials, and, sometimes, state officials. Although this process satisfied the procedural requirements of representative democracy, it did not incorporate all the potentially interested parties.

The reality now is different. In the late 1960s it became obvious to many that locally based siting decisions have substantial impacts on neighboring communities, regions, and ultimately entire states. Air and water pollution recognize no municipal boundaries; dense buildup in one community affects traffic and congestion in the next. As many communities sought to increase their tax base by developing every available parcel of land, the once readily accessible open spaces such as ocean and lakefront shoreline and outdoor recreational areas were disappearing. Few public officials seemed willing to protect these valuable community or regionwide assets. The effects of urban congestion and increasing population were taking their toll.

This triggered the quiet revolution in land-use planning in the 1970s, which was marked by a notable shift of land-use authority away from the localities. Laws began to require state-level review of local decisions, state permitting of major facilities, and more comprehensive local plans that incorporated social and environmental considerations.[17]

NIMBYism is an extension of these trends.[18] Though some decision-making authority shifted away from the localities, the wider arena for participation in siting decisions vastly expanded the opportunities for local opposition. Although not everyone is equally active, experience has shown that most any locally organized group can insert itself in the decisionmaking process. And "just say no" became the dominant strategy.

The case of hazardous waste facilities is instructive. In the beginning, businesses tried to muscle their way through local siting procedures. When this met with failure, waste generators and waste managers united behind efforts to convince state legislatures that NIMBYism would prevent them from ever siting their needed facilities, and that the states must preempt local siting decisions. Several did, but to little avail. NIMBY resistance only increased—hazardous waste facilities still could not be sited. Many politicians and public agencies responded by calling for greater dialogue and public involvement. They assumed that once people were involved and "knew the facts," responsible local leaders would find some accommodation with industry, if only to secure their own economic future. This, too, did not prove to be the case. Public involvement only gave NIMBY groups more clout and visibility.

Citizen involvement at the local level seems like the epitome of democracy. But when citizens have the power only to stop proposed facilities, the process is far from complete. Few mechanisms have yet been devised to bring competing interests together in ways that allow them to identify their shared values and goals, narrow their differences, and move forward to appropriately site genuinely necessary industrial and public facilities that today are being vetoed. No suitable democratic process has been devised that can effectively mesh society's collective needs with those of individuals and localities. Several promising approaches, however, have emerged over the course of the past decade.

Moving Beyond NIMBY to Successful Facility Siting

One strategy to resolve the siting gridlock is to return these decisions more fully to the marketplace. This idea was first broached by the political right, where environmental problems are seen as the product of government mismanagement. In the "tragedy of the commons," it is in everyone's self-interest to overconsume what is held in common and to shepherd what is theirs.[19] The solution? Privatize public lands, auction off ownership rights to water and other natural resources, and establish private property where it has never previously existed, such as in the oceans.[20] When disputes or injuries occur, one can rely on private claims and tort law, not on government regulators, to secure relief. Advocates of privatization argue that better facility-siting decisions could be achieved through auctions, with the highest bidder deciding the use of the land in question. In this way, proponents and opponents are forced to reveal their "true" preferences and to place a monetary value on them.[21]

The more populist left has proposed another approach to privatization, but for vastly different reasons. The argument here is made on behalf of a "citizens' bill of rights" to environmental and health protection. All polluters would be held accountable to these requirements. If a clean and healthy environment were an individual's legal right, then anyone polluting could be brought to account through private litigation.

Privatization clearly has potential to help resolve NIMBY controversies and achieve successful facility siting. It does not, however, provide a complete solution. The policing that would occur under tort law and the citizen-monitoring potentials are all after-the-fact remedies; they are triggered only after the harm has occurred to human health and environment. Moreover, as many questions are raised as are answered by this scheme. Would an environmental bill of rights mean that no person or business could generate pollution, at any time? If so, would all productive activities come to a halt? Where *is* the line to be drawn? Also, although auctioning development sites may sound attractive, especially in this period of siting gridlock, the process would inevitably be tipped in favor of those with the most money, not in favor of health, ordinary citizens, or the environment. Furthermore, auctions would resolve siting controversies one at a time. The approach is not well suited to coordinated regional programs for hazardous waste and materials management, nor does it fit obviously into a program of source reduction and waste minimization.

Successful siting in the new environmental epoch needs to be guided by a broader set of principles than self-interested market behavior. A set of five guidelines has been suggested by Roger Kasperson:

1. The general well-being of society requires that some individuals will have to bear risks on behalf of others.

2. Wherever reasonable, such risks should be avoided rather than mitigated or ameliorated through compensation.
3. Reasonably unavoidable risks should be shared, not concentrated, in the population of beneficiaries.
4. The imposition of risk should be made as voluntary as reasonably achievable within the constraints of deploying sites in a timely manner, and the burden of proof for site suitability should be on the developer.
5. Reasonably unavoidable risks should be accompanied by compensating benefits.[22]

It is unlikely that all these principles can be satisfied by working strictly within a market framework. Equally true, they probably cannot be satisfied fully by a top-down, command-and-control form of government. And surely they are not met by the ineffective, fragmented regulatory regimes that exist today. The challenge is to devise approaches to siting that incorporate the five principles within a democratic framework, while remaining sensitive to the complex political, economic, technical, and social contexts of American society.

The *process* of site selection and approval for hazardous waste and hazardous materials facilities must gain greater legitimacy by improving early public access to decisions, planning more effectively, avoiding state preemption, and providing for community oversight of facility operations. Likewise, the *substance* of facility proposals will best be improved by encouraging development of smaller facilities to lessen local inequities, using transportable units, and insisting on stricter safety standards.

Industry and government both need to change their approach to the siting dilemma if the genuine concerns of citizens are to be addressed. This is a monumental challenge, but not an impossibility. Three approaches for moving beyond NIMBY gridlock while satisfying the Kasperson principles can serve as models for the coming decade.[23]

Siting a Single Facility: The Siting Contract

The best way to democratically and successfully site a facility that handles hazardous materials is suggested in the quasi-experimental work of Michael Elliott.[24] He finds that most project proponents become preoccupied with technical issues and, not surprisingly, with technical solutions. In contrast, those in the surrounding community are more worried about detecting health and environmental risks that may develop at the plant and about implementing measures to lessen or reverse the danger. They worry more about whether those measures will be applied speedily should a problem arise than about the capabilities of exotic, technically advanced equipment. NIMBYism is born out of these concerns.

Community members might accept a technically less sophisticated facility if its operator placed greater emphasis on a rapid, effective detection and response system. In addition, Elliott concludes that the only realistic way of convincing an ever-wary community that a facility's operator is committed to detection and mitigation is to open the plant's operations to community scrutiny and to subject its safety practices to close community review. In this context, the problems of democratic discourse relate to discussing health risks, technical complexity, industrial design, and cost and risk sharing as they affect the beneficiaries in the broader community and those who live near the proposed new facility.

These lessons were gleaned from the single major new hazardous waste facility in North America built in more than a decade and operating today. The people of Alberta, Canada, avoided the NIMBY outcome by squarely addressing these issues. An open, participatory process was devised in Alberta that involved the major local and regional interests from the very outset. The issues of siting usually framed in zero-sum terms, with clear winners and clear losers, were transformed so that all the major stakeholders chose negotiation over conflict and, through the process, came to believe that they could all reap the benefits of cooperation.[25] The process involved a local plebiscite on siting, state funding to hire consultants and experts for the local community, many public forums, government assurances of additional economic and infrastructure benefits to the community, and a permanent consultant to monitor the facility's operation. Though the particulars of the situation may not be replicable everywhere, they show that a positive, democratically inspired discourse can result in a positive solution even for the most complex and fear-invoking facility.

This suggests that to increase the likelihood of siting good facilities in good locations, one needs to establish long-term oversight arrangements that provide for greater community involvement, power sharing, and risk sharing. These are requisites to doing business in a modern, complex democratic society. In the American context, it may be necessary to formalize precisely what this entails between the facility operator and the host community through an enforceable contract between the owner/operator and the local community. With such a facility-siting and operations contract in place, the facility's neighbors would no longer have to rely on notoriously weak government permitting processes and regulatory enforcement activities.

The contract's specific terms would be negotiated during the siting process. It would typically contain the operational provisions normally placed in the facility's regulatory permits. The contract could also embody the source reduction/siting compromise noted earlier. Violation of the contract's terms could be addressed by the community directly, through traditional breach-of-contract judicial proceedings. A court could even be asked to issue a temporary restraining order requiring the facility to cease operations until it was again able to fully observe its formal contractual obligations.

With an oversight committee of community members and an open dialogue at the facility, resort to legal remedies should seldom be necessary. But having this option may be the price a community will need to exact for its siting approval. The bargain is simple: no contract, no approval.

Inviting the community to participate in the oversight of a facility is obviously a radical departure from past practices, yet it is clearly inclusive, community-based, and democratic. It provides a mechanism for ensuring that many of Kasperson's principles will be addressed, even if not fully satisfied in every instance. If Elliott is correct in observing that the public does not so much fear technology and chemical substances per se but, rather, how they are managed, then the contract approach may be useful not only in securing needed siting but also in overcoming chemophobia.

A Public Utility Approach to Hazardous Waste Management

For more than a decade, local communities have vetoed modern facilities designed to recycle, neutralize, detoxify, incinerate, or provide short- or long-term storage of hazardous wastes. In Europe the introduction of technically sophisticated and effective facilities for hazardous waste management is further along, in part because hazardous waste management has been treated as just one more public obligation, like highway building and sewage treatment.

Bruce Piasecki and Gary Davis have proposed a variation on the European approach for the United States. They believe the regulated public utility model of close public-private cooperation can be used to move the United States to closed systems that recycle, treat, store, and protect society from hazardous wastes. This would be accomplished through independently operated, managed, and profit-making corporations. Closely watched and regulated, they would receive liability waivers, charge reasonable prices, and operate within a given geographic or functional area. Piasecki and Davis note:

> In exchange for treating all of the waste generated in an area, including hard-to-treat waste and household toxics, at set prices and using specified technologies, the private firm would have no competition in its service areas and would receive a guaranteed return on its investment in treatment facilities.[26]

Offering a comprehensive system of modern treatment facilities, the public utilities approach has much to recommend it and may prove a vital piece of tomorrow's hazardous waste and materials management strategy. Local governments and citizens would presumably be more receptive to siting such a facility if they felt confident that it would be operated like a utility, with close public scrutiny and with the goal of safe waste-management practices. At the same time, new facilities would be operated with the effectiveness of a private business. The closest example today is the Gulf Coast Waste Disposal Authority in Houston, Texas. It operates as an independent, quasi-governmental, nonprofit corporation that plans and operates needed waste facilities. It has the power to issue tax-exempt bonds for financing and to condemn land to site its facilities.

In view of continued NIMBYism, gridlock, and little or no progress toward successful siting, the public utility model for hazardous waste management may be the most viable option available. The inherent problem of winning public assent for siting would not disappear, of course. Moreover, dealing with hazardous wastes is only one, albeit important, component of the revolution needed in hazardous materials management and of the overall siting dilemma facing society.

An Equity-Based Regional Design for Hazardous Wastes

An unusual effort, which in many ways incorporates some of the best features of both the siting contract and public utility models, has been tested in California.[27] This hazardous-waste planning and siting process was initiated in the mid 1980s in response to the state's facility-siting gridlock. Its objective is to enable every county to map its own plans for managing hazardous wastes and materials. Under the process, each county has developed a profile of the hazardous wastes generated within its borders, including projections of waste volumes through the year 2000. Each has had to stipulate criteria for siting new facilities and, in general, to identify where they might be located. Some counties have entered into intercounty compacts for waste management on a regional basis. The county plans are prepared and must be updated with extensive involvement of their cities, industry, environmental and health groups, and the general public. Anyone with a strong vested interest in the outcome has a right to participate. Local participants recognize that if they cannot agree among themselves, the law provides that the state's hazardous waste regulatory agency will make decisions for them.

This statewide process builds directly on earlier experiences in Southern California, where eight counties and their associated cities carried out a regional planning process whose hallmark was the equitable distribution of needed new facilities based on each county's share of the region's total waste generation. The Southern California Hazardous Waste Management Authority first initiated this "YIMBY" (yes in many backyards) solution as an equity-based alternative to the NIMBYesque controversy over siting.[28] The YIMBY concept lies at the heart of the planning process now in place in all the counties.[29] In this way, communities throughout California have been challenged to chart their own future and take responsibility for their hazardous wastes. Serious conflicts have arisen between the state hazardous waste agency and the counties over the equity basis of county plans. Yet if the process proves successful in the coming years in guiding hazardous waste management and facility siting, California will be unique in the nation in having locally determined, community-based strategies for hazardous waste management. Developers will be able to request, and stand a reasonable chance of receiving, approval for those new hazardous waste management facilities that are consistent with a county's plan. If the siting proposal meets all the technical and procedural requirements in a locally based plan yet is still turned down by local authorities under NIMBY-style pressure, for example, the developer can then appeal to a state review board for an override of the local decision. (In the single case to date that has gone through the appeal process, the panel decided in favor of siting the facility.) Local vetoes of good facilities in good locations may thus no longer be the case in California. If diverse business, environmental, and other interests actually agree to negotiate, bargain, and cooperate through this new planning and siting process, there is hope that the era of gridlock over facility siting may be ebbing away. If so, it will be due in no small part to the widespread local involvement and, in turn, commitment to a process that addresses the issue of siting in the context of the broad need for a regional hazardous wastes and materials management plan grounded in equity and open dialogue.

Conclusion

Opposition to new industrial facilities—the NIMBY syndrome—underscores the failure of democratic discourse in the United States over the past decade. This has happened even as formal access to the public policy process has been extended to a much wider array of interests. The participatory nature of American politics assures that contending interests can have access to the process and a major say in the outcome of decisions. With its many checks and balances, however, neither those in favor of the siting of proposed new facilities, nor those opposed, have been able to emerge supreme. Both sides have dug in their heels; the result has been policy gridlock. To the extent that democratic political empowerment is the right to say no, the system has clearly worked. The problem is that this is only a negative power, and, ultimately, everyone will end up worse off.

Although this situation will not be remedied overnight, some potent harbingers of change are visible. Public-private partnerships are beginning to emerge, as all parties recognize the futility of continuing along the traditional path. Facility-siting contracts and cooperative siting can allow long-term community oversight of facility operations and provide a focus for effective mitigation and compensation measures and siting/source reduction compromises. Most significantly, regional and statewide siting efforts based explicitly on the politics of equity and fair share, built from the bottom up, offer the potential to meld successfully the interests of proponents and opponents in conventional facility-siting disputes. Guided by Kasperson's ethical principles of risk sharing, YIMBY based on equity may replace NIMBY based on parochialism as the way the United States resolves its facility-siting needs and manages its hazardous wastes and toxic materials.

Notes

The authors would like to thank Michael Stanley-Jones, Michael Kraft, and Norman Vig for their review of and helpful comments on this chapter. The epigraph quoting H. D. Forbes is taken from his "Dahl, Democracy, and Technology" in *Democratic Theory and Technological Society*, ed. Richard B. Day, Ronald Beiner, and Joseph Masciulli (Armonk, N.Y.: M. E. Sharpe, 1988), 229.

1. Susan G. Hadden, Joan Veillette, and Thomas Brandt, "State Roles in Siting Hazardous Waste Disposal Facilities: From State Preemption to Local Veto," in *The Politics of Hazardous Waste Management*, ed. James P. Lester and Ann O'M. Bowman (Durham, N.C.: Duke University Press, 1983), 197-211.
2. William Glaberson, "Coping in the Age of 'Nimby'," *New York Times*, June 19, 1988.
3. Some observers allege that the public suffers from an absence of the requisite technical information and a misperception of the genuine risk involved. See Paul Slovic and Baruch Fischhoff, "How Safe Is Safe Enough? Determinants of Perceived and Acceptable Risk," in *Too Hot to Handle? Social and Policy Issues in the Management of Radioactive Wastes*, ed. Charles Walker, Leroy Gould, and Edward Woodhouse (New Haven, Conn.: Yale University Press, 1983). However, this is certainly not always the case. For those opposing the siting of radioactive waste facilities, the opposition has been well apprised of the risks involved. See Michael E. Kraft and Bruce B. Clary, "Citizen Participation and the NIMBY Syndrome: Public Response to Radioactive Waste Disposal," *Western Political Quarterly* 44 (June 1991): 299-328.
4. Peter M. Sandman, "Risk Communication: Facing Public Outrage," *EPA Journal* (November 1987), 21-22.
5. U.S. Council on Environmental Quality, "Public Opinion on Environmental Issues: Results of a National Public Opinion Survey" (Washington, D.C.: U.S. Government Printing Office, 1980), 31.
6. Seymour Martin Lipset and William Schneider, *The Confidence Gap: Business, Labor, and Government in the Public Mind*, rev. ed. (Baltimore: Johns Hopkins University Press, 1987).
7. Dennis J. Brion, *Essential Industry and the NIMBY Phenomenon* (New York: Quorum Books, 1991).
8. Daniel Mazmanian and David Morell, *Beyond Superfailure: America's Toxics Policy for the 1990s* (Boulder: Westview, 1992).
9. See A. Myrick Freeman's discussion, in chapter 9 of this volume, of the market-type incentives that have been introduced into environmental policy.
10. The case for banning hazardous substances from use as the most effective environmental policy is presented in Barry Commoner, "The Environment," *New Yorker*, June 15, 1987, 46-70.

11. U.S. Congress, Office of Technology Assessment, *Superfund Strategy*, OTA-ITE-253 (Washington, D.C.: U.S. Government Printing Office, March 1985); and Mazmanian and Morell, *Beyond Superfailure*, chaps. 2 and 3.

12. Paul Slovic, "Perception of Risk," *Science* 236 (April 17, 1987): 280-285.

13. Sheldon Krimsky and Alonzo Plough, *Environmental Hazards: Communication Risks as a Social Process* (Dover, Mass.: Auburn House, 1988); Committee on Risk Perception and Communication, National Research Council, *Improving Risk Communication* (Washington, D.C.: National Academy Press, 1989); and K. S. Shrader-Frechette, *Risk and Rationality: Philosophical Foundations for Populist Reforms* (Berkeley and Los Angeles: University of California Press, 1991).

14. J. Ronald Engel and Joan Gibb Engel, eds., *Ethics of Environmental Development: Global Challenge, International Response* (Tucson: University of Arizona Press, 1990).

15. Christopher D. Stone, *Earth and Other Ethics: The Case for Moral Pluralism* (New York: Harper and Row, 1988).

16. Susan G. Hadden, "Public Perception of Hazardous Waste," *Risk Analysis* 11 (March 1991): 47-57.

17. See Robert Healy and John Rosenberg, *Land Use and the States*, 2d ed. (Baltimore: Johns Hopkins University Press, 1979).

18. David Morell and Christopher Magorian, *Siting Hazardous Waste Facilities: Local Opposition and the Myth of Preemption* (Cambridge, Mass.: Ballinger, 1982), 87-88.

19. Garrett Hardin, "The Tragedy of the Commons," *Science* 162 (December 13, 1968): 1243-1248.

20. Terry L. Anderson and Donald R. Leal, *Free Market Environmentalism* (Boulder: Westview, 1991).

21. For an overview of market approaches to siting, see David E. Ervin and James B. Fitch, "Evaluating Alternative Compensation and Recapture Techniques for Expanded Public Control of Land Use," *Natural Resources Journal* 19 (January 1979): 21-44.

22. Roger E. Kasperson, "Hazardous Waste Facility Siting: Community, Firm, and Governmental Perspectives," in *Hazards: Technology and Fairness* (Washington, D.C.: National Academy Press, 1986), 139.

23. A fourth strategy, "risk substitution," has been proposed recently by Kent Portney. Here, new hazardous waste facilities would be sited at already degraded (e.g., Superfund) locations as part of an overall cleanup effort. Although such a trade-off should have the net result of improving the site, it is tantamount to extracting siting approval for the new facility from the affected community as the price of cleaning up the already polluted situation. Pragmatically this may make sense, but a less coercive approach is obviously preferable. See Kent E. Portney, *Siting Hazardous Waste Treatment Facilities: The NIMBY Syndrome* (Westport, Conn.: Auburn House, 1991).

24. Michael L. Poirier Elliott, "Improving Community Acceptance of Hazardous Waste Facilities Through Alternative Systems of Mitigating and Managing Risk," *Hazardous Waste* 1 (1984): 397-410.

25. Barry G. Rabe, "Beyond the NIMBY Syndrome in Hazardous Waste Facility Siting: The Albertan Breakthrough and the Prospects for Cooperation in Canada and the United States," *Governance: An International Journal of Policy and Administration* 4, no. 2 (April 1991): 184-206.

26. Bruce W. Piasecki and Gary A. Davis, *America's Future in Toxic Waste Management: Lessons from Europe* (New York: Quorum Books, 1987), 229.

27. Daniel A. Mazmanian, Michael Stanley-Jones, and Miriam J. Green, "Breaking Political Gridlock: California's Experiment in Public-Private Cooperation for Hazardous Waste Policy" (Claremont: California Institute of Public Affairs, 1988).

28. David Morell, "Siting and the Politics of Equity," *Hazardous Waste* 1 (1984): 555-571.

29. An analysis of several regional collaborative planning processes has identified seven conditions, in addition to the YIMBY principle, that are necessary for successful siting of otherwise unwanted facilities. These include the presence of an issue crisis, political legitimacy, interest representation, a representative structure, iterative bargaining, resource sharing, and development of trust. See Daniel Mazmanian and Michael Stanley-Jones, "Reconceiving LULUs: Changing the Nature and Scope of Locally Unwanted Land Uses," in *Confronting Regional Challenges: Approaches to LULUs, Growth, and Other Vexing Governance Problems*, ed. Joseph DiMento (Cambridge, Mass.: Lincoln Land Institute, 1991).

IV. TOWARD GLOBAL ENVIRONMENTAL POLICIES

12

Environmental Policy and Management in the European Community

Regina S. Axelrod

The building of the European Community (EC) has transformed western Europe. The objective of establishing a common internal economic market has contributed to the openness of national borders and the harmonization of many policies once in the exclusive domain of individual member states. The EC has also established some of the strongest and most innovative environmental protection measures in the world, and has increasingly taken the lead on international environmental issues such as global warming. In principle, environmental protection now enjoys equal weight with economic development in Community policymaking.

Political will and public support have been the key to EC success in approaching the environment from an integrated perspective. First, the legal foundations have been firmly established so that the Community has an unchallenged right to protect the environment. Second, all states recognize that without common environmental policies, barriers to free trade will emerge. Common environmental policies thus strengthen the prospects for creation of a single economic market. Third, political, economic, and geographic diversity has challenged policymakers to develop innovative strategies for overcoming differences and sharing burdens equitably. The EC is moving into the forefront in such areas as carbon/energy taxes, waste reduction, environmental auditing, and "ecolabeling."

The European Community is thus an important model to study, both as the most advanced regional organization of states and as an experiment in sustainable environmental development or "green capitalism." If it succeeds in strengthening environmental protection while liberalizing trade, the EC may provide a model for other regions of the world such as North America and East Asia.

The Political Origins of the EC

The quest for political and economic union in Europe had its origins in the 1920s and 1930s, when it was recognized that some kind of supranational organization was needed to avoid brutal competition, protectionism, and war. But it was the experience of World War II that convinced statesmen to seek a new type of unity. U.S. economic assistance under the postwar Marshall Plan also called for regional cooperation.

The first step toward building a more integrated Europe was the formation of the European Coal and Steel Community (ECSC). The idea of French foreign minister Robert Schumann and French businessman Jean Monnet, it was created by the Treaty of Paris on April 18, 1951. The original ECSC members were Belgium, France, Germany, Italy, Luxembourg, and the Netherlands. Its economic goal was to pool the production of coal and steel for the benefit of all six countries. Its other purpose was to lock Germany politically and economically into a stable partnership with western Europe.

Other cooperative activities were slow to develop, but in June 1955 the six ECSC members decided to move toward closer economic integration. They saw a European free trade area or "common market" as a means to increase industrial and agricultural exports, to redistribute resources to economically depressed areas, and to encourage travel among countries. The result was the 1957 Treaty of Rome, which established the European Economic Community (EEC) and the European Atomic Energy Authority (Euratom). In the 1970s the United Kingdom, Ireland, and Denmark joined the EEC, and Spain, Portugal, and Greece followed suit by 1986, bringing the total membership to twelve.[1]

There were no explicit provisions for protection of the environment in the original Treaty of Rome. Community policy for the environment dates instead from the 1972 Paris summit of the heads of state and government of the EEC, which proposed that an Environmental Action Programme be established under Article 235, which permits legislation in new areas if consistent with Community objectives. In effect, an environmental agenda was added to the Treaty of Rome.[2]

The Single European Act (SEA) of 1986 was the next milestone in the development of the treaties. This act accelerated the integration process by calling for establishment of a single internal economic market by the end of 1992. It set out more precise goals for harmonizing economic policies and eliminating border controls and other barriers to the free movement of goods, services, labor, and capital across Europe. Equally important, the SEA added a new section to the Treaty of Rome (articles 130r, 130s, 130t) that formally defined the goals and procedures of EC environmental policies and called for "balanced growth" by integrating environmental policy into all other areas of Community decisionmaking.

The Maastricht Treaty signed on February 7, 1992, called for closer political and monetary union—including development of a common European currency—by the end of the decade. Since Denmark failed to ratify the treaty in its original form—and at this writing it has yet to be ratified in the United Kingdom and Germany—it is unclear whether the Maastricht Treaty will be implemented within the original time frame. Insofar as the momentum toward closer integration continues, environmental policy is likely to be determined increasingly in Brussels.

The EC as an Ecological and Socioeconomic Bioregion

To fully comprehend the environmental issues associated with EC integration, it is important to recognize that the twelve member states differ from each other not only in population distribution, culture, and socioeconomic characteristics, but also in climate, topography, hydrology, and natural resources. The 325 million people in the EC live in a land area that reaches from Scotland in the north to Spain and Italy in the south, and from Ireland and Portugal in the west to Greece in the east (approximately 3,600 km in each direction). The population density varies from 3,700 per square km in Ireland to 60,500 in Germany (excluding the former East Germany). Also, 7.9 million resident aliens live primarily in Germany, France, and the United Kingdom.[3] Climate varies from the cool maritime areas of the North Sea to the sunny, dry regions of the Mediterranean. The terrain ranges from mountainous Alpine regions in France and Italy to areas below sea level in the Netherlands. There are 300 soil types, 200 kinds of vegetation, more than 600 species of birds, 130 species of mammals, and 60 fish species, with great local diversity.[4]

Environmental problems in Europe are quite similar to those in the United States (see box). Economic growth and industrial development have taken a similar toll. Many species are threatened with extinction. Air and water pollution is most severe in the more industrialized north, but the Mediterranean region is now severely threatened as well. In the late 1980s CO_2 emissions ranged from 8 million tons in Ireland and 11 million tons in Portugal, to 166 million for the United Kingdom and 201 million for Germany.[5] Acid precipitation is estimated to cost 300 million ECU a year,[6] and has killed or damaged large areas of forests (what the Germans call *Waldsterben*). Industrial regions have high concentrations of toxic and hazardous wastes. Agricultural areas have been subject to intensive farming for centuries, leaving soils depleted and threatened by waste accumulations. Lost agricultural production is estimated at 1 billion ECU per year.[7] Pollution emissions and discharges easily cross national frontiers in the air or rivers (many of which flow through several countries).

The energy sector demonstrates some of the most important differences among states and highlights the complexities of achieving common environmental policies. Differences in basic fuel sources lead to different policy orientations toward allowable emissions and risks. Germany subsidizes its coal industry and France does the same for nuclear power. Because 75 percent of France's electricity is nuclear-generated, it is less concerned about fluctuations in oil prices. France actually generates a surplus of electric power that it would like to sell to other countries. But the Germans prefer to utilize their extensive coal resources by developing

Major Environmental Threats in the European Community

Air. "Air quality . . . continues to give cause for concern in most towns and cities due to the increasing emissions of the principal pollutants into the air from motor vehicles. . . . Simulations for the year 2000 suggest there will be some improvement, but at the same time further deterioration in urban and industrial growth areas."

Water. "Despite the investments made over the last 20 years or so, on the whole there has been no improvement in the state of the Community's water resources. There have been more cases of deterioration in quality than of improvement. With demand rising as it is at present, the impending depletion of freshwater resources in certain regions may create major problems in the future, particularly in the Mediterranean countries."

Soil. "Physical degradation of the soil is widespread throughout the Community. The soil was long thought to have unlimited absorptive capacity, but now it is becoming increasingly difficult for it to perform its many vital functions, as a source of biomass in the form of crops and timber, as a habitat and as an ecosystem stabilizer. An increase in the pollution content has been observed at many sites. Pollution . . . by heavy metals and organic products is increasing not only . . . around industrial centres . . . but also in some rural areas, as a result of the combination of air pollution and farming."

Waste. "The volume of waste generated is increasing at a far greater rate than treatment and disposal capacity. A major effort to set up . . . household refuse collection networks has ensured that virtually all the urban waste in the Community is actually collected. Nevertheless, landfill remains the commonest disposal method. Processes such as composting or recycling are gaining ground but remain too limited to alleviate the growing landfill problem."

The quality of life. "Urban population growth will continue at a rapid rate in the cities of southern Europe, particularly along the coast, putting further pressure on the population's quality of life. Without rigorous measures to protect the rural environment in places where desertification is becoming acute, the countryside will continue to deteriorate."

High-risk activities. "As man learned to protect himself from natural risks, he also began to apply more and more high-risk techniques. Not only the workers employed in these activities are at risk but also the local population as well. The nuclear power industry, the chemical industry, the transport of hazardous substances and, more recently, the genetic engineering industry all pose new risks."

Source: Fifth Programme on the Environment of the European Commission, 1992.

cleaner coal-burning technologies. The Dutch have no interest in either nuclear power or coal but have some of the largest fields of natural gas in Europe, which they would like to market as a less polluting fuel. Fossil fuels (coal, oil, gas) predominate in the United Kingdom, but this country tends to lag in pollution control technologies. Italy relies on imported oil for electricity generation and also imports natural gas from Algeria and the former Soviet Union. It faces a serious problem because electricity consumption has risen faster than supplies. Belgium relies on nuclear power for nearly half of its electricity, while Denmark has no nuclear plants and is a leader in developing renewable energy sources such as wind power. These national differences in resource endowments, government subsidies, employment patterns, and vested economic interests make it difficult to legislate common EC policies for mitigating the environmental impacts of energy production and consumption.

Other political differences also complicate the Community environmental agenda. The northern, more industrialized states have a history of stringent environmental legislation and a high level of public awareness on environmental issues. They oppose policies that would compromise their level of environmental protection. Germany is particularly concerned about the effects of acid rain on its forests and the dangers of nuclear waste. Not coincidentally, it has the largest Green party and perhaps the most respected national environmental ministry. The Netherlands, a "low country," has a special interest in the potential sea-level rise from global warming and has developed the most comprehensive national environmental plan for addressing this issue. Denmark also has high environmental standards in part because of close ties to its Scandinavian neighbors.

The southern tier of states and Ireland tend to place greater emphasis on economic development than on the environment. Rural areas in these countries have different environmental problems than urban areas to the north, although large cities in Spain, Italy, and Greece also have major pollution problems. These states argue that they cannot meet the same environmental standards as more wealthy states. Spain, for example, has been undergoing rapid industrialization and claims it will need to increase its CO_2 emissions for some time. Spain, Portugal, Greece, and Ireland all benefit from special EC funds to help them improve their environmental infrastructures. The entire Mediterranean Basin is threatened by soil erosion, water pollution, and toxic waste accumulations that will require massive cleanup efforts and strain Community resources.

Public Opinion and the Green Movement

Public opinion polls indicate that Europeans are deeply concerned about the environment and becoming more so. A Eurobarometer opinion survey conducted in the summer of 1989 asked respondents in all EC

Table 12-1 European Opinion on the Urgency of Environmental
Problems, 1986-1992 (in percentages)

Perceived Urgency of the Environmental Problem	1986	1988	1992
An immediate and urgent problem	72%	74%	85%
More a problem for the future	22	20	11
Not really a problem	3	3	2
Don't know/no answer	3	3	2

Source: Eurobarometer, no. 37, June 1992.

Note: The question asked was: "Many people are concerned about protecting the environment and fighting pollution. In your opinion, is this . . . ?"

countries to rank the twelve most important national and international issues facing them; an astounding 94 percent ranked environmental policy very important, second only to unemployment. The difference among countries was slight, ranging from 98 percent among Germans to 91 percent for the Portuguese and Irish.[8] A study completed for the European Commission in the spring of 1992 indicates that the percentage of Europeans who consider the environment "an immediate and urgent problem" has risen dramatically since 1988 to a high of 85 percent (table 12-1). Concern is greatest in France, eastern Germany, Greece, the Netherlands, and the United Kingdom.[9] On specific issues, the Italians and Spaniards are worried most about water pollution, while air pollution concerns are greatest among the Germans, Dutch, Greeks, and Italians. Industrial waste disposal is the problem of most general concern throughout the Community.[10]

But does this mean that Europeans are willing to give up national control over environmental policy to the European Community? Yes, according to another recent survey: 69 percent said environmental policy should be a Community responsibility (28 percent disagreed). Support for joint decisionmaking ranged from 83 percent in the Netherlands to 52 percent in Ireland (table 12-2).

The Community's northern countries have the strongest ecological and conservation movements.[11] Green parties have won representation in the national parliaments of Belgium, Germany, Greece, Ireland, Italy, Luxembourg, the Netherlands, Portugal, and several other European countries.[12] They also have done well in elections to the European Parliament, electing a total of twenty-nine members in the 1989 election (from Belgium, France, Germany, Italy, and the Netherlands). But the green movement has had a larger impact through its influence on other political parties and on European public opinion generally.[13]

Table 12-2 Support for the European Community's
Environmental Decisionmaking

Nation	Support for Joint Decisionmaking (in percentages)
The Netherlands	83%
Italy	71
Germany	70
Spain	70
France	68
United Kingdom	67
Belgium	63
Greece	61
Portugal	58
Denmark	57
Luxembourg	55
Ireland	52

Source: Commission of the European Communities, *Protecting Our Environment,* 1992.

Note: The question asked was whether environmental policy should be decided jointly within the European Community or by national governments.

EC Institutions and Policymaking Processes

Community Institutions

The primary institutions of the EC are the council, the commission, the parliament, and the European Court of Justice.

The EC Council in Brussels consists of representatives from the governments of each of the member states. When the heads of state meet, it is known as the "European Council," but normally council meetings involve the twelve ministers responsible for the topic under discussion. The council is the most important EC body because it must approve all legislation. Its "directives" must be adopted by the individual member states and incorporated into national law within a specified period of time (usually two years). EC "regulations" that automatically apply to the states can also be enacted, but they are less common. In general, the council's actions reflect the national interests of the states. Under the Single European Act, many decisions can now be taken by a "qualified majority" of the council, that is, by a special voting procedure that gives greater weight to larger states than smaller ones but does not require unanimity.

The EC Commission is a body of seventeen commissioners (and their staffs) who head twenty-three directorates-general (DGs). DG XI is responsible for the environment, nuclear safety, and civil protection. The commission's task is to initiate Community legislation and to oversee its implementation by member states. Its president, currently Jacques Delors, is sometimes referred to as the "European president." A large multinational bureaucracy serves the commission and its directorates in Brussels.

The European Parliament, by contrast, is elected directly by people from constituencies in each country and tends to reflect the diverse interests of political parties and groupings across Europe. The parliament has a moving seat. It holds plenary sessions in Strasbourg, France, its staff is in Luxembourg, and it holds most of its committee meetings in Brussels. Draft legislation from the commission is submitted to parliament, which can either accept the draft as is or propose amendments. In the latter case, the commission and council can agree to the amendments or may override parliament's position.

On the one hand, parliament is not a true legislature because it cannot initiate or block legislation. On the other hand, parliamentary committees can influence policy formation by the commission, and in areas of law where the council votes by qualified majority, a unanimous vote is required to override the wishes of parliament. This "cooperation procedure" gives parliament more leverage on some issues than in the past, but members (MEPs) argue that the EC will suffer from a "democratic deficit" until parliament receives full legislative powers.[14]

The weakness of the European Parliament is unfortunate also because it has the strongest environmental orientation among the EC institutions. After the 1989 election the Greens were the fourth-largest grouping in parliament. Besides providing an omnipresent environmental constituency, they have been successful in the "greening" of the more traditional parties and in lobbying the commission and council to keep environmental issues on the Community agenda. Other parties also play an influential role on the Committee on Environment, Public Health, and Consumer Protection, which handles some 40 percent of all parliamentary business. But committee members of all shades tend to support environmental legislation.

The European Court of Justice, located in Luxembourg, considers cases brought before it by the commission, the council, or member states concerning the application of EC treaties. Its decisions are binding on member states, though there is no mechanism for directly enforcing them (national courts are relied on to carry out decisions). The court is frequently asked for advisory opinions on legal disputes between the EC and the states as well. Some of the court's decisions have played an important role in defining the rights of member states to enact environmental legislation under Article 100a that may violate Community treaty provisions prohibiting restraints on trade. For example, in the 1988 "Danish bottle case" the court upheld Denmark's law requiring the use of returnable bottles for beer and soft drinks on grounds that its environmental benefits

were sufficient to justify a minor restraint on trade.[15] Like courts in the
United States, the European Court is emerging as an important policy-
maker in balancing economic and environmental interests (chap. 7).

The Policy Process

Policymaking within the EC is more "political" than a formal review
of the institutions might suggest.[16] Because the EC is a fluid and developing institution, policymaking is complicated by uncertainty over roles,
powers, and decision rules. As we have seen, the council, commission, and
parliament perform different functions from those of the three branches of
U.S. government.

The commission and parliament can be viewed as supranational bodies, whereas the council remains essentially intergovernmental. Under
their terms of appointment, the commissioners and their staffs are international civil servants who are not supposed to serve any national interest.
Thus the commission's proposed legislation tends to favor greater "harmonization" of Community-wide policies. Parliament also tends to favor
stronger EC policies, especially in such fields as environmental and consumer protection that are popular at home. The council, by way of contrast, is usually more cautious because of its sensitivity to national political
interests and the costs of implementing EC policies (which largely de-
volve on national governments). The council is more likely to invoke the
principle of subsidiarity, under which actions are to be taken at the Community level only if they cannot be carried out more efficiently at the
national or local level.

Conflicts of interest among the states are evident in the council. A
fluid coalition of Germany, Denmark, and the Netherlands has pushed
the hardest for environmental protection. These countries often have
higher standards than the Community to start with and they would like
other states to adopt their norms. In some cases they have succeeded. For
example, Germany was influential in proposing tough air pollution controls on large combustion plants, while the Netherlands convinced the
council to essentially adopt its high standards for small car and truck
emissions (see discussion below).[17] By contrast, the poorer countries of
southern Europe, occasionally with the United Kingdom and Ireland, have
been more reluctant to support such measures.

Lobbying by private interests is also omnipresent in the EC. Industry
is very concerned about the impact of new environmental legislation on
business, and maintains an army of lawyers in Brussels. Both the commission directorates and parliamentary committees regularly consult such interests, which tend to represent the largest companies and trade associations. Parliament is now considering requiring the registration of
lobbyists. Environmental, consumer, and other public interest groups also
have representation. An umbrella organization in Brussels, the European

Environmental Bureau, represents some 120 national groups. It closely monitors DG XI and tries to influence proposed legislation.[18] Other international environmental organizations such as the World Wildlife Fund and Greenpeace also lobby intensely.

Environmental policy is closely related to other issues such as completion of the internal market, taxation, research and development, energy, and transportation. Effective policymaking thus requires interaction and cooperation among many EC directorates and parliamentary committees. Formal and informal working groups and task forces try to work out mutually compatible strategies. For example, the development of efficiency standards for electrical appliances involves a working group of members from DG XI and the energy directorate (DG XVII). The divergent perspectives of these directorates often lead to different policy preferences, as do those of the agriculture, transportation, trade, and other "economic" directorates. In the absence of formal mechanisms for resolving differences, the leadership skills of the individual commissioners and the president of the commission are often critical in achieving agreement.

Final policy resolution by the commission and council usually involves extensive political compromise. Sometimes this takes the form of "side payments." For example, to gain approval for a tax to reduce CO_2 emissions, a burden-sharing plan was worked out under which some states agreed to exceed EC norms so that other states could proceed more slowly in meeting the targets. Such arrangements are creating what is often referred to as a "multispeed" Europe.

The Harmonization of Environmental Standards

The rationale for creating common EC policies and "harmonizing" standards is to level the economic playing field. The danger is always that the lowest common denominator will prevail. In the case of environmental standards, this could result in Community norms that are considerably weaker than those of the leading states.

Article 130r of the Treaty of Rome guarantees that the Community will take action "to improve the quality of the environment." This implies that there will be a minimum standard which is not the lowest; all areas should be brought up to an acceptable level. Article 130s allows the council to define which environmental matters can be decided by "qualified majority," in which case they do not require unanimous agreement among states (unless parliament votes against the measure). It may thus take several states to block a decision. Article 130t further specifies that "measures taken by the Community do not prevent any Member State from maintaining or introducing more stringent protective measures, provided that these are compatible with the treaty."[19]

The lead states such as Germany can thus retain higher environmental standards than other countries so long as the European Court does not find them in violation of other sections of the treaty. Naturally they would rather bring the EC norms up to their level so they are not at a competitive economic disadvantage. But they have often moved ahead of the Community. For example, Denmark, the Netherlands, and Germany require high levels of materials recycling. Denmark regulates the content of gasoline more strictly, while the Netherlands has a variety of taxes and charges on energy consumption and automobile pollution emissions.

Such policies have met a good deal of opposition from the slower states. In one case, Italy, Greece, and France claimed that German standards for use of the chemical pentachlorophenol (PCP) were more stringent than required under a 1989 EC directive (91/73/EEC), and therefore represented a barrier to trade (PCP is used on leather imported into Germany). The commission upheld the German standard on grounds that it applied equally to German and non-German companies.[20] In the case of the Dutch tax on "dirty" cars, France threatened legal action but later dropped it when it became evident that public opinion favored stricter auto emission standards for the EC as a whole.[21]

Despite these difficulties, the EC has made considerable progress toward accommodating national differences on the environment. As mentioned above, a "multispeed" Europe is already emerging in which some countries move faster than others, but all are moving in the direction of higher environmental standards. One method for achieving this is to set high EC standards with two "tracks" for achieving them. Some states will adopt the mandatory standards (based on currently available technology), while others may adopt even higher standards based on the latest advances in science and technology. Another approach is for the less-developed states to be given additional time to meet the Community standard; but all states must eventually achieve it. This is effectively what is being done on CO_2 emissions (see below), and it may become the pattern in many other areas as well. Political realities and considerations of equity cannot be ignored in pursuit of the elusive level playing field.

A large area of uncertainty remains over the compatibility of individual national actions with the elimination of barriers to trade under Article 100a of the treaty. The Danish bottle case described earlier suggests that the European Court will allow strict national standards to stand if they do not present barriers to trade or contribute to arbitrary discrimination, and if there is a sufficiently clear environmental basis for them. However, these decisions are made on a case-by-case basis, and the criteria will continue to evolve.

Another area of uncertainty is which environmental decisions can be made by qualified majority in the council. The Maastricht Treaty would appear to place most environmental decisions in this category (whereas previously unanimity was normally required). At the same time, the treaty places greater emphasis on the principle of subsidiarity, under which actions should be taken by the member states unless EC objectives can be better achieved through Community actions. Maastricht's ambiguity and uncertain status leave the application of these principles unclear.

The European Environment Agency

Perhaps the greatest failure in EC environmental policy thus far is the inability of member states to agree on a Community-wide environmental agency to implement its directives. A proposal to create a European Environment Agency (EEA) was introduced in the European Parliament by EC president Jacques Delors in January 1989. The limited resources of DG XI to gather environmental data, improve enforcement of environmental directives, and achieve harmonization of legislation seemed to justify a stronger institutional capacity.

Differences quickly developed, however, over the powers of the new agency. The commission proposal, reflecting the views of the council, limited the role of the proposed body to data gathering and monitoring, whereas parliament wanted the EEA to have powers of inspection and enforcement to make it more comparable to the U.S. Environmental Protection Agency. There was also disagreement over the structure and management of the proposed agency.

After vigorous debate and more than two years of negotiations, a compromise regulation was adopted on May 7, 1990 (90/1210/EEC). The agency is to concentrate on developing information programs on air and water pollution, soil and land use, waste management, noise abatement, hazardous chemicals, and protection of coastlines. The resolution provided, however, for review of EEA's functions after two years with the possibility of enlarging them at that time. The agency is to be governed by a management board with representation from the states and the commission as well as scientists designated by parliament.

Unfortunately the EEA does not yet exist because no agreement has been reached on where it should be located. The EEA has become a hostage to a larger controversy within the EC over the future location of Community institutions. In particular, there has been a widespread desire to move the seat of parliament from Strasbourg to Brussels, where most of its actual work is done. France has consequently blocked the siting of the EEA in order to bring pressure on other states to maintain the parliament in Strasbourg. It is not clear how or when this issue can be resolved. In the meantime, a task force made up of a shadow group of experts (acting as consultants to DG XI) is planning a work program for EEA, collecting information, and working on a "state of the environment" report for all of Europe.

The Fifth Programme and Current Legislation

The Fifth Programme

Since 1972 the commission has developed an agenda to guide its activities for a five-year period, called action programmes. The guiding principle of the Fifth Programme, adopted in 1992, is "sustainability."[22] This principle, derived from the 1987 Report of the World Commission on Environment and Development, *Our Common Future*, goes beyond the concept of balanced growth espoused by the Single European Act. It attempts to operationalize the report's definition of sustainability: "development which meets the needs of the present without compromising the ability of future generations to meet their own needs."[23] This principle is seen as especially critical if Europe is to reconcile its push for economic growth under the "1992" single market with preservation of the environment.

The new program calls for "integration of environment considerations in the formulation and implementation of economic and sectoral policies, in the decisions of public authorities, in the conduct and development of production processes, and in individual behavior and choice."[24] All Community policies are said to be dependent on achieving sustainable practices. New strategies are suggested for dealing with such problems as cross-media pollution, pollution prevention at the source, and alternatives to command-and-control regulation. The program goes beyond environmental cleanup and pollution mitigation in calling for more fundamental behavioral changes. The key sectors targeted are industry, energy, transportation, agriculture, and tourism.

A significant management innovation of the Fifth Programme is the establishment of several new environmental committees to bring about such changes. A new consultative forum will bring together actors from industry, business, government, trade unions, public interest groups, and the appropriate directorate-general of the commission. It will provide opportunities for sharing responsibility in developing and implementing policy with the individuals and groups that will be most critical to its success. A second committee will track the application of Community environmental law in the states and work directly with the responsible parties to improve state implementation. This will involve information exchange and assistance on how to achieve better compliance. This may raise questions in the future about the EC's legal competence to advise states on the application of Community law. A third committee, composed of directors-general and representatives of the states, is also anticipated to exchange views on more general issues to improve mutual understanding. All of these committees represent efforts to improve follow-up to Community actions in the states and to make the policy process more open and transparent.

The Current Legislative Agenda

The Community has approximately two hundred environmental laws in force. The following section describes some of the most important concerns now being addressed.

Reduction of carbon dioxide. Concern over global climate change due to the accumulation of CO_2 and other greenhouse gases in the atmosphere has been particularly strong in Europe. It is widely perceived that continued burning of fossil fuels could produce major disruptions in weather patterns and cause rising sea levels that could imperil such countries as the Netherlands. Recognizing that industrial nations are largely responsible for the problem, a June 1990 summit meeting of the European Council (EC heads of state) in Dublin called for a Community strategy to reduce greenhouse emissions. The Dublin summit was followed by a council meeting of EC environment and energy ministers in October 1990, at which it was agreed that CO_2 emissions should be stabilized at 1990 levels by the year 2000 in the Community as a whole. The council asked the commission to develop a strategy to meet this target, including fiscal and economic instruments to promote energy efficiency.

The most exciting and politically controversial proposal is for the use of economic instruments such as a carbon tax to reduce fuel consumption and pollution, improve energy efficiency, and encourage development of alternative energy sources. The commission proposed a Community-wide tax on oil beginning at $3 a barrel in 1993 and rising $1 per year up to $10 a barrel in 2000.[25] Other fuels, including coal and nuclear, would be taxed at rates according to their energy and carbon content. Because the EC does not have the competence to levy taxes directly, the tax would have to be adopted by individual states and harmonized like the value added tax (VAT) to avoid competitive disadvantages.[26]

Carlo Ripa di Meana, the former EC environment commissioner, was a strong supporter of this concept and hoped to be able to take a Community agreement on the carbon tax to the Earth summit in Río de Janeiro in June 1992. The council anticipated approval of the text by May.[27] Because of further disagreements among member states, however, the council was unable to act on the proposal in time. With nothing to show for his efforts, and the United States blocking a global climate treaty with targets for CO_2 reduction, Ripa di Meana ultimately refused to attend the summit. It may be more difficult for Europe to move ahead on the tax unless the United States and other industrial nations are willing to take similar actions.

The EC is pursuing other means of improving energy efficiency, even though Europeans utilize only half as much energy per capita as

Americans. It is supporting a variety of research and development (R&D) programs such as the Joule program for nonnuclear energy research and the Thermie program for bringing renewable energy, conservation, and clean fossil fuel technologies to the marketplace. Also, interest in least-cost planning would create incentives for electric power utilities to save energy by reducing customer demand. The Special Actions for Vigorous Energy Efficiency (SAVE) program was launched in October 1991 to encourage energy savings through consumer information, new energy efficiency standards, environmental audits, and least-cost planning.

Transportation presents other problems. Although the EC has passed legislation to reduce automobile air pollution, the full impact of the new standards will not be felt for several years. It is predicted that auto ownership will continue to increase rapidly (by 45 percent between 1987 and 2010), thereby offsetting even these gains. There is thus interest in expanding rail and other public transportation. The commission is developing a strategy for "sustainable mobility," which includes such things as standards for the sulfur content of fuels, state aid for combined inland water/rail transportation, and taxes and charges on dirty fuels and vehicles.[28]

Transfer of hazardous wastes. The creation of the internal market poses some interesting questions about hazardous waste management. Although hazardous waste is only about 20 percent of the total waste stream, it is already routinely shipped across borders in Europe. France and the United Kingdom are net importers, while Germany and the Netherlands are exporters. It is predicted that the volume of such waste will increase with higher rates of economic growth after 1992, raising "the specter of large quantities of dangerous waste moving freely across Europe in search of the cheapest and least regulated outlets."[29] The elimination of border checks will make it more difficult to monitor this movement.

The EC is considering revising some laws to improve monitoring and other controls over hazardous waste shipment. Existing legislation requiring "informed consent" from importing nations is no longer considered adequate.[30]

Packaging. Another component of the commission's comprehensive waste management plan is the reduction of solid waste through changes in packaging standards and increased reliance on recycling and reuse of materials. Packaging is a large contributor to the waste stream, accounting for 50 million tons per year in the EC, of which only 18 percent is currently recycled.[31]

Some of the northern countries have already begun to enact stringent packaging and recycling laws, which could pose barriers to trade. Germany has the most ambitious program, requiring manufacturers and/or store owners to take back packaging for reuse or recycling. Industries are allowed to establish their own collection sites alongside government recycling centers. A green dot on the package reminds consumers of their obligation to return it. By 1995 industry is required to collect and recycle 80 percent of its packaging. There are similar standards for glass, tin, and aluminum. The Flemish region of Belgium and the Netherlands have packaging reduction programs, and France is also considering a plan.

On July 15, 1992, the EC Commission approved a packaging directive that would establish a recovery target of 90 percent by weight, which states are to meet through their own programs. Within ten years, 60 percent of all recovered waste must be recycled, 30 percent may be incinerated with energy recovery, and not more than 10 percent can receive final disposal (e.g., in landfills). States are allowed to set intermediate targets to demonstrate that they can meet the ten-year goal.[32] The directive must now achieve council approval.

That the proposed directive of the commission sets lower recycling targets than existing German law may be reassuring to industry, but there is still concern that implementation will not be responsive to local needs and conditions. Industry would like to put incineration on a more equal footing with recycling. In any case, to be successful, the program will require close cooperation among the Community, states, and affected industries.

Ecolabeling. Consistent with the principles of green capitalism and of encouraging consumers to adopt sound environmental policies, the EC Council adopted a regulation on "ecolabeling" on March 23, 1992.[33] The purpose is to identify products that are environmentally "friendly" with special labels. The criteria for rating products will stress eliminating pollution at the source and minimizing environmental impacts throughout the life-cycle of the product, including disposal costs. The impacts on the health and safety of workers, the use of best available technologies in manufacturing, and use of recyclable and recycled materials will also be weighed in the labeling process.

Germany has led the way in this area as well, having had its "Blue Angel" environmental label since 1978. France, the United Kingdom, the Netherlands, Ireland, and Denmark are all considering their own national labeling programs. Because these plans have different criteria, labeling procedures, and logos, it is important for the Community to implement a common system to avoid market confusion. Although the EC program would not require industry participation, there would be a strong incentive to apply for the "green" label because of growing consumer awareness and sophistication.

Implementation

The success of the EC commitment to environmental protection will depend on the extent to which states actually take the actions required by Community legislation. States must enact Community law into national law (transposition of law), but this is not always accomplished within the prescribed time periods. They are also responsible for applying and enforcing the law. A great many political and administrative forces within the states affect the outcomes. The greener states with a tradition of national environmental regulation generally have the best record of EC environmental enforcement. They have more sophisticated administrative infrastructures for putting Community mandates into operation. The extent to which regions within states (and their citizens) comply with EC law also varies. Thus, as one scholar puts it, "achieving compliance with the directive once it is transformed into national law is far more complex and problematic than simply incorporating Community directives into national legal codes."[34]

The EC does have enforcement mechanisms at its disposal. Article 169 of the treaty allows citizens, local authorities, businesses, or interest groups to lodge complaints on the inadequate application or transposition of EC law directly before the commission. Once a complaint is brought, efforts are made to mediate the dispute or to informally persuade the national government to take appropriate action. If a party is found to be in violation of EC law, the commission can issue a formal notice to the state. If all else fails, a case can be brought before the European Court of Justice to force compliance.

In 1984, in the environment and consumer protection sector, there were 65 cases in which formal notice was given to a state; 2 cases were referred to the European Court. In 1991 this had increased to 136 formal notices and 8 court referrals. Enforcement of Community law varies widely among individual states. For example, for all policy sectors (agriculture, transportation, internal market, and so forth) in 1991, 86 formal letters of notice were given to Portugal, 64 to the United Kingdom, 62 to Germany, 60 to France, and 118 to Italy.[35]

Some of the variation in compliance is related to differences in levels of citizen and interest group awareness. Some states may have proportionately more complaints lodged because their citizens are more alert, informed, and able to bring matters to the attention of the Community. But differential enforcement is also the result of variations in the budgets and other resources of governments to carry out EC mandates. Because states choose their own means of compliance, differences are inevitable in the instruments used and in the severity of penalties levied against violators.

Some examples will help to illustrate these problems. A 1985 EEC directive (85/337/EEC) requires member states to conduct environmental impact assessments (EIAs) on public and private projects. Some states have incorporated this requirement into existing national law, while others passed new laws. But the legal requirements for EIAs, the level and competence of the administering authorities, the extent of public participation, the role of judicial review, and the quality of resulting assessments vary greatly across countries.[36]

The United Kingdom and the European Commission disagree over the need for an EIA for the proposed high-speed rail link between London and the Eurotunnel being constructed under the English Channel. The commission initiated proceedings against the United Kingdom in October 1991, arguing that an assessment should have been done in this case as well as in a number of others. The British government countered that it was grandfathered in because the EC law had not been transposed at the time of the siting decision. Although disagreement persists over the date for implementing the law, the case will probably not be taken to the European Court of Justice for fear that it could affect British ratification of the Maastricht Treaty.[37] Nevertheless, in November 1992 the Court of Justice condemned the United Kingdom for failing to implement a 1980 directive on water quality. It was the first time the United Kingdom was condemned for a breach of environmental standards.[38]

In perhaps a more typical case, the court found Italy guilty of noncompliance with an EC directive on protection of wild birds (79/409/EEC). Because Italy had not limited bird hunting nor incorporated an amendment (86/411/EEC) to the original directive into Italian law, it was ordered to pay legal costs. In another case, France was censured by the court for failing to comply with EC directives on air pollution. As a consequence, in October 1991 France incorporated the directives directly into French law.[39]

Conclusion

This review of environmental policy does not cover all the issues addressed by the EC. One can nevertheless conclude that the Community is committed to protecting its environment during the process of economic and political integration. Environmental concerns are to be integrated into all EC policy at the earliest stages of planning. DG XI has proposed institutional reforms to deal with new problems and has taken seriously its mandate to improve compliance and enforcement. There is greater consultation with industry, other Community institutions, and environmental and consumer groups. The latter, which are not as well organized or funded as in the United States, have increasing access to the commission and its staff.

The EC recognizes that environmental problems are serious and that managing them effectively is vital to the success of the entire common market project. Most EC civil servants and parliamentarians see the Community as better suited to dealing with transboundary pollution problems and other issues than the individual countries. They share an optimism that accommodations, although difficult, can be made to ensure progress toward solving environmental problems in all of the states. It is doubtful that this could be achieved by countries acting individually.

At the same time, to be successful, the EC must maintain its popular support. Current divisions over monetary policy, agricultural subsidies, and ratification of the Maastricht Treaty suggest that direct representation through the European Parliament must be strengthened. The Greens have opposed the treaty on grounds that it actually increases the "democratic deficit" by giving even greater powers to the council. They have linked this issue to environmental politics by arguing that if the parliament were more powerful, the environment would receive greater attention. Together with the status of the European Environmental Agency, this remains a critical question to be resolved.

Nevertheless, the EC now has an opportunity to set an example of sustainable development for the rest of the world. It has already made its mark in the global climate debate by proposing to stabilize CO_2 emissions by the end of the decade and agreeing in principle to a carbon/energy tax. The EC has also begun to address the more serious environmental needs of central and eastern Europe and provides a useful model there.[40]

There is thus good reason to be optimistic, despite recent setbacks for the Maastricht Treaty. Several of the member states will continue to push the EC toward greener heights. The gradual disappearance of national frontiers and the building of political as well as economic union should contribute to keeping environmental issues high on the European and world agenda.

Notes

1. On the general history and development of the EC see, e.g., Clifford Hackett, *Cautious Revolution: The European Community Arrives* (New York: Praeger, 1990); and William Nicoll and Trevor C. Salmon, *Understanding the European Communities* (Savage, Md.: Barnes and Noble, 1990).

2. For a summary of the first four plans and a general description of EC environmental legislation, see Stanley P. Johnson and Guy Corcelle, *The Environmental Policy of the European Communities* (London: Graham and Trotman, 1989). An overview of EC policies is also given in *Environmental Policy in the European Community*, 4th ed. (Luxembourg: Office for Official Publications of the European Communities, 1990).

3. *Environmental Indicators* (Paris: Organization for Economic Cooperation and Development, 1991), 65; and Statistical Office of the European Communities, *A Social Portrait of Europe* (Luxembourg: Office for Official Publications of the European Communities, 1991), 18.

4. *"1992" The Environmental Dimension*, Task Force Report on the Environment and the Internal Market, at the request of the Commission of the European Communities (Bonn: Economica, 1990), 44-45.

5. *Environmental Indicators*, 19.

6. The ECU or "European Currency Unit" is a monetary unit based on all of the national European currencies. At exchange rates prevailing in mid 1993, one ECU equaled approximately $1.20.

7. *Environmental Policy in the European Community*, 13.

8. Ibid., 34.

9. *Europe Environment* (Brussels: Europe Information Service), N. 389, June 19, 1992, I, 7.

10. *A Social Portrait of Europe* (Luxembourg: Office for Official Publications of the European Community, 1991), 106-107.

11. Ibid., 107.

12. Extensive documentation on all the European Green parties, including those in the European Parliament, can be found in Mike Feinstein, *Sixteen Weeks With European Greens* (San Pedro, Calif.: R and E Miles, 1992). See also Sara Parkin, *Green Parties: An International Guide* (London: Heretic, 1989).

13. Ferdinand Muller-Rommel, ed., *New Politics in Western Europe: The Rise and Success of Green Parties and Alternative Lists* (Boulder: Westview, 1989).

14. See Francis Jacobs and Richard Corbett, *The European Parliament* (Boulder: Westview, 1990).

15. "Commission of the European Communities v. Kingdom of Denmark—Case 302/86," *Report of Cases Before the Court,* vol. 8 (Luxembourg: Office for Official Publications of the European Communities, 1988).

16. See, e.g., Stephen George, *Politics and Policy in the European Community*, 2d ed. (New York: Oxford University Press, 1991); and Alberta M. Sbragia, ed., *Euro-Politics* (Washington, D.C.: Brookings, 1992).

17. Nigel Haigh, "New Tools for European Air Pollution," *International Environmental Affairs* 1:1 (Winter 1989): 33; and Charlotte Kim, "The Cats and Mice: The Politics of Setting EC Car Emission Standards," CEPS Standards Programme: Paper No. 2 (Brussels: Centre for European Policy Studies, May 1992), 19.

18. See "European Federation of Environmental NGOs" (Brussels: European Environmental Bureau, n.d.); and Christian Hey and Jutta Jahns-Bohm, *Ecology and the Single Market* (Brussels: European Environmental Bureau, 1989).

19. Johnson and Corcelle, *Environmental Policy*, 344.

20. *Europe Environment* (Brussels: Europe Information Service), N. 389, June 19, 1992, I, 9.

21. For excellent analyses of this case, see Kim, "Cats and Mice"; and Henning Arp, "Interest Groups in EC Legislation: The Case of Car Emission Standards" (Paper presented at a workshop held at the University of Sussex, March 22-28, 1991).

22. Commission of the European Communities, *Toward Sustainability: A European Community Programme of Policy and Action in Relation to the Environment and Sustainable Development*, I,1, COM(92)23 final (Brussels, March 27, 1992), 18.

23. World Commission on Environment and Development, *Our Common Future* (New York: Oxford University Press, 1987).

24. *Toward Sustainability*, 3.

25. Paul L. Montgomery, "Heavy Energy Tax Is Proposed to Curb Emissions in Europe," *New York Times*, September 26, 1991; "A Community Strategy to limit carbon dioxide emissions and to improve energy efficiency," Communication from the Commission to the Council, SEC(91)1744 final, Brussels, October 14, 1991.

26. *Europe Environment*, N. 387, "Dossier on CO_2 Tax," May 19, 1992, V.3.

27. "A Community Strategy to limit carbon dioxide emissions and to improve energy efficiency," Council Conclusions, SN/283/91, Brussels, Dec. 13, 1991, 3-4.

28. "Green Paper on the Impact of Transportation on the Environment: A Community Strategy for Sustainable Mobility," Communication from the Commission, COM(92)46 final, Brussels, Feb. 20, 1992, 37, 44.

29. *Environmental Policy in the European Community*, 35.

30. "Report from the Commission of the European Communities to the United Nations Conference on Environment and Development, Río de Janeiro, June 1992," SEC(91)2448 final, Brussels, March 29, 1992, 29.

31. "Draft Proposal for a Council Directive on packaging and packaging waste," DG XI-A4, XI/369/91, 21/2/92, final draft, 2.
32. Ibid., 6.
33. OJ No. L99/92, 92/880/EEC.
34. Alberta Sbragia, "Environmental Policy in the European Community: The Problem of Implementation in Comparative Perspective," in *Towards a Transatlantic Environmental Policy* (Washington, D.C.: European Institute, 1991), 52.
35. *Europe Environment*, N. 385, April 14, 1992, I, 3-4.
36. R. Coenen and J. Jorissen, "Environmental Impact Assessment in the Member Countries of the European Community" (Karlsruhe, Germany: Kernforschungszentrum Karlsruhe), 1989, 7-8.
37. *Europe Environment*, N. 393, September 8, 1992, I, 6; and press release, "United Kingdom Infringement, Environment, Termination/Reasoned Opinion," Brussels, July 31, 1992.
38. *Europe Environment*, N. 399, December 1, 1992, I, 10.
39. *Europe Energy*, N. 367, November 15, 1991, I, 7.
40. *Newsletter: Environmental Research*, N. 8, SP-1.91.42 (Brussels: Commission of the European Communities, December 1991), 1.

13

Environment, Population, and Economic Development

Richard J. Tobin

E nvironmental problems occasionally make life in the United States unpleasant and inconvenient, but most Americans contribute to or willingly tolerate this unpleasantness in exchange for the benefits, comforts, and life-styles associated with a developed, industrial economy. Most Europeans, Japanese, and Australians share similar life-styles, so it is not unexpected that they too typically take modern amenities for granted.

When life-styles are viewed from a broader perspective, however, much changes. Consider, for example, what life is like for most of the world's population. In the early 1990s the United States' gross national product per capita was almost $420 per week, but more than 60 percent of the world's population lived in countries where per capita incomes were less than $20 per week. In India and China the weekly average in 1990 was less than $8. In Mozambique, the world's most impoverished country, per capita income—of $120 per year—was about four-tenths of 1 percent of that in the United States.

Low incomes are not the only problem facing many of the world's inhabitants. In some developing countries, women, often illiterate with no formal education, will marry as young as age thirteen or fourteen. During their childbearing years, these women will deliver as many as six or seven babies, most without the benefit of trained medical personnel. This absence is not without consequences. As the United Nations Children's Fund (UNICEF) notes, the risk of dying because of pregnancy or childbirth is up to 150 times higher in the world's poorest countries than it is in Europe or the United States.[1]

Many of the world's children are also at risk. Only one out of a hundred American children die before the age of five; in many Asian and African countries as many as 20 to 25 percent do. *Every day* nearly forty thousand children under five die in developing countries from diseases that rarely kill Americans. Most of the deaths are caused by one or more of the following six diseases: tetanus, measles, malaria, diarrhea, whooping cough, or acute respiratory infections.[2]

Of the children from these poor countries that do survive their earliest years, some will have brain damage because their pregnant mothers had no iodine in their diets; others will go blind from lack of proper vitamins. Many will face a life of poverty, never to taste clean water, visit a doctor, enter a classroom, or eat nutritious food regularly or sufficiently. To the extent that shelter is available, it is rudimentary, rarely with electricity or proper sanitary facilities. When a poor child in Jakarta wants to bathe, as an example, he might lower himself into the open sewer that flows through his family's squatter settlement. Because their surroundings have been abused or poorly managed, millions of those in the developing world will also become victims of floods, famine, desertification, waterborne diseases, infestation of pests, and exceedingly noxious levels of air and water pollution.

As these children grow older, many will find that their governments do not have or cannot provide the resources to ensure them a reasonable standard of living. Yet all around them are countries with living standards well beyond their comprehension. The average American uses about thirty-three times more energy and consumes about 65 percent more calories per day—far in excess of minimum daily requirements—than does the average Indian. The Indian might wonder why Americans consume a disproportionate share of the world's resources when she has a malnourished child she cannot afford to clothe or educate.

In short, life in the many countries in Asia, Africa, and Latin America provides an entirely different array of problems than those encountered in developed nations, which are responding to the benefits and consequences of development. The residents of poor countries, however, must cope with widespread poverty and the relative lack of economic development. Yet both developed and developing nations often undergo environmental degradation. Those without property, for example, may be tempted to denude tropical forests for land to farm. Alternatively, pressures for development often force countries to overexploit their base of environmental resources.

All of this leads to the key question addressed in this chapter: can the world's poorest countries, with the overwhelming majority of the world's population, improve their lot through sustainable development? According to the World Commission on Environment and Development, sustainable development requires meeting the essential needs of the present generation for food, clothing, shelter, jobs, and health without "compromising the ability of future generations to meet their own needs." To achieve this goal, the commission emphasizes the need to stimulate higher levels of economic development without inflicting irreparable damage on the environment.[3]

Whose responsibility is it to bring about sustainable development? One view is that richer nations have a moral obligation to assist less fortunate ones. If the former do not meet this obligation, not only will hundreds of millions in developing countries suffer but the consequences will be felt in the developed countries as well. Others assert that the poorer nations must accept responsibility for their own fate; outside efforts to help them only worsen the problem and lead to an unhealthy dependence. As an illustration, biologist Garrett Hardin insists that it is wrong to provide food to famine-stricken nations because they have exceeded their environment's carrying capacity. In Hardin's words, "if you give food and save lives and thus increase the number of people, you increase suffering and ultimately increase the loss of life."[4]

The richer nations, whichever position they take, cannot avoid affecting what happens in the developing world. It is thus useful to consider how U.S. actions influence the quest for sustainable development. To a large extent, two related factors affect this quest. The first is a country's population; the second is a country's capacity to support its population.

Population Growth: Cure or Culprit?

Population growth is one of the more controversial elements in the journey toward sustainable development. Depending on the perspective used, the world is either vastly overpopulated or capable of supporting as many as thirty times its current population (slightly more than 5.5 billion in mid 1993 and increasing at an annual rate of about 1.7 percent).[5] Many of the developing nations are growing faster than the industrial nations (table 13 1), and nearly three-quarters of the world's population live outside the developed regions. If current growth rates continue, the proportion of those in developing countries will increase even more. Between 1990 and 2025 more than 95 percent of the world's population increase will occur in the latter regions, exactly where the people and the environment can least afford such a surge.

Africa is particularly prone to high rates of population growth. In the last decade of this century, Kenya, Zambia, Tanzania, and the Côte d'Ivoire are expected to increase their populations by at least 3.8 percent per year.[6] This may not seem to be much until we realize that such rates will double the countries' populations in less than nineteen years. The continent has another twenty-eight countries that are expected to increase their populations by 3 percent or more per year in the 1990s. Of the three-dozen countries that had crude birth rates of at least forty-five per thousand in 1990, all but three are in Africa. Fertility rates measure the number of children an average woman has during her lifetime. Thirty-seven of the forty-five countries with fertility rates at six or above are in Africa. By comparison, the birth rate in the United States is fifteen per thousand, and its fertility rate is less than two.

High rates of population growth are not necessarily undesirable, and criticisms of high rates often bring rebuke. In the early 1970s, for example, when the United States and other industrial nations urged developing countries to stem their growth, more often than not the latter responded with hostility.

Table 13-1 Estimated Populations and Projected Growth Rates

Region or Country	Estimated Population (millions)			Population Growth Rate (percentage)	Number of Years to Double Population Size
	1990	2000	2025	1990-2000	
Developed countries	1,207	1,264	1,354	0.5	149.0
United States	249	266	300	0.7	105.8
Japan	123	128	127	0.4	174.3
Canada	27	28	32	0.7	96.8
Developing regions	4,086	4,997	7,150	2.0	34.4
China	1,139	1,299	1,513	1.3	52.7
India	853	1,042	1,442	2.0	34.7
Bangladesh	116	151	235	2.7	26.2
Africa	642	867	1,597	3.0	23.1
Kenya	24	35	79	3.9	18.3
Tanzania	27	40	85	3.8	18.6
Mexico	89	107	150	1.9	36.3
Brazil	150	179	246	1.8	39.2
World total	5,293	6,261	8,504	1.7	41.2

Source: United Nations Population Division, *World Population Prospects 1990* (New York: United Nations, 1991).

To pleas that it initiate family-planning programs, China complained that they represented capitalist efforts to subjugate the world's poorer nations. China viewed a larger population as desirable because it contributed to increases in domestic production.[7]

African delegates to a conference on population in 1973 reported that many of their countries prize high levels of fertility and resent foreigners lecturing them about population growth. Pointing to the vast natural resources and low population density of Africa, the delegates insisted that their continent could accommodate a much larger population and that Africa's anticipated economic growth would easily satisfy the needs of a growing population. The Africans also offered an alternative view of the world situation that criticized the West's profligate waste of scarce resources. Developed nations, the delegates believed, wanted to resolve shortages of world resources, not by restricting their own use or reducing their own populations, but by restricting growth in poor countries so that more resources would be available to the West.[8]

By the late 1970s and early 1980s, however, many developing countries no longer viewed high population growth as desirable. They found themselves with a large number of young, dependent children; increasing rates of unemployment; a cancerous and unchecked growth of urban areas; and a general inability to provide for the social and economic demands of ever larger populations. Many developing countries also realized that if their living standards were to improve, their economic growth would have to exceed their rate of population increase.

Although many countries altered their attitudes about population growth, they soon realized the immensity of the task. The prevailing theory of demographic transition suggests that societies go through three stages. In the first stage, in premodern societies, birth rates and death rates are high, so populations remain stable or increase at low rates. In the second stage, death rates are lower and populations grow more rapidly because of vaccines, better health care, and more nutritious foods. As countries begin to reap the benefits of economic growth, they enter the third stage. Infant mortality declines, but so does the desire or need to have large families. Population growth slows considerably.

This model explains events in the United States and many European countries: as standards of living increased, birth rates declined. The model's weakness is that it assumes economic growth; in the absence of such growth, many nations are caught in a "demographic trap."[9] They get stuck in the second stage. This is the predicament of many developing countries today. In some of these countries the situation is even worse. Their populations are growing faster than their economies, and living standards are declining. According to UNICEF, average incomes dropped by as much as 10 to 25 percent in much of Africa and Latin America in the 1980s. The immediate prospects for improvement are not bright. The World Bank predicts that many African and Latin American nations will face even lower average incomes in the 1990s.[10]

These declines create a cruel paradox. Larger populations produce increased demands for health and educational services; deteriorating economies make it difficult to provide the services. Evidence for the latter is found in governmental budgets. In the African nation of Zaire, the national government devoted slightly more than 15 percent of its expenditures to education in 1972; by 1990 education's share of the budget was slightly more than 1 percent. Over the same time period, the amount the Kenyan government spent on health declined by almost 50 percent.[11]

Economic decline is not the only barrier to reducing population growth, but in the absence of sufficient levels of economic development, large families are either imperative or difficult to avoid. With economic futures so uncertain, children provide families with additional labor, sometimes as early as age seven or eight. Children also provide a source of income security for their parents during illnesses or retirement. In addition, because infant mortality is high, having many children is necessary to ensure the survival of at least a few.

Abortions and contraceptives can contribute to lower growth rates, but these approaches may not be followed because of social and religious objections. Consider the example of the Philippines. Its population increased by more than 250 percent between the mid 1940s and the mid

1970s. Demographers estimated the growth rate to be about 2.4 percent per year in the 1980s.

If this rate continued, they argued, the Philippines would be unable to improve its standard of living. The Catholic Bishops Conference, which called contraceptives "dehumanizing and ethically objectionable," condemned recommendations that contraceptives be provided to all Filipino men and women of reproductive age.[12] The Philippines is overwhelmingly Catholic, so the church's objections have nearly paralyzed the country's response to its high growth rates.

Another barrier to slower growth can be found in the opportunity to lower death rates significantly. In some Asian and African countries the average life expectancy at birth is less than forty-five years (compared with seventy-six in the United States and seventy-nine in Japan). If these Asians and Africans had access to the medicines, vaccines, and nutritious foods readily available in the developed nations, then death rates would drop substantially. Life expectancies could be extended by twenty years or more.

Indeed, there is good reason to expect death rates to decline. Over the past two decades the United Nations and other development agencies have attempted to reduce infant mortality by immunizing children against potentially fatal illnesses and by making available inexpensive cures for diarrhea, the single largest cause of death among children under five.[13] These programs have met with enormous success and more is anticipated. The consequence of this success, matched with higher birth rates, is that at least ten low-income countries, all in Africa, will experience even faster growth in the 1990s than they did in the 1960s, 1970s, and 1980s. Reduced infant mortality rates should also reduce fertility rates, but the change will be gradual and millions of children will be born in the meantime. Most of the first-time mothers of the next twenty years have already been born.

Given these problems, the success that Cuba, Sri Lanka, South Korea, and Thailand have had in lowering their population growth rates is all the more remarkable. Thailand reduced its growth rate by half in fifteen years. The Thais have used both humor and showmanship to achieve this reduction. A private association distributes condoms at movie theaters and traffic jams, sponsors condom-blowing contests, and organizes a special cops-and-rubbers program each New Year's Eve. The association also offers free vasectomies on the king's birthday; for those who cannot wait, the normal charge is $20.[14]

Perhaps the best known but most controversial population control programs are in India and China. India's family-planning program started in the early 1950s as a low-key educational effort that achieved only modest success. The government changed course from volunteerism to compulsion in the mid 1970s. The minimum age for marriage was increased, and India's states were encouraged to select their own methods to reduce growth.

Several states chose coercion. Parents with two or more children were expected to have themselves sterilized. To ensure compliance, states threatened to withhold salaries or to dismiss government workers from their jobs. Public officials were likewise threatened with sanctions if they did not provide enough people for sterilization. One result was a massive program of forced sterilization that caused considerable political turmoil.[15] Although the program was eventually relaxed, India was able to cut its fertility rate by almost 30 percent between 1960 and 1990. This is remarkable progress, but cultural resistance may stifle further gains. India currently adds another 18 million inhabitants each year to all those it now has trouble feeding and clothing. If such growth continues, India could become the world's most populous country within the next half-century.

Whether India becomes the world's most populous nation in the next century depends on what happens in China. Sharply reversing its earlier position in the late 1970s, the Chinese government conceded that too-rapid population growth was leading to shortages of jobs, housing, and consumer goods, further frustrating efforts to modernize its economy.[16] To reduce the country's population growth rate, the government now discourages early marriages. Beginning in 1979, it also adopted a one-child-per-family policy. The government gives one-child families monthly subsidies, free education for their child, preference for housing and health care, and higher pensions at retirement. Families that choose to have more than one child are deprived of these benefits and penalized financially if they had previously agreed to have only one child.

The controversial element of the program involves the government's monitoring of women's menstrual cycles; allegations of forced abortions and sterilizations, some occurring as late as the last three months of pregnancy; and even female infanticide in some rural areas. Chinese officials admit that abortions have occasionally been forced on some unwilling women. These officials quickly add, however, that such practices represent aberrations, not accepted guidelines, and that they violate the government's birth control policies.

In its initial years the program in China successfully lowered annual rates of population growth by 50 percent—from 2.2 percent in the 1970s to only 1.1 percent by 1985. Perhaps because of this success, the program encountered considerable resistance and, in some areas, outright disregard. Consequently, the government relaxed its restrictions and exempted certain families, particularly in rural areas, from the one-child policy. These policy changes led to a 20 percent increase in the birth rate between 1985 and 1987, and China soon announced that it had abandoned its goal of a population of 1.2 billion by 2000.[17] Abandoning this goal does not mean that China has forsaken its entire population control strategy. Renewed concern about population growth in the late 1980s caused the Chinese government to reassess the effectiveness of its programs. If these programs fail and current birth rates continue, China's population could approach 2 billion by the middle of the next century.

The position of the U.S. government toward China's population control efforts has not been consistent. For many years the American government viewed rapidly growing populations as a threat to economic development. The United States backed its rhetoric with money; it was the single largest donor to international population control programs. The official U.S. position changed dramatically during the Reagan administration. Due to its opposition to abortion, the administration said the United States would no longer contribute to the United Nations Fund for Population Activities (UNFPA) because of its association with some population programs in China. None of UNFPA's money is used to provide abortions anywhere in the world, but the U.S. ban on contributions nonetheless continued during the Bush administration. Within a day of taking office, President Bill Clinton announced his intention to alter this policy, to provide financial support to this U.N. program, and to fund international population control programs that rely on abortions.

Concerns about abortion are not the only reason that many people have qualms about efforts to control population increases. Their view is that large populations are a problem only when they are not used productively to enhance economic development. The solution to the lack of such development is not government intervention, they argue, but rather individual initiatives and the spread of capitalist, free-market economies. Advocates of this position also believe that larger populations can be advantageous because they enhance political power, contribute to economic development, encourage technological innovation, stimulate agricultural production, and increase prospects that more geniuses will be available to solve human problems.[18] Other critics of population control programs also ask if it is appropriate for developed countries to impose their preferences on others.

As one scholar has asked: "Isn't it time wealthy white people stopped telling Third World peasants who aspire to a better life how many children and what kind of economy to have?"[19]

These views are not limited to a few academics. Several developing countries are dissatisfied with their rates of population increase. Among them are Bolivia, Iraq, North Korea, the Congo, and Laos. All of them would like to see larger populations. In Singapore the government became so concerned about a declining birth rate that it virtually started a dating service, including "Love Boat" cruises, for the country's unmarried adults.

Clearly, the appropriateness of different population sizes is debatable. There is no clear answer to whether growth by itself is good or bad. The important issue is a country's carrying capacity. Can it ensure its population a reasonable standard of living?

Providing Food and Fuel for Growing Populations

Sustainable development requires that environmental resources not be overtaxed so that they are available for future generations. As Lester Brown points out, however, when populations exceed sustainable yields of their forests, aquifers, and croplands, "they begin directly or indirectly to consume the resource base itself," gradually destroying it.[20] The eventual result is an irreversible collapse of biological and environmental support systems. Is there any evidence that these systems are now being strained or will be in the future?

The first place to look is in the area of food production. Nations can grow their own food, import it, or, as most nations do, rely on both options. Earth is richly endowed with agricultural potential and production. Millions of acres of arable land remain to be cultivated, and farmers now produce enough food to satisfy the daily caloric and protein needs of a world population exceeding 10 billion, far more than are already alive.[21] These data suggest the ready availability of food as well as a potential for even higher levels of production. This good news must be balanced with the sobering realization that nearly a billion people in the developing world today barely have enough food to survive.

As with economic development, the amount of food available in a country must increase at least as fast as the rate of population growth; otherwise per capita consumption will decline. If existing levels of caloric intake are already inadequate, then food production (and imports) must increase faster than population growth in order to meet minimum caloric needs. Assisted by the expanded use of irrigation, pesticides, and fertilizers, many developing countries, particularly in Asia, dramatically increased their food production over the past two or three decades. Asia's three largest countries—China, India, and Indonesia—are no longer heavily dependent on imports. Between 1965 and 1989, China and Indonesia were able to increase their populations' average daily caloric supply by more than 35 percent.[22] In fact, the average citizen in both countries now consumes more calories than the minimum daily requirement.

Despite these and a few other notable successes, much of the developing world is in the midst of a long-term agricultural crisis. Of the fifty poorest countries (thirty of which are in Africa), thirty-two actually produced less food per person in the late 1980s than they had ten years earlier. Not surprisingly, daily caloric consumption decreased in many of these countries, in some cases by as much as 20 percent. The remaining eighteen countries experienced modest to sizable increases in per capita production, but a majority of these were still unable to meet minimum subsistence levels in 1990. In many developing countries the average daily caloric consumption, already below subsistence levels in 1965, declined still further by 1990 as agricultural productivity per capita plunged by as much as 20 to 30 percent in some places (table 13-2).[23]

Table 13-2 Changes in Agricultural Production and Daily Caloric
Intake

Country	Index of Food Production Per Capita (1969-1971=100) Years 1988-1990	Daily Caloric Supply Per Capita Years 1965	Daily Caloric Supply Per Capita Years 1989	Per Capita Average Calories Available (as percent of need) Years 1987-1989
Mozambique	59	1,712	1,680	71%
Somalia	61	1,718	1,906	84
Honduras	66	1,967	2,247	99
Niger	66	1,996	2,308	98
Sierra Leone	72	2,014	1,799	80
Rwanda	80	1,856	1,971	84
Uganda	82	2,361	2,153	92
Peru	84	2,323	2,186	96
Kenya	90	2,208	2,163	93
United States	107	3,234	3,671	138
Canada	108	3,127	3,482	130
India	126	2,021	2,229	99
China	154	1,929	2,639	112

Sources: World Bank, *World Development Report, 1983* (New York: Oxford University Press, 1983);
World Bank, *World Development Report, 1992* (New York: Oxford University Press, 1992); United
Nations, Food and Agriculture Organization, *Agrostat PC* (Rome: FAO, 1991).

Of course, some people consume more and others less than the average daily caloric intake in each country. The result is that in many countries that exceed average caloric requirements, some people are on the
brink of starvation. In Iran, Laos, Indonesia, Guatemala, Sri Lanka, and
Myanmar the average resident consumes more than the required number
of calories each day, but more than one-third of the children in these
countries suffer from moderate to severe malnutrition.[24]

In many of these countries the low levels of production can be
attributed to inefficient farming practices: lack of irrigation, pesticides,
and fertilizers, and in some instances corruption or incompetence. Zaire
exemplifies several of these problems. According to the United Nations
Food and Agriculture Organization (FAO), Zaire is "land abundant."
With few agricultural inputs (in other words, with traditional farming
practices), Zaire was capable of producing almost twelve times as much
food as it needed in 1975, according to FAO calculations. With a higher
level of inputs, the country could feed all Africans several times over.
Despite its potential, Zaire's increase in food production between 1980
and 1990 lagged behind its population growth. This was not at all unusual. Among the ten "land abundant" African countries, few increased

their agricultural production faster than their populations over this time period.[25]

If current agricultural practices are continued, more than half of the 117 developing countries studied by the FAO will not be able to provide minimum levels of nutrition by the turn of the century. If, however, their agricultural practices are improved significantly to include complete mechanization and other high-technology approaches, then ninety-eight of the countries could feed themselves by 2000.[26]

It is theoretically possible to expand agricultural outputs, as the FAO found, but its calculations did not incorporate practical limitations. No consideration was given to whether money would be available to purchase the higher level of inputs.[27] The calculations also assumed that all land that could be cultivated would be cultivated; no cropland would be lost to degradation or soil erosion; no livestock would be allowed to graze on land that had the potential to grow food; and no nonfood crops, such as tea, coffee, or cotton, would be grown! The study also assumed that only minimum nutrition levels would be satisfied and that production could be distributed appropriately. In short, the current-practice scenario is likely to offer a better indication of the state of agricultural production over the near term.

This scenario is discouraging. In many countries there is not enough arable land to support existing populations, and some developing countries have already reached or exceeded the sustainable limits of production. Kenya had the agricultural potential to support less than 30 percent of its population in 1975. With its anticipated growth, Kenya will be able to provide for an even smaller share of its population, at least with continued low levels of agricultural inputs. Many other Asian and African countries face similar predicaments. Their populations are already overexploiting the carrying capacity of their environments. These people are thus using their land beyond its capacity to sustain agricultural production. One estimate suggests, as an illustration, that farmers in India, Pakistan, Bangladesh, and West Africa are already farming virtually all the land that is suitable for agriculture.[28] Unless changes are made soon, production will eventually decline and millions of acres of land will become barren.

Increased use of fertilizers can boost agricultural production, but increases in production rarely match (and often lag) increases in the use of fertilizer. Pakistan's use of fertilizer increased by more than 600 percent between 1970 and 1990, but this produced only a 1 percent increase in agricultural production per capita in the decade of the 1980s. Guatemala more than doubled its use of fertilizer but this was not enough to prevent a decline in agricultural production per capita.

Food imports offer a possible solution to deficiencies in domestic production, but here, too, many developing countries encounter problems. In order to finance imports, countries need foreign exchange, usually acquired through their own exports or from loans. Few developing countries outside of Asia have industrial products or professional services to export, so they must rely on minerals, natural resources (such as timber or petroleum), or cash crops (such as tea, sugar, coffee, cocoa, and rubber).

Economic recessions and declining demand in the developed world caused prices for many of these commodities to drop precipitously in the 1980s. The price that exporting nations received for coffee beans in 1992 was the lowest it had been in twenty years. The drop in the value of coffee and other exported commodities cost African nations more than $50 billion between 1986 and 1990. To cope with declining prices for export crops, farmers are forced to expand the area under cultivation in order to increase production. Unfortunately, this seemingly rational reaction is likely to depress prices even further as supply outpaces demand. As the area used for export crops expands, less attention is given to production for domestic consumption.

There are opportunities to increase exports, but economic policies in the developed world often prevent or discourage expanded activity in the developing countries. Farmers in Europe and North America received more than $175 *billion* in subsidies from their governments in 1991,[29] often resulting in overproduction and surpluses. In turn, these surpluses discourage imports from developing countries, further reduce prices, and remove incentives to expand production. These subsidies as well as protectionist trade policies in the developed nations prevent access to many markets. In 1992, for example, the United Nations estimated that subsidies and trade barriers cost developing countries about $500 billion a year in lost income,[30] about ten times as much as they received in foreign aid. There is obvious irony in these figures. Without access to export markets, developing countries are denied their best opportunity for economic development, which, historically, has provided the best cure for rapid population growth and, of course, poverty.

At one time developing countries could depend on loans from private banks or foreign governments to help finance imports. Now, however, many developing countries are burdened with massive debts, which exceeded $1.35 trillion in early 1992. This debt often cannot be repaid because of faltering economies. Failures to make interest payments are common, and banks are increasingly hesitant to lend more money.

Developing countries that attempt to repay their debts find that interest payments alone take a huge share of their earnings from exports. Consider as well the change in the flow of money. In the late 1970s about $40 billion in net aid per year was transferred to the developing countries. By the late 1980s and early 1990s, the flow of resources had actually reversed. Poor countries' payments of principal and interest were four times higher than the value of new loans and foreign aid received from rich countries.[31] Many developing countries have asked that their repayments be rescheduled or that their debts be forgiven. Many banks have been forced to accept the former; most have rejected the latter. In sum, at a time when many countries are not able to grow enough food, they also find that they cannot afford to import the short-fall, particularly when droughts and poor harvests in exporting countries cause prices to rise.

Shortages in developing countries are not limited to food. Rather than rely on electricity or natural gas, as is common in developed countries, more than 2 billion people in these countries depend on wood or other traditional fuels for heating and cooking. In much of the world, however, fuelwood is in short supply, and efforts to acquire it are time-consuming and environmentally destructive. One estimate suggests that a typical household in some parts of East Africa spends as many as three hundred days per year searching for and collecting wood. Despite such efforts, the FAO believes that about 100 million people, half in Africa, are unable to meet their daily minimum needs for fuelwood. Another 1 billion, mostly in Asia, are able to satisfy their needs, but only through unsustainable exploitation of existing resources.[32]

The Destruction of Tropical Forests

Shortages of fuelwood point to a much larger and potentially catastrophic problem—the destruction of tropical rain forests. The rain forests of Africa, South America, and Southeast Asia are treasure chests of incomparable biological diversity. These forests provide irreplaceable habitats for as much as 80 percent of the world's species of plants and animals, most of which remain to be discovered and described scientifically. Among the species already investigated, many contribute to human well-being. More than one-quarter of the prescription drugs used in the United States have their origins in tropical plants. Viable forests also stabilize soils, reduce the impact and incidence of floods, and regulate local climates, watersheds, and river systems.[33] In addition, increasing concern about the effect of excessive levels of carbon dioxide in the atmosphere (the greenhouse effect) underscores the global importance of tropical forests. Through photosynthesis, trees and other plants remove carbon dioxide from the atmosphere and convert it into oxygen. In short, the functions that tropical forests perform are so ecologically priceless that some might argue that these forests should be protected as inviolable sanctuaries. However desirable such protection might be, what often occurs is exactly the opposite. Tropical rain forests, contend biologists Paul and Anne Ehrlich, "are the major ecosystems now under the most determined assault by humanity."[34]

At the beginning of this century, tropical forests covered approximately 10 percent of the Earth's surface, or about 5.8 million square miles. The deforestation of recent decades has diminished this area by about one-third. Estimates of current rates of deforestation vary, but some experts believe that the pace of destruction is accelerating, with a total loss of about 2 percent of all tropical forests each year. In some areas the pace is much quicker, as nations seemingly rush to destroy their biological heritage and the Earth's life-support systems. If current rates of deforestation continue unabated, only a few areas of forest will remain untouched. Humans will have destroyed a natural palliative for the greenhouse effect and condemned to extinction perhaps half of all species.

Causes and Solutions

Solutions to the problem of tropical deforestation depend on the root cause. One view blames poverty and the pressures associated with growing populations and shifting cultivators.

Landless peasants, so the argument goes, invade tropical forests and denude them for fuelwood or to grow crops with which to survive.[35] Frequent clearing of new areas is necessary because tropical soils are often thin, relatively infertile, and lack sufficient nutrients. In other words, these areas are ill suited for sustained agricultural production. As one researcher explains, "Deprived of its protective cover [a tropical forest] becomes an ugly wasteland—huge expanses of coarse scrub, unusable grassland and lateritic hardpan."[36]

In spite of this knowledge, some governments have actively encouraged resettlement schemes that require extensive deforestation. In Brazil, which has about 30 percent of the world's tropical forests, the government opened the Amazon region in the name of land reform. The results were spectacular. After the government built several highways into the interior and offered free land to attract settlers, the population of some Amazonian states soared by as much as a hundredfold between the mid 1960s and the late 1980s. Thousands of square miles of forest were cleared each year to accommodate the new arrivals and to provide them with permanent settlements.

Indonesia's transmigration program moves people from the densely populated island of Java to sparsely populated, but heavily forested, outer islands. Other forested land is being cleared to increase the acreage allotted to cocoa, rubber, palm oil, and other cash crops intended for export.

Another explanation for deforestation places primary blame on commercial logging intended to satisfy demands for tropical hardwoods in developed countries. Whether strapped for foreign exchange, forced to repay loans from foreign banks, or subjected to domestic pressure to develop their economies, governments in the developing world frequently regard the resources of tropical forests as sources of ready income. Exports of wood now produce about $8 billion in annual revenues for developing countries, and some countries impose few limits in their rush to the bank. In the early 1990s Southeast Asia contained about 25 percent of all tropical forests, but the region accounted for nearly 80 percent of the value of all exports of tropical hardwoods.

If tropical forests were managed in an environmentally sustainable manner, the flow of income and benefits to local populations could continue indefinitely. In fact, however, few tropical forests are so managed, and many countries are now becoming victims of past greed and too-rapid exploitation. About three-dozen countries were net exporters of tropical hardwoods in 1988, but fewer than ten of these countries will have enough wood to export at the end of the 1990s.[37] Some countries, such as Nigeria and Thailand, have already shifted from being net exporters to net importers.

The consequences of deforestation are not only economic. Nearly 1 billion people are "periodically disrupted by flooding, fuelwood shortages, soil and water degradation and reduced agricultural production caused directly or indirectly by the loss of tropical-forest cover."[38] In late 1988 separate floods devastated much of Bangladesh and southern Thailand. In seeking explanations, officials in the two countries pointed to severe deforestation that had contributed to soil erosion and exacerbated the flooding. Unfortunately, floods would become regular occurrences, these officials predicted, because of deforestation.

Recognizing the causes and consequences of deforestation is not enough to bring about a solution. Commercial logging is profitable, and few governments in the developing countries are equipped to manage their forests properly. Governments in developing countries often let logging concerns harvest trees in designated areas under certain conditions. All too frequently, however, the conditions are inadequate or not well enforced because there are too few forest guards. Paltry wages for guards also create opportunities for corruption—and not only among low-level employees. The director general of Thailand's forestry department was once suspended because he had granted a private firm illegal access to a government-owned forest reserve.

Penalties can be imposed on those who violate the conditions, but violators are rarely apprehended. When they are, the fine is often less than the profits associated with the violation. Some countries require companies with concessions to post bonds, which are returned once the companies complete mandatory reforestation projects. Here again, however, the amounts involved are generally so low that many companies would rather forfeit their bonds than reforest.[39] Moreover, concessions are typically granted for brief periods that discourage reforestation. When a logging company receives a twenty-year concession, granting it a right to cut for twenty years, no incentive exists to replant trees for someone else's benefit when many trees take forty to fifty years to reach maturity. One estimate suggests that for every one hundred acres of tropical forests that are cleared, only about one acre is reforested and managed in an environmentally sound manner.[40]

An Alternative View of the Problem

As the pace of tropical deforestation has quickened, so have international pressures on developing countries to halt or mitigate it. In response, leaders of developing countries quickly emphasize how ironic it is that developed countries, whose consumption of tropical woods is increasing, are simultaneously calling for a reduction of logging and shifting cultivation in developing countries.

In addition, the developing countries correctly note Europe's destruction of its forests during the industrial revolution and the widespread cutting in the United States in the nineteenth century. Why then should developing countries be held to a different standard than the developed ones? Just as Europe and the United States decided how and when to extract their resources, developing countries insist that they too should be allowed to determine their own patterns of consumption. The prime minister of Malaysia, the world's largest exporter of tropical timber, made clear his feelings about environmental groups that want to restrict the timber trade. Speaking in early 1992, Mahathir Mohamad complained that these groups are "advocating that forest dwellers remain in the forest, eating monkeys, and suffering from all kinds of diseases."[41] One observer, examining the situation in Indonesia, cast the problem somewhat differently. He wondered how bureaucracies in poor countries can overcome domestic pressures for economic development. He raised this question after hearing the views of an Indonesian involved with logging. As the Indonesian businessman declared, "We are a profit-oriented company, and if that means destroying the environment within the legal limit, then we will do it."[42]

Fortunately, such a view is not universally shared, and there is evidence of change in many developing countries. Thailand imposed a nationwide ban on logging in early 1989, despite projections that the ban would cause thousands of people to lose their jobs. Ghana, Côte d'Ivoire, and the Philippines similarly announced restrictions on logging in the late 1980s. These are well-intentioned efforts, but in each instance the restrictions were imposed well after they could do much good.

International collaboration between wood-producing and wood-consuming nations offers one hope in the battle against deforestation. To date, however, such collaboration has a pitiful record. The U.N.-sponsored International Tropical Timber Organization (ITTO), formed in 1985, was on the brink of collapse just a few years later.[43] Several importing nations had refused to pay their full dues, Japanese importers boycotted ITTO's meetings, and the organization could claim few accomplishments other than its tenuous survival.

Will tropical forests survive? Solutions abound. What is lacking, however, is a consensus about which of these solutions will best meet the essential needs of the poor, the reasonable objectives of timber-exporting and timber-importing nations, and the inflexible imperatives of ecological stability. Fortunately, there is a growing realization that much can be done to stem the loss of tropical forests. Rather than seeing forests solely as a source of wood or additional agricultural land, for example, many countries are now examining the export potential of forest products other than wood. The expectation is that the sale of such products will provide economic incentives to maintain rather than destroy forests. Likewise, a multinational drug company signed an agreement with Costa Rica to explore ways in which the country's genetic resources might contribute to the creation of new drugs. Other companies and countries are likely to reach similar agreements that serve the needs of both developing and developed countries.

Debt-for-nature swaps provide still another means to protect fragile environments. Put as simply as possible, these swaps allow countries to reduce their foreign debts, which are usually denominated in dollars, in exchange for agreements to increase expenditures of local currencies on environmental activities. Sustained concern about tropical forests suggests that many other imaginative ways to protect these forests will soon emerge. Having noted these causes for optimism, it is important to emphasize that much remains to be done if the world's tropical forests are to be preserved.

Conflicting Signals from the Industrial Nations

Improvements in the policies of many developing countries are surely necessary if sustainable development is to be achieved. As already noted, however, industrial countries sometimes cause or contribute to environmental problems there.

Patterns of consumption provide an example. Although the United States and other industrial nations can brag about their own low rates of population growth, developing nations reply that patterns of consumption, not population increases, are the real culprits.[44] This view suggests that negative impacts on the environment are a function of population growth plus consumption and technology.

Applying this formula places major responsibility for environmental problems on rich nations, despite their relatively small numbers of global inhabitants. The inhabitants of these nations consume far more of the Earth's resources than their numbers justify. Consider that the richest one-quarter of the world's nations consume about 60 percent of its food, more than 70 percent of its metals and energy, and 85 percent of its wood. These nations similarly generate over 90 percent of all hazardous and industrial wastes.[45] Consider as well that these relatively few rich nations are likewise responsible for releasing more than 80 percent of all ozone-depleting chlorofluorocarbons into the atmosphere.

More specifically, much of the responsibility for this situation can be placed on Americans. They represent less than 5 percent of the Earth's inhabitants yet consume almost 30 percent of the world's commercial energy. Much of this energy is used to fuel Americans' love for the automobile, one of the most environmentally harmful technologies known to humans. While Americans increased their numbers by about 20 percent in the 1970s and 1980s, the total number of automobiles in use in the United States grew by more than 50 percent.

Although some gains were made in fuel efficiency during this period, the typical American still uses about two and one-half times more gasoline per year than does the typical German (who, incidentally, does not encounter any speed limits on the *autobahns*). Americans' profligacy with fossil fuels provides part of the explanation for U.S. production of almost 18 percent of the emissions that contribute to global warming.

As environmental scholar Paul Harrison has noted, because of such inequalities in consumption, continued population growth in rich countries is a greater threat to the global environment than it is in the developing world.[46] He adds that if relative consumption and levels of waste output remain unchanged, the 57 million extra inhabitants likely to be born in rich countries in the 1990s will pollute the globe more than the extra 900 million born elsewhere. Other experts suggest that if Americans want to maintain their present standard of living and levels of energy consumption, then the ideal population for the United States is between 40 and 100 million.[47]

Causes for Optimism?

Although there is cause for concern about the prospects for sustainable development among developing countries, the situation is neither entirely bleak nor beyond hope. Many of these countries are gradually reducing their rate of population growth and are far more appreciative of its linkage to development and environmental quality than in the past. A survey of policies in developing countries also reveals a growing awareness of the inseparable relation between a healthy environment and economic development. Countries that once favored development over environmental protection now recognize that pollution and neglect of the environment are no longer preconditions for economic development.

At the international level, multilateral lending institutions such as the World Bank, the Asian Development Bank, and the Inter-American Development Bank are increasingly sensitive to the need to mitigate damage to the environment and are incorporating concern for sustainable development into their activities. Several of these banks now refuse to fund projects that irreparably damage the environment. Moreover, the World Bank has established an environment department with a specific mandate to focus on tropical deforestation, the loss of biological diversity, and the environmental problems of sub-Saharan Africa.

The international community is also demonstrating a new recognition of the Earth's ecological interconnectedness. At the request of the U.N. General Assembly, the World Commission on Environment and Development was established in 1983 and asked to formulate long-term environmental strategies for achieving sustainable development. In its report, *Our Common Future*, the commission forcefully emphasized that although environmental degradation is an issue of survival for developing nations, failure to address the degradation satisfactorily will guarantee unparalleled and undesirable global consequences from which no nation will escape.[48] This report's release in 1987 provided at least some of the reason for the increased international attention to environmental issues in the late 1980s and early 1990s. This attention manifested itself most noticeably in the United Nations Conference on Environment and Development in Río de Janeiro in 1992 (chap. 14).

Most of the developing nations at this "Earth summit" recognized their obligations to protect their environments as well as the global commons. At the same time, however, these nations argued that success would require technical and financial assistance from their wealthy colleagues. However desirable the protection of tropical forests and biological diversity and the prevention of global warming and a depleted ozone layer, the poor nations said they could not afford to address these problems in the absence of cooperation from richer nations. The prospects for achieving such cooperation are uncertain. On the one hand, for example, developing nations like China and India want to provide refrigerators to as many of their inhabitants as possible. These hundreds of millions of refrigerators will require extraordinary amounts of chlorofluorocarbons (CFCs) unless companies in developed nations are willing to share or give away the scientific secrets associated with substitutes for the CFCs. These companies are reluctant to do so, arguing that they are in business to make money, not to give away valuable trade secrets. Similarly, when a group of developing countries sought $20 million from the United States to finance conversions from CFCs to safer chemicals, President George Bush initially balked at the request.

On the other hand, providing assistance to the developing nations requires leadership and a willingness to compromise national interests for global ones. The nations at the Earth summit approved international agreements covering biological diversity, the protection of tropical forests, and reductions in emissions that contribute to global warming. The United States initially refused to sign the first, irritated advocates of the second, and worked vigorously to weaken the third. Without cooperation from the United States, the prospects for successful implementation of these agreements may be diminished.

Delegates at the conference also approved Agenda 21, a plan for cleaning the global environment. The price tag for the recommended actions is huge—an estimated $125 billion per year, of which developed nations would be expected to provide a major share. Cast in other terms, however, rich nations could afford to provide this amount if they donated as little as .70 percent (*not* 7 percent, but seven-tenths of one percent) of their total economic output to the developing world each year. Only Norway, Sweden, Denmark, and the Netherlands exceeded this target in 1992. The Japanese pledged to move toward the recommended target, but U.S. foreign aid as a percentage of gross national product (GNP) declined steadily between the 1960s and the early 1990s. At .17 percent of GNP in 1991, U.S. aid to developing nations was well below the target level.[49] The prospects for increasing U.S. aid to address environmental problems in developing countries are not good. Most Americans (unlike most residents of France and Japan) believe Asians and Africans should solve their own environmental problems. Most Americans are similarly opposed to providing additional money and technology to foreign countries if it will be used to improve the environment.[50]

Despite Americans' apparent reluctance to share their wealth, other nations have demonstrated an increased willingness to address globally shared environmental problems. Within the last few years many international agreements covering environmental protection have been signed, and many more are likely in the future. Most of the world's industrial nations have agreed to eliminate the use of key CFCs by the middle of the decade, the international community is gradually beginning to make some headway in protecting endangered species of plants and animals that find themselves in international trade, and this community now operates a Global Environment Facility (GEF), a multibillion-dollar effort to finance environmental projects in developing countries. The World Bank administers the GEF and distributes funds to address four priority areas: global warming, loss of biological diversity, pollution of international waters, and depletion of the ozone layer.

However promising, these institutional changes and agreements will not be sufficient to protect the environment without concerted and effective international action. The economic, population, and environmental problems of the developing world dwarf those of the industrialized nations and are not amenable to immediate resolution, but immediate action is imperative. To meet their daily needs for food and fuel, millions of people are steadily destroying their biological and environmental support systems at unprecedented rates. Driven by poverty and the need to survive, they have become ravenous souls on a planet approaching the limits of its tolerance and resilience. Whether this situation will change depends on the ability of residents in the developing countries not only to reap the benefits of sustained economic development but also to meet the demands of current populations while using their natural resources in a way that accommodates the needs of future generations. Unless the developing nations are able to do so soon, their future will determine ours as well. It is both naïve and unreasonable to

assume that the consequences of population growth, environmental degradation, and abysmal poverty in developing countries will remain within
their arbitrary political boundaries.[51]

Notes

1. United Nations Children's Fund (UNICEF), *State of the World's Children 1989*
(New York: Oxford University Press, 1989), 42.
2. Ibid., 37.
3. World Commission on Environment and Development, *Our Common Future* (London: Oxford University Press, 1987), 8, 43.
4. John N. Wilford, "A Tough-Minded Ecologist Comes to Defense of Malthus,"
New York Times, June 30, 1987, C3.
5. United Nations Population Division, *World Population Prospects 1990* (New York:
United Nations, 1991); Colin Clark, *Population Growth and Land Use*, 2d ed.
(London: Macmillan, 1977), 153 ("the world's potential agricultural and forest
land could supply the needs of 157 billion people"); Paul Ehrlich and Anne
Ehrlich, *Extinction* (New York: Random House, 1981), 243 (starting a gradual
decline of the human population is "obviously essential").
6. United Nations Development Programme (UNDP), *Human Development Report
1992* (New York: Oxford University Press, 1992), 171.
7. Richard Bernstein, "World's Surging Birthrate Tops the Mexico City Agenda,"
New York Times, July 29, 1984, sec. 4, 3.
8. "African Seminar on Population Policy," in National Academy of Sciences
(NAS), *In Search of Population Policy: Views from the Developing World* (Washington, D.C.: NAS, 1974), 57-60; and United Nations Food and Agriculture Organization (FAO), *The State of Food and Agriculture 1983* (Rome: FAO, 1984), 66.
9. Lester R. Brown, "Analyzing the Demographic Trap," in *State of the World, 1987*,
ed. Lester R. Brown (New York: Norton, 1987), 20.
10. UNICEF, *Children 1989*, 1, 20; Steven Greenhouse, "Third World Economies
Shrink Again," *New York Times*, April 16, 1992, D1.
11. World Bank, *World Development Report 1992* (New York: Oxford University Press,
1992), 238.
12. James Clad, "Genesis of Despair," *Far Eastern Economic Review*, October 20,
1988, 24-25.
13. UNICEF, *Children 1989*, 8-9.
14. "The Good News: Thailand Controls a Baby Boom," *Time*, Asian international
ed., January 2, 1989, 37.
15. K. Srinivasan, "Population Policy and Programme," in U.N. Economic and Social
Commission for Asia and the Pacific, *Population of India* (New York: United Nations, 1982), 161. For a recent discussion of India's family planning programs, see
Sharon L. Camp and Shanti R. Conly, *India's Family Planning Challenge: From
Rhetoric to Action* (Washington, D.C.: Population Crisis Committee, 1992).
16. U.N. Department of International Economic and Social Affairs, *World Population
Policies*, vol. 1 (New York: United Nations, 1987), 127-129.
17. Marshall Green, "Is China Easing Up on Birth Control?" *New York Times*, April
23, 1986, A25; "The Mewling That They'll Miss," *Economist*, August 13, 1988,
27. Summaries of recent developments in efforts to control population in China
can be found in Sharon L. Camp and Shanti R. Conly, *China's Family Planning
Program: Challenging the Myths* (Washington, D.C.: Population Crisis Committee,
1992). See also Nicholas D. Kristof, "A U.N. Agency May Leave China Over
Coercive Population Control," *New York Times*, May 15, 1993, A1.

18. Chief among these advocates is Julian Simon. See his *The Ultimate Resource* (Princeton, N.J.: Princeton University Press, 1981). See also Ester Boserup, *The Conditions of Agricultural Growth* (London: Allen and Unwin, 1965); and Malcolm S. Forbes, Jr., "The World Is Overpopulated. Not" *Forbes*, June 8, 1992, 25. For a response to some of Simon's positions, see U.N. Fund for Population Activities, *State of the World's Population 1987* (New York: United Nations, 1987), 6-8.

19. Sheldon L. Richman, letter to the editor, *New York Times*, June 30, 1992, A22.

20. Brown, *State of the World*, 21.

21. U.N. Environment Programme, *The State of the Environment 1987* (Nairobi: United Nations, 1987), 47.

22. World Bank, *World Development Report 1992*, 272.

23. Ibid.

24. UNICEF, *Children 1992*, 74-75.

25. FAO, *Potential Population-Supporting Capacities of Lands in the Developing World* (Rome: FAO, 1982), 137.

26. Ibid., 49.

27. Brown, *State of the World*, 24. The criticisms of the study are from Brown's analysis of the FAO report.

28. FAO, *The State of Food and Agriculture, 1983*, 66; Paul Harrison, *The Third Revolution: Environment, Population and a Sustainable World* (New York: I. B. Taurus, 1992), 45.

29. "Featherbedded Farmers," *Economist*, May 23, 1992, 112.

30. UNDP, *Human Development Report 1992*, 67.

31. Anthony Rowley, "Harvest of Ill Will," *Far Eastern Economic Review*, January 12, 1989, 51.

32. World Commission on Environment and Development, *Our Common Future Reconvened* (Geneva: Centre for Our Common Future, 1992), 14.

33. National Academy of Sciences, *Population Growth and Economic Development: Policy Questions* (Washington, D.C.: NAS, 1986), 31; FAO, Committee on Food Development in the Tropics, *Tropical Forest Action Plan* (Rome: FAO, 1985), 2, 47.

34. Ehrlich and Ehrlich, *Extinction*, 160.

35. FAO, *Tropical Forest Action Plan*, 2.

36. "The Vanishing Jungle: Ecologists Make Friends with Economists," *Economist*, October 15, 1988, 26.

37. Ibid.

38. This view of the World Resources Institute is quoted in Margaret Scott, "The Disappearing Forests," *Far Eastern Economic Review*, January 12, 1989, 34.

39. Michael Richardson, "Indonesia Wonders If Timber Boom Will Backfire," *International Herald Tribune*, September 5, 1988, 1.

40. Scott, "Disappearing Forests," 35.

41. "Tropical Heat," *Economist*, February 15, 1992, 38.

42. Michael Vatikiotis, "Tug-of-War Over Trees," *Far Eastern Economic Review*, January 12, 1989, 41.

43. Margaret Scott, "Unequal to the Task," *Far Eastern Economic Review*, January 12, 1989, 38.

44. Harrison, *Third Revolution*.

45. UNDP, *Human Development Report 1992*, 35; Harrison, *Third Revolution*, 256.

46. Harrison, *Third Revolution*, 256-257.

47. David Pimentel and Marcia Pimentel, "Land, Energy and Water: The Constraints Governing Ideal U.S. Population Size," *NPG Forum*, January 1990, 5.

48. World Commission, *Our Common Future*.

49. UNDP, *Human Development Report 1992*, 198; Stuart Auerbach, "Europe Crisis Likely to Hurt 3rd World Aid," *Washington Post*, September 25, 1992, F1.

50. Marcy E. Mullins, "How Three Nations View the Future," *USA Today*, June 1, 1992, 8A; Rae Tyson, "Poll: Environment Tops Agenda," *USA Today*, June 1, 1992, 1A. Both articles report the results of public opinion surveys conducted in May 1992 by Gordon S. Black Corp. in the United States and by *Sankei Shimbun*, a Japanese newspaper, in Japan and France. The surveys questioned approximately one thousand adults in each country. *USA Today* provided additional information on the surveys to the author.
51. Moni Nag, "Overpopulation Becomes Our Problem Too," *New York Times*, May 21, 1992, A28.

14

From Stockholm to Río:
The Evolution of Global Environmental Governance

Marvin S. Soroos

O nly three decades ago concern about the deteriorating state of the
natural environment was confined largely to the scientific community and groups of environmental activists. Since then the environment
has risen rapidly to prominence as a public issue and by the late 1980s
had become a leading policy problem on both national and international
agendas. Two major United Nations conferences held twenty years apart
are important landmarks in the emergence and rise of the environment as
a global issue, the first being the Conference on the Human Environment
in Stockholm in June 1972, the second the Conference on Environment
and Development, otherwise known as the Earth summit or ECO 92, in
Río de Janeiro in June 1992.

The Stockholm conference added the environment to the array of
global policy problems on the agenda of the United Nations. Prior to the
conference, several United Nations specialized agencies had taken up
various discrete environmental problems, such as conservation of fisheries,
radioactive contamination, oil pollution from ships, and the impact of
pollutants on human health. The conference theme, "Only One Earth,"
conveyed the importance of addressing the myriad of threats to the natural environment in a comprehensive and integrated manner in the organs
and agencies of the United Nations.[1] The most significant outcome of the
conference was the creation of the United Nations Environment Programme (UNEP) as part of a broader action plan that was proposed for
addressing international environmental problems.

A greater sense of urgency pervaded the 1992 Earth summit, as
reflected in its slogan, "Our Last Chance to Save the Earth." Its organizers hoped the conference would significantly revise and strengthen the
international response to what is rapidly becoming an even more ominous
array of environmental problems. The Earth summit was a historical landmark for being the first global summit conference on environmental problems, which is indicative of the swift rise of the environment to the realm
of "high politics" that receives the attention of the top-level officials of
national governments.

Several significant changes have taken place in the environmental
situation during the era bounded by the Stockholm and Río conferences.

First, the ecological crisis has deepened significantly as a result of a 40 percent growth in the human population; further industrial development and a higher material standard of living in much of the world; the continued buildup of air pollutants, including those responsible for acid rain, depletion of the ozone layer, and the greenhouse effect; the accelerating degradation of agricultural land; the rapid clearing of tropical rain forests in South America and Asia; and the extinction of countless species as a result of habitat loss.[2]

Second, scientific research has contributed to a much richer, but by no means complete, understanding of what is happening to environmental systems, including the impact of human activities on the basic physical processes of the planet. During the late 1980s scientific revelations that human impacts on the environment were of a greater magnitude than was anticipated led to the coining of the term "global change" to refer to such trends as depletion of the ozone layer, global warming, and loss of biodiversity.[3] The International Council of Scientific Unions in 1984 launched the International Geosphere-Biosphere Programme, a major international research effort by the world's scientists to continue the rest of the century and beyond, which aims to enhance significantly knowledge about interrelationships among the atmosphere, the oceans, and the land, as well as the extent to which they are being altered by human beings.[4]

A third development is the evolution in thinking about the complex relationships between the environment and economic development. The development issue arose as a contentious issue in the preparations for the Stockholm conference but was not addressed in a comprehensive way until it was taken up in the mid 1980s by the twenty-two-member United Nations Commission on Environment and Development, chaired by Prime Minister Gro Harlem Brundtland of Norway. The commission's influential report, *Our Common Future*, which emphasized that the desperate economic plight of much of the developing world is a major cause of environmental degradation, provided an intellectual framework for the Río conference.[5]

Finally, significant changes have taken place since the Stockholm conference in the realm of institutions and policies, both internationally and nationally. UNEP has become the focal point for environmental cooperation throughout the world and a number of the United Nations' specialized agencies and regional organizations, most notably the European Community (EC), have become more active in addressing environmental problems. Numerous international agreements and programs have been adopted that address a broad range of environmental problems. Most states now have environmental ministries and have adopted major bodies of environmental law.

This chapter examines the evolution of global environmental governance during the era bounded by the Stockholm and Río conferences.

Governance does not necessarily imply a formally established government with coercive power to enforce its edicts, something that does not exist at the global level, but simply the existence of laws and policies that regulate behavior, as well as the institutions that facilitate the adoption and implementation of them. The overriding question is whether global environmental governance can keep pace with the deepening ecological predicament that humankind faces in the form of the global change *problematique*.[6]

The Foundations of Global Environmental Governance

To begin an assessment of global environmental governance, let us consider three of its principal foundations: single-issue world conferences, international environmental institutions, and international environmental law and policy.

Conference Diplomacy

The Stockholm conference of 1972 ushered in an era of major U.N. theme conferences, otherwise known as "megaconferences" or "global town meetings," that focused on single policy problem areas. These conferences were convened to focus worldwide attention on specific economic, social, or environmental problems and to set forth principles and propose action plans for addressing them. In the environmental realm, conferences were held on population (1974, 1984), food (1974), human settlements (1976), water (1977), desertification (1977), agrarian reform (1979), climate (1979, 1990), new and renewable sources of energy (1981), and outer space (1982).[7]

The Stockholm conference became the model for the later theme conferences, some of which were more successful than others. Scheduling the conference four years in advance permitted an extensive series of preparatory meetings to assemble information and to negotiate drafts of documents that could be finalized and adopted at the relatively brief official conference. Furthermore, not only did the conference draw delegates from 113 states and 19 intergovernmental agencies, but it also facilitated the participation of several hundred nongovernmental organizations (NGOs). Accredited NGOs were given an opportunity to present their perspectives on the conference agenda at a concurrently held Environmental Forum. Activists gathered at an informal People's Forum to listen to prominent environmentalists and to express their generally more radical views.[8]

Several documents adopted at the Stockholm conference lay the groundwork for the subsequent development of international environmental governance. One was the Declaration of the Stockholm Conference, which set forth twenty-six principles that would guide international and national policies and programs on the environment. Two principles have had considerable impact, one being the often quoted Article 21, which reinforces the right of states to exploit their resources but in doing so to ensure that they do not damage the environment beyond their borders. The other principle calls on states to cooperate in developing international law on liability and compensation for environmental damage.[9]

Ultimately, the impact of major theme conferences depends on the adoption of an action plan that is bold enough to address the primary policy problems but also sufficiently practical to be implemented. The ambitious action plan of the Stockholm conference contained 109 separate recommendations on subjects as diverse as atmospheric testing of nuclear weapons, fisheries, forests, pollution of river systems, and toxic chemicals.

International Institutions

In the aftermath of the Stockholm conference, the General Assembly adopted a resolution establishing UNEP. It was not to be a specialized agency that would centralize responsibility for developing and implementing the environmental programs of the United Nations. Rather, it was designed to stimulate, coordinate, and facilitate the environmental activities of the existing specialized agencies, some of which were already well established. For example, the World Health Organization had been dealing with the effects of pollutants on human health; the World Meteorological Organization with the consequences of air pollution for climate; the Food and Agricultural Organization with the impacts of environmental degradation on food production and of overharvesting ocean fisheries; the International Maritime Organization with vessel-source pollution of the marine environment; and UNESCO (United Nations Educational, Scientific, and Cultural Organization) with scientific knowledge about the environment.

UNEP has had to overcome many obstacles in pursuing its multifaceted mission, not the least of which is its small annual budget of less than $40 million, which supports a staff of only 230 professionals (1990 figures).[10] The work of the organization has also been hampered by being headquartered in Nairobi, Kenya, far from other centers of U.N. activity. But perhaps UNEP's greatest challenge, as a new international organization with limited resources, has been to gain the respect and cooperation of well-established international agencies, which initially were not receptive to sharing responsibility for addressing environmental problems that had previously been their exclusive domain. With time, however, UNEP has established fruitful partnerships both with numerous international agencies and with international NGOs such as the International Council of Scientific Unions, the International Union for Conservation of Nature and Natural Resources, and the World Wildlife Fund.

Many of UNEP's activities involve the collection and dissemination of information about the environment through its Earthwatch Program. The principal component of Earthwatch is the Global Environmental Monitoring System (GEMS), which is an institutional umbrella for a variety of monitoring networks that UNEP sponsors cooperatively with other international agencies. Data are collected regularly on such environmental trends as air pollutants, climate, forest cover, water quality, and rare and endangered species. Another GEMS initiative known as GRID, the Global Resource Information Database, banks and organizes environmental data for users throughout the world.

Two other Earthwatch projects gather and disseminate information. The International Register of Potentially Toxic Chemicals (IRPTC) is a repository for scientific information on risks that a myriad of humanly created chemicals pose for workers, the general population, and the environment. INFOTERRA is a clearinghouse for international sharing of a wide range of information on the environment and resource management. The service puts countries seeking information on environmental problems in contact with those who may be able to supply it. IRPTC and INFOTERRA are especially helpful to countries that have insufficient means to investigate a broad range of environmentally related questions.[11]

UNEP has also taken an active role as an initiator and manager of international efforts to address various environmental problems. One of its first major management projects was the Regional Seas Programme, which was directed at cleaning up partially enclosed seas that had become the most heavily polluted parts of the oceans. UNEP supervised negotiations on the so-called Med Plan through which sixteen nations bordering the Mediterranean Sea committed themselves to reduce the flow of pollutants from ships and land sources. The plan became the model for similar programs for ten other regional seas, including the Red Sea, the Persian Gulf, the Caribbean Sea, and several coastal seas around Africa and the Pacific Rim.[12]

UNEP has been involved in the creation and implementation of other major international environmental agreements and programs, including the 1985 Vienna convention and 1987 Montreal protocol, both of which addressed the ozone depletion problem, and the 1989 Basel convention, which regulates transboundary movements of hazardous wastes. UNEP serves as the secretariat for the 1973 Convention on International Trade in Endangered Species and the 1979 Convention on Conservation of Migratory Species.[13] Along with the World Bank and the United Nations Development Programme, UNEP sponsors the Global Environment Facility, which was created in 1990 with $1 billion in funding to provide interest-free loans for environmental projects in the developing world.

International Law and Policy

The international agreements UNEP has fostered are only a very small part of an expanding body of international environmental law and policy, a second foundation of global environmental governance. Numerous principles of customary law can be applied to international environmental issues, an example being liability of states for causing damage to other states. This principle was affirmed by the landmark decision in the Trail Smelter Case (1941) in which a specially convened tribunal ruled that Canada should compensate the United States for damages to orchards in the state of Washington that were caused by air pollutants drifting over the border from a smelter in Trail, British Columbia.[14]

The often vague and ambiguous tenets of customary law, which are susceptible to divergent interpretations, are being gradually supplanted by treaties that spell out specific regulations and responsibilities on a wide variety of environmental matters. A UNEP compendium lists 152 multilateral treaties and other agreements adopted through 1990 that address environmental problems. The rate of adoption of environmental treaties has accelerated during recent decades: only twenty were concluded between 1921 and 1959, twenty-six during the 1960s, forty-nine during the 1970s, and forty-eight during the 1980s.[15] UNEP's listing does not include numerous bilateral agreements, such as the 1909 Canada–United States Boundary Waters Agreement, which has played a significant role in the environmental relations between the two countries.

Existing multilateral treaties on environmental subjects do not constitute a comprehensive or integrated body of international environmental law. Many treaties are a response to a specific environmental problem by a small number of concerned states. As a result, some environmental problems are much more thoroughly covered than others. Approximately sixty multilateral agreements deal with the marine environment, such as pollution from oil tankers, dumping of toxic wastes, depletion of fisheries, and pollution of regional seas.[16] By contrast, only a few of the agreements regulate use of the atmosphere as a sink for pollutants; and while the Convention on the Law of the Sea, adopted in 1982, is quite comprehensive, no negotiations have taken place on a comparable law of the atmosphere. International law has been in place to protect the Antarctic region for more than three decades, but only recently have talks begun on preserving the Arctic's fragile environment.[17]

The impact of existing international environmental agreements can be questioned on several grounds. Treaties bind only those states that voluntarily agree to comply with them. Thus, they are often lowest-common-denominator agreements designed to maximize the number of states willing to become parties. Even after a treaty is negotiated, many years may pass before there are enough ratifiers for the agreement to come into force. Because international enforcement mechanisms are generally weak, if they exist at all, compliance with treaty obligations depends largely on the good faith of the states being regulated. Despite these intrinsic limitations of international law, some notable successes have nevertheless occurred in the environmental field; for example, nuclear weapons are not being tested in the atmosphere, less oil is discharged from oil tankers, the populations of some endangered species are recovering, fewer toxic substances are being dumped in the oceans, and internationally shared river systems are being cleaned up.

In summary, much has been accomplished since the 1972 Stockholm conference in establishing the foundations for global environmental governance. But are these foundations strong enough to provide for effective international environmental management in the face of increasingly serious challenges that are looming? Can UNEP provide the type of leadership that will be necessary to coordinate the diverse programs of various environmental agencies that will be needed to address complex global problems such as climate change? Will states accept needed international regulations that impinge on their traditional sovereign prerogatives, such as population policies, exploitation of forests and other natural resources within their boundaries, and the use of the oceans and other international commons?

Differing Perspectives on the Global Environment

Developing the foundations of global environmental governance would be a challenging undertaking even if the world community were of essentially one mind on what should be done. Unfortunately, the three major contemporary groups of countries—the industrial nations, the developing world, and the former Communist countries—have had markedly different perceptions about global environmental problems, the priority they should receive relative to other problems, who is responsible, and how the cost of addressing them should be shared.

The Stimulus From Industrial Nations

The impetus for international environmental regulations and programs has come largely from the advanced industrial countries, which have had much longer experience with the environmental havoc caused by industrialization and the dangers that it poses to human health. Highly publicized episodes, such as London's smog in 1952 and the mercury poisoning of the residents of Minamata, Japan, in the 1960s, underscored the need in these countries for much stronger environmental rules and for government agencies created specifically to carry out national environmental policies.[18]

Their assertiveness on international environmental matters can also be attributed to several other factors. Extensive scientific research programs in the industrial countries have brought to light the seriousness of numerous environmental problems, including some that might otherwise go unnoticed for decades, such as depletion of the ozone layer. Furthermore, having achieved a relatively high standard of living that satisfies most of the basic material needs of their populations, these countries have more resources to devote to other priorities—such as a cleaner, healthier environment—which in poorer countries are looked on as unaffordable luxuries. Finally, environmental activism is much more highly developed in the advanced industrial countries, which allow relatively open access to information on environmental threats and permit environmental interest groups to mobilize public opinion and lobby governments.

In the late 1960s Swedish scientist Svante Odén presented evidence that the acid rain that had been killing fish in many of southern Scandinavia's rivers and lakes was caused by pollutants carried long distances by wind currents from the heavily industrialized regions of the British Isles and central Europe.[19] As significant net importers of acid rain-forming pollutants, the Scandinavian countries and Canada became the leading advocates of regulations that would reduce the flow of transboundary air pollution. The Convention on Long-Range Transboundary Air Pollution (LRTAP), adopted under the auspices of the United Nations Economic Commission for Europe (ECE) in Geneva in 1979, calls on countries to voluntarily begin limiting, if not reducing, air pollution using the "best available technology that is economically feasible."[20]

Serious negotiations on international rules that establish deadlines for reductions in emissions of air pollutants began in 1982. That year, the West German government responded to public alarm over damage to the forests of the region by dramatically announcing at a scientific conference on acidification in Stockholm that it was changing its position from opposition to support for international action on sulfur pollution.[21] A 1985 protocol to the LRTAP treaty mandates that parties reduce their sulfur emissions, or the transboundary fluxes of sulfur that originate in their country, by 30 percent of 1980 levels by 1993. The United States and United Kingdom, major net exporters of transboundary air pollutants, refrained from making commitments to cut sulfur emissions, arguing that the evidence was not conclusive on the severity and the causes of the acidification problem and the extent to which reducing emissions would mitigate the problem.[22] Subsequent protocols adopted in 1988 and 1991 regulate emissions of nitrogen oxides and volatile organic compounds.

With the demise of the Eastern bloc and its military and ideological threats, the democratic, industrial nations now regarded ominous environmental trends as being one of the primary sources of insecurity for both current and future generations.[23] Given the international, and global, character of these environmental threats (such as depletion of the ozone layer and climate change), these countries have been accelerating their efforts to create and strengthen international regulatory mechanisms that will slow the pace of environmental degradation and change. In doing so, they seek a partnership with the rest of the world, which could have an enormous impact on the environment as it seeks to industrialize and achieve a higher standard of living.

Reservations in the Developing World

The developing world has been decidedly less enthusiastic about the development of global environmental governance since the environment first appeared on the agenda of the United Nations in the late 1960s. At the time of the Stockholm conference, policymakers from developing nations approached the environmental issue with both lack of interest and suspicion. They were indifferent because economic development was a much higher priority for their societies than preserving the environment; some even expressed the view that polluted air over rapidly growing urban areas was a welcome sign of modernization. If unrestrained resource exploitation and environmental degradation were integral to development, as appeared to have been the case for the highly developed societies, this was the price that they were willing to pay to achieve modernization.

The developing world also viewed with suspicion the motivations that inspired the first major wave of environmentalism. Would developed countries cite the new burden of funding environmental programs as an excuse for diverting money from development assistance programs? Moreover, would publications such as the Club of Rome's highly visible report, *The Limits to Growth*, encourage the view that the planet's natural resource base was being rapidly depleted and would therefore not permit further industrialization (unless, of course, the advanced countries were willing to make deep sacrifices in their life-styles)?[24] These suspicions were further inflamed by Garrett Hardin's controversial theory of "lifeboat ethics," which argued that food aid should be discontinued so that developing countries would be compelled to limit their population growth.[25]

By threatening to boycott the Stockholm conference, the developing nations succeeded in influencing the early direction of international environmental policy. The first article of the Stockholm Declaration begins with the phrase "Man has the fundamental right to freedom, equality, and adequate conditions of life." Other principles assert that underdevelopment is a cause of environmental degradation and that environmental policies should enhance, and not adversely affect, economic development and better living conditions for all.[26] Developing countries also prevailed in having UNEP headquarters located in Nairobi and in designating "human settlements" (including the region's mushrooming megalopolises) as one of UNEP's "environmental" missions, as well as making them the subject of a global conference in 1976.[27]

During the remainder of the 1970s, the developing nations, caucusing as the Group of 77, repeatedly used international theme conferences as forums for pressing demands for a "new international economic order" that would pose fewer obstacles to their economic development. Such was the case at the World Population Conference in Bucharest in 1974, where representatives annoyed many delegates from the industrial nations by arguing that the underlying problem in their countries was not overpopulation but underdevelopment. Shunning proposals to assist in making contraceptives universally available (as being motivated by the developed countries' desire to maintain their world dominance), they argued that economic development assistance would be a more effective and just strategy for limiting population growth.[28]

By the 1980s it was becoming increasingly apparent throughout the developing world that pollution, soil erosion, deforestation, the spread of deserts, and other forms of environmental degradation were undermining prospects for development. Most governments accepted the need to restrain the growth of their populations and, thus, were dismayed when the U.S. delegation to the 1984 International Conference on Population, representing the Reagan administration, backed away from the United States' previous staunch commitment to family planning, arguing instead that economic growth spurred by market forces would reduce population growth rates to acceptable levels.[29]

The increasing environmental consciousness, however, ran up against the economic realities of the 1980s. Referred to as the "lost decade of development," the decade was a disastrous period of negative growth and declining standards of living in much of Africa and Latin America, where many countries were saddled with heavy foreign debts, hyperinflation, weak markets, and declining prices for the commodities they exported. Pressured to generate foreign revenues to pay the interest and principal on their huge debts and to address the desperate economic needs of their populations, governments of the developing countries therefore see no alternative to intensively using their natural resources, such as fossil fuels and tropical forests. In doing so, however, they are contributing to a global "tragedy of the commons," which will have serious consequences to which they are less able to adapt than are the developed countries.

Passive Support From the Soviet Bloc

The Soviet Union and the Eastern bloc boycotted the Stockholm conference to protest the exclusion of East Germany on procedural grounds. The Soviet bloc nevertheless expressed support for the conference objectives and, over the past two decades, for the cause of global environmental governance generally.

From a purely ideological standpoint, support of international environmental policy required few sacrifices from the Socialist states, whose theoreticians had been arguing that environmental degradation was primarily a consequence of capitalists seeking to maximize their profit by shirking responsibility for environmental damages caused by their economic activities. Conversely, Socialist managers, unmotivated by personal profit, could strike a better balance between economic and environmental values. If the onus for environmental damage was on capitalism, then the burdens of reform were disproportionately those of capitalist countries. The Socialist countries therefore saw something to gain and little to lose from international action on the environment.[30]

During the era of detente in the 1970s, the environment became the subject of efforts to defuse East-West tensions. In 1972 the United States and Soviet Union agreed on a program of bilateral environmental cooperation. Following up on a provision of the Helsinki Accord of 1975 that specified the environment as one of several subjects for East-West cooperation, Soviet president Leonid Brezhnev pushed hard for the high-level conference on atmospheric pollution, which adopted the Convention on Long-Range Transboundary Air Pollution mentioned above.[31] The Soviet bloc generally supported the adoption of supplemental protocols on sulfur and nitrogen oxide emissions, presumably at least in part because they were net importers of air pollutants from central and western Europe. It is questionable, however, whether the Soviet Union and Eastern bloc states had the commitment and the means to comply with international limits on transboundary pollution.

With the veil of official secrecy lifted in the former Soviet Union and its allies, government-caused environmental catastrophes have come to light. For decades driven almost exclusively by the goals of maximizing production and enhancing military power, the Soviet Union gained international notoriety on environmental matters, a notoriety that was reinforced by two recent disasters: the nuclear accident at Chernobyl in 1986 that spewed radioactive pollutants at dangerous levels throughout much of Europe, and the drying up of the Aral Sea, caused by the large-scale diversion of rivers to irrigate cotton fields.[32] The outside world also became aware that the heavily industrialized regions of the Eastern bloc countries, in particular a zone encompassing parts of Poland, East Germany, and Czechoslovakia, were among the most polluted places in the world and were taking a heavy toll on the health of the residents.[33]

Soviet president Mikhail S. Gorbachev became one of the most outspoken advocates of multilateral cooperation to address environmental problems.[34] In a speech in Murmansk in 1987, he pledged Soviet cooperation regarding the Arctic's environmental problems, bringing an end to the policy of secrecy about Arctic affairs that had closed off much of the region to the international research community. The Soviet Union concluded treaties with Norway and Finland for reducing transboundary pollution, in particular emissions from large smelting operations in the Kola Peninsula near its western border.[35]

It remains to be seen whether the non-Communist governments of eastern Europe and the newly independent states of the former Soviet Union will have a very strong commitment to global environmental governance. Popular discontent over environmental degradation was a factor in the overthrow of the old regimes, but without substantial technical and economic assistance, the new governments are likely to be preoccupied with the economic crisis they face.

Sustainable Development as an Integrating Concept

The challenge of reconciling the often divergent perspectives of developed and developing countries on global environmental governance was taken up by the Brundtland Commission in *Our Common Future*. The report elaborates the argument made by developing world representatives as early as the preparatory meetings for the 1973 Stockholm conference; to wit: poverty and underdevelopment are major causes of environmental degradation. It follows, then, that the environment of the developing countries and the former Soviet bloc cannot be preserved or repaired without an economic development approach that allows for growth and satisfies basic human needs while avoiding profligate resource exploitation and pollution. The report also emphasizes the importance of reforming aspects of the international economic order, such as burdensome international debt, that contribute to the desperate economic plight of so many countries and hamper their efforts to develop.[36]

The commission adopted the concept "sustainable development" to focus thought on the task of reconciling environmental and economic priorities throughout the world. Defined as "development that meets the needs of the present without compromising the ability of future generations to meet their own needs,"[37] the concept is vague and subject to many and diverse interpretations. Critics argue that sustainable development is an oxymoron that offers a convenient way of obscuring what are still profound differences of perspective between the richer and poorer societies of the world on the issues of environment and development. Nevertheless, the terminology has stimulated a reassessment of the meaning of development in an era fraught with environmental perils, in addition to becoming a conceptual bridge for efforts to forge a critical partnership between North and South for addressing the problems of environment and development.

The New Challenge of Global Change

Scientific evidence has mounted over the past decade that human beings, by virtue of their numbers and activities, are causing changes in the basic physical processes of the planet that are many times faster than occurs naturally. Concern over what is commonly referred to as "global change" is largely directed at alterations in the chemistry of the atmosphere due to pollution. Many fear it is bringing about a thinning of the stratospheric ozone layer and raising the average global temperature.[38]

A Convergence of Scientific Opinion

International negotiations on mitigating environmental problems usually succeed only after scientific opinion converges as to the seriousness of the situation. The first major scientific breakthrough regarding the human impact on the ozone layer occurred in 1973 when two scientists at the University of California at Irvine, Sherwood Rowland and Mario Molina, calculated that chlorofluorocarbons (CFCs), when broken down by intense solar radiation at high altitudes, release chlorine with an immense ability to break apart ozone molecules.[39] For the next decade, scientific projections of the potential rate of ozone loss fluctuated within a range generally not considered a serious cause for alarm.

Concern about ozone depletion intensified in the mid 1980s. An authoritative study sponsored by UNEP, the World Meteorological Organization (WMO), and several national agencies projected a 9 percent reduction of the ozone layer by the last half of the twenty-first century.[40] About the same time, a British scientific expedition reported the startling finding that concentrations of ozone over the south polar region during the spring of 1985 were only half what they had been in the 1960s, a phenomenon that has become known as the "Antarctic ozone hole." Varying degrees of seasonal ozone thinning were noted in subsequent years, but the cause remained a mystery until 1988 when an international scientific panel assembled conclusive evidence linking the phenomenon to human pollutants, in particular to CFCs, thus discrediting the theory that the "hole" might be caused by the seasonal wind currents of the polar vortex. In recent years evidence has also mounted that a more gradual, but nevertheless alarming, thinning is occurring globally, and there are signs of a seasonal ozone hole over the northern polar region.[41]

The possibility that human pollutants might have an impact on weather was conjectured a century ago by Swedish scientist Svante Arrhenius, who calculated the amount of warming that would result from a doubling of carbon dioxide, or CO_2. It wasn't until the 1970s, however, that the possibility of climate change was seriously studied. At the time, scientists had widely divergent opinions on whether the net effect of pollutants would be a general warming or cooling. By the 1980s the preponderance of scientific evidence pointed toward warming. Monitoring programs begun in the 1950s revealed that atmospheric concentrations of greenhouse gases—in particular CO_2, methane, and CFCs—were steadily and rapidly increasing. Scientists also found that fluctuations in temperature between ice ages and interglacial periods over the past 160,000 years correlated with concentrations of CO_2 found in air trapped in Antarctic glacial ice.[42] The Intergovernmental Panel on Climate Change, which was sponsored by WMO and UNEP and involved one thousand experts from sixty countries, concluded in 1990 that global mean temperatures had already risen .3-.6 degrees centigrade over the past one hundred years and predicted they would rise another .3 degrees centigrade per decade over the next century if present trends continue.[43]

There is less agreement on the consequences of climate change and for the environment and human populations. Higher temperatures and altered rainfall amounts are likely to have substantial impacts on agriculture and cause the spread of deserts. Altered precipitation patterns will also affect river flows, with implications for hydroelectric and irrigation projects and urban water supplies. A more rapid melting of polar ice and expansion of ocean waters is likely to cause sea levels to rise, inundating coastal cities and even causing some small island nations to disappear. Unable to adapt to the new climate or migrate with the changing environment, numerous species will die off; others, such as noxious weeds and disease vectors, may flourish. Societal disruptions, including vast migrations of people forced from their homes by drought or rising water, could be immense.[44]

International Policy to Preserve the Ozone Layer

The negotiations sponsored by UNEP to address ozone depletion, which led to three increasingly strong international agreements between 1985 and 1990, constitute perhaps the most remarkable chapter in the history of global environmental diplomacy. The first agreement, the 1985 Vienna Convention for the Protection of the Ozone Layer, was a typical framework treaty. Rather than mandating any specific reductions of the use of ozone-depleting substances, the convention simply called on the parties to take "appropriate measures" to protect the ozone layer and to cooperate on monitoring, research, and the exchange of information on the ozone layer and the extent to which it is affected by CFCs and other chemicals.

Revised scientific projections of a more rapid thinning of the ozone layer than had previously been anticipated, coupled with the alarming news of the Antarctic ozone hole, prompted the parties to the Vienna convention to conduct follow-up negotiations on limiting production and use of the chemicals responsible for the problem. The next agreement, the Montreal protocol, adopted in September 1987, obliged parties to reduce production of certain CFCs and halons by 20 percent by 1993 and 50 percent by 1998, using 1986 as the base year. Developing countries were allowed a ten-year grace period.

When it was signed, the Montreal protocol was regarded as a major diplomatic breakthrough and a large step toward mitigating the ozone depletion problem. In the months following its adoption, however, further scientific revelations, in particular linking the Antarctic ozone hole to human-generated pollutants, demonstrated that stronger international measures were needed. Thus, ninety-three countries, meeting in London in June 1990, amended the protocol by mandating a complete phasing out of ozone-depleting substances by 2000. Again, developing countries were given a grace period and a fund was established to assist them in adopting substitutes.[45] Further scientific evidence that the ozone loss is occurring more rapidly than previously projected has prompted most of the developed countries, including the United States, to announce earlier target dates in the mid 1990s for the total phaseout of CFCs.[46]

Richard E. Benedict, the chief U.S. delegate to the ozone negotiations, attributes the remarkable diplomatic breakthroughs to a number of factors: the critical role played by scientists; the willingness of political leaders to act in the face of scientific uncertainties; the pressure for action from an educated and mobilized public opinion; the leadership of UNEP and the U.S. government in mobilizing an international consensus; the preemptive environmental measures of several countries in advance of a global agreement; the participation of industry and environmental organizations; the adapting of regulations to economic and structural inequalities among nations; and the efforts made to create a level playing field among nations that compete economically. It remains to be seen whether these lessons from the ozone negotiations can be incorporated into what Benedict calls a "new global diplomacy" that will successfully address an even more challenging array of future environmental problems.[47]

Negotiations on Climate Change

Global warming poses a much greater challenge for international policymakers than did ozone depletion, which is caused by relatively few chemicals that can be replaced at reasonable cost. A greater variety of greenhouse gases are created by a myriad of essential human activities, including the generation of power, industrial production, transportation, agriculture, and forestry. Mitigating climate change will require major changes in life-style, especially those that consume large amounts of fossil fuels.

The Changing Atmosphere Conference held in Toronto in June 1988, which was sponsored by the Canadian government along with WMO and UNEP, was the first major international, policy-oriented meeting on climate change. The conference report recommended that CO_2 emissions be reduced 20 percent from 1988 levels by 2005.[48] The possibility of an across-the-board reduction in CO_2 emissions was discussed at a subsequent series of ministerial meetings leading up to the second World Climate Conference held in Geneva in 1990, but the opposition of the United States and a dwindling group of like-minded states thwarted a consensus. After the 1990 defections of Japan and the United Kingdom to the ranks of those committed to reducing CO_2 emissions, the United States stood alone among the industrial states in refusing to make such a commitment.[49]

The U.N. General Assembly created the Intergovernmental Negotiating Committee to be the venue for talks on a first climate change treaty that was to be ready for adoption at the Earth summit the following year. The negotiations, which began in Chantilly, Virginia, in February 1991, were hampered by the United States' continued refusal to agree to a timetable for limiting CO_2 emissions, which most other advanced states felt was a prudent precautionary measure in view of the scientific evidence already available on climate change. The document finally adopted at the Earth summit is an example of a lowest-common-denominator type of framework treaty. Although it requires the parties to limit emissions of greenhouse gases, to protect forests that absorb those gases, and to report on what they are doing to achieve these ends, it specifies no targets or deadlines, a concession to U.S. intransigence.[50] Representatives from thirty-seven small island nations, which are highly vulnerable to rising sea levels, were especially vocal in protesting what they regarded as a toothless treaty on climate change.[51]

U.S. participation is critical to an effective climate change accord because it accounts for 25 percent of energy-related CO_2 emissions.[52] The United States is also among the highest per capita consumers of fossil fuels and the least efficient in energy use per unit of GNP of the industrial countries.[53] For these reasons, the international community expects it to make the most significant contribution to retarding global warming and is determined not to give the United States a free ride on sacrifices borne by other countries to reduce their emissions of greenhouse gases.

One irony of the official U.S. position is that much of the research suggesting the likelihood of global warming—including the development of the large general circulation models used to project long-term climate change on a global basis—has been conducted in the United States. The Bush administration rationalized its opposition to internationally mandated reductions on the grounds that scientific evidence on climate change was not sufficiently conclusive to warrant what it contended would be costly economic adjustments. To its credit, the United States continues to invest heavily in global change research.

The Bush administration had also maintained that international policy on climate change should encompass not only CO_2, but also the other principal greenhouse gases, including methane, much of which is generated by agricultural operations in the developing world such as wet rice cultivation. It has argued that phasing out production of CFCs, a much more potent greenhouse gas than CO_2 on a per-molecule basis, is enough of a first step toward mitigating global warming until there is more compelling scientific evidence that stronger measures are needed on other gases. This position was consistent with the Bush administration's receptivity to "no regrets" measures that can be justified on the basis of other benefits, in this case curbing ozone depletion.[54]

The Earth Summit

Climate change was only one of the prominent issues on the agenda of the Earth summit in Río de Janeiro, which took place after two years of extensive preliminary discussions and negotiations involving the three working groups of the Intergovernmental Preparatory Committee. The official conference held June 3-14, 1992, drew representatives from 179 states, including 118 heads of states who participated in the final sessions. The conference organizers established procedures that permitted the numerous interested NGOs more opportunities than at previous world conferences to have their perspectives taken into account, especially in the preparatory meetings. The '92 Global Forum, held concurrently with the official conference at a site close to downtown Río, gave representatives of more than seven thousand NGOs, as well as thousands of interested private individuals, a smorgasbord of opportunities to engage in lively discussions on the issues of the summit and to present and view exhibits describing their environmental activities and projects.[55]

Delegates to the Earth summit focused much of their efforts on achieving as broad a consensus as possible on several key documents. The nonbinding Río Declaration on Environment and Development sets forth twenty-seven broad principles to guide efforts to strengthen global environmental governance. The eight-hundred-page Agenda 21 presents a detailed, long-term plan of action for implementing the goals of the conference. The Climate Change Convention was one of two binding treaties adopted, the other one being the Biodiversity Convention designed to protect endangered species and to ensure that nations with genetic resources be able to share in the fruits of the biotechnology derived from them. The United States led efforts to reach an agreement on a binding treaty to preserve tropical forests, but eventually settled for a watered-down Statement on Forest Principles. Concern about implementation of the decisions made at the Earth summit prompted creation of a U.N. Commission on Sustainable Development, which would be a forum for continuing meetings and work on the issues of the Earth summit. This innovative body would also be a watchdog group—monitoring nations and international organizations on their commitments to preserve the global environment.[56]

The Earth summit revealed much about the intensity of the international politics of global environmental governance, in particular the contrasting positions of the advanced industrial states and the developing nations. Representatives from the latter countries repeatedly sought explicit acknowledgment that the blame for global environmental change resides primarily with the highly developed countries, which, as they industrialized over many decades, made profligate use of the world's resources, including global commons such as the atmosphere. It was thus argued that these same countries should pay the lion's share of the cost of mitigating the world's environmental problems.

Moreover, the developing countries would not agree to forgo use of what they contend to be their fair share of these global resources, on which their development plans are based, unless they are compensated with economic and technological assistance from the rich countries that are asking them to sacrifice for the good of the global community.[57] Several Northern countries announced modest increases in their environmental assistance but balked at making specific commitments to the level of financing sought by the South, which included a doubling of economic assistance to .7 percent of the GNPs of the donor countries, a standard the United Nations set three decades ago. They did agree, however, to achieve this standard "as soon as possible."

The conference was also remarkable for exposing how isolated the United States under the Bush administration had become on issues of global environmental governance. U.S. opposition to targets and deadlines for limiting emissions of greenhouse gases continued to exasperate leaders from other industrial countries, as was evident in the sharply worded remarks of German chancellor Helmut Kohl. But in the end they yielded to the U.S. position in order to secure its signing of the Climate Change Convention. To those who argued that the United States should reduce its consumption of fossil fuels and other natural resources, the Bush administration refused to compromise.[58]

The United States alone refused to sign the Biodiversity Convention, arguing that the economic and intellectual property rights of the biotechnology industry were not adequately protected. U.S. proposals for a forest convention were strongly opposed by developing countries, the most outspoken being Malaysia and other tropical timber-producing states, which asserted defiantly that their forests were a national resource subject to their sovereign control. They also accused the United States of seeking to apply a double-standard in view of its national policies that permit extensive clear-cutting of species-rich, old-growth forests in the Pacific Northwest.[59]

The Earth summit posed an awkward political dilemma for President George Bush. On the one hand, aware of the American public's widespread support for the conference's objectives, he wished to avoid the diplomatic embarrassment of worldwide condemnation for single-handedly thwarting a consensus on major new international environmental initiatives. At Río, the administration's positions were sharply criticized by congressional members of the U.S. delegation, in particular Democratic senators Tim Wirth and Al Gore. Moreover, American environmental activists attending the Global Forum staged public demonstrations on the Río beaches to express their outrage over the official policies of their government. Nevertheless, President Bush's political advisers apparently concluded that standing alone in opposition to international agreements would play well with his conservative constituency, which did not concede the seriousness of global environmental problems and had exhorted him not to attend a conference dominated by the world's "environmental extremists." Tommy Koh of Singapore, chairman of the summit's main working sessions, sagely opined that the United Nations would be prudent not to hold such conferences during an American election year.[60]

Future Prospects

Only time will tell whether the 1992 Earth summit was a landmark event in the evolution of global environmental governance. The conference was not as successful as had been initially hoped in achieving binding commitments from states to take action on leading environmental problems, such as climate change and tropical deforestation. On a more positive note, the conference did not collapse into disarray, as many had feared it would owing to the intransigence displayed by key countries and blocs earlier in the negotiations. In the end, compromises were reached on the language of the Río Declaration and Agenda 21. Based on the impact of parallel documents from the Stockholm conference twenty years earlier, this augurs well for strengthened international environmental institutions, laws, and programs.

The summit was notable for exposing deep lines of conflict, both among and within states, on how the interrelated issues of environment and development should be addressed. Seeing these divisions so openly expressed at Río is reason for concern about whether there is enough commonality of outlook in the world community to enable a significant strengthening of global environmental governance. The politically charged atmosphere of the conference is evidence, however, that the global environment has graduated from being a peripheral concern, dealt with primarily by environmental ministries, to the ranks of the era's most salient issues that command the attention of the world's political leaders and the constituencies they represent. The magnitude of life-style changes needed to mitigate the global change *problematique* will not be possible without the environment achieving this level of prominence.

Leadership in the development of global environmental governance is needed from the United States. Unfortunately, the Reagan and Bush administrations backed away from playing such a role, except on selected issues, such as ozone depletion. A peace dividend derived from the end of the Cold War could be invested in preserving the global environment, but the economic malaise of recent years and the relative absence of a military threat have caused politicians to respond to public pressures for a shift of resources from international to national priorities. The Clinton administration, which took office in 1993, will probably move the United States more into line with other industrial countries on the issues discussed at Río and quite possibly fill the leadership vacuum that has hindered the development of global environmental governance.[61]

Notes

1. See the study commissioned for the conference by Barbara Ward and René Dubos, *Only One Earth: The Care and Maintenance of a Small Planet* (New York: Norton, 1972).
2. See Constance Mungall and Digby J. McLaren, eds., *Planet Under Stress: The Challenge of Global Change* (New York: Oxford University Press, 1990).
3. See Martin F. Price, "Global Change: Defining the Ill-Defined," *Environment* 31 (October 1989): 18-20, 42-44.
4. See Thomas F. Malone, "Mission to Planet Earth," *Environment* 28 (October 1986): 6-11, 39-42; and Thomas F. Malone and Robert Corell, "Mission to Planet Earth Revisited," *Environment* 31 (April 1989): 7-11, 31-36. The International Social Science Council is sponsoring a parallel project called the Human Dimensions of Global Environmental Change Programme. See Paul C. Stern, Oran R. Young, and Daniel Druckman, eds., *Global Environmental Change: Understanding the Human Dimensions* (Washington, D.C.: National Academy Press, 1992).
5. World Commission on Environment and Development, *Our Common Future* (New York: Oxford University Press, 1987). For further analysis, see Linda Starke, *Signs of Hope: Working Towards Our Common Future* (New York: Oxford University Press, 1990).
6. A *problematique* is an interrelated group of problems that cannot be effectively addressed apart from one another.
7. For a discussion of the role and dynamics of world conferences, see A. LeRoy Bennett, *International Organizations: Principles and Issues*, 3d ed. (Englewood Cliffs, N.J.: Prentice-Hall, 1984), 293-323.
8. For a description and analysis of the political dynamics of the Stockholm conference, see John R. Handelman, Howard B. Shapiro, and John A. Vasquez, *Introductory Case Studies for International Relations: Vietnam/Middle East/the Environmental Crisis* (Chicago: Rand McNally, 1974), 60-83.
9. For the Declaration of the Stockholm Conference, see *Report of the United Nations Conference on the Human Environment*, UN Doc. A/Conf. 48/14, 1972.
10. United Nations Environment Programme, *1990 Annual Report of the Executive Director* (Nairobi: UNEP, 1991), 89-106.
11. For a description and assessment of UNEP's early projects, see Lynton K. Caldwell, *International Environmental Policy: Emergence and Dimensions*, 2d ed. (Durham, N.C.: Duke University Press, 1990), 71-88. See also *Annual Report of the Executive Director 1990* (Nairobi: UNEP, 1991).
12. See Peter M. Haas, *Saving the Mediterranean: The Politics of International Environmental Cooperation* (New York: Columbia University Press, 1990).
13. See Carol A. Petsonk, "The Role of the United Nations Environment Programme (UNEP) in the Development of International Environmental Law," *American University Journal of International Law and Policy* 5 (Winter 1990): 362-367.
14. See James Barros and Douglas M. Johnston, *The International Law of Pollution* (New York: Free Press, 1974), 177-195.
15. Tabulated from *Register of International Treaties and Other Agreements in the Field of the Environment* (Nairobi: UNEP, 1991), UNEP/GC.16/Inf.4.

16. Ibid.
17. See Marvin S. Soroos, "The Odyssey of Arctic Haze: Toward a Global Atmospheric Regime," *Environment* 34 (December 1992): 6-11, 25-27.
18. For a description of the London smog, see Peter Brimblecombe, *The Big Smoke: A History of Air Pollution in London Since Medieval Times* (London: Methuen, 1987), 165-169. For background on the Minamata mercury poisonings and subsequent court cases, see Donald R. Kelley, Kenneth R. Stunkel, and Richard R. Wescott, *The Economic Superpowers and the Environment: The United States, the Soviet Union, and Japan* (San Francisco: Freeman, 1976), 192-194.
19. See Ellis B. Cowling, "Acid Rain in Historical Perspective," *Environmental Science and Technology* 16 (February 1982): 110a-123a.
20. Convention on Long-Range Transboundary Air Pollution, Geneva (November 13, 1979), E/ECE/1010.
21. Gregory S. Wetstone, "A History of the Acid Rain Issue," in *Science for Public Policy*, ed. Harvey Brooks and Chester Cooper (New York: Pergamon, 1987), 189.
22. See John McCormick, *Acid Earth: The Global Threat of Acid Pollution*, new exp. ed. (London: Earthscan, 1989).
23. See Jessica Tuchman Mathews, "Redefining Security," *Foreign Affairs* 68 (Spring 1989): 162-177. See also chap. 15 in this volume.
24. Donella H. Meadows, Dennis L. Meadows, Jørgen Randers, and William W. Behrens III, *The Limits to Growth* (New York: Universe Books, 1972).
25. Garrett Hardin, "Living on a Lifeboat," *BioScience* 24 (October 1974): 561-568.
26. See Stockholm Declaration, *Report of the U.N. Conference on the Human Environment.*
27. For a discussion of the issues addressed at this conference, see Barbara Ward, *The Home of Man* (New York: Norton, 1976).
28. See Marcus F. Franda, "The World Population Conference: An International Extravaganza," *Fieldstaff Reports: South East Asia Series* 21 (September 1974).
29. See Jason L. Finkle and Barbara B. Crane, "Ideology and Politics at Mexico City: The United States at the 1984 International Population Conference on Population," *Population and Development Review* 11 (March 1985): 1-28.
30. See Charles E. Zeigler, *Environmental Policy in the Soviet Union* (Amherst: University of Massachusetts Press, 1987); and Barbara Jancar, *Environmental Management in the Soviet Union and Yugoslavia* (Durham, N.C.: Duke University Press, 1987).
31. C. Ian Jackson, "A Tenth-Anniversary Review of the ECE Convention on Long-Range Transboundary Air Pollution," *International Environmental Affairs* 2 (Summer 1990): 218-219.
32. For a general overview of the condition of the environment in the former Soviet Union, see Murray Feshbach and Alfred Friendly, Jr., *Ecocide in the USSR: Health and Nature Under Siege* (New York: Basic Books, 1992). On specific problems, see Chris Park, *Chernobyl: The Long Shadow* (New York: Routledge, 1989); and V. M. Kotlyakov, "The Aral Sea Basin: A Critical Environmental Zone," *Environment* 33 (January-February 1991): 4-9, 36-38.
33. See Hilary F. French, "Restoring the East European and Soviet Environments," in *State of the World 1991* (New York: Norton, 1991), 93-112; and Jon Thompson, "East Europe's Dark Dawn: the Iron Curtain Rises to Reveal a Land Tarnished by Pollution," *National Geographic* 179 (June 1991): 36-69.
34. Mikhail Gorbachev, "Our Grandchildren Will Never Forgive Us," *Vetsnik* (March 1990), 41-43.
35. See Gail Osherenko, "Environmental Cooperation in the Arctic: Will the Soviets Participate?" *Current Research on Peace and Violence* 3 (1989): 144-157.
36. World Commission on Environment and Development, *Our Common Future*, 67-91.

37. Ibid., 43.
38. For overviews of the scientific aspects of "global change," see National Academy of Sciences, *One Earth, One Future: Our Changing Global Environment* (Washington, D.C.: National Academy Press, 1990).
39. See Sharon L. Roan, *Ozone Crisis: The 15-Year Evolution of a Sudden Global Emergency* (New York: Wiley, 1989), 1-19.
40. World Meteorological Organization et al., *Atmospheric Ozone 1985*, 3 vols. (Geneva: WMO, 1986).
41. For an overview of the evolution of scientific knowledge on ozone depletion, see Peter M. Haas, "Banning Chlorofluorocarbons: Epistemic Community Efforts to Protect Stratospheric Ozone," *International Organization* 46 (Winter 1992): 147-186.
42. See Stephen H. Schneider, *Global Warming: Are We Entering the Greenhouse Century?* (New York: Vintage Books, 1989).
43. Intergovernmental Panel on Climate Change, "Policy Makers' Summary of the Scientific Assessment of Climate Change" (Report prepared by Working Group I, June 1990), 1.
44. World Resources Institute, *World Resources 1990-91* (New York: Oxford University Press, 1990), 18-24.
45. For a description and analysis of the ozone depletion agreements and the negotiations that led to them, see Richard E. Benedict, *Ozone Diplomacy: New Directions in Safeguarding the Planet* (Cambridge: Harvard University Press, 1991).
46. Marnie Stetson, "Saving Nature's Sunscreen," *World Watch* 5 (March-April 1992): 34-36.
47. Richard E. Benedict, "Protecting the Ozone Layer: New Directions in Diplomacy," in *Preserving the Global Environment: The Challenge of Shared Leadership*, ed. Jessica T. Mathews (New York: Norton, 1991), 143-149.
48. *The Changing Atmosphere: Implications for Global Security*, proceedings of a conference held June 27-30, 1988, in Toronto (Geneva: WMO, 1989), 296.
49. For the positions of the developed countries on policies to address climate change, see Karen Schmidt, "How Industrialized Countries Are Responding to Global Climate Change," *International Environmental Affairs* 3 (Fall 1991): 292-317.
50. William K. Stevens, "With Climate Treaty Signed, All Say They'll Do Even More," *New York Times*, January 13, 1992, 1, 4.
51. James Brooke, "U.N. Chief Closes Summit With an Appeal for Action," *New York Times*, June 15, 1992, 8.
52. Schmidt, "How Industrialized Countries Are Responding," 317. The World Resources Institute calculates that the United States emits 17.8 percent of all global greenhouse gasses. See *World Resources 1992-93* (New York: Oxford University Press, 1992), 208.
53. World Resources Institute, *World Resources 1990-91*, 18-24.
54. See Peter M. Morrisette and Andrew J. Plantinga, "How the CO_2 Issue Is Viewed in Different Countries," discussion paper ENR91-03.
55. Brad Knickerbocker, "Alternative Earth Summit Gives Voice to Grass Roots," *Christian Science Monitor*, June 8, 1992, 3.
56. Paul Lewis, "Storm in Río: Morning After," *New York Times*, June 15, 1992, 1, 5. See also Michael McCoy, "Post Río: Phase Two," *Development Forum* 20 (July-August 1992): 1, 7.
57. See Anil Agarwal and Sunita Narain, "We Can No Longer Subsidize the North," *Development Forum* 20 (May-June 1992): 15.
58. Paul E. Lewis, "U.S. at the Earth Summit: Isolated and Challenged," *New York Times*, June 10, 1992, 8.
59. William K. Stevens, "Bush Plan to Save Forests Is Blocked by Poor Countries," *New York Times*, January 9, 1992, 1, 8.

60. William K. Stevens, "The Lessons of Río: A New Prominence and an Effective Blandness," *New York Times*, January 14, 1992, 10.
61. See recent books on climate change by two Democratic senators, George W. Mitchell, *World on Fire: Saving an Endangered Earth* (New York: Scribner's, 1990), and Al Gore, *Earth in the Balance: Ecology and the Human Spirit* (Boston: Houghton Mifflin, 1992).

15

National Security and the Environment
Odelia Funke

*Environmental degradation imperils nations' most fundamental
aspect of security by undermining the natural support systems on
which all of human activity depends.*

—Michael Renner, 1989

How in today's world do we frame national security policies so that they
give adequate attention to environmental factors? Traditional definitions of and approaches to national security have assumed that the principal
sources of danger to national security and welfare were other states (or
political groups) and that therefore national defense and security were best
served by being prepared for war against other states. The narrow focus on
outside threats, while ignoring environmental health and safety dangers,
made it difficult to confront the damage resulting from our strategic and
economic choices. To make matters worse, the national security imperative
erected barriers to accountability. Both the United States and the former
Eastern bloc countries are still evaluating the full extent and implications of
the environmental damage incurred during the Cold War.

Within the past several years, an increasing number of analysts and
policymakers have recognized that environmental concerns are basic to
our national well-being. The integrity of our national resource base and
the health of our people are fundamental elements of national security.

All nations, but particularly the United States in its role as the
world's most powerful nation, must do a better job of integrating environmental considerations into national security analysis. Otherwise, security
policies will tend to decrease rather than increase our ability to sustain
complex social and economic systems. Rethinking traditional assumptions
about national security involves redefining the elements of national security and considering the environmental consequences of past and present
military activities.

The Concept of "National Security"

National security is typically defined in terms of protecting internal
values and interests from external threats. Although directly related to

values, security itself is not the goal; rather, security is a *condition* that allows a nation to maintain its values. By this definition, actions that make a nation physically more secure yet degrade its values are counterproductive. The concept of "national security," in fact, has been evolving over the past several decades to accommodate a broader understanding of security. I will argue that this expansion is necessary because U.S. national security depends on the country's environmental resources and is fundamentally affected by pressing environmental issues facing the planet.

Prior to World War II, national security concerns fell under the umbrella of foreign affairs. Environmental factors such as natural resource base, population, soil productivity, and climate were taken into account as influences on a nation's strength and interests, or sometimes as objectives of foreign policy (to increase the resource base, for example). After World War II, relations among states changed substantially. With the advent of nuclear weapons, national security emerged as a separate, often paramount, concern of international relations. In both the academic and defense realms, national security studies during the Cold War emphasized protection from external attack and were dominated by a narrow focus on military strategy and on the objectives, concepts, and resources required to support a powerful and flexible military force. Concentrating almost exclusively on the East-West balance of power (such as alliance structures, military power, and nuclear deterrence) resulted in neglect of other vital factors, especially preservation of natural resources and ecological balance.

The economic dimensions of security were often underappreciated in theory, though usually not ignored in the actual conduct of foreign affairs, as evident in policies ranging from the Marshall Plan to the creation of the Agency for International Development (AID) and the Peace Corps. In the last several decades, economics gained a more prominent role in national security discussions. However, the concept of power, including economics but focused primarily on military capabilities, remained the centerpiece. If environmental goals were addressed at all, they were generally referred to in terms of securing natural resources and understood as an element of economic power.

These postwar ideas of national security are inadequate to address evolving international and environmental challenges. Although a few scholars have taken a broader perspective, only in recent years do we find significant public attention given to global ecology, including natural resources, human health, and demographics. Security issues can no longer be the exclusive or primary domain of the military. The consensus of the Brundtland Commission of the U.N. Environmental Programme was that:

> The deepening and widening environmental crisis presents a threat to national security—and even survival—that may be greater than well-armed, ill-disposed neighbors and unfriendly alliances. . . . The arms

race—in all parts of the world—pre-empts resources that might be used more productively to diminish the security threats created by environmental conflict and the resentments that are fueled by widespread poverty. . . . There are no military solutions to "environmental insecurity."[1]

Lester Brown of the Worldwatch Institute has reached more radical conclusions: traditional approaches to national security are outmoded, he says, and national defense establishments are useless against new threats. Nonmilitary threats are extremely complex, much less clearly defined than military ones, and growing more formidable; they present great challenges of information gathering and analysis, which governments seem ill prepared to meet. The very concept of "national" security is inadequate.[2] Another Worldwatch scholar has concluded that "national security is a meaningless concept if it does not include the preservation of livable conditions within a country—or on the planet as a whole." Traditional national defense strategies undermine national security. Individuals as well as nations depend "on economic vitality, social justice, and ecological stability. Pursuing military security at the cost of these other factors is akin to dismantling a house to salvage materials to erect a fence around it."[3]

The Role of the Environment and Resources

At least two decades ago, Lynton K. Caldwell called for a realignment of our understanding of security and a reevaluation of the priority we give to environmental matters. Caldwell argued that a fundamental change, perhaps a major alteration in how humans perceive themselves on Earth, was under way: there was an emerging awareness that humans were an integral part of the biosphere.[4] The overriding priority of modern governments, Caldwell observed, has been military expenditures, and their thinking has been dominated by technological developments. Government policies should not focus on military or economic issues in isolation, he said, and their orientation must change to avoid accelerating environmental deterioration.[5]

Unfortunately change in governments and other large bureaucratic institutions always lags behind developments in attitudes and values. Today's more holistic approach to security requires that we analyze elements such as the natural resource base, population growth and migration, and trade patterns and trends. Societies must learn to live within their ecological resources, or suffer terrible consequences that will affect the global commons. Western societies have embraced a vision of expanding technologies and limitless progress, treating resources as an "externality" in their quest for economic growth. But Western growth has been at the cost of damaging the environment, threatening ecological systems, and depleting the natural resources of less developed countries (LDCs). Manmade substitutes have overcome resource scarcity for some products, but they, too, can be costly to the environment. Environmental consequences have to be part of the calculus of economic development.

As resources disappear, insufficient food and large-scale migration are direct results. Impoverishment creates environmental refugees, who in turn further crowd other (often urban) areas. As population pressures increase and the number of desperate people grows, marginal lands are overexploited, destroying large areas and threatening local ecosystems. Massive forest loss affects global weather patterns; overuse of croplands and poor irrigation practices cause desertification. We know that soil erosion and deforestation are expanding globally, silting and flooding are accelerating, air pollution is severe in many areas, and waterborne disease is widespread internationally. Permanent loss of species continues at an estimated rate of two per hour. For the first time, life expectancy is declining in industrial countries, in eastern Europe, and in the states of the former Soviet Union, with environmental pollution clearly linked to high disease rates.

The link between the demand for natural resources and the use of aggression is an important facet of the environmental dimensions of national security. Nations have often fought over natural resources; in this century alone, control of natural resources was an important factor in over a dozen wars.[6] Nations have sought to increase their wealth by using violence to acquire resources, but lack of resources is probably a stronger motivation for aggressive expansion. Rapidly increasing populations in poorer countries will lead to environmental overload and resource depletion in the next century, which will most likely result in political upheaval and violence as well as mass starvation. Like toxins poured into the environment, political destabilization tends to spill across national borders. Countries are increasingly finding their security undermined by transborder pollution problems, which require regional or global solutions.

The International Dimension

Jessica Tuchman Mathews of the World Resources Institute has argued persuasively that "changes in sovereignty are blurring the once sharp dividing line between foreign and domestic affairs and altering our notions of national security. . . . Our most fundamental concepts of international governance are shifting beneath our feet." She has observed further that borders are becoming increasingly porous, and "security is seen to rest more and more on international—rather than strictly national—conditions. Security in the military sense remains important, but it is now only a part of the essential equation."[7]

For some, the gravity and scope of ecological threats clearly indicate an overwhelming need for international rather than national action. The requirements of environmental security transcend national borders and suggest the inadequacies of traditional concepts of national interest and military strategy. Environmental security cannot be sought at the expense of other nations, nor can nations achieve it unilaterally. This kind of security necessitates cooperation to safeguard a healthy environment and manage resources in an ecologically sound manner.

Nations faced with the possibility of global environmental disaster and the unprecedented threat posed by environmental problems to national security must coordinate policies with one another, as purely national efforts are bound to fail. The United States has not fully addressed the international complexities of environmental security. But there has been some progress in addressing global environmental threats; for example, international agreements on chlorofluorocarbon (CFC) phaseout provide a model of pragmatic cooperation. However, the requirements for environmental security go far beyond dealing sequentially with a few global issues. Supporting international stability also requires attention to nationally or regionally based environmental issues that either could lead to conflict within the nation or region, or could spread across national borders.

As we learn more about the movement of pollutants and delicate ecological balances, it becomes increasingly clear that each nation is at the mercy of other nations' actions. The dramatic shifts in power relations and alliance structures that have been occurring since the end of the Cold War may serve to boost environmental negotiations, for agreement across traditional alliances is required to meet many environmental challenges. The 1992 Earth summit in Río de Janeiro brought together interests and forces that will probably continue to mobilize support for a new global environmental agenda. Social scientists and policymakers must change their frames of reference to understand the opportunities for and constraints on security strategies in the contemporary world.

The Consequences of Defense-Related Activities

In addition to considering how environmental problems affect national security interests, it is important to look at the impacts security policies have on the environment. The ecological disruptions and destruction wrought by war are clear, but peacetime activities also have adverse effects. Ecological damage occurs with everything from training troops, to building, testing, and practicing with weapons systems, to research for a wide variety of defense-related products, including biological and chemical weapons. There are indirect costs too, relating to the allocation of resources.

The defense establishment has been a major source of the total toxic and hazardous wastes generated each year. Lands have been destroyed through abuse and contamination, and the health and safety of some citizens have been compromised or sacrificed. Workers as well as populations

living around defense facilities—many operated by the private sector—
have been exposed to elevated risks in the name of "national security"
imperatives. Much of the damage was done according to the practices of
the day, now recognized as unacceptable. Some facilities continued gross
abuses, even after more was learned about health and environmental
impacts, until intense public pressure forced changes. Defense facilities
in the United States are only now being held accountable in a way at all
comparable to nondefense industries. But because defense research and
preparedness are still shrouded in secrecy, it is difficult to know whether
significant abuses are continuing.

Although we still do not know the scope of the environmental damage associated with research and development activities; with improper
manufacture, use, storage, and disposal of toxics; and with releases at
defense-related facilities, we do know that the treatable problems will
take many generations to rectify. Highly contaminated areas can be controlled but not returned to precontaminated conditions. The economic
costs for cleanup or containment are still being estimated. At a minimum,
remediation will cost hundreds of billions of dollars over the next several
decades in the United States alone.

Outlined below are the principal categories of defense impacts: (1)
regular training and preparedness activities and production; (2) cleanup
of toxic and hazardous wastes generated by the departments of Defense
and Energy; and (3) disarmament, including programs to dispose of chemical and nuclear weapons. As with most of our national toxic cleanup
problems, some resulted from industrial processes, some from malfunc-
tion, mismanagement, or negligence; and some from ignorance of the
consequences.

Training and Preparedness

Routine training and exercises—from heavy equipment and troop
movements, to jet aircraft, naval ships, and munitions use—require large
amounts of energy, including burning of fossil fuels, and cause substantial
environmental disruption. Troops on land and ships at sea deposit huge
quantities of trash. Deploying nuclear submarines heightens the risks associated with accidents. Producing nuclear submarines and weapons is
particularly damaging, and currently no safe way exists to either destroy
large quantities of nuclear components or to dispose of spent nuclear
wastes. The size and scope of maneuvers directly affect the degree of
environmental disruption, and the amount of land destruction or sea pollution. Equipment design heavily influences minimum land and sea areas
required for training exercises and the noise it produces. Noise alone can
permanently damage human hearing and disrupt animal habitats and mat-
ing patterns. Equipping and training troops and producing weapons systems and munitions during peacetime entail large quantities of toxic ma-

terials. Storing or moving these materials, and disposing of them, all create additional pollution and environmental risks. Thus, the size of the defense force, its training and deployment strategies, and its equipment have important environmental implications.

Cleanup

The Department of Defense (DOD) has direct control over about 25 million acres, including ninety sites listed on the National Priority List for cleanup under Superfund. These are only the worst sites; there are many more contaminated areas to clean. Estimated costs for DOD cleanup have varied widely depending on the source and have escalated markedly over the past several years—from $14 billion in 1987 to $200 billion or $250 billion in 1991.[8] In 1992 the General Accounting Office (GAO) estimated $200 billion cleanup costs for DOD and DOE (Department of Energy) sites.[9] These costs do not include nuclear production facilities. Ultimate costs will depend on numerous factors, including the level of cleanup sought.

The Defense Environmental Restoration Program (DERP) is responsible for hazardous waste cleanups, compliance activities, and environmental restoration at military bases scheduled to close. The largest and most widely publicized DOD contamination occurred at Rocky Mountain Arsenal near Denver, Colorado. This one site will require hundreds of millions of dollars and many years to clean up. At the end of FY 1991, DERP included assessment and possible remedial action for 17,660 sites at 1,877 installations. The Department of Defense plans to assess sites and clean up the worst hazards first. DERP grew tenfold between FY 1984 and FY 1992 ($150 million to $1.4 billion), with anticipated costs climbing to more than $3.7 billion in FY 1993. Total DOD expenditure on the environment (from FY 1990 to FY 1993) will probably exceed $11 billion.[10] Even at these levels of funding, progress is slow. GAO has conducted several assessments of DOD cleanup efforts and has found that its Superfund cleanups are moving even more slowly than those at nongovernment sites.[11]

U.S. responsibility for cleanup of its overseas bases is an unresolved and politically sensitive issue. Host nations such as the Philippines have little capability for cleanup and far less leverage than Germany in negotiating remedial activities. Whatever the outcome, it is likely to require at least some additional funding and will certainly affect the perceived benefit for both the United States and host nations of having such bases in the future. The significance of this issue is also evident in attempts by former Eastern bloc nations to negotiate with Russia on compensation for bases contaminated by Soviet troops.

Contamination at DOE weapons production facilities appears to be a graver situation. The United States has produced seven hundred times more high-level wastes for weapons than for power plants, measured by volume. DOE facilities constitute a huge industrial enterprise (with more than 100,000 employees) covering thousands of square miles in thirteen states. They include some of the most contaminated sites in the world, and assessments of the contamination are far from complete.[12] Because records were not kept on all disposals, and leaks have further mixed toxic and radioactive contaminants, disposal constituents or amounts are currently unknown. Huge volumes of waste in liquid and solid form stored and disposed on-site contaminated billions of cubic meters of soils and sediments, as well as ground and surface waters. With current technology, containment is the best that can be accomplished for much of this contamination. As DOE admits, the government will have to cordon off large tracts of land indefinitely (some call them "national sacrifice zones") and concentrate on remediating highly contaminated areas, stabilizing soils, and stopping the spread of toxics in groundwater.[13]

For four decades DOE and its predecessor, the Atomic Energy Commission, acted in secrecy, under the umbrella of "national security," without oversight and with little attention to environmental consequences (showing "neglect bordering on contempt for environmental protection" as Sen. John Glenn [D-Ohio] put it).[14] Near- and long-term health effects are not known, and systematic studies of nearby populations have not been conducted. For years practices were lax because there was no information about health and environmental effects; for example, radioactive wastes were discharged directly into the ground through the 1960s. Abuses and violations of legal standards continued, however, even after impacts were better understood. The Department of Energy's attitude was reflected in its policy of paying noncompliance penalties for its contractors and in its decision to award multimillion-dollar bonuses to a company with severe safety problems and in serious noncompliance with Environmental Protection Agency (EPA) standards. Production goals were paramount. Mishaps, including large fires and other significant releases, have occurred at nuclear production facilities in both the United States and the former USSR. Both governments failed to warn residents or take action to protect them.[15] But disregard for public and environmental safety was more egregious in the former Soviet Union, where there were no mechanisms for challenging the government.

The EPA, states, and citizens have tried to force the Department of Energy to honor environmental and health standards, but complex legal issues are involved. There is an ongoing debate about the authority of one agency (particularly EPA) over another in environmental matters. Under the Reagan and Bush administrations, the White House limited EPA's ability to force other federal agencies to comply with environmental regulations. The Supreme Court has consistently upheld a very narrow interpretation of the constitutional principle of sovereign immunity, which constrains the ability of states or citizens to force the federal government to comply, or to collect penalties for noncompliance. In September 1992 the Federal Facilities Compliance Act was enacted; this law establishes the right for EPA or states to sue federal facilities for violation of certain environmental standards. In 1992-1993, court rulings involving Ohio and Colorado somewhat expanded states' authority regarding federal sites within their borders. The balance of federal-state authority is evolving.

In the late 1980s the Energy Department finally started giving more serious attention to cleanup. Its FY 1989 cleanup budget was $1.7 billion, climbing to $4.4 billion in FY 1992. It planned to spend about $5.5 billion in FY 1993. By mid 1992 estimates for cleaning up known contamination, which have been escalating rapidly, stood at hundreds of billions of dollars over a thirty-year period. The five-year plan (1993-1997) does not offer a total cost estimate. As with DOD cleanups, assessments are not complete and estimates depend on assumptions about cleanup levels.

According to a GAO official, between 1980 and 1990 GAO issued more than seventy separate assessments of DOE problems in reports and congressional testimony. In a 1991 report DOE's Advisory Committee on Nuclear Facility Safety found continuing deficiencies in programs to protect human health and the environment. GAO and the Office of Technology Assessment (OTA)—both congressional agencies—have found that, despite recent significant reforms and programs, DOE still lacks the management tools to do this massive job properly.[16] Private sector and government officials responsible for weapons production (and contamination) in the past are in some cases being chosen for cleanup efforts.[17]

How to dispose of DOE's nuclear wastes safely is a thorny issue, technically and politically. Two sites have been targeted by the federal government as permanent repositories. The first is the Waste Isolation Pilot Project (WIPP) in New Mexico, built more than two thousand feet underground in the desert to store nuclear wastes from atomic weapons production that are contaminated with plutonium. This site has cost the public about $1 billion but had not yet received its first shipment by early 1993. Many technical experts believe the site is completely safe and was overengineered because of political concerns; they emphasize that WIPP will store only relatively low-level transuranic wastes. But opponents raise safety issues, or those involving oversight and compensation for New Mexico. There is considerable public skepticism about DOE's assurances of safety, given its record. The controversy in Congress has been fierce as competing oversight committees fight over jurisdiction; and substantive issues regarding safety standards, compensation, and EPA's role in DOE oversight delayed action.[18] In New Mexico, some resent being chosen as the nation's dump, charging that the federal government imposed its will on the state. The state legally prevented shipments of waste for several months in 1991.

Yucca Mountain, Nevada, is the second proposed permanent repository. This site is for high-level radioactive wastes. Preparations for this facility are further behind, and it is similarly embroiled in controversy. Nevada has also delayed federal activity through its permitting process. Until disposal issues are resolved, there can be no long-term solution to the cleanup problems at DOE facilities. The United States currently has no place for these highly contaminated wastes, so DOE faces strong political pressures from states with DOE nuclear facilities to remove wastes from cleanup activities as well as from any continuing nuclear weapons production.

The significance of these issues goes beyond past contamination of the ecosystem. The huge cost of remediation means that expenditures on other national programs are precluded. The distrust of DOD and DOE engendered by environmental abuses will have long-lasting consequences, affecting public acceptance of not only their cleanup programs, but of other activities relating to national security as well.

Disarmament

One of the most difficult security and environment problems facing the United States and the former USSR is getting rid of existing arsenals. Both nations reduced their stocks of weaponry in the past through sales to other nations, dumping, or burning. Indeed, a great deal of concern has been expressed both within and outside the former Soviet Union (now partially reconstituted as the Commonwealth of Independent States [CIS]) that sales (both legal and black market) from the CIS might escalate under the tremendous economic and political pressures they are experiencing. Such sales are constantly rumored. The greatest fear involves nuclear armaments. The precarious political structure and fragmented control resulting from the breakup of the Soviet empire exacerbates the threat, including the possibility of sales to terrorist groups. A related fear is that nuclear scientists from the former Soviet Union will be drawn to other nations and thereby aid in the spread of nuclear weapons. Proliferation increases environmental as well as political risks. Yet, at the same time, the opportunity for arms reduction has not been this great since 1945. For the first time since the end of World War II, both the United States and the former Soviet Union seem determined to reduce stockpiles, both conventional and nuclear. U.S.-CIS arms control agreements raise a difficult set of problems about the disposal of weapons in an environmentally safe manner. The problem goes beyond the territories of the two former adversaries. Germany, both East and West, has stockpiles of armaments, some going back to World War II. The location of many older armaments is not known (some are buried), and they might not be stable.

Disposal of chemical and nuclear weaponry has been widely discussed over the past few years. Biological weapons are still an issue but are generally believed to be a less pressing concern. By 1972 they had already been banned by the Biological Weapons Convention Treaty (signed by 111 nations, including the superpowers), which prohibits development, production, and stockpiling. In the 1980s both the United States and the USSR continued research and development, ostensibly for "defensive" and not "offensive" purposes. Some scientists assert that this distinction is not possible or legitimate. In any case, public protests have limited activities.

Stockpiles of chemical and nuclear weapons in the CIS and the United States are very large, and substantial technical and logistical (as well as political) problems remain to be resolved. Given the dismal state of the economies in the former Soviet republics, much of the money to finance these expensive undertakings may have to come from the rich industrial nations. The CIS appears anxious about securing such assistance.

Chemical Weapons

U.S. efforts to deal with the destruction of chemical weapons (nerve and blister agents) started in the early 1980s and were broadened as tensions with the USSR relaxed; eventually an estimated 22,680 metric tons were destroyed. The United States and CIS agreed in principle in 1992 to eliminate these highly toxic weapons, though the processes for doing so have not yet been determined. For many years the United States disposed of unwanted chemical weapons by various means, including open burning and ocean dumping; the last dumping was in 1970.[19] The USSR disposed of many of its chemical weapons in the ocean. Discussions are under way regarding how to handle large numbers of chemical weapons dumped in the Baltic Sea, where massive amounts were deposited after World War II, and are now feared to be an environmental time bomb in that valuable ecosystem.

By 1984 the U.S. Army, which has responsibility for disposing of these weapons, chose incineration as the best option. After approximately four years of assessment and public consultation under the National Environmental Policy Act (NEPA), the army started a pilot project (a sophisticated automated incinerator) at Johnston Atoll in the Pacific. Judging it the least risky approach, the army decided to build incinerators at the eight continental U.S. locations with chemical weapons. Predictably, localities want to be rid of the toxins but fear on-site destruction. The army has concluded that moving these wastes to a distant disposal site poses far greater risks than on-site destruction. Timeliness is also a factor, as some of these weapons are unstable, especially those with propellants, and delay increases the chances for leaks or other mishaps.

The pilot phase has taken longer than planned, and costs for the entire project have soared. The stockpile at Johnston Atoll increased as Germany insisted that U.S. chemical weapons on its soil be moved there for destruction. As time passes and costs continue to mount (more than $6 billion over the next decade), political forces are gathering. The latest Senate proposal would not only extend the deadline to 2004 but also force a reevaluation of the army's decision to incinerate in place because of local pressure to ship the weapons elsewhere for destruction.[20] Small island nations near Johnston Atoll oppose using it as the hazardous waste receptacle; they fear that, despite promises to the contrary, incineration at the atoll will continue even after the weapons currently stored there are all burned. These same peoples saw Pacific islands used for U.S. nuclear testing and do not want their ecosystem to be placed at risk again for U.S. convenience. Several alternative techniques are under development, but they are not near readiness and their feasibility is not assured.

The CIS faces parallel difficulties and more serious cost limitations. Public opposition closed the plant it intended to use. Neutralization and controlled underground nuclear explosions are two disposal methods being discussed in the CIS. The former was used for several years in the United States and abandoned as slow, costly, and unreliable (it also leaves vast amounts of hazardous waste); the second method is rejected outright by most people but is seriously supported by others as the best option.

Nuclear Weapons

Estimates of current nuclear arsenals vary. The CIS may not know how many warheads or how much weapons material it has stockpiled; the U.S. government will not disclose a total. The CIS is said to have a total of 25,000 to 30,000 nuclear warheads. One source suggests that the United States has produced about 60,000 warheads since World War II. Both sides may eventually reduce their stockpiles to about 3,000 to 4,000 warheads each.

As with chemical weapons, options for the disposal of nuclear warheads are unattractive and even less technically sound. Both the United States and the CIS have agreed to dismantle a large portion of their arsenals. Political and environmental problems afflict their storage and transport, their dismantling, and the disposal of their component parts in an environmentally safe manner. Nuclear proliferation is one threat, along with misuse, mishap, or secret rearmament. Some suggest that the International Atomic Energy Agency, whose credibility and strength have increased considerably with its role in Iraq, might evolve to deal with some of these issues. Some materials might be sold for nuclear power, but only if made unfit for reprocessing into weapons. In any case, the world has more processed materials than it is likely to use commercially for some time, particularly if fears about nuclear energy continue to slow that industry. Under any foreseeable approach, many weapons will have to be stored indefinitely. The Bush administration resolved a number of important issues with the CIS; as of late 1992, however, no clear set of procedures was in place—verification being one obvious area of vagueness and indecision.[21]

Nuclear armaments development and testing, to which the Bush administration remained committed, is controversial on political and economic as well as environmental grounds. Continued U.S. weapons development raises some caution and distrust in the CIS regarding its own disarmament and test ban policies. Environmental consequences did not seem to figure in the U.S. decision. A major motive might be to protect the industry and its jobs; traditional national security concerns about maintaining overall production capability might also have affected the decision. The Clinton administration's policy is still evolving. The new president has enthusiastically endorsed arms reduction. But he has also promised to keep U.S. defense technically superior, which some argue could require testing. Congress established a nine-month moratorium in FY 1993 and plans to end testing by 1996. Some in the Clinton administration are advocating limited underground testing after 1996; the issue is still under debate. Political instability in the CIS and the technical difficulties of disposing of nuclear weapons will undoubtedly make nuclear armaments a continuing issue for negotiation.

The Environmental Consequences of War

Limiting the development, production, or testing of weapons based on environmental impacts has proved very difficult. Even more difficult is limiting the conduct of hostilities abroad. The environmental costs of military actions, particularly warfare, have dramatically increased as a result of modern weaponry. Military strategy over the past few decades has magnified environmental destruction by emphasizing the use of high volumes of munitions against ill-defined targets.[22] Studies conducted in numerous battle areas years after hostilities confirm that the toll on human life and the environment continues long after the fighting stops.

Environmental damage has frequently been a strategic or punitive aim in warfare—from the Romans salting the soil of Carthage to the United States denuding Vietnam of tree cover. Whether or not the environment is a direct target, warfare brings profound and long-term destruction. Concern about environmental damage in foreign lands does not seem to be a significant factor when nations decide to go to war, however. Rarely are environmental effects calculated (attention to environmental impacts during the Gulf war was unusual), yet the costs are extraordinarily high. Land and water damage last for many years or even permanently, species are depleted, ecosystems are disrupted or destroyed. Large numbers of weapons do not explode on impact but will do so if disturbed. In place, shells pose risks of leaking chemicals and metals into soil and groundwater. In addition to severely diminished soil productivity, farmers are hampered by unexploded bombs, which cause injuries and death for many years after the hostilities stop. Animals continue to be victims of unexploded munitions or of toxins from the war. In one Vietnamese province, for instance, three hundred people and one thousand water buffalo were killed by explosions during a twelve-month period after the war. Fifteen years later there were still new victims. To find and clean up contaminants and unexploded munitions, some in urban areas, is an expensive and dangerous undertaking. The United States seeded eleven thousand sea mines in Haiphong Harbor and in inland waterways. Subsequent recovery in the harbor took a large naval task force five months, even though mines were laid with recovery in mind.[23]

Vietnam and the Gulf war provide recent examples of the extensive nature of modern warfare's impacts. Both Vietnam and Iraq were subjected to an extraordinary barrage of weapons. In Vietnam, 13 million tons of bombs left 25 million bomb craters. Nineteen million gallons of herbicides (including Agent Orange) were spread over the countryside. The United States and South Vietnam also bulldozed and napalmed huge areas. The land was stripped, including an estimated 5.43 million acres of tropical forest. Some estimate that 80 percent of Vietnam's forests and swamplands were destroyed. Today, about 40 percent remains deforested. Waterways were mined. Many babies have been born deformed; in a heavily sprayed area near the Cambodian border, a National Academy of Sciences study after the war found sixty-four out of one thousand babies were born braindead. Babies with serious defects are still being born. The war and the economic blockade promoted poaching, which continued long after the war ended. Conditions of desperation and struggle resulted in ongoing erosion and destruction of forests, rice fields, and other food sources. Years after the war, devastating scars on the environment and disruption of ecosystems are still evident. With a population that is 85 percent farmers, 20 percent of agricultural land is still unusable.[24]

The Gulf war provides another example, perhaps second only to the Vietnam War in destruction of wildlife—estimated at 15,000 to 30,000 of various bird species and 8,000 (of 10,000) of Kuwait's camels. The greatest impacts on animals are not from direct killings (though there were many in the Gulf war) but from habitat destruction.[25] Oil wells that were booby-trapped or bombed resulted in fires and spills; 4 to 8 million barrels of oil were spilled into the sea. The smoke plume reached several miles high and emitted tens of thousands of tons of sulfur dioxide and other gases per day for several months. The oil and burning oil wells brought severe damage to nearly five hundred miles of coastline, causing great harm to a fragile marine ecosystem as well as loss of marine life and birds. Some deem the Gulf war a greater environmental disaster than Vietnam.[26]

The war was conducted primarily through air power, with massive tonnage of bombs dropped over very wide areas. In six weeks, one thousand bombing missions were flown, dropping six thousand bombs that contained more than two thousand tons of munitions.[27] In addition to the many human deaths, massive bombing in the desert and disruption from heavy equipment, armaments and troops (almost 2 million) destroyed delicate balances in the ecosystem from which it may not recover. In addition to toxic pollutants from equipment, which might seep through sandy soil to aquifers, large volumes of solid waste and sewage were suddenly added to the desert environment.

Devastation from war creates poverty and disease, and it disrupts social, economic, and political infrastructures. A weakened nation is often a target for attack from internal and external enemies. All of these factors contribute to instability, reducing international security in the region. Such conditions can lead to the emergence of aggressive leaders to divert attention from issues at home. Victory may well come at the cost of long-term animosity, which will continue to fuel security threats far into the future.

States have been reluctant to accept limits on the use of weaponry during war, particularly if such limits might prolong battle. International sanctions are weak or nonexistent, though there are some internationally recognized limits to legitimate military destruction. For example, the Geneva Protocol I of 1977 prohibits warfare that can be expected to result in widespread, long-term, and severe damage to the environment, especially that which endangers human life. The Convention on the Prohibition of Military or Any Other Hostile Use of Environmental Modification Techniques seeks to outlaw manipulation of natural processes for hostile purposes when it would have widespread, severe, and long-lasting effects. Though enforcement mechanisms are weak, particularly given the ambiguity of treaty terms, there is international consensus that nations should respect such limits. That is, an emerging international public opinion acts as something of a check on governments.

It is notable that environmental tactics and consequences were widely discussed during the preparation and conduct of the Gulf war. According to Greenpeace, this unprecedented level of attention "reflected the global rise of environmental awareness, due in part to urgent warnings from the environmental movement and the scientific establishment about crises in the natural environment, and of mankind's global destructive capacity."[28] Criticism of the United States for the use of herbicides in Vietnam seems to have affected U.S. conduct of the Gulf war. The U.S. government was vocal in opposing Iraqi "environmental terrorism" and talked of bringing Iraqis accused of environmental atrocities to an international tribunal. It was less eager, however, to inform the public of the great environmental destruction caused by allied war actions. Some charge that the U.S. government made a concerted effort to stifle information; the lack of Iraqi casualty estimates is one example. Perhaps the United States feared that the scope of the damage would diminish public support for the war or trust in U.S. ability to deliver surgical strategic strikes with little civilian destruction.

The ultimate environmental catastrophe facing the planet is a large-scale thermonuclear war. Much has been written about probable or possible effects on the environment. Aside from near-term consequences of massive human casualties, poisoned air and airborne particles, poisoned crops and croplands, and radioactive rain and water supplies, scientists have speculated about long-term effects on the atmosphere and on weather patterns. Many scientists agree that the dust storms and particulate concentrations would block out vital sunlight and dramatically lower temperatures in much of the Northern Hemisphere, creating a so-called nuclear winter. If thermonuclear reactions blanketed the Earth in clouds of ash and soot, most living things under the cloud would die. This vision of a dying planet has been a powerful force in antinuclear movements. The possibility of nuclear winter, of near-destruction of the global environment through warfare, emphasizes the radical insecurity on which nuclear security in the Cold War was built.

Changing Policy

Over the past few years, the intimate connection between security and environmental integrity has been much more widely acknowledged in the United States—even in establishment publications, among government officials, and in the military. Articles in the *New York Times* and *Washington Post* have addressed the changing definition of national security and the destabilizing potential of environmental problems, internally and internationally. This evolution of opinion has coincided largely with the discovery of widespread toxic damage associated with defense activities. The demise of the Cold War also permitted revelations about the profound extent of environmental destruction in the former Soviet bloc. In addition, widespread press coverage of the 1992 Earth summit in Río de Janeiro stressed the link between security and the environment. Given that governments change very slowly, it is particularly important to look at signs of change in this sector.

Policymakers

In the August 1991 "National Security Strategy of the United States," President Bush stressed the need to broaden the United States' understanding of national security in light of the increased interdependence of the world. It is instructive to note, however, that despite the report's initial emphasis on important changes in the world, President Bush's outline of U.S. security objectives made scant mention of environmental challenges and issues; where they are mentioned, it is as a subtopic to "national security and economic strength." Environment merits no separate attention in the section on trends where it is especially relevant. The focus of this document was still primarily on military, economic, and alliance strength and reflected no appreciation of the profound influence and importance of environmental degradation on economic and political strength. President Bush also ignored the environment in his August 1992 speech accepting his party's nomination for reelection.

More dramatic prospects in presidential policy are evident in the election of Bill Clinton and in his choice for vice president, Al Gore. Gore is known as a strong environmental advocate, one who clearly sees environmental protection as a component of security; he criticized the Bush administration for its lack of leadership at the Earth summit. As one indication of policy change, Clinton has now endorsed the biodiversity treaty, which Bush refused to sign (chaps. 4 and 17).

There are other developments as well. One is in the mission and function of the intelligence community. A White House memorandum, signed by President Bush, referred to "dramatic changes in U.S. defense planning" and the breakup of the Soviet empire and notes the consequent growing interest "in our intelligence services tackling new issues and problems." Principal policy officials were asked to identify their intelligence support needs, looking to nontraditional areas of interest; the suggested list began with "environment, natural resource scarcities."[29]

Congress is reflecting a similar awareness and has taken several actions recognizing the importance and complexity of DOD and DOE environmental activities and the growing public interest and concern with these matters. One sign is that members of Congress have asked the GAO and OTA for a large number of studies on DOD and DOE environmental cleanup and compliance programs. Another clear signal of redirection is the Strategic Environmental Research and Development Program (SERDP). This program attracted bipartisan support to earmark national security expenditures for environmental research and development. Speaking for the program on the Senate floor, Sen. Sam Nunn (D-Ga.) presented it as part of the peace dividend, reasoning that with changes in defense requirements, we can "redirect this tremendous national resource toward the environmental challenges we face in the 1990s"; he called reversing the growing rate of destruction "a key national security objective."[30] Senator Nunn recognized that "a new and different threat to our national security [is] emerging—the destruction of the environment." He argued that the defense establishment should be at the forefront of environmental activity, because (1) environmental problems threaten national and international security, (2) the defense establishment has unique data collection and technology capabilities, and (3) it helped to create the problems in the first place.

Public opinion is also changing. The managing editor of a defense journal reported in 1991 that "the U.S. public now considers global envi-

ronmental issues as the greatest threat to national security."[31] That conclusion is supported by the 1990 Roper survey on the environment, which
found that environmental concerns ranked fourth on a list of national
priorities, above traditional military concerns regarding arms control and
limiting nuclear weapons, or improving relations with Russia.[32] Reflective
of this shifting climate of opinion, Earth summit secretary-general Mau-
rice Strong identified as one of the three major shortcomings of the Río
conference its failure to deal with military activities and their contribution
to environmental degradation.[33]

Progress is slow, but the issue is taking hold in the military as well.
DOD leadership has begun to recognize that fulfilling its traditional mission of protecting the nation has environmental implications. This includes minimizing the environmental impact of defense activities at home
and abroad and practicing stewardship of the lands DOD holds in trust.
Public tolerance for abuses has decreased. Convictions for violation of
environmental standards at Aberdeen Proving Ground in the late 1980s
and tighter enforcement of the Endangered Species Act (with two army
personnel indicted in 1992) are clear signals of stricter environmental
accountability. Public opposition to allocating new lands for military use
will likely increase if perceived abuses continue.

The Military and the "Peace Dividend"

As military budgets shrink, DOD must find more creative, less re-
source-intensive ways to guarantee national security. The army, for example, is looking beyond cleanup and compliance for ways to prolong the
useful life of training facilities, and to train with minimum disruption to
the ecosystem. It has developed environmental training programs and
sophisticated computer-modeling systems to evaluate the carrying capacity of its installations.

Furthermore, in a time of cutbacks, self-interest suggests that the
military will identify ways that its expertise and programs best serve
evolving national needs. Army long-range planning documents have begun including environmental assessments as part of their analytical framework. The assistant secretary of the army (for installations, logistics, and
the environment) delivered a speech to army personnel in September of
1991 on the environmental dimensions of national security. Primary motivations for this change are not necessarily environmental. Some argue that
the military should seriously address the link between security and environmental considerations because a "threat to U.S. national security could
well occur as a result of the environmental movement's impact upon the
Army."[34]

The future of defense spending has important implications for national
security and the environment. A smaller defense establishment would reduce environmental impacts from research and development, manufactur-

ing, training, and equipment. Lower defense spending could free funds for environmental projects and research; or there might be a larger infusion of funds for cleanup activities. The disintegration of the Soviet Union and the widely hailed "outbreak of peace" encouraged the United States to expect large defense reductions over the next few years. This expectation has led to considerable speculation and debate about the best uses of the "peace dividend." A major issue has been whether the funds should be used to retire the U.S. debt, to support domestic programs, particularly education and rebuilding the infrastructure, or be channeled to the private sector (for example, through tax cuts).[35] Some support the policy embodied in the SERDP program—to convert defense expertise in research and development to environmental programs. How quickly or successfully such a conversion could happen is a matter of debate. Clinton has endorsed a transition from military to environmental productivity. Because environmental products are believed to be an area of economic growth internationally, the Clinton administration has announced that it will pursue a conversion strategy for at least some portion of the defense establishment.

DOD's budget has experienced some cutbacks, and a downsizing in personnel levels is now under way. It should be noted, however, that these reductions began from the plateau of the Reagan administration's defense buildup. The government has not yet moved toward large cutbacks, especially when compared with other post-war cuts in defense spending. Therefore, the question of how to spend the peace dividend has yet to emerge in any real sense. Furthermore, several aspects of U.S. defense obligations may swallow any savings from canceled or downsized programs for years to come, particularly if the massive DOE cleanup program is counted in this equation. One is the high cost of the Desert Storm operation that delayed downsizing. Another is the U.S. decision to increase military operations under U.N. auspices, as in the December 1992 intervention in Somalia. A third element is that expected payoffs from closing bases have diminished as the nation realized that, in addition to the costs for planning and executing the moves, the government would have to remediate many of those sites before walking away, much less before selling them. It is also clear that taxpayers will have to pay for cleanups at active DOD and DOE sites for decades to come. Finally, current policy calls for DOE to continue to produce weapons and to conduct research on nuclear systems. Restarting the old plants or building new ones will be very expensive. And greater public and state oversight would necessitate increased expenditures for environmental compliance at operating facilities.

There is some good news as well. Funds used to develop new technologies and techniques for environmental cleanup and perhaps for disarmament will be transferable in large part to the private sector. These federal resources could have a positive effect on the U.S. economy, subsidizing cleanups in the private sector and increasing U.S. industry's ability to compete for available cleanup funds in eastern Europe and the CIS.

Conclusion

Environmental issues are slowly becoming part of our national security vocabulary, though the environment is not yet an integrated, much less central, part of security thinking in the United States. In industrial nations, environmental quality is a popular and well-developed theme, and governments have redirected programs to address at least some of the defense-related pollution. But they have not substantially modified their ideas about the sources of power and stability, nor have they incorporated concepts of sustainability and environmental integrity into their defense assumptions and programs. That sound ecosystems are essential to survival is most obvious to marginalized populations; but populations struggling for survival are forced to deplete their ecosystems further, to do whatever is necessary to meet immediate needs. Richer nations or groups may assume they are not yet stressing the limits, or may not recognize limits, as they expect to find technological alternatives before crisis strikes, or they may simply be callous to the severe environmental stress their activities cause elsewhere.

At the rhetorical level, at least, governments profess that they are trying to meet environmental challenges and understand that environmental protection is fundamental to the stability of the planet's life systems. Taking the concept of environmental security seriously would have a profound effect on how nations define problems and acceptable alternatives for action. It would influence not only how they allocate resources but also how they define and control their power and interests and, consequently, design their military defense operations. This entails much broader implications for the range of foreign and domestic policies that affect the use and abuse of natural resources as well—from trade relations to loan policies to domestic policies promoting or subsidizing products or activities. Recognizing the legitimacy of ecological considerations in security policy will surely not guarantee their resolution, or even a consensus for taking action. Perceptions about the issues at stake, the urgency of solving various problems, and who should pay vary widely. But a better definition is the first step to changing policy.

Governments are usually slow to act, particularly when large costs or powerful interests are involved, and they will probably be pulled along rather than lead. A loose international network of nongovernmental organizations (NGOs) is very active in environmental issues, and their influence has been growing. Some organizations have become quite sophisticated in the use of political techniques, including mass media. Greenpeace, for example, has been able to garner considerable support because of its education efforts and its effectiveness in presenting symbols and images to move public opinion.

Experience with global environmental issues, such as CFCs, a growing scientific consensus on global environmental problems, increasing numbers of political and social elites who want to place more emphasis on ecology, and strong public opinion for environmental protection are all indicators that change may be possible. Additional factors are the growing influence of environmental NGOs, the increasingly vocal call of poor nations, and the sheer cost of traditional military defense. If these fragmented elements do not combine to push nations in a new direction, it may be that a momentous environmental catastrophe will be needed to provide a sufficiently strong impetus for change.

Notes

Michael Renner's thoughts, quoted in the chapter epigraph, were taken from his article, "National Security: The Economic and Environmental Dimensions," *Worldwatch Paper* 89 (May 1989): 29-30.

1. World Commission on Environment and Development (Brundtland Commission), *Our Common Future* (New York: Oxford University Press, 1990), 6-7, 19.
2. Lester Brown, "Redefining National Security," *Worldwatch Paper* 14 (Washington, D.C.: Worldwatch, 1977).
3. Renner, "National Security," 6, 7.
4. Lynton K. Caldwell, *In Defense of Earth: International Protection of the Biosphere* (Bloomington: Indiana University Press, 1972; exp. version, in *International Environmental Policy*, 2d ed., Durham, N.C.: Duke University Press, 1990).
5. Lynton K. Caldwell, *Between Two Worlds* (New York: Cambridge University Press, 1990), 67-69.
6. Stockholm International Peace Research Institute (SIPRI), "The Global Ecology," in *Warfare in a Fragile World* (London: Taylor and Francis, 1980); see also Arthur H. Westing, "Global Resources and International Conflict: An Overview," in *Global Resources and International Conflict*, ed. Arthur H. Westing (New York: Oxford University Press, 1986).
7. Jessica Tuchman Mathews, "Redefining Security," *Foreign Affairs* 68 (Spring 1989): 162-177; see also Mathews's "Nations and Nature: A New Look at Global Security" (Twenty-first J. Robert Oppenheimer Memorial Lecture, Los Alamos, N.M., August 12, 1991).
8. James Kitfield, "The Environmental Cleanup Quagmire," *Military Forum* 5 (April 1989): 37; Vincent P. Grimes, "DOD Cleans Up," *National Defense* 76 (September 1991): 9; Kent H. Butts, "The Army and the Environment: National Security Implications" (Carlisle, Pa.: U.S. Army War College, June 3, 1991), 16.
9. General Accounting Office (GAO), "Federal Facilities: Issues Involved in Cleaning Up Hazardous Waste," Testimony by Richard L. Hembra Before the House Subcommittee on Investigations and Oversight, Committee on Public Works and Transportation, July 28, 1992, 4 (GAO/T-RCED-92-82); subsequently referenced as GAO, "Federal Facilities."
10. Statements by Thomas E. Baca, deputy assistant secretary of defense (environment) and Lewis D. Walker, deputy assistant secretary of the army (environment, safety, and occupational health), Defense Subcommittee, Senate Appropriations Committee, May 12, 1992; see also DOD, *Defense Environmental Restoration Program*, annual report to Congress for FY 1991, February 1992 (ADA 244196).
11. GAO, "Federal Facilities."
12. Office of Technology Assessment (OTA), *Complex Cleanup: The Environmental Legacy of Nuclear Weapons Production*, summary, February 1991 (OTA-O-484).

13. U.S. Department of Energy, *Environmental Restoration and Waste Management Five-Year Plan for FY 1993-1997*, August 1991, 48 (FYP DOE/S-0089P).

14. Karen Dorn Steele, "Hanford: America's Nuclear Graveyard," *Bulletin of the Atomic Scientists* 45 (October 1989): 17.

15. Bryan Abas, "Rocky Flats: A Big Mistake From Day One," *Bulletin of the Atomic Scientists* (December 1989): 18-24; see also "Mayak Military Plant's Waste Irradiated 500,000," *Foreign Broadcast Information Service: Central Eurasia*, daily report 92-112, June 10, 1992, 3-4, reprinted from *Kyodo*.

16. Victor S. Rezendes, "Long Road to Recovery Begins at DOE Plants," *Forum for Applied Research and Public Policy* 6 (Spring 1991): 19; OTA, *Complex Cleanup*; "DOE Lacks Tools to Manage Cleanup Costs at Nuclear Weapons Sites, GAO Report Says," *Environment Reporter* 23 (June 12, 1992): 650-651.

17. Dick Russell, "In the Shadow of the Bomb," *Amicus Journal* 12 (Fall 1990): 27-28; Brian Bremmer, "Spoils of Peace: A Texas Tussle," *Business Week*, March 9, 1992, 87-88; see also "If You Can't Build Weapons, Destroy 'Em," *Business Week*, March 9, 1992, 86-87.

18. Elizabeth A. Palmer, "Senate Clears Bill to Start Tests at New Mexico Nuclear Dump," *Congressional Quarterly*, October 10, 1992, 3156.

19. S. A. Carnes and A. P. Watson, "Disposing of the U.S. Chemical Weapons Stockpile," *Journal of the American Medical Association* 262:5, August 4, 1989, 653-659; S. A. Carnes, "Disposing of Chemical Weapons: A Desired End in Search of an Acceptable Means," *Environmental Professional* 11 (1989): 279-290; and S. A. Carnes, "NEPA Compliance for the Chemical Stockpile Disposal Program," 434-446.

20. National Defense Authorization Act for 1993, Bill S.3114, August 1992.

21. Spurgeon M. Keeny and Wolfgang K. H. Panofsky, "Controlling Nuclear Warheads and Materials: Steps Toward a Comprehensive Regime," *Arms Control Today* 22 (January-February 1992): 3-9; Christopher Paine and Thomas Cochran, "So Little Time, So Many Weapons, So Much To Do," *Bulletin of the Atomic Scientists* 48 (January-February 1992): 13-16.

22. SIPRI, *Warfare;* and Harry H. Almond, Jr., "Weapons, War and the Environment," *Georgetown International Environmental Law Review* 3 (Summer 1990).

23. Arthur H. Westing, "Explosive Remnants of War: An Overview," in *Explosive Remnants of War*, ed., Arthur Westing (London: Taylor and Francis, 1985), 6-7; see also Westing et al., "Explosive Remnants of Conventional War: A Report to UNEP," in ibid.; and John M. Miller, *The Hidden Casualties: The Environmental Consequences of the Gulf Conflict*, vol. 1 (San Francisco: Arms Control Research Center, 1991), 21.

24. Richard Wolkomir and Joyce Wolkomir, "Caught in the Crossfire," *International Wildlife* 22 (January-February 1992): 4-11; and "Vietnam—Legacy of Agent Orange," ECONET, July 13, 1992, reprinted from *Worldnews*, citing Elizabeth Kemp, *Months of Pure Light*.

25. Wolkomir and Wolkomir, "Caught in the Crossfire," 4-11.

26. Kristen Ostling and Joanna Miller, *Taking Stock: The Impact of Militarism on the Environment*, Science for Peace Report (Toronto: University of Toronto, February 1992), 3.

27. William M. Arkin, Damian Durrant, and Marianne Cherni, *On Impact: Modern Warfare and the Environment, A Case Study of the Gulf War* (New York: Greenpeace, 1991), 6.

28. Ibid., 1.

29. White House memorandum signed by George Bush, November 15, 1991.

30. Senator Sam Nunn, Senate Floor Speech, June 28, 1990.

31. Grimes, "DOD Cleans Up," 9-11.

32. Roper Survey, "The Environment: Public Attitudes and Individual Behavior" (The Roper Organization, July 1990).
33. John Miller, "Bypassing UNCED on Militarism," ECONET, July 14, 1992, reprinted from *Peace News.*
34. Butts, "Army and the Environment," 1.
35. C. Alan Garner, "The Effect of U.S. Defense Cuts on the Standard of Living," *Economic Review* 76 (Federal Reserve Bank of Kansas City, January-February 1991): 33-47; Karen Pennar and Michael J. Mandel, "The Peace Economy," *Business Week*, December 11, 1989, 50-55; Mark A. Wynne, "The Long-Run Effects of a Permanent Change in Defense Purchases," *Economic Review* (Federal Reserve Bank of Dallas, January 1991): 1-16.

V. ENVIRONMENTAL ETHICS
AND THE FUTURE

16

Environmental Values and Public Policy
Robert C. Paehlke

A corporation wants to locate in your community but would alter a wetland habitat for its new facility. Should your municipal government approve construction in that location? Epidemiological evidence suggests that releases of a particular chemical would likely induce a small number of cancers per 1 million human exposures. Avoiding future releases will cost millions of dollars. What should be done? In this latter case, some would argue, even a portion of the money involved might save more lives if it were spent on medical research. These are the sorts of questions that arise when one thinks about the ethical dimensions of environmental politics.

Recently the problems confronting environmental ethics have grown even larger. For example, because the world's climate may be negatively affected by carbon dioxide (CO_2) emissions, many new questions arise. Should we increase the taxes on gasoline in order to encourage more selective automobile use? Should government subsidize fuel-efficient forms of public transportation? Should Vice President Al Gore, as an environmentalist, oppose (presumably quietly) President Bill Clinton's proposed infrastructure expenditures on the grounds that highway construction provides a subsidy to automobiles (and thereby increases CO_2 emissions)? It is vitally important that citizens and decisionmakers learn to think ethically about environmental matters.

This chapter treats environmental politics as an expression of a set of values. It presumes David Easton's definition of politics as the authoritative allocation of values.[1] It sets out the value dimensions of contemporary environmentalism and identifies some of the difficult issues that the wide acceptance of these values urges onto the political agenda.[2] It also develops a framework for integrating these values with other prominent political values. This framework might be called a "triple E" perspective, for environment, economy, and equity.

Much of nineteenth and early- to mid-twentieth-century politics centered on the struggles between economic values (capital accumulation, enhanced trade, economic growth) and equity values (wages, working conditions, social welfare, public health, and public education). Although these issues have not been resolved, it might be argued that with the end of the Cold War, other issues and tensions will come to the fore. Two sets of issues are of particular concern to us here—those that arise between environment and economy, on the one hand, and environment and equity on the other. Points of mutual support as well as of conflict occur in both cases. There is little doubt, however, that many contemporary political issues can be better understood within this wider framework.

The Principal Dimensions of Contemporary Environmental Values

Historians as well as philosophers have observed that the contemporary environmental movement is based on a transformation of human social values. The historian Samuel Hays noted that new values, rooted in the advances in prosperity and educational levels following World War II, have emerged in virtually all wealthy societies.[3] Others have suggested that these recent value shifts run deeper than those that sustained the earlier conservation movement. The philosopher George Sessions has concluded that the ecological "revolution" is fundamentally religious and philosophical and involves "a radical critique of the basic assumptions of modern western society."[4] More recently many analysts have suggested that the churches must take an important role in environmental politics if they wish to remain the leading institution within which values are considered.[5]

Using opinion survey instruments, Ronald Inglehart and other social scientists have measured related shifts in popular attitudes, postulating a "silent revolution" that entails the spread of "postmaterialist" values.[6] Riley Dunlap, Lester Milbrath, and others have identified a "new environmental paradigm."[7] Whatever name one attaches to the change, the environmental movement is the political manifestation of a significant shift in societal values.

But what values constitute the essential core of an environmental perspective? In an earlier work, I set out a list of thirteen central environmental values, and others have developed lists similar to this one:

1. An appreciation of all life forms and a view that the complexities of the ecological web of life are politically salient.
2. A sense of humility regarding the human species in relation to other species and to the global ecosystem.
3. A concern with the quality of human life and health, including an emphasis on the importance of preventive medicine, diet, and exercise to the maintenance and enhancement of human health.
4. A global rather than a nationalist or isolationist view.
5. Some preference for political and/or population decentralization.

6. An extended time horizon—a concern about the long-term future of the world and its life.
7. A sense of urgency regarding the survival of life on Earth, both long term and short term.
8. A belief that human societies ought to be reestablished on a more sustainable technical and physical basis. An appreciation that many aspects of our present way of life are fundamentally transitory.
9. A revulsion toward waste in the face of human need (in more extreme forms, this may appear as asceticism).
10. A love of simplicity, although this does not include rejection of technology or "modernity."
11. An esthetic appreciation for season, setting, climate, and natural materials.
12. A measurement of esteem, including self-esteem and social merit, in terms of such nonmaterial values as skill, artistry, effort, or integrity.
13. An attraction to autonomy and self-management in human endeavors and, generally, an inclination to more democratic and participatory political processes and administrative structures.[8]

This list and others like it can be distilled to three core items: (1) the protection of biodiversity, ecological systems, and wilderness; (2) the minimization of negative impacts on human health; and (3) the establishment of sustainable patterns of resource use. These core items are relatively new as significant actors on the stage of political ideas. They are all ideas with an extended history but were for at least a century swamped by the larger ideological battles of left and right—over and between economy and equity.

Ecology as a Core Value

The first of the three core environmental values is captured to a large extent in the concept of ecology. All life forms are bound up each with the other in a complex, and frequently little understood, web of life. Fruit bats are essential to the propagation of many tropical trees and numerous other plant species in other climactic zones. Forests, in turn, help to determine the climate of the planet as a whole. The transformation of forest to agriculture in Latin America can dramatically affect migratory songbird populations in North America. The web of life ties all species together inextricably.

Human well-being, indeed human survival, depends on the success of an almost endless list of plant and animal species, often in ways we barely understand. Our global food reserves would endure for but a matter of months should our food production capabilities suddenly decline. That capability is determined in turn by rainfall and temperature, by the activities of many insect species such as bees, and by microbiological life within the soils of the planet. All of these in turn are affected by both plants and animals. Our well-being is determined by other species in other ways as well, not the least of which is our deep need for contact with, or awareness of the existence of, wild nature. The significant place of wild nature in human history has been captured in an important recent book by Max Oelschlaeger, who writes:

> By abandoning the view that nature is no more than an ecomachine or a stockpile of resources to fuel the human project, preservationists tend not to be bulls in an ecological china shop. They typically reject a strictly economic approach to valuing wilderness, and entertain other considerations such as rarity, species diversity, and even beauty. And by adopting a holistic view, preservationists are attentive to the pervasive linkages and interactions essential to any concept of a wilderness ecosystem.[9]

The deep ecologists, who express biocentric or ecocentric values, go further than this. They see preservationism (as distinct from the mere conservation of "resources") as itself anthropocentric and therefore suspect. In other words, biocentrism and ecocentrism go beyond strict preservationism by questioning "speciesism": the idea that humankind is somehow superior to, and therefore entitled to impose its values on, nature.[10] Deep ecology is a philosophical perspective that sees humans as no higher or lower than other life forms. All life forms are equally valued, and the ecological whole that they comprise cannot and should not be "managed" in the interests of any particular species.[11] Human interference in the natural processes of the living planet should be kept to a minimum. For some, animal rights and vegetarianism follow logically from a deep ecology perspective.

Consider some of the political and policy implications of a deep ecology perspective (or even a strict preservationist perspective). Should we continue to permit the cutting of forests? Forests, after all, from the perspective of other species, are home and indeed the source of life. Should we not, for example, strictly control the number of humans and the character of their transportation within wilderness areas, including national parks? Should we not disallow the testing of toxic substances on animals, and, indeed, all animal experimentation?[12] Should farmers be allowed to fill in hedgerows on their lands given that these provide corridors essential to the local survival of many animal species? What of filling in wetlands for shopping malls? And what of ultimate situations where humans and other species both require use of the same land for survival? The way we understand and value ecology clearly has very important political implications, and each of the questions posed above has gained in political salience in recent years. As Oelschlaeger put it in the preface to his book: "*The Idea of Wilderness* . . . is . . . subversive, for I have assumed that what the members of a democratic society think ultimately makes a difference."[13] Ideas and values, if widely shared, can establish a new political agenda.

Health as a Core Value

Where deep ecology values are presently a minority view, health, the second core belief of environmentalism, is not. The present era is highly health-conscious, and most Americans are concerned about their exposure to toxic chemicals. Strong parallels also exist between an increased interest in outdoor recreational activities and public concern regarding wilderness protection. Concerns regarding diet, food additives, and "natural" foods are often linked to environmental concerns regarding pesticides and herbicides. Keeping fit often produces an increased concern for air and water quality. Health is more than the absence of illness, and physical well-being is very hard to separate from environmental well-being.

Nonetheless, the minimization of impacts on human health can also be politically contentious. Here one might consider the opposing views of two noted social scientists. Aaron Wildavsky argues that in a clash between health values and wealth values, the latter should be encouraged by public policy. Wealth, in his view, largely determines health.[14] That is, the wealthier the nation, the healthier the nation. Wildavsky would thus never expend more public funds on health than the calculable value of the lives saved, or improved, by such expenditures. A contrasting view is put forward by Mark Sagoff. As he sees it, health and environmental protection must sometimes come first, economics second. In Sagoff's words:

> Since the New Deal, environmental law and policy have evolved as a continuous compromise between those who approach the protection of public health, safety, and the environment primarily in ethical terms and those who conceive it primarily in economic terms. The first attitude is moral: It regards hazardous pollution and environmental degradation as evils society must eliminate if it is to live up to its ideals and aspirations. The second attitude is prudential or practical. It argues that the benefits of social regulation should be balanced more realistically against the costs.[15]

In recent years the views of those who would balance costs and benefits economically have prevailed, both in the executive branch (through President Ronald Reagan's Executive Order 12291) and in the courts (in, for example, the decisions on the exposure standards for benzene and cotton dust). In Sagoff's view this trend has run counter to the historic intent of most environmental health legislation. Sagoff would prefer a balance between economic costs and benefits and an ethical assertion of the right to health protection. In effect, Wildavsky might be asked if additional wealth automatically produces increments of health. His view does not account for the inferior health performance in some very wealthy nations, including the United States. Nor for the enormous health costs of the single-minded (if ineffective) drive for economic growth in eastern Europe and the former Soviet Union.

There is agreement that environmental health is an important societal value. There is disagreement as to how to maximize health outcomes. Should we emphasize the avoidance of risks, or should we take chances in the name of increased wealth and assume that health improvements will follow? Wildavsky draws an analogy with a jogger who must run a greater short term risk of a heart attack while running in order to achieve a lower long term risk of heart disease. If automobiles, toxic chemicals, or nuclear power advance our economy significantly while adding a small increment to overall health risks, these are risks worth taking. Most environmentalists would disagree, both on moral grounds (the risks are mostly involuntary) and on practical grounds (the risks are large, the economic gains minimal). It is not as if there would be no transportation, chemical industry, or energy industry. They would just be different and possibly more economically advantageous, not less.

Sustainability as a Core Value

The third core belief of environmentalism, sustainability, has frequently come to the fore in recent years. It may be the most important dimension of environmentalism because it implies a thoroughgoing transformation of industrial society. As a goal, sustainability requires a radically reduced dependence on nonrenewable resources, a commitment to extract renewable resources no more rapidly than they are restored in nature, and a minimization of all human impacts on natural ecosystems. In sum, sustainability sets the economic opportunities and ecological foundations of future generations on the same ethical level as those of present generations. Those who promote sustainability assume that now is the time to acknowledge how finite and fragile Earth is.

Perhaps the most important aspect of sustainability is the recognition that fossil fuels are not renewable. There is no obvious substitute that can supply comparable amounts of energy at a comparable cost. Nor can humankind continue to extract wood from forests or fish from the seas at present rates; they are not being replenished at those rates. Nor can we continue to burn combustible fuels at present rates lest we significantly alter the global climate, if we have not already done so. Sustainability, then, shifts the focus of societal concern from the present to the future and presumes a fundamental obligation to future generations.

Lester Milbrath, a political scientist, argues that the need to focus public policy on sustainability is an urgent one. Our "entire social system is in jeopardy," he writes, and "we cannot continue on our present trajectory." He argues that "open-minded recognition of the deep systemic nature of our problem would allow a planned gradual transition, with minimal dislocation and pain."[16] Milbrath and many others come to this view in a consideration of human population trends and the long-term potential for food supply and adequate resources, global climate change, and numerous other patterns and trends. Joel Kassiola entitles his inquiry *The Death of Industrial Civilization* and argues that future economic growth is fundamentally limited by ecological and resource constraints.[17] Indeed, there is a widespread sense that the Western standard of living, or anything like it, cannot ultimately be enjoyed by humankind as a whole, nor even indefinitely by those who enjoy it now. Yet human numbers continue to grow, as does the rate at which we extract nonrenewable resources (or remove renewable resources too rapidly for recovery). At the same time, a variety of possible futures are attainable that are both less resource dependent and profoundly comfortable. Advocates of sustainable development are seeking a viable future for postindustrial society.[18]

Competing Values and an Environmental Ethic

The three core values of the environmental movement are clearly important, but they must compete with other values (especially those of economy and equity). To complicate matters further, they also sometimes conflict with each other. For example, high-yield, sustainable forests may lack the diversity that would otherwise provide habitats for many animal species. Similarly, even the act of protecting human health, and thereby ensuring that human population will rise, reduces resource sustainability and virtually guarantees the diminution of nonhuman habitat. Such dilemmas do not absolve us of the task of sorting out difficult value questions; indeed politics, as the authoritative allocator of values, requires it. Technical solutions to some environmental problems exist, but are usually partial solutions that sometimes create their own problems.

There is in the end no avoiding hard questions. An environmental ethic helps us to establish priorities. Acknowledging that all nonhuman species have a right to a wild existence carries implications for the meaning and character of property rights. If all humans have a right to a healthy environment, some industries must begin to behave very differently. A societal commitment to sustainability—as we will see—suggests that we may all need to adjust many dimensions of our everyday behavior, including what we buy, what we throw away, and which mode of transportation we select in various circumstances.

Environmental values, then, involve much more than just concern for attractive animals and the protection of scenic beauty. The core values of environmentalism, if taken seriously, challenge nothing less than how we organize our society and live our lives. These values provoke policy dilemmas and can lead to choices so hard as to be almost impossible. Yet we must make them. The following three sections focus on the tough questions in the hope that considering challenging cases will deepen our understanding of the political significance of environmentalism. These cases arise out of each of the three core values of environmentalism: ecology, health, and sustainability. I have also identified one case that arises out of all three simultaneously.

The Ethical Challenge of Ecology

Throughout the developing world humans and other large animals compete for space. In the wealthy nations this competition has largely been resolved in favor of the human species. Lions and bears no longer roam the forests of Europe. Few bison populate the vast prairies of North America; gone, too, are the nonhuman predator populations they once supported. Now much of the wild habitat of the elephant is threatened, and the rhino, and the cheetah, and the tiger, and a long list of other creatures less grand. So too are the tropical rain forests as a whole—as well as the nontropical rain forests of the Pacific Northwest. These are popular issues in part because it was one thing for humankind to appropriate some of the planet, another thing to appropriate nearly all of it. Few would disagree with the assertion that the lives of future humans would be profoundly less rich should we as a species appropriate most of the space required by other species. Yet here is the dilemma: both the animals and humans now need the same land. Who will decide what to do? And how?

Particularly perplexing issues include how best to protect the spotted owl, the tiger, and the elephant. The case of the spotted owl is familiar to most North Americans. Its protection was assured by the U.S. Endangered Species Act. The logging of some old-growth forests, its habitat, was blocked by a federal judge in Seattle. Intense political conflict erupted in the Pacific Northwest following this decision. Loggers, industry, small businesses, and the local media rallied against both the decision and the owl. In the process, some environmental positions have been widely misunderstood. The owl itself, however deserving of protection, has been seen by environmentalists as but one species under threat. In their view, the ancient forest itself deserves protection. As Patrick Mazza puts it, "the spotted owl is a 'canary in a coal mine', whose troubles signal a warning for the entire old growth ecosystem."[19] The jobs are soon to be lost in any case because little old-growth forest remains. The larger question is, should humankind remove and replace all the forests of the world? The replacement forest may be vastly different ecologically. The issue for most environmentalists is not the economic value of forests, but whether all the world exists simply for our benefit. Jobs that might have existed for a few years more must, in this view, come to an end a few years sooner.

The "spotted owl" dilemma is difficult—very difficult if one's life is directly affected—but it is not nearly so tough as the case of tigers and elephants, both of which require vast wilderness habitats. The land the tiger needs is also coveted by Indian peasants who would hope to grow crops there and nearby. Given the numbers of humans in India, and their present rate of growth, it is only a matter of time before this is literally a matter of human lives versus tiger lives. Additionally, as humans encroach on tiger populations, fatalities are inevitable.

In East Africa humans who hunt elephants are now themselves hunted and killed regularly by protection authorities. Something near to a state of war exists. Most African nations are cooperating in seeking an end to trade in ivory worldwide. Other African nations with more stable elephant populations (Zimbabwe, Botswana, and South Africa) issue permits to hunt elephants. This strategy has been partially successful against poaching, and elephant populations appear, for now, to be secure in these countries.[20] But should the existence of elephants in the wild depend on the desire of some humans to kill them? Do not both tigers and elephants have an absolute right to a safe habitat somewhere on the planet?

Most people—if unaffected personally—would answer the last question affirmatively. But the implications may be far more radical than most understand. As George Sessions has stated:

> Population biologists have argued that 1 to 2 billion people living lightly on the planet would be sustainable given the ecological requirements of maintaining carrying capacity for all species. A human population decrease from its present level to that level (by humane needs such as steady low birth rates) would also be good for humans and for the diversity of human cultures, as well as for wild species and ecosystems.[21]

The individual policy dilemmas, however difficult, pale to insignificance if one accepts the profound nature of the challenge posed by this view. Those human numbers may be optimal, but that conclusion hardly provides our species with a means of humanely achieving a significant population reduction. There is no general agreement that such a goal is either feasible or desirable. Some feel, however, that it is possible in the long run, and from this perspective our zoos and parks are seen as arks for a very different planetary future.

The Ethical Challenge of Health

A particularly difficult ethical question has to do with attaching a price to human lives. Yet this is virtually required in a benefit-cost analysis on standards for toxic substance exposures. The cost of changing an industrial process is calculated and compared to the additional health costs of continued human exposures at present levels. Environmental exposures of other species are usually ignored. Indeed, calculations are usually for *either* human occupational exposures or human environmental exposures, but not both.[22] Typically, a small number of human fatalities is set against an estimate by industry of the cost of cleaning up. The costs of nonfatal illnesses are often underestimated or ignored and so too are some nonhealth gains to industry associated with most retooling of industrial processes. Thus, the price assigned to the estimate of human lives lost is a significant part of the overall calculation.

What is important here is seeing that all of the above objections are technical objections. The ethical objection is, simply put, that a human life is beyond price. If a life can be saved, it should be saved. Yet if that were literally true governments might be expected to set speed limits at 10 mph or to close down all oil refineries. One is drawn back to Sagoff's view that what is appropriate is some compromise, some balancing, between the two approaches to matters of environmental and occupational health. Cost-benefit calculations can be made, but governments should not imagine that they are utterly bound by them. Other factors must be considered. Do technologies exist that would ameliorate or eliminate the problem? How deep are the polluters' pockets relative to the cost of cleaning up? How important to society is the product associated with the imposed risk? Regarding this latter question, consider that it is possible that some human lives may be lost to achieve dandelion-free suburban lawns. Does that make ethical sense even if risking those lives generates millions of dollars in economic activity? In the case of asbestos (a known potent carcinogen), does it not matter if the substance is used in protective garments for fire persons or for a more trivial purpose? Should we not also ask whether or not substitutes are readily available?

Releases of chemicals into the wider environment raise additional important questions. In particular, one must consider the likely duration of the environmental impact. If a risk will exist in perpetuity, the price is infinite regardless of the value one assigns to any one life. But in practice we more frequently err in an opposite way. We site toxic chemical dumps, or municipal solid waste containing hazardous chemicals, on clay soils because they delay movement through the ground. But ultimately those chemicals will reach larger bodies of water. Arguably, it makes more sense to bury toxic wastes in sand, but to bury them in an amount and form that will release no more than we can tolerate in nearby aquifers. Otherwise all we are doing is assigning a toxic world to distant future generations. We are unable, it seems, to reason morally beyond our own grandchildren.

The Ethical Challenge of Sustainability

Any number of policy complexities arise from sustainability values as well. In the mid 1970s and again in the early 1980s North Americans were acutely aware of the long-term nonsustainability of fossil fuel supplies. This reality remains, though it has slipped for the present from public consciousness. Acutely in the public mind at present, however, are the limits of future lumber supplies from old-growth sites. So, too, in many locations are acceptable sites for the disposal of municipal solid waste. But lest all the news appear to be bad, feasible options are available in many cases. Building materials can be made from recycled household and industrial wastes, slowing the speed with which we "run out" of both lumber and landfill sites. Even more dramatically, by changing the rules by which electrical utilities and their customers make supply-and-demand decisions, we could save enough electricity to eliminate any need for new coal-burning power plants. This latter assertion perhaps needs a brief elaboration.

Electrical utilities traditionally worried almost exclusively about supply, while demand management was primarily the customer's concern. The more the utility supplied, the more money they made. Utilities also rarely considered for long how durable or expandable their supply sources were; it was assumed that other supply sources could always be found, if necessary. Demand management frequently fell between the cracks as neither builders nor building managers were concerned about electricity bills because they did not pay them—tenants did. Builders avoided the higher capital costs of more efficient lighting and other devices. Many commercial tenants were unconcerned about electrical efficiency because they paid a share of electricity costs related to the square footage they occupied rather than the amount of electricity they actually used. In the late 1980s utilities in several states were ordered by state regulatory agencies to treat efficiency improvements as a supply source and awarded a rate-of-return on efficiency improvement investments made on behalf of their customers. The savings have been considerable: for the utilities, for their customers, for the economy as a whole, and for the sustainability of energy supplies.[23] Demand reduction has proved to be cheaper than new supply; there are, it would seem, some win-win possibilities.

Nonetheless, there remains a difficult policy choice because some jobs might be lost and some firms may suffer significant economic losses. Those who supply or build new power plants are, or would be, hit very hard by these changes. So, too, might some employees of utilities. Achieving greater sustainability may well require very significant transformations throughout industrial society.

A final example will provide a clearer appreciation of the importance of this issue and lead toward a discussion of integrating environmental, economic, and equity values. Automobiles, their manufacture and repair, and related industries, generate at least 25 percent of the gross national product (GNP) of North America. Related industries include road building, tires, auto parts, and significant proportions of the steel industry, the cement industry, aggregates (sand and gravel) extraction, fast foods, motels, advertising, and so forth. Yet the automobile itself may well be unsustainable—at least in present numbers, traveling current average annual distances. Automobiles consume land, pollute the air, use up the least durable of fossil fuels, contribute to global warming, reduce the habitat of other species, and are a major source of acid precipitation. All three core environmental values are simultaneously offended. It has increasingly been argued in recent years that a sustainable future will see more compact cities which in turn are less dependent on automobile transportation, however fueled.[24] European cities are at present typically twice as compact as North American cities, and citizens of those cities typically use half the transportation fuel of their North American counterparts.[25] Yet Europeans are equally prosperous overall and the cities in question are arguably more pleasant (Paris, London, Amsterdam). In addition, several European cities have very recently carved out core areas from which automobiles are completely excluded. Such efforts may soon spread to North America.

The principal point to be appreciated here is that environmental values, if taken seriously, could transform the future of industrial societies. The economic, social, and political implications of these changes are very important. Governments will require, then, ways to integrate these new values with the other important values that have always served as at least implicit guides to public policy. Here one might speak of three fundamental value sets: environment, economy, and equity. Below, I consider the relationships between two pairs of value sets: environment/economy and environment/equity. Many such considerations have been implicit within the preceding analysis as well. Economy and equity are so central to politics as a value-integrating process that they deserve additional attention here.

The Environment and the Economy

As Charles Lindblom has observed, contemporary political leaders are held to be responsible for the success or failure of the economy.[26] Accordingly, rising unemployment or falling profits often result in electoral difficulties for incumbents. Increasingly now our political leadership is also seen to be responsible for environmental damage. To the extent that environmental protection and economic growth are in conflict, political leaders are thus held to an impossible mandate. Much has been written on this subject, but in recent years the emphasis on win-win scenarios, on the possibility of sustainable development, has been growing. In other words, the perhaps impossible mandate is seen by some to be achievable—the simultaneous maximization of environmental values and economic values taken to lie somewhere between assumption and hope. But, putting aside equity considerations for the moment, *can* environment and economy be simultaneously advanced?

On the positive side, some significant economic sectors are highly compatible with environmental protection.[27] Growth in public transport systems result in improved air quality and the more efficient use of land, materials, and energy. Demand-side management by electrical utilities has similarly positive environmental effects, and it can also be a considerable economic stimulus to manufacturers and installers of electrical equipment for heating, cooling, lighting, and electrical motors. Recycling-based manufacturing of paper, building materials, packaging, metal products, and plastic products also enhances environmental quality on a variety of fronts. So, too, of course, does the production, installation, and maintenance of pollution abatement equipment. Similarly, reduced dependence on agricultural chemicals can result in more economically viable farming operations. To the extent that governmental policies advance economic transformations of this sort, economy and environment can improve simultaneously.

In addition, many sectors of a modern economy have only very small, or readily avoidable, effects on the environment. Significant growth in these sectors would have negligible environmental effects. Additional expenditures on education, social services, health care, or the arts, for example, would add little to the burden borne by the environment. This is an aspect of the debate on the appropriate level of public expenditures (as a proportion of the economy) that has largely been left aside. But other economic sectors also have quite modest net impacts. These include some of the more dynamic sectors of the global economy. Computers, automation, and telecommunications have modest impacts per dollar of value added. In addition, they may make offsetting contributions. Communications can substitute for travel with very significant energy savings. Robots need little lighting or heat and do not add to highway congestion at rush hour. Equity effects aside for the moment, automation has enormous potential for reducing the total energy and materials devoted to manufacturing workspaces. Energy and materials use, much more than GNP, determines total environmental impact.

One cannot have one's cake, however, and eat it too. Some economic sectors would appear irretrievably in conflict with environmental values in the long term—especially ecological and sustainability values. No one would propose eliminating any economic sector by fiat. Yet it is hard to imagine how environmental values will not increasingly come into conflict with the growth goals of some sectors of the contemporary economy. Sectors where clashes are likely include the automobile industry (and thereby the steel, rubber, cement, oil, and other attendant industries), the forest industry, the chemical industry, coal mining and use, the packaging industry, and the construction industry (as regards suburban sprawl). And one should not omit tobacco producers. Clearly the political challenges here are enormous. We are, in a very real sense, in conflict with two different dimensions of our own best interests and intentions.

Comfortable, happy, healthy lives for ourselves and our families are, it would appear, in conflict with exactly those same goals. The automobile that keeps us out of the rain on our way to basketball practice pollutes the air we breathe. The materials used to produce the extra rooms in our home may require the diminution of habitat and perhaps outdoor recreational space. Our drycleaned clothes mandate the production and use of hazardous chemicals.[28] The suburban life-style we have collectively embraced since the 1940s and 1950s may be environmentally inappropriate for the population levels and energy reserves of the early twenty-first century. The potential value conflicts are clearly very deep and must be resolved both at the many points where polity and economy intersect and in the inner recesses of present and future minds. When we cannot have both economy and environment, which is the more important to us? (And exactly when can we not have both?)

These tensions, both potential and immediate, could be resolved in a number of ways. Even being able to step back and ask questions is, of course, a luxury. In poor nations the choices are more stark: Food or nature? Economic collapse or forests for tomorrow? A manufacturing sector or clean air? Choice is the ultimate luxury, and North Americans still have greater increments of such luxury.

Changes in governmental tax and subsidy regimes could, in all nations, spur rapid adaptations. Many now agree that the extraction of energy and raw materials should not be subsidized in any way. At present it is.[29] Also, some environmentalists urge that automobile transportation no longer be subsidized.[30] Taxation burdens might, in general, be shifted at least in part from work (income tax), property ownership, and gross sales to energy, materials use, land use, and waste disposal. Such structural changes would allow the marketplace to gradually handle the multitude of production and consumption decisions associated with improving sustainability.

Combined with more effective protection of environmentally sensitive lands and effective regulations to protect human health, government could help to integrate environmental and economic values. Also, through green products, green investment options, environmental audits, and other techniques, the private sector and individual consumers can take significant initiatives irrespective of the government's commitment. Even those industries identified above as likely to be in conflict with environmental values could make fundamental breakthroughs in both profitability *and* improved environmental protection. The electrical utilities are a crucial case in point here: the new commitment to demand-side management has improved their profits. Gains may not be achieved by every industry challenged by environmental values, but losses can be minimized or turned around within those firms and sectors that are best able to anticipate change.

The Environment and Equity

The integration of environmental values and economic values has received a lot of consideration in recent years. A good deal of attention has been devoted as well to the great challenges associated with achieving

improved North-South equity and environmental protection simultaneously.[31] But political leaders have given little sophisticated consideration to the linkages between environmental values and improvements in
equity within wealthy economies. Such linkages are nonetheless both real
and complex. They are so significant in some cases as to suggest that
environmental values are not likely to find effective political expression
unless and until major environment-equity tensions are at least partly
resolved. Important points of value intersection—sometimes conflictual,
sometimes mutually supportive—exist as regards gender and environment, class and environment, race and environment, and regional equity
and environment.

Gender provides an interesting starting point because a commonality
of interests between environmentalists and feminists has been frequently
asserted in recent years.[32] Many of the complexities of these debates need
not be reiterated here, but three matters are fundamental. The first is
human population, the second is the parallel dominance of women and
nature, and the third is women's distinctive perspective on sustainability.

All three core values of environmentalism would be more easily
achieved if the total human population were stabilized or in gradual decline toward an optimal level. This is particularly true for ecology and
sustainability values which in all likelihood are unobtainable unless human population growth is halted. Many of the major objectives of the
women's movement are thus essential to environmentalists. Access to
family planning services and freedom of choice regarding abortion are
obviously important. But perhaps even more important are improved educational and economic opportunities for women. There is no stronger
determinant of ultimate family size than equal opportunity for women.
Environmentalists and the women's movement concur, then, in a fundamental way on an issue significant to both.

Second, there are parallels between the domination of women and
the domination of nature. These parallels are so strong that they reach
into the very structure of our language as in the "rape" of the land,
"virgin" forests, and "mother" Earth. Another dimension of the parallel
character of male-female and human-nature domination is that in both
cases subjectivity is denied. The domination arises out of a self-regarding
lack of respect. The habits and attitudes born of one form of domination
re-create themselves within the other.

Third, women's distinctive biological (and cultural) role in childbearing and early nurture may well have other environmental implications.
Whether or not this distinctiveness has been overstated in the past, bearing children may well incline women to a greater sensitivity to the needs
of future generations.

Sustainability issues are seen in perhaps a different light than they
are seen by men. So, too, may be the habitat needs of other species.
Women have frequently assumed leadership roles within the environmen-

tal movement.[33] Overall, there is some potential for cooperation between those advancing gender equity and those seeking environmental protection, and there would appear to be few points of tension.

The linkages between environmental values and class equity values are quite different. Here, tensions have been widespread, particularly over perceived threats to employment opportunities. A sense of threat has been particularly striking in the forest industry, but it has also arisen for workers in the nuclear industry, for coal miners, for ranchers (as regards protection of predators), for highway construction and packaging workers, and for farmers (regarding pesticide use). It exists as well within a variety of polluting industries where the cost of cleanup may, or appears to, threaten competitiveness. It could also exist in the auto industry in the future, though the United Auto Workers' union has had a very long history of positive involvement with conservation and environmental protection.[34]

These tensions are both real and politically significant, but they do not reveal the whole story. As noted above, environmental protection initiatives also generate significant employment opportunities.[35] Renewable energy supply sources are more employment intensive and less environmentally threatening than are energy supply megaprojects. Energy efficiency improvements create jobs in manufacturing, installation, and construction. Recycling is highly labor intensive. Bottle bills, pushed through in ten states by environmental organizations, are net generators of employment. Urban reconfiguration and public transport expenditures create employment, as do pollution abatement and environmental restoration. Overall, the jobs gained may well be more numerous than the jobs put at risk. This does not necessarily help those who lose their jobs, but it could if transitions were accomplished in a more orderly and gradual fashion. Nonetheless, some political tension on the class-environment front is unavoidable.

Environmentalists have become somewhat more thoughtful on such questions in recent years. Some have suggested that the time has or will come when there should be some decoupling of employment and income. Wealthy societies could perhaps afford to replace present transfer payments (social security, unemployment insurance, welfare, food stamps) with a universal social income. Net income would remain the same for most people, but a significant proportion would come from a nonemployer source. The income level for some unemployed persons might rise, but only modestly. But the largest difference would be that all adults would receive the income and thus there would be no disincentive to working (as with welfare) and no disincentive to education (as with unemployment insurance). The problem with the present situation is that any risk to employment is taken to be tragic, regardless of the tragedy attendant on continued employment (as in the cutting of the last of the old-growth forests). In effect, the problem lies in the equitability of the distribution of both work and income. It may be the single largest political problem involved with the integration of equity values and environmental values, and it thus deserves a great deal of attention in the future.

Also increasingly important are the linkages between racial equity and environmental protection. However, here—as with gender—the interests tend to be parallel, though, as with class, perceptions sometimes diverge. In the 1970s many African American leaders saw environmental protection as likely to divert funds from social justice needs. Given government's limited domestic budget, this was, and remains, an appropriate concern. But as with the issue of employment (itself, of course, a central concern of all visible minorities) there is another side captured in the new movement for environmental justice. Minorities have historically borne the brunt of occupational hazards, pollution, and waste disposal, including hazardous waste disposal.[36] The realization of this fact has had a very real political effect in recent years, especially in the South. Robert Bullard's recent book *Dumping in Dixie* carefully portrays the growing environmental awareness among African Americans in their opposition to the disproportionate siting of hazardous waste dumps, incinerators, municipal landfills, plants using heavy metals, and chemical factories in their neighborhoods.[37] More than this, major environmental organizations are paying increasing attention to the environmental issues that affect minorities disproportionately, such as lead poisoning, the hazards faced by farm workers, and the general level of toxic exposures in minority communities.[38] Early opinion studies that suggested that African Americans were less likely to show high environmental concern have, in recent years, given way to those that indicate more balanced views across racial lines.

Regionally based environment-equity matters also have a potential for future value conflict. For example, the strong push for recycling may have a negative effect on already depressed resource-producing regions. This is particularly pronounced in isolated regions of Canada, where many communities depend on pulp and paper production to survive. New plants to produce paper products from recycled stock will likely locate in high population areas near to the source of supply. Closure of distant mills will hurt some already economically marginal regions. Conversely, older urban cores in the United States, particularly in the Northeast, are as regionally underadvantaged as any location in North America. They may well benefit from recycling and, as well, from any turn toward more compact urban areas and the corresponding increase in public transport expenditures. Also, it is arguable that wood alcohol may come to be an important (sustainable) substitute for oil. Should that prove to be the case, alternative employment opportunities would increase for some disadvantaged rural regions.

Thus, on the whole, the prospects for integrating equity and environmental values would seem promising, though neither easy nor simple. What is clear is that adding environment to the traditional political agenda will forever change the face of politics. Multidimensionality is accentuated and accelerated. Not that politics was ever simple. But ideology can no longer be seen in simplistic left-right/liberal-conservative terms. Not only the end of the Cold War assures this new reality. Widely held environmental values will enormously diversify each citizen's coherent intellectual options, while increasing the variety of possible political coalitions and combinations.

Conclusion

The integration of economy, equity, and environment is and must be a political process, one fraught with ethical dilemmas and disputes. These matters cannot be resolved solely on the basis of either facts or expertise. Solutions require a thoughtful collective sense of what kind of society we want. In a democracy, fundamental values are matters each of us must establish for ourselves. Democratic institutions succeed or fail on the basis of their ability to integrate citizen values within effective collective decisions. But more than that, our society itself will not succeed in the long run unless we face up to the difficult issues and choices now before us. That in turn requires that most, if not all, citizens understand environmental, economic, and equity values. It also requires both a widespread tolerance for the values of others and an ongoing prospect for broad participation in the political process.

Notes

1. David Easton, *The Political System* (New York: Knopf, 1953).
2. Evidence of the level of acceptance of environmental values is contained in *Wildlife and the Public Interest* (New York: Praeger, 1989), and Riley E. Dunlap, "Polls, Pollution and Politics: Public Opinion on the Environment in the Reagan Era," *Environment* 29 (July-August, 1987): 6-11, 32-37.
3. Samuel P. Hays, "From Conservation to Environment: Environmental Politics in the United States Since World War Two," *Environmental Review* 6 (Fall 1982): 20.
4. George Sessions, "The Deep Ecology Movement: A Review," *Environmental Review* 11 (Summer 1987): 107.
5. See Max Oelschlaeger, ed., *After Earth Day: Continuing the Conservation Effort* (Denton: University of North Texas Press, 1992), chapters by Susan Bratton and Oelschlaeger.
6. Ronald Inglehart, *The Silent Revolution: Changing Values and Political Styles Among Western Publics* (Princeton, N.J.: Princeton University Press, 1977).
7. Riley E. Dunlap and K. VanLiere, "The New Environmental Paradigm," *Journal of Environmental Education* 9 (1978): 10-19; and Lester W. Milbrath, *Environmentalists: Vanguard for a New Society* (Albany: State University of New York Press, 1984).
8. Robert C. Paehlke, *Environmentalism and the Future of Progressive Politics* (New Haven, Conn.: Yale University Press, 1989), 144-145.

9. Max Oelschlaeger, *The Idea of Wilderness: From Prehistory to the Age of Ecology* (New Haven, Conn.: Yale University Press, 1991), 292.
10. Ibid.
11. See Warwick Fox, *Toward a Transpersonal Ecology* (Boston: Shambhala, 1990); see also Bill Devall and George Sessions, *Deep Ecology: Living as if Nature Mattered* (Salt Lake City: Peregrine Smith Books, 1985); and Arne Naess, *Ecology, Community and Lifestyle: Outline of an Ecosophy*, (Cambridge: Cambridge University Press, 1989).
12. See, for example, Tom Regan, *All That Dwell Therein: Animal Rights and Environmental Ethics* (Berkeley and Los Angeles: University of California Press, 1982); and the extensive work of Peter Singer.
13. Oelschlaeger, *Idea of Wilderness*, ix.
14. Aaron Wildavsky, *Searching for Safety* (New Brunswick, N.J.: Transaction, 1988).
15. Mark Sagoff, *The Economy of the Earth* (New York: Cambridge University Press, 1988), 195-196.
16. Lester Milbrath, *Envisioning a Sustainable Society* (Albany: State University of New York Press, 1989), 338.
17. Joel J. Kassiola, *The Death of Industrial Civilization* (Albany: State University of New York Press, 1990).
18. See World Commission on Environment and Development, *Our Common Future* (New York: Oxford University Press, 1987), and the many works that have followed from it.
19. Patrick Mazza, "The Spotted Owl as Scapegoat," *Capitalism, Nature, Socialism* (June 1990): 100.
20. Oelschlaeger, *After Earth Day*, chapter by Michael L. Nieswiadomy, at pp. 123-124.
21. Oelschlaeger, *After Earth Day*, 19.
22. Robert C. Paehlke, "Occupational and Environmental Health Linkages," in *Controlling Chemical Hazards*, ed. Raymond P. Côté and Peter G. Wells (London: Unwin Hyman, 1991), 175-197.
23. See, for example, David Moscovitz, Steven Nadel, and Howard Geller, *Increasing the Efficiency of Electricity Production and Use: Barriers and Strategies* (Washington, D.C.: American Council for an Energy-Efficient Economy, 1991).
24. See, for example, Marcia D. Lowe, "Rethinking Urban Transport," in *State of the World, 1991*, ed. Lester R. Brown (New York: Norton, 1991), 56-73.
25. Peter Newman and Jeffrey Kenworthy, *Cities and Automobile Dependence: An International Sourcebook* (Hants [Eng.]: Gower, 1989).
26. Charles E. Lindblom, *Politics and Markets* (New York: Basic Books, 1977).
27. For more information on simultaneous gains noted in this paragraph see, for example, Moscovitz, Nadel, and Geller, *Increasing Efficiency*; and Brown, ed., *State of the World, 1991 and 1992* (New York: Norton, 1991 and 1992), esp. chaps. 2, 3, and 4 in 1991 and 3, 8, and 9 in 1992.
28. Kirk R. Smith, "Air Pollution: Assessing Total Exposure in the United States," *Environment* 30 (October 1988): 10-15, 33-38.
29. See Jim MacNeill, Pieter Winsemius, and Taizo Yakushiji, *Beyond Interdependence* (New York: Oxford University Press, 1991).
30. Francesca Lyman, "Rethinking Our Transportation Future," *E Magazine* 1 (September-October 1990): 34-41.
31. See, for example, MacNeill, Winsemius, and Yakushiji, *Beyond Interdependence*.
32. Perhaps the best single introductory article is still Karen J. Warren, "Feminism and Ecology: Making Connections," *Environmental Ethics* 9 (1987): 3-20. See also Judith Plant, ed., *Healing the Wounds: The Promise of Ecofeminism* (Toronto: Between the Lines, 1989); I. Diamond and G. Orenstein, eds., *Reweaving the World: The Emergence of Ecofeminism* (San Francisco: Sierra Club Books, 1990);

and Janet Biehl, *Finding Our Way: Rethinking Ecofeminist Politics* (Montreal: Black Rose Books, 1991).

33. Carolyn Merchant, "Earth Care: Women and the Environmental Movement," *Environment* 23 (June 1981): 6-13, 38-40.

34. Robert Paehlke, "Environnementalisme et syndicalisme au Canada anglais et aux Etats-Unis," *Sociologie et Sociétés* 13 (April 1981): 161-179.

35. See Paehlke, *Environmentalism and the Future of Progressive Politics;* and Michael Renner, "Creating Sustainable Jobs in Industrial Economies," in *State of the World, 1992,* ed. Brown.

36. James C. Robinson, *Toil and Toxics: Workplace Struggles and Political Strategies for Occupational Health* (Berkeley and Los Angeles: University of California Press, 1991).

37. Robert D. Bullard, *Dumping in Dixie: Race, Class, and Environmental Quality* (Boulder: Westview, 1991); and Charles Lee, *Toxic Waste and Race in the United States* (New York: United Church of Christ Commission for Racial Justice, 1987).

38. See, for example, the extensive treatment of environmental justice issues in *Environmental Action* (January-February 1990), 19-30, and the extensive sources cited therein. In this special issue, Environmental Action, a large environmentalist organization, faces up to the white middle-class past of the environmental movement.

17

Conclusion: The New Environmental Agenda

Norman J. Vig and Michael E. Kraft

*Modern industrial civilization, as presently organized, is collid-
ing violently with our planet's ecological system. . . . We must
make the rescue of the environment the central organizing principle for civilization.*

—Sen. Al Gore, 1992

Bill Clinton and Al Gore espoused an ambitious environmental agenda
in their 1992 campaign. Even more significantly, they redefined the
scope of environmental policy. As Mr. Gore implies in the above passage
(from his book, *Earth in the Balance*), environmental concerns are now
potentially important to virtually all areas of policy. Economic growth and
competitiveness, national security, foreign policy, and the general health
and welfare of society are all contingent on environmental sustainability.
Although the environment has occupied an important place on the national policy agenda for more than two decades, it may now be integrated
into the mainstream of policymaking as never before.

A number of public and private commissions have called for a broadening and deepening of the national environmental agenda. The National
Commission on the Environment, a prestigious group of individuals including former EPA administrators Douglas Costle, Lee Thomas, and
William Ruckelshaus, issued a report in late 1992 outlining a new national strategy based on the principle of sustainable development:

> U.S. leadership should be based on the concept of *sustainable develop-
> ment*. By the close of the twentieth century, economic development and
> environmental protection must come together in a new synthesis:
> broad-based economic progress accomplished in a manner that protects
> and restores the quality of the natural environment, improves the qual-
> ity of life for individuals, and broadens the prospects for future genera-
> tions. This merging of economic and environmental goals in the con-
> cept of sustainable development can and should constitute a central
> guiding principle for national environmental and economic policy-
> making.[1]

The President's Commission on Environmental Quality, a little-no-
ticed committee of corporate, foundation, and environmental group exec-

utives set up by President George Bush, issued a report in early 1993 that
called for establishing a national council on sustainable development. The
council would promote management practices in the private sector that
would encourage sustainable development.[2] The Carnegie Endowment
National Commission on America and the New World, in a report on the
role of the United States in the post-Cold War era, also endorsed the
integration of environmental costs into all economic decisionmaking.[3]

The global environmental agenda is rapidly expanding. The U.N.
Conference on Environment and Development (Earth summit) held in
Río de Janeiro, Brazil, in June 1992 brought representatives of 179 nations together to address environmental threats. Although the treaty
agreements signed were weaker than had been hoped and, in some instances, failed to gain U.S. approval (chap. 14), the summit inaugurated a
process for initiating and coordinating international actions on a wide
range of environmental problems. A major outcome of the conference was
Agenda 21, an extensive action plan outlining principles and strategies for
achieving sustainable development in the coming decades.[4] Nongovernmental organizations (NGOs) from around the world participated in the
Río conference to an unprecedented degree and are forming international
networks to pressure governments to implement such policies. The
United Nations has also established the Commission on Sustainable
Development to monitor national actions.

It remains to be seen how effectively any of these initiatives are
implemented. To recognize environmental integrity as a universal value
will not solve the problem of making difficult policy choices that involve
other important social values. Although many of these choices may no
longer be regarded as zero-sum trade-offs, they will often require financial
sacrifices and changes in social behavior. This means that environmental
policies will continue to generate strong political resistance from established economic and bureaucratic interests. Political opposition is also
likely to grow among antienvironmental and property rights organizations
(chap. 3). And as environmental protection deepens, success in policy
implementation will increasingly depend on public understanding and
acceptance of the need for social and behavioral change.

Environmental policy success will thus require more innovative strategies and tools than have characterized past regulation. Many chapters in
this book have emphasized the need for new policy approaches, including
more use of economic incentives, comparative risk assessment, and alternative means of conflict resolution, as well as more thoughtful policy
evaluation and greater attention to the ethical dimensions of environmental trade-offs. The remainder of this chapter discusses new mechanisms
for integrating environmental values into national policymaking; identifies
seven of the most pressing environmental issues on the agenda of the
Clinton administration; outlines seven innovative approaches to environmental management; and concludes with some general reflections on the

need to rethink political strategies and the long-term choices that must be made if we are to maintain the health of the planet.

Integrating Environmental Policies

As the authors of chapters 1 and 6 point out, national environmental legislation has accumulated in piecemeal fashion over a long period of time in response to specific problems and crises. As a result, environmental administration is deeply fragmented and inconsistent, often pitting agencies and departments (or divisions within them) against each other and their authorizing committees in Congress. Environmental goals, missions, and priorities are often conflicting and unclear, and no adequate mechanism exists for coordinating policies and resolving disputes. In the Reagan and Bush administrations, supervision by the White House staff and Office of Management and Budget focused too narrowly on controlling regulatory costs. The Council on Environmental Quality (CEQ) lacked the authority and status needed to play a coordinating role.

To remedy this weakness, President Clinton created the Office of Environmental Policy (OEP), which will seek to integrate environmental considerations into all areas of policy formulation in the White House. Its director is to attend meetings of the Domestic Policy Council, the National Security Council, and the new National Economic Council to ensure the consideration of environmental values. The new office will replace CEQ under Clinton's reorganization plan, but it will have an even smaller staff, and its success will depend heavily on the effectiveness of its director and how seriously it is taken by other senior policy advisers in the White House.

Some of CEQ's functions, such as its responsibilities for compiling statistics on environmental trends, will presumably be transferred to the revamped Environmental Protection Agency (EPA), which is likely to achieve full cabinet status as the Department of the Environment. As a department, EPA would have increased leverage with other departments but would not by itself overcome conflicting statutory mandates and missions. Agencies within the departments of Interior, Agriculture, and Energy would still be responsible for most natural resource policies. Congressional committees and interest group constituencies will fight to maintain their jurisdictional authority and channels of access to these agencies.

The need to institutionalize policy coordination will increase greatly as domestic and international policymaking converge in many fields. This will certainly be the case if environmental considerations are to become integral to defense planning, trade negotiations, and foreign policy generally. Agencies such as the Defense Department, the State Department, and the Office of Trade Representative will have to strengthen their environmental policy capabilities considerably and build much stronger institutional links with EPA and other environmental agencies. Scientific agencies like the White House Office of Science and Technology Policy (OSTP), the National Oceanic and Atmospheric Administration (NOAA), and the National Aeronautics and Space Administration (NASA) should also be reoriented toward environmental problems and incorporated more fully into the policymaking process. President Clinton has already reorganized the White House structure for scientific advice, and has given OSTP a larger role in coordinating science, technology, and environmental policy.[5]

In addition to interagency communication and coordination, environmental policy integration will require changing the institutional cultures within traditional resource departments and agencies. The Department of the Interior contains several major subcultures ranging from the consumptive orientation of the Minerals Management Service and the Bureau of Land Management to the more preservationist values of the Fish and Wildlife Service.[6] Employees within the Agriculture Department's Forest Service are forcing a shift in that agency to more ecologically sensitive management practices. But the Department of Energy still reflects many of the values of the old Atomic Energy Commission and the traditional energy producers. Unless major changes are made in personnel and procedures, it will be difficult to reorient these agencies toward sustainable development.

Key Policy Issues

Although strengthening the institutional capabilities of government, especially in the executive branch, is clearly necessary for improved environmental policymaking, this will not obviate the need to make difficult political choices on many contentious issues at both ends of Pennsylvania Avenue. Some of these issues involve environmental problems that have long been discussed but not seriously addressed; others involve problems that have only recently been recognized. The following is a short overview of substantive issues likely to occupy Congress and the Clinton administration in the coming years.

Energy Consumption

In the early 1990s energy supplies in the United States were plentiful and fuel prices remained low. Yet for the first time since the Carter administration energy policy has returned to the national agenda and is likely to become a contentious issue for President Clinton. There are several reasons. First, petroleum imports have risen dramatically since 1986 and now make up nearly half of total U.S. oil consumption. Under current policies they will continue to increase well into the next century. Oil imports have high costs to our economy—accounting for roughly half of our current foreign trade deficit—and threaten our national security by maintaining our dependence on Middle East producers. Second, our inefficient use of energy is increasingly perceived as a threat to our international economic competitiveness. Other nations such as Japan and Germany have already taken the lead in developing many energy-efficient technologies. Third, consumption of fossil fuels is the principal source of greenhouse gas emissions that may cause global warming. In his 1993 Earth Day address, President Clinton pledged to cut U.S. CO_2 emissions to 1990 levels by the year 2000. The threat of global warming is likely to require a transition to noncarbon fuel sources such as solar and wind power and biomass in the first decades of the next century.

The Energy Policy Act of 1992 contained some provisions for energy conservation and efficiency (especially in government buildings and vehicle fleets) and limited incentives for developing renewable energy technologies (chap. 5). But its general thrust was to enhance production and use of all fuels, including fossil fuels. The act did not address the problems of global warming or raise corporate average fuel economy (CAFE) standards for automobiles, partly because the Bush administration was unwilling to confront the powerful oil and auto-manufacturing industries.[7] As the Democratic nominee, Bill Clinton pledged during the election campaign to raise the CAFE standard from 27.5 to 40 miles per gallon by 2000, but he later backed away from a specific timetable when Bush made an issue of potential job losses.

In his first budget, President Clinton proposed an energy tax based on the Btu (British thermal unit) heat content of fuels (except those from certain renewable sources) to be phased in over four years. The broad-based tax was designed to equalize burdens across different regions of the country and to offset costs to low-income people.[8] Although the tax would be relatively small (adding possibly eight cents per gallon of gasoline), the administration claimed it would raise $22 billion a year in revenue when fully implemented in 1996 and would encourage energy efficiency and reduce pollution.

But even this relatively modest tax proposal encountered strong opposition in the Senate. A coalition of Republicans and Democrats from energy-producing and farm states and an array of other special interests forced Clinton to abandon the Btu tax in favor of a smaller energy consumption tax that would not discriminate among fuels on the basis of heat or carbon content.[9]

Nevertheless, it is likely that pressures will mount for additional measures to reduce fossil fuel use. Other approaches such as higher CAFE standards will remain on the agenda. The Clinton administration has proposed a new technology policy that will shift substantial research and development (R&D) funding from military to civilian projects, including a joint venture with the auto industry to develop a "clean car" (see below). A number of other proposals for conservation and development of renewable energy resources are pending in Congress.

Hazardous and Nuclear Waste

The volume of hazardous, toxic, and radioactive waste continues to increase more rapidly than facilities for safely disposing of it. Many hazardous waste facilities have been closed down, while others such as incinerators are meeting increasing public opposition. Nuclear power plants are running out of space for storing spent fuel rods long before a permanent repository for high-level nuclear wastes is available (it remains uncertain whether the proposed facility at Yucca Mountain, Nevada, will ever be built). Interim storage technologies such as placement in aboveground steel and concrete casks are being constructed at several plant sites but remain controversial and are likely to generate strong NIMBY (not in my backyard) opposition (chap. 11). The cleanup of highly contaminated military weapons plants and other federal energy and defense facilities is proceeding at a snail's pace, while the federal Superfund program for remediating other hazardous waste sites has fallen far behind schedule. According to one widely cited study, cleanup of all sites will cost $750 billion over the next thirty years under current policy assumptions.[10] This would require average annual expenditures at twice the current level of about $12 billion—in a period of severe budget deficits. A major overhaul of our entire national hazardous and toxic waste program is thus considered necessary by many.[11]

The Resource Conservation and Recovery Act (RCRA), which regulates the storage, treatment, and disposal of most hazardous wastes, is up for reauthorization in the 103d Congress, and major efforts are also likely to reform the Superfund program. Among suggested amendments to RCRA are proposals for mandatory waste reduction, waste recovery, and recycling programs in industry; numerical requirements for recycled content of paper and other products, and federal-purchasing requirements for such products; restrictions on packaging; tighter controls on solid and hazardous waste incineration; and new requirements for state hazardous waste management planning and recycling. All of these proposals are likely to meet strong resistance in Congress. Changes in the Superfund program—especially efforts to exempt various parties from liability, to concentrate on stabilizing and containing waste sites rather than on complete cleanups, and to cut the costs and delays of projects by streamlining administrative processes and reducing litigation and fraud—are also likely to be highly contentious and difficult.[12] President Clinton will probably attempt to reduce the federal share of Superfund cleanup costs and shift more of the burden to private parties.

Clean Water and Wetlands

The Clean Water Act, last amended in 1987, is also up for reauthorization.[13] Although it is not considered in need of major revision, several important issues will need to be addressed. One is how to control "nonpoint" pollution from farm fields, construction sites, mining, forestry, and urban runoff, which together account for as much as two-thirds of all surface water pollution. Solutions may require tighter regulation of pesticide and fertilizer use as well as new land use controls to protect watersheds. Under the act, states are required to develop nonpoint source controls, but Congress has provided little funding for this purpose and state laws are weak and poorly enforced. Congress is also phasing out federal wastewater treatment grants, to be replaced by state-financed revolving loan funds. Clinton has proposed increased authorizations for these funds and would create similar funds to help states and localities meet the requirements of the Safe Drinking Water Act.

The most explosive issue in the clean water reauthorization concerns Section 404, which regulates the dredging and filling of wetlands. After promising a policy of "no net loss" of wetlands during the 1988 campaign, President Bush found himself mired in controversy when members of his staff rejected a proposed revision of the government wetlands manual by the four agencies charged with wetlands protection (the Army Corps of Engineers, Environmental Protection Agency, Soil Conservation Service, and Fish and Wildlife Service). The new manual redefined various types of wetlands according to scientific criteria such as plant growth in wet soils rather than using traditional measurements of standing water. Responding to opposition from a coalition of land developers, farmers, and energy interests, the White House quickly stepped in to block the more restrictive definitions. After consideration by Vice President Dan Quayle's Council on Competitiveness, new definitions were proposed that would have eliminated nearly half the wetland areas from protection.[14]

President Clinton has promised a "real no net loss policy," and environmentalists will seek to strengthen the scientific criteria for wetlands protection in Section 404. The new administration has also indicated, however, that it will seek to avoid open confrontation on controversial land use issues of this kind. EPA administrator Carol Browner had considerable success in working out compromises among land developers, farmers, and environmentalists to restore sections of the Everglades National Park when she was Florida's secretary of environmental regulation, and it appears she will attempt to extend this pattern of cooperation.[15] But it is unlikely that a major battle can be avoided over both Section 404 and the broader issue of whether wetlands protection constitutes a "taking" of property that requires economic compensation to owners (chap. 7).

Biodiversity and Endangered Species

Few issues have aroused more emotional controversy than the conflict between environmentalists and loggers over preservation of the northern spotted owl in the ancient forests of the Pacific Northwest. The conflict began in June 1990 when the Fish and Wildlife Service classified the owl as a threatened species under the provisions of the Endangered Species Act (ESA). As in the case of wetlands, President Bush rejected a scientific committee's recommendation to protect much of the owl's habitat, and attempted to impose an alternative plan opening more acreage to logging in order to protect local jobs. But a federal judge blocked most logging in the area, leading President Bush to call for major revision of the ESA during the presidential campaign of 1992. The president condemned the act, calling it "a sword aimed at the jobs, families and communities of entire regions like the Northwest." He argued that the law must be rewritten to give priority to economic considerations in conflicts of this kind. Clinton and Gore defended the ESA and proposed a summit meeting to try to resolve the issues in the Northwest; but no resolution was achieved before Bush left office.[16]

President Clinton honored his campaign promise by convening a "forest summit" in Portland, Oregon, in April 1993. After listening to extensive testimony on both sides, he appointed a special task force to develop compromise solutions for the old-growth area. One such solution might be to curtail logging permanently but provide compensation to affected communities for job retraining and economic diversification. This would not resolve, however, the larger questions of how much priority should be given to preserving biodiversity generally and how our approach to species preservation can be made more effective in the future.

Many environmentalists believe the Endangered Species Act is obsolete and should be revised to place greater emphasis on preserving whole ecosystems rather than individual species and their habitats. The Clinton administration appears to agree. Secretary of the Interior Bruce Babbitt has announced his intention to shift toward a more proactive ecosystem protection approach in order to avoid the kind of costly single-species conflicts sparked by the ESA.[17] Forest Service policy is also shifting toward more selective harvesting and ecosystem management, a policy President Clinton could institutionalize in coming years.

International Aid and Cooperation

Vice President Gore was a leading critic of the Bush administration at the Río conference and has called for much greater global environmental cooperation. During the campaign he and Clinton indicated that their administration would support a stronger climate change treaty and sign the biodiversity treaty. In his 1993 Earth Day speech the president announced he would sign the biodiversity treaty, having interpreted its language to be compatible with the concerns of U.S. business. He also pledged to develop an action plan to meet the goals of the climate treaty by reducing CO_2 emissions.[18] Other potential areas for stronger international cooperation include rainforest protection, international hazardous waste shipment, export and use of agricultural pesticides and chemicals, and a host of issues relating to nuclear fuel reprocessing, destruction of nuclear weapons, and weapons proliferation.

A number of other initiatives, such as restoration of U.S. funding for U.N. population programs,[19] increased support for the Global Environmental Facility at the World Bank, and negotiation of "debt for Nature" swaps in developing countries, will require additional financial commitments at a time of high budget deficits and little popular enthusiasm for foreign aid programs. In his first major statement on trade and aid policies, President Clinton indicated that aid to developing countries will emphasize environmental values:

> Our aid policies must do more to address population pressures, to support environmentally responsible sustainable development, to promote more accountable governance, and to foster a fair distribution of the fruits of growth among an increasingly restive world population, where over 1 billion people still exist on barely a dollar a day. These efforts will reap us dividends of trade, of friendship and peace.[20]

Trade and the Environment

One of the newer issues on the president's agenda is the relationship between international trade agreements and environmental protection. Until recently environmental problems were considered outside the scope of trade negotiations. But the proposed North American Free Trade Agreement (NAFTA) with Mexico and Canada raised serious environmental concerns about pollution along the Mexican border and became a major issue in the 1992 presidential campaign. Mr. Clinton endorsed the treaty on condition that additional environmental and labor safeguards would be added. Conversely, negotiations on the General Agreement on Tariffs and Trade (GATT) have raised the question of whether certain kinds of national environmental policies might be construed as unfair barriers to trade. As in the European Community (chap. 12), new policies are needed to ensure that opening markets to free trade does not accelerate resource depletion or undermine other conservation efforts.[21]

At the same time, energy efficiency and good environmental design are increasingly viewed as advantages in trade competition. During the 1992 campaign the argument was frequently made that the United States was falling behind nations such as Germany and Japan in taking advantage of these opportunities. Clinton and Gore have proposed targeted incentives and increased government aid for developing "green" technologies (see below).

Environmental Justice

Another general issue that is rapidly gaining attention is environmental justice. Although dating from the same era, the civil rights and environmental movements have had little in common until recently. It is increasingly recognized, however, that low-income individuals and minorities are disproportionately exposed to environmental hazards such as lead poisoning, industrial air pollution, and toxic waste sites. This is particularly true in poor urban neighborhoods and in the South, but research indicates that it holds for the nation as a whole when factors such as socioeconomic status are controlled.[22] African Americans, Hispanics, Asians, and Native Americans have formed hundreds of new grass-roots organizations to fight pollution in their communities, and in late 1991 a National People of Color Environmental Leadership Summit meeting was held in Washington, D.C.[23] Mainstream environmental groups such as the Sierra Club Legal Defense Fund have also joined civil rights and other organizations in bringing lawsuits against environmental discrimination.

The Environmental Protection Agency issued a report in June 1992 confirming that racial minorities suffer disproportionately from various kinds of pollution.[24] Administrator William Reilly vowed to make environmental equity a new agency priority, but EPA denied responsibility for lax enforcement of the laws. There is some evidence, however, that environmental policies have been implemented less effectively in minority areas. For example, a 1992 study found that the government acted much more slowly and levied much lower fines when cleaning up Superfund sites in minority neighborhoods than in white areas. Fines averaged $333,556 in largely white communities but only $55,318 in areas with the greatest minority populations.[25] The EPA and Justice Department will be hard-pressed to deal with such inequalities in the future. New language requiring equal treatment under environmental laws is likely to be included in legislation establishing the Department of the Environment.

New Strategies and Methods

The need to "reinvent government" to encourage innovation and experimentation was a prominent theme during the 1992 elections.[26] Environmental regulation has been singled out as a leading candidate for such experimentation for some time, but relatively few departures have yet been made from the traditional standards-and-enforcement approach adopted in the 1970s. In most areas EPA is still charged with writing detailed regulations requiring individual polluters to install specific technologies to mitigate emissions or discharges at "the end of the pipe." Such "command and control" regulation of major pollution sources has had some success in improving environmental quality (chap. 1), and will continue to be needed to protect public health and environmental resources against many immediate threats. But a broad consensus has now developed among economists, business leaders, government officials, and environmental professionals that more efficient and cost-effective methods are necessary if we are to address the expanding environmental agenda of the 1990s and beyond. The following section lists seven areas in which new policy approaches are receiving wide discussion.

Pollution Prevention

Perhaps no idea has received more widespread general support than the wisdom of preventing pollution before it occurs rather than trying to clean it up later. Prevention is usually far less expensive for companies and eliminates potential liability. It spares people from harmful exposure to wastes. It is the only way to halt deterioration of the environment in the long run. Yet only a tiny fraction of EPA's resources is devoted to *prevention*, while the remainder is essentially spent on end-of-the-pipe cleanups (chap. 6). The reason is that most of the environmental statutes (app. 1) require after-the-fact controls. They are based on the assumption that environmental problems can be managed without significant changes in existing production technologies and consumption patterns. This assumption can no longer be sustained.[27]

The Bush administration deserves credit for passage of the Pollution Prevention Act of 1990, which established prevention as an EPA priority for the first time and authorized cooperative programs with industry to install energy-efficient lighting and to encourage source reduction of toxic wastes. Several hundred companies are voluntarily participating in these programs, mainly because pollution prevention pays; that is, investments in waste reduction, materials recovery, and recycling often pay large dividends in the form of cost savings and liability avoidance.[28] Public information programs such as the annual Toxic Release Inventory on chemical discharges from industrial plants also give polluters an incentive to eliminate use of toxic materials to avoid community criticism. Some companies, such as Monsanto, Polaroid, and McDonald's, have made great strides toward waste minimization, and many others are committed to doing so. Yet many of the nation's largest corporations continue to generate enormous pollution. A study released in late 1992 identified Cargill, Ciba-Geigy, DuPont, Exxon, General Electric, General Motors, Georgia Pacific, Maxxam, Rockwell, and USX as the ten worst toxic polluters in America.[29]

Pollution prevention can be extended to all sectors of the economy and government, including energy and transportation, agriculture, and defense. In many cases relatively simple process changes or materials substitution can produce dramatic results at low cost. It is also the most effective strategy for reducing pollution from many small, decentralized sources such as garages and dry cleaners that are difficult to regulate directly. The Clinton administration and Congress should strengthen the pollution prevention emphasis of environmental laws such as the Resource Conservation and Recovery Act and Clean Water Act and provide other new incentives for waste reduction. Other policy changes, such as higher energy taxes and proactive land use regulation, can also be considered prevention strategies because they seek to reduce future environmental costs.

Environmental Restoration

Like pollution prevention, environmental restoration is not really a new idea but one that is increasingly recognized as an effective supplement to traditional resource management practices. The fundamental idea is that once environmental degradation in a specific region is halted, with proper management the damaged ecosystem can be restored to much better health. Some current restoration plans are much more ambitious than in the past. For example, in February 1993 scientists meeting in Chicago revealed a plan for the recovery of the large and biologically rich oak savanna that once stretched from the Great Lakes to Texas. It calls for working with public and private landowners to set aside sufficient land to assure the ecosystem's health. Similar efforts are under way in California for the coastal sage ecosystem, one of the state's ten bioregions.[30]

Environmental restoration of lakes, rivers, and wetlands is becoming a more common policy goal. Under the Great Lakes Water Quality Agreement, remedial action plans are being developed for the forty-three most seriously degraded areas—in river mouths, ports, harbors, and wetlands in the Great Lakes ecosystem. In addition, the federal Omnibus Water Act of 1992 mandated major changes in water use in California's Central Valley to restore ecosystems damaged by years of water diversion for intensive agriculture in the area.

These plans, and others like them, represent a radical departure from most pollution and land management policies. By intervening before an ecosystem becomes so degraded that few options are left, this approach facilitates carefully planned trade-offs between environmental protection and economic growth and thus supports the goal of sustainable development. We will likely see increasing pressures for environmental restoration projects in the United States and globally in the coming decade, but they will succeed only with strong and determined leadership from both public and private sectors.

Comparative Risk Assessment

Comparative risk assessment is discussed in chapters 6 and 10. The logic of this approach lies in the variable magnitude of risk to public and ecosystem health posed by environmental threats ranging from the deterioration of the ozone layer to urban smog. Environmental policies attempt to reduce these risks, but they do so with wildly different efficiency. Hence a great deal of money can be spent by governments and private parties without an appreciable return in risk reduction, that is, in improved public health and environmental quality.

Comparative risk assessment is intended to facilitate the setting of priorities for action by the EPA and other agencies and thus to increase the rationality of environmental policy. The case for such an approach has been made by the EPA since 1987, and it became a major policy objective under William Reilly in the early 1990s. The agency's Science Advisory Board strongly endorsed comparative risk assessment in its widely read 1990 report *Reducing Risk*, in which it urged the agency to target its environmental protection efforts based on opportunities for the greatest reduction in risk. The report recommended giving far more attention to reduction of ecological risk, in effect putting it on a par with reducing human health risk.[31]

More extensive use of risk assessment for setting priorities depends on improved methodologies for measuring risk. As Richard N. L. Andrews notes in chapter 10, present methods are subject to significant limitations, which have led to uncertainty about the actual risks posed and thus about the need for corrective action. The uncertainty fuels controversy over the use of these methods to set public policy, for example, over the level of pesticide residues permitted in the nation's food supply or allowable concentrations of chemicals in drinking water.

Another major challenge is the need to reconcile public and expert perceptions of risks. The two are often sharply at odds. In some cases the public is more concerned about environmental and health risks (for example, from hazardous wastes and oil spills) than are the experts. In other cases (such as indoor air pollution, drinking water quality, and loss of biological diversity) the experts are more worried than is the public. More often than not, congressional policies reflect the public's view of risk. The result is that EPA is often mandated to devote time and resources to relatively low-priority risks while ignoring greater ones.

We will need to think more seriously about comparative risk assessment and priority setting in the years ahead. If for no other reason, limited budgetary resources demand that we put the considerable money we spend on environmental protection to the best possible use. Scarce resources will also force us to make difficult societal choices about the level of risk we are prepared to bear in exchange for the benefits we receive, and about who should make such intrinsically controversial decisions.

Environmental Taxes, Incentives, and Markets

Economists have long espoused the concept of internalizing environmental costs by taxation or other means of pricing "externalities." The idea of utilizing market signals to encourage behaviors that prevent pollution and conserve resources now has general support. The late senator John Heinz (R-Pa.) and former senator Tim Wirth (D-Colo.) sponsored a series of studies known as *Project 88* proposing a wide range of market-based alternatives to direct regulation.[32] Leading environmental think tanks such as the Worldwatch Institute and the World Resources Institute have proposed a broad array of environmental taxes that would harness market forces to change consumer behavior.[33] President Clinton and Vice President Gore have also spoken in favor of such "green thumb" approaches.

Energy taxes have been among the most widely discussed market-oriented approaches, and the Btu tax initially proposed by Clinton was expected to motivate changes in both consumer preferences and industrial production. For example, auto manufacturers were reportedly considering production of more small cars.[34] Other taxes or fees could be designed to discourage use of toxic chemicals and virgin materials, to reduce the generation of solid and hazardous waste, and to discourage the purchase of "gas guzzler" cars. Tax credits are being targeted for renewable energy technologies and other pollution-reducing products and processes, and rebates could be given for the purchase of environmentally benign products. Research and development for new environmental technologies can also be directly subsidized (see below).

Conversely, government subsidies to environmentally destructive activities like timber harvesting on public lands and cheap water supply to western farmers can be eliminated. Secretary of the Interior Bruce Babbitt announced in early 1993 sweeping plans to raise grazing, timber, mining, and water use fees to market levels, reversing a "century of practices that have promoted development of the West at government expense." The Agriculture Department's Forest Service has also announced plans to end below-cost timber sales in the national forests.[35]

As A. Myrick Freeman explains in chapter 9, tradable permit systems that create private "pollution markets" are an alternative to pollution taxes. Although EPA has been experimenting with emissions trading since the 1970s, the first major attempt to implement a pollution credit-trading system was made in the acid rain provisions of the 1990 Clean Air Act. It appears this program will be difficult to implement, both because regulated electrical utilities have little incentive to cut costs and because some trades may actually increase pollution in certain regions such as the Northeast.[36] Many other proposals, however, have been made for utilizing the emission-trading principle. For example, Vice President Gore has proposed a market trading system for CO_2 emissions both within the United

States and internationally.[37] Until more experience is gained with these systems, environmental taxes and credits may provide a more feasible alternative.

Green Consumerism and Environmental Design

A more direct way to utilize the marketplace is to encourage the design, manufacture, and sale of "green" consumer products. Many products are already being marketed as environmentally safe because they contain no toxic substances, are energy efficient to operate, or contain recycled materials or are themselves recyclable. Evidence suggests that many consumers prefer buying such products and will often pay at least a modest premium for them, and several green consumer guides have been published. One problem is that environmental advertising is often misleading. The Federal Trade Commission has issued voluntary guidelines for such advertising and there are two private "green label" services, but Congress has not yet set binding standards for green marketing.[38] Several proposals have been made for federal legislation to regulate environmental claims and to establish a national environmental labeling system comparable to those in European nations (chap. 12). Ideally, such ecolabels should advise consumers of the environmental costs of products over their entire life-cycle from materials processing and manufacturing to ultimate disposal.

In anticipation of future markets, as well as of imminent regulation, many companies are redesigning products to be environmentally competitive. Some auto manufacturers, for example, are following the example of BMW and Volkswagen, which are beginning to design cars for total disassembly and recycling of parts. Engineers are being trained in "design for the environment" (DFE) in some corporations.[39] A recent report of the Office of Technology Assessment, *Green Products by Design*, suggests a broad range of incentives that could be used to encourage better environmental design not only of products but also of their entire systems of manufacturing and consumption.[40]

Environmental Research and Technology Development

Increased support for scientific R&D is essential if we are to deal effectively with the growing list of domestic and global environmental problems demanding attention. As mentioned above, more precise and systematic knowledge is needed in many areas of science if we are to set environmental priorities on the basis of relative risks and benefits. Although support for environmental research has recovered from its low point in the Reagan administration, it remains a small fraction of the $73 billion federal R&D budget. Funding for the EPA's Office of Research and Development was lower (in constant dollars) in FY 1992 than in FY

1980.[41] The largest spending increase in the Bush administration was for global climate research, which rose fivefold to more than $1.1 billion in 1992. Yet nearly 60 percent of federal R&D was still devoted to military purposes despite the demise of the Soviet Union and the end of the Cold War.

We now have an opportunity to redirect R&D in many of the government's seven hundred research laboratories toward environmental and energy problems. During the campaign Clinton and Gore proposed to shift a substantial share of defense R&D to civilian purposes. Shortly after taking office, Clinton announced a broad new technology policy that called for spending $17 billion over four years to support civilian technologies, including a $272 million increase for EPA technology programs and a joint venture with the auto industry to develop a "clean car." Although no new civilian technology agency was created, funding for the National Institute of Standards and Technology in the Commerce Department would be sharply increased (to $1.2 billion by 1997). Department of Energy support for renewable energy and energy conservation would rise by $1.3 billion over four years, while funding for nuclear power would be reduced. Overall, under Clinton's plan the civilian share of the R&D budget would rise from 41 percent to 50 percent.[42]

One area in which more R&D could pay the greatest dividends is in developing highly energy-efficient technologies and renewable energy sources. A 1991 report by four major environmental and energy organizations concluded that the United States could reduce its energy consumption by 30 percent to 50 percent and cut CO_2 emissions by as much as 71 percent over the next forty years if it developed renewable energy technologies. Moreover, such a sustainable energy transition would result in at least *$1.8 trillion* in savings to the economy.[43] The Union of Concerned Scientists carried out an extensive study of renewable energy supply in the Midwestern states; it found enormous potential for wind generation and biomass fuel production in this region.[44] Energy conservation and renewable energy production are relatively labor-intensive compared with current practices, so such a transition could create substantial employment. One study calculates that a major effort in this direction could lead to a net increase of 1 million jobs by 2010.[45] Such findings should be rapidly assessed and exploited by government laboratories in cooperation with private industry.

Environmental Accounting

Many of our difficulties in utilizing economic efficiency criteria to guide environmental policy stem from the inaccuracy of our accounting systems in measuring environmental costs and benefits. The national index of output, gross national product (GNP), has come under increasing criticism. Although widely used as the primary indicator of the state of our economy and national welfare, GNP counts all expenditures for pollution control and cleanup as part of our output of goods and services but does not subtract the economic value of losses caused by environmental degradation and depletion of nonrenewable resources.[46] Increased pollution thus counts positively rather than negatively, while depreciation of environmental capital is ignored. As Al Gore has put it, "For all practical purposes, GNP treats the rapid and reckless destruction of the environment as a good thing!"[47]

A number of economists and international agencies have developed alternative measures of national welfare that more accurately value environmental goods and services and overall quality of life. The United States does considerably less well on some of these scales than on conventional economic indexes.[48] The Clinton administration and Congress, in cooperation with experts from other nations, should jointly develop a new definition of GNP that more accurately estimates environmental costs and benefits. Corporate accounting systems could also be improved to better represent their environmental liabilities. Gore has proposed that governments adopt "measures to encourage full disclosure of companies' responsibility for environmental damage."[49]

Rethinking Environmental Politics

Broadening the definition of environmental policy presents great challenges and opportunities for political action. The monumental scope of the ecological problems now recognized is mind-boggling and calls for environmental activism on nearly every front. Insofar as the fundamental problems are long term and global, they are likely to command an increasing share of intellectual and financial resources for decades to come. The concept of sustainable development touches every aspect of human life, from individual life-styles and tastes to the corporate strategies of multinationals. We are still in the early stages of conceptualizing many of the implications, but they undoubtedly carry far beyond our preoccupations of the past two decades with national regulation of specific types of pollutants or preservation of individual species and landscapes.

Environmental policy itself thus has to be rethought in "ecological" terms; that is, reconsidered in relation to the larger social, economic, political, and moral systems within which it is embedded. To be successful, environmentalists will be challenged to develop new skills and broaden their understanding of other human values. As Robert C. Paehlke suggests in the preceding chapter, there is great potential for integrating and balancing the "three Es"—environment, economy, and ethics. But alliances with civil rights, social justice, and community development groups may require greater tolerance of differences and, in many cases, more flexibility and modesty in advocating particular solutions.[50] A willingness to try less intrusive and centralized approaches such as market incentives and local education and consensus building might often lead to superior results. At the same time, we need to become much more aware of our responsibilities to the global ecological system.

A strong case can be made, as Christopher J. Bosso does in chapter 2, that an environmental "movement" no longer exists. Instead, thousands of independent local community organizations and protest groups are proliferating alongside the two-dozen or so large and well-established national conservation and environmental organizations in Washington, D.C. Although the latter are often effective in lobbying on national policy, pressure from the grass-roots organizations may be even more important in mobilizing public opinion and effecting change. For example, companies are often far more sensitive to local citizen pressures than to regulatory controls from above. Conversely, environmentalists are more likely to find constructive solutions when they are forced to consider the fears and concerns of their neighbors. In any case, the 1990s will likely bring increased pluralism and fragmentation among environmental groups working at different levels on different issues.

On the broadest level, there are reasons to believe that ecological awareness and a new environmental ethic are steadily advancing in this country and in most areas of the world. In chapter 1 we spoke of a deep current of cultural change that undergirds public concern for the environment. Lester Brown of the Worldwatch Institute has noted that a "perceptual threshold" has been crossed, and that it is beginning to affect the way people everywhere think about their place in the biosphere. Survey evidence from many nations supports this conclusion:

> Results from a 1992 Gallup International Institute survey conducted in 24 countries show widespread concern for the environment among citizens of all types of countries. While the specific problems that generate concern vary from country to country, Gallup's *Health of the Planet* survey reveals a surprisingly high level of citizen awareness of environmental deterioration and support for environmental protection. Concern over the environment has clearly become a worldwide phenomenon.[51]

Although the recent economic recession has reduced financial and membership support for environmental groups in the United States and for green parties in Europe since 1990, there is no reason to believe that underlying public concerns over the future health of the environment have been weakened.[52]

Indeed, long- and short-term trends favoring environmental protection seem to have converged in the election of Clinton and Gore. Despite constraints posed by budget deficits and congressional divisions, we expect to see the most active environmental presidency in two decades. But the success of the Clinton administration will depend on its ability to convince the American public that environmental economics makes sense and that some traditional behavioral patterns must be changed. This will require not only acceptance of technical and economic change, including higher costs and less convenience in many cases, but also a continuing shift toward deeper ethical commitments. We need to rethink the values of the "consumer society" itself.[53]

Governing the Future

It has been said that for the first time in evolutionary history human beings have achieved a greater measure of influence over the future of their planet than evolution itself. If this is so, we have no alternative but to decide what kind of future we want. One possibility is to continue on our present course of human development. However, a growing world consensus holds that this course cannot be sustained without triggering catastrophic changes in the Earth's natural systems. A 1992 report of the U.S. National Academy of Sciences and the Royal Society of London opened with a dire warning: "If current predictions of population growth prove accurate and patterns of human activity on the planet remain unchanged, science and technology may not be able to prevent either irreversible degradation of the environment or continued poverty for much of the world."[54] We do not know whether changes in the planetary life support system, such as deterioration of the atmospheric ozone layer, are irreversible. Yet most environmental experts believe we have time to preserve our essential life support systems if we act with sufficient foresight in the next few decades.

In a follow-up to their pathbreaking 1972 study, *Limits to Growth*, Donella Meadows, Dennis Meadows, and Jørgen Randers have recently projected ten different computer-generated scenarios of the next century in which differing assumptions are made about economic, technological, and human development.[55] Most of the scenarios, including those based on current policies and practices, lead to ecological collapse. They demonstrate, however, that with rapid adoption of new industrial technologies, slower population growth, and other changes in human values and behavior, ecological stabilization and global economic needs can be reconciled.

Stephen Schneider, a respected climatologist, has distinguished three strategic responses to major environmental threats such as global warming: *technological countermeasures, adaptation, and prevention.*[56] Until now we have relied heavily on the first strategy of developing technical fixes for such problems as air and water pollution. But it is far less certain that corrective measures can be engineered to deal with disturbances to planetary systems such as atmospheric cycles or ocean pollution. An alternative is adaptation to global change; we can "seek to adjust society to environmental changes without attempting to counteract or prevent those changes."[57] Under this approach, which is supported by many economists, we could rely on price fluctuations and other warning signals to avoid environmental "overshoot." We could also devise strategies for anticipating problems such as global warming by developing more heat-resistant crop strains, building dikes to prevent coastal flooding, or even moving populations to higher elevations or cooler regions. The third approach, prevention, calls for stopping or reversing current activities that are likely to produce adverse ecological changes. This approach is obviously preferred by environmentalists, but it will require far-reaching changes in both technology and human life-styles on a global scale.

Worldwide prevention will demand far more international cooperation and "governance" than we now have. The challenges we face are ultimately human and political: meeting basic human needs, limiting population growth, restricting consumption of nonrenewable resources, building a sense of world community, and negotiating mutually beneficial agreements among nations. These problems can be resolved only with a much longer time horizon than we are accustomed to in democratic societies. Political leadership is therefore essential. Democracies have proved capable of sustaining national and international efforts to defeat enemies in war and to contain them for decades in peacetime. But our success in defeating communism hardly means "the end of history," as Francis Fukuyama has suggested.[58] Rather, the coming decades will bring even more pressing challenges if we are to stabilize life on the planet for ourselves and for the generations to come.[59]

Notes

The quotation from Al Gore is taken from his book, *Earth in the Balance: Ecology and the Human Spirit* (Boston: Houghton Mifflin, 1992), 269.

1. *Choosing a Sustainable Future*, The Report of the National Commission on the Environment (Washington, D.C.: World Wildlife Fund, 1992), v.
2. *Partnerships to Progress: The Report of the President's Commission on Environmental Quality* (Washington, D.C.: President's Commission on Environmental Quality, January 1993). See also Business Council for Sustainable Development, Stephen Schmidheiney, chairman, *Changing Course: A Global Business Perspective on Development and Environment* (Cambridge: MIT Press, 1992).
3. *Changing Our Ways: America and the New World* (New York: Carnegie Endowment for International Peace, 1992), 38-46.
4. See United Nations, *Agenda 21, Rio Declaration, and Forest Principles* (New York: United Nations Publications, 1993); and Peter M. Haas, Marc A. Levy, and Edward A. Parson, "Appraising the Earth Summit," *Environment* 34 (October 1992): 6-11, 26-33.
5. "Jack Gibbons: Plugging into the Power Structure," *Science* 259 (February 19, 1993), 1115-1116.
6. Tom Kenworthy, "Tangled Web of Policy Faces Babbitt at Interior," *Star Tribune* (Minneapolis), February 21, 1993, 8.
7. See "National Energy Strategy Provisions," *Congressional Quarterly Weekly Report*, November 28, 1991, 3722-3730; and Holly Idelson, "After Two-Year Odyssey, Energy Strategy Clears," *Congressional Quarterly Weekly Report*, October 10, 1992, 3141-3146.

8. Steven Greenhouse, "Fuels Tax: Spreading the Pain," *New York Times*, February 18, 1993, 12; and Robert D. Hershey, Jr., "Indirect Effects of the Energy Tax," *New York Times*, February 20, 1993, 6.

9. Steven Greenhouse, "Manufacturers and Farmers Join in Opposing a Tax on Energy," *New York Times*, May 6, 1993, 14; Michael Wines, "Using Taxation in a Good Cause Often Backfires," *New York Times*, June 6, 1993, E3; David E. Rosenbaum, "Clinton Backs Off Plan For New Tax on Heat in Fuels," *New York Times*, June 9, 1993, 1.

10. Milton Russell, E. William Colglazier, and Bruce E. Tonn, "The U.S. Hazardous Waste Legacy," *Environment* 34 (July-August 1992): 12-14, 34-39.

11. See especially Daniel Mazmanian and David Morell, *Beyond Superfailure: America's Toxics Policy for the 1990s* (Boulder: Westview, 1992); and Kent E. Portney, *Siting Hazardous Waste Treatment Facilities* (Westport, Conn.: Auburn House, 1991). President Clinton has been highly critical of the Superfund program.

12. See, e.g., Barnaby J. Feder, "In the Clutches of the Superfund Mess," *New York Times*, June 16, 1991, F1; "Little of Superfund Settlements Go to Cleanup," *New York Times*, April 26, 1992, 6.

13. For an excellent overview of the issues, see Debra S. Knopman and Richard A. Smith, "Twenty Years of the Clean Water Act," *Environment* 35 (January-February 1993): 17-20, 34-41.

14. On the wetlands controversy, see Philip J. Hilts, "U.S. Aids Retreat on Wetlands Rule," *New York Times*, November 23, 1991, 1; Michael Weisskopf, "Is the Idea to Protect Wetlands or Open Them Up?" *Washington Post National Weekly Edition*, January 20-26, 1992, 31-32; and Joseph Alper, "War Over the Wetlands: Ecologists v. the White House," *Science* 257 (August 21, 1992), 1043-1044. The Bush administration decided against putting its weaker regulations into effect before leaving office.

15. Keith Schneider, "The Nominee for E.P.A. Sees Industry's Side Too," *New York Times*, December 17, 1992, 13.

16. Michael Wines, "Bush, in Far West, Sides with Loggers," *New York Times*, September 15, 1992; Keith Schneider, "For Clinton and Bush, Contradictions in Balancing Jobs and Conservation," *New York Times*, October 13, 1992, 11; "Lujan Leaves Spotted Owl Decision to Successor," *Washington Post*, January 15, 1993, 10.

17. William K. Stevens, "Interior Secretary Is Pushing a New Way to Save Species," *New York Times*, February 17, 1993, 1; and Stevens, "Babbitt to Map Ecosystems Under Policy Shift," *New York Times*, March 14, 1993, 14.

18. Richard L. Berke, "Clinton Supports Two Major Steps for Environment," *New York Times*, April 22, 1993, 1.

19. Robin Toner, "Clinton Orders Reversal of Abortion Restrictions Left by Reagan and Bush," *New York Times*, January 23, 1993, 1. One of the five orders Clinton signed lifted the prohibition on aid to the U.N. program. See also Steven Greenhouse, "Family Planning Officials Laud Clinton Move on Bans," *New York Times*, January 24, 1993, 13.

20. "President's Speech: Prosperity Aids Freedom," *New York Times*, February 27, 1993, 4.

21. See Hilary F. French, *Costly Tradeoffs: Reconciling Trade and the Environment*, Worldwatch Paper 113 (Washington, D.C.: Worldwatch Institute, March 1993); and U.S. Congress, Office of Technology Assessment, *Trade and the Environment: Conflicts and Opportunities* (Washington, D.C.: U.S. Government Printing Office, May 1992).

22. Robert Bullard, *Dumping in Dixie* (Boulder: Westview, 1991); Bunyan Bryant and Paul Mohai, eds., *Race and the Incidence of Environmental Hazards* (Boulder:

Westview, 1992); and Robert F. Kennedy, Jr., and Dennis Revira, "Pollution's Chief Victims: The Poor," *New York Times*, August 15, 1992, 15.

23. Roberto Suro, "Pollution-Weary Minorities Try Civil Rights Tack," *New York Times*, January 11, 1993, 1; and Karl Grossman, "From Toxic Racism to Environmental Justice," *E Magazine* 3 (May-June 1992): 28-35.

24. EPA, *Environmental Equity: Reducing Risk for All Communities* (Washington, D.C.: EPA, June 1992). See also *EPA Journal* 18 (March-April 1992), issue entitled "Environmental Protection—Has It Been Fair?"; and John R. Cushman, Jr., "E.P.A.'s New Focus on Threat to the Poor," *New York Times*, January 21, 1992, B7.

25. "Minorities Get Slower EPA Action, Report Says," *Star Tribune* (Minneapolis), September 14, 1992, 7. The findings were published in a special insert of the *National Law Journal* on September 14, 1992.

26. *Reinventing Government*, an influential book by David Osborne and Ted Gaebler (Reading, Mass.: Addison-Wesley, 1992), was frequently mentioned during the campaign. An endorsement by Bill Clinton appears on the jacket of the book.

27. World Commission on Environment and Development, *Our Common Future* (New York: Oxford University Press, 1987); Business Council on Sustainable Development, *Changing Course.*

28. See Joel S. Hirschhorn and Kirsten U. Oldenburg, *Prosperity Without Pollution* (New York: Van Nostrand Reinhold, 1991); Richard Andrews, "Heading Off Potential Problems," *EPA Journal* 18 (May-June 1992): 41-45; Business Council on Sustainable Development, *Changing Course;* and "Reducing Toxic Waste Produces Quick Results," *Wall Street Journal*, August 11, 1992, B1.

29. See "Toxic Ten: America's Truant Corporations," *Mother Jones* (January-February 1993). Detailed reports on the environmental records of these and other companies are available from the Council on Economic Priorities in New York.

30. William K. Stevens, "Restoring an Ancient Landscape: An Innovative Plan for the Midwest," *New York Times*, March 2, 1993, B2.

31. EPA, *Reducing Risk: Setting Priorities and Strategies for Environmental Protection* (Washington, D.C.: EPA, September 1990). For a discussion of the pros and cons of risk assessment, see Graeme Browning, "Taking Some Risks," *National Journal*, June 1, 1991, 1279-1282.

32. Tim Wirth and John Heinz, *Project 88: Harnessing Market Forces to Protect Our Environment* (Washington, D.C.: n.p., December 1988); and *Project 88—Round II: Incentives for Action, Designing Market-Based Environmental Strategies* (Washington, D.C.: n.p., May 1991). See also Robert N. Stavins, "Harnessing the Marketplace," *EPA Journal* 18 (May-June 1992): 21-25; and *Ecological Economics: The Science and Management of Sustainability*, ed. Robert Constanza (New York: Columbia University Press, 1991).

33. Robert Repetto, Roger C. Dower, Robin Jenkins, and Jacqueline Geoghegan, *Green Fees: How a Tax Shift Can Work for the Environment and the Economy* (Washington, D.C.: World Resources Institute, 1992); Lester R. Brown "Launching the Environmental Revolution," in *State of the World 1992*, ed. Lester R. Brown (New York: Norton, 1992), 174-190.

34. Thomas C. Hayes, "How Industries View Energy Tax," *New York Times*, February 26, 1993, C1.

35. Timothy Egan, "Sweeping Reversal of U.S. Land Policy Sought by Clinton," *New York Times*, February 24, 1993, 1; and Keith Schneider, "U.S. Would End Cutting of Trees in Many Forests," *New York Times*, April 30, 1993, 1.

36. Matthew L. Wald, "Risk-Shy Utilities Avoid Trading Emission Credits," *New York Times*, January 25, 1993, C2; and James Dao, "A New, Unregulated Market: Selling the Right to Pollute," *New York Times*, February 6, 1993, 1.

37. Gore, *Earth in the Balance*, 345.

38. Keith Schneider, "Guides on Environmental Ad Claims," *New York Times*, July 29, 1992, C3. Several states regulate environmental claims; see Michael Specter, "Making Sense of Labeling on Products," *Washington Post*, December 16, 1991, B1.

39. Elizabeth Corcoran, "Thinking Green: Can Environmentalism Be a Strategic Advantage?" *Scientific American* (December 1992), 44-46.

40. Office of Technology Assessment, Congress of the United States, *Green Products by Design: Choices for a Cleaner Environment* (Washington, D.C.: U.S. Government Printing Office, September 1992).

41. Carnegie Commission on Science, Technology, and Government, *Environmental Research and Development: Strengthening the Federal Infrastructure* (New York: Carnegie Commission, December 1992), 116. The commission estimates that all federal environmental R&D funding amounted to 6.8 percent of the total federal R&D budget (p. 46).

42. John Markoff, "Clinton Proposes Changes in Policy to Aid Technology," *New York Times*, February 23, 1993, 1; Edmund L. Andrews, "Clinton's Technology Plan Would Redirect Billions From Military Research," *New York Times*, February 24, 1993, 8. The military share of the federal R&D budget fell under 50 percent in the Carter administration, but rose to nearly 70 percent under President Reagan.

43. Alliance to Save Energy, American Council for an Energy-Efficient Economy, Natural Resources Defense Council, and Union for Concerned Scientists (UCS), *America's Energy Choices* (Cambridge, Mass.: UCS, 1991).

44. Michael C. Brower, Michael W. Tennis, Eric W. Denzler, and Mark M. Kaplan, *Powering the Midwest: Renewable Electricity for the Economy and the Environment* (Cambridge, Mass.; UCS, March 1993).

45. Howard Geller, John DeCicco, and Skip Laitner, *Energy Efficiency and Job Creation* (Washington, D.C.: American Council for an Energy-Efficient Economy, 1992); see also Michael Renner, *Jobs in a Sustainable Economy*, Worldwatch Paper 104 (Washington, D.C.: Worldwatch Institute, September 1991).

46. See Robert Repetto, "Earth in the Balance Sheet: Incorporating Natural Resources in National Income Accounts," *Environment* 34 (September 1992): 12-20, 43-45; and Herman E. Daly and John B. Cobb, Jr., *For the Common Good* (Boston: Beacon, 1989), 62-84.

47. Gore, *Earth in the Balance*, 185.

48. One such index is the "Index of Sustainable Economic Welfare"; see Daly and Cobb, *For the Common Good*, 401-455.

49. Gore, *Earth in the Balance*, 346. The Securities and Exchange Commission is encouraging companies to disclose potential environmental liabilities; see John Holusha, "Market Place," *New York Times*, March 9, 1993, C6.

50. See, for example, Martin Lewis, *Green Delusions: An Environmentalist Critique of Radical Environmentalism* (Durham, N.C.: Duke University Press, 1992); and Robert C. Paehlke, *Environmentalism and the Future of Progressive Politics* (New Haven: Yale University Press, 1989).

51. Riley E. Dunlap, George H. Gallup, Jr., and Alec M. Gallup, "International Public Opinion Toward the Environment," *Impact Assessment* 11 (Spring 1993): 3-4. See also Richard Morin, "Giving the Green Light to the Environment: The World Would Pay the Price to Breathe Easier," *Washington Post National Weekly Edition*, June 15-21, 1992, 37; and Lester R. Brown, Christopher Flaven, and Sandra Postel, "A World at Risk," in *State of the World 1989*, ed. Lester R. Brown (New York: Norton, 1989), 5-8.

52. See Riley E. Dunlap and Angela G. Mertig, eds., *American Environmentalism: The U.S. Environmental Movement, 1970-1990* (Philadelphia: Taylor and Francis, 1990); and Riley E. Dunlap and Rik Scarce, "The Polls—Poll Trends: Environ-

mental Problems and Protection," *Public Opinion Quarterly* 55 (Winter 1991): 651-672.

53. Alan Thein During, *How Much Is Enough? The Consumer Society and the Future of the Earth*, Worldwatch Environmental Alert Series (New York: Norton, 1992).

54. Quoted in Lester Brown, "A New Era Unfolds," *State of the World 1993* (New York: Norton, 1993), 3.

55. Donella H. Meadows, Dennis L. Meadows, and Jørgen Randers, *Beyond the Limits: Confronting Global Collapse, Envisioning a Sustainable Future* (Post Mills, Vt.: Chelsea Green, 1992).

56. Stephen H. Schneider, *Global Warming: Are We Entering the Greenhouse Century?* (San Francisco: Sierra Club, 1989), 249ff.

57. Ibid., 253.

58. Francis Fukuyama, *The End of History and the Last Man* (New York: Free Press, 1992).

59. For example, see Paul Kennedy, *Preparing for the Twenty-first Century* (New York: Random House, 1993); and Christopher D. Stone, *The Gnat Is Older Than Man: Global Environment and Human Agenda* (Princeton, N.J.: Princeton University Press, 1993).

APPENDIX

APPENDIX.

Appendix 1 Major Federal Laws on the Environment, 1969-1992

Legislation	Implementing Agency	Key Provisions
	Nixon Administration	
National Environmental Policy Act of 1969, PL 91-190	All federal agencies	Declared a national policy to "encourage productive and enjoyable harmony between man and his environment"; required environmental impact statements; created Council on Environmental Quality (CEQ).
Resources Recovery Act of 1970, PL 91-512	Health, Education, and Welfare Department (later the Environmental Protection Agency)	Set up a program of demonstration and construction grants for innovative solid waste management systems; provided technical and financial assistance to state and local agencies in developing resource recovery and waste disposal systems.
Clean Air Act Amendments of 1970, PL 91-604	Environmental Protection Agency (EPA)	Required administrator to set national primary and secondary air quality standards and certain emission limits; required states to develop implementation plans by specific dates; required reductions in automobile emissions.
Federal Water Pollution Control Act (Clean Water Act) Amendments of 1972, PL 92-500	EPA	Set national water quality goals; established pollutant discharge permit system; increased federal grants to states to construct waste treatment plants.
Federal Environmental Pesticides Control Act of 1972 (amended the Federal Insecticide, Fungicide, and Rodenticide Act of 1947), PL 92-516	EPA	Required registration of all pesticides in U.S. commerce; allowed administrator to cancel or suspend registration under specified circumstances.

(Continued on next page)

Appendix 1 *(Continued)*

Legislation	Implementing Agency	Key Provisions
Marine Protection Act of 1972, PL 92-532	EPA	Regulated dumping of waste materials into the oceans and coastal waters.
Coastal Zone Management Act of 1972, PL 92-583	Office of Coastal Zone Management, Commerce Department	Authorized federal grants to the states to develop coastal zone management plans under federal guidelines.
Endangered Species Act of 1973, PL 93-205	Fish & Wildlife Service, Interior Department	Broadened federal authority to protect all "threatened" as well as "endangered" species; authorized grant program to assist state programs; required coordination among all federal agencies.
Ford Administration		
Safe Drinking Water Act of 1974, PL 93-523	EPA	Authorized federal government to set standards to safeguard the quality of public drinking water supplies and to regulate state programs for protecting underground water sources.
Toxic Substances Control Act of 1976, PL 94-469	EPA	Authorized premarket testing of chemical substances; allowed EPA to ban or regulate the manufacture, sale, or use of any chemical presenting an "unreasonable risk of injury to health or environment"; prohibited most uses of PCBs.
Federal Land Policy and Management Act of 1976, PL 94-579	Bureau of Land Management, Interior Department	Gave Bureau of Land Management authority to manage public lands for long-term benefits; officially ended policy of conveying public lands into private ownership.

| Resource Conservation and Recovery Act of 1976, PL 94-580 | EPA | Required EPA to set regulations for hazardous waste treatment, storage, transportation, and disposal; provided assistance for state hazardous waste programs under federal guidelines. |
| National Forest Management Act of 1976, PL 94-588 | U.S. Forest Service, Agriculture Department | Gave statutory permanence to national forest lands and set new standards for their management; restricted timber harvesting to protect soil and watersheds; limited clearcutting. |

Carter Administration

Surface Mining Control and Reclamation Act of 1977, PL 95-87	Interior Department	Established environmental controls over strip mining; limited mining on farmland, alluvial valleys, and slopes; required restoration of land to original contours.
Clean Air Act Amendments of 1977, PL 95-95	EPA	Amended and extended Clean Air Act; postponed deadlines for compliance with auto emission and air quality standards; set new standards for "prevention of significant deterioration" in clean air areas.
Clean Water Act Amendments of 1977, PL 95-217	EPA	Extended deadlines for industry and cities to meet treatment standards; set national standards for industrial pretreatment of wastes; increased funding for sewage treatment construction grants and gave states flexibility in determining priorities.
Public Utility Regulatory Policies Act of 1978, PL 95-617	Energy Department, states	Provided for Energy Department and Federal Energy Regulatory Commission regulation of electric and natural gas utilities and crude oil transportation systems in order to promote energy conservation and efficiency; allowed small co-generation and renewable energy projects to sell power to utilities.

(Continued on next page)

Appendix 1 *(Continued)*

Legislation	Implementing Agency	Key Provisions
Alaska National Interest Lands Conservation Act of 1980, PL 96-487	Interior Department, Agriculture Department	Protected 102 million acres of Alaskan land as national wilderness, wildlife refuges, and parks.
Comprehensive Environmental Response, Compensation, and Liability Act of 1980 (Superfund), PL 96-510	EPA	Authorized federal government to respond to hazardous waste emergencies and to clean up chemical dump sites; created $1.6 billion "Superfund"; established liability for cleanup costs.
Reagan Administration		
Nuclear Waste Policy Act of 1982, PL 97-425; Nuclear Waste Policy Amendments Act of 1987, PL 100-203	Energy Department	Established a national plan for the permanent disposal of high-level nuclear waste and authorized the Energy Department to site, obtain a license for, construct, and operate geologic repositories for spent fuel from commercial nuclear power plants. Amendments in 1987 specified Yucca Mountain, Nevada, as the sole national site to be studied.
Resource Conservation and Recovery Act Amendments of 1984, PL 98-616	EPA	Revised and strengthened EPA procedures for regulating hazardous waste facilities; authorized grants to states for solid and hazardous waste management; prohibited land disposal of certain hazardous liquid wastes; required states to consider recycling in comprehensive solid waste plans.

Food Security Act of 1985 (the Farm Bill), PL 99-198	Agriculture Department	Limited federal program benefits for producers of commodities on highly erodible land or converted wetlands; established a conservation reserve program; authorized Agriculture Department technical assistance for subsurface water quality preservation; revised and extended the Soil and Water Conservation Act (1977) programs through the year 2008.
Safe Drinking Water Act of 1986, PL 99-339	EPA	Reauthorized the Safe Drinking Water Act of 1974 and revised EPA safe drinking water programs, including grants to states for drinking water standards enforcement and groundwater protection programs; accelerated EPA schedule for setting standards for maximum contaminant levels of eighty-three toxic pollutants.
Superfund Amendments and Reauthorization Act of 1986 (SARA), PL 99-499	EPA	Provided $8.5 billion through 1991 to clean up the nation's most dangerous abandoned chemical waste dumps; set strict standards and timetables for cleaning up such sites; required that industry provide local communities with information on hazardous chemicals used or emitted.
Clean Water Act Amendments of 1987, PL 100-4	EPA	Amended the Federal Water Pollution Control Act of 1972 and extended and revised EPA water pollution control programs, including grants to states for construction of wastewater treatment facilities and implementation of mandated nonpoint-source pollution management plans; expanded EPA enforcement authority; established a national estuary program.

(Continued on next page)

Appendix 1 *(Continued)*

Legislation	Implementing Agency	Key Provisions
Global Climate Protection Act of 1987, PL 100-204	State Department	Authorized the State Department to develop an approach to the problems of global climate change; created an intergovernmental task force to develop U.S. strategy for dealing with the threat posed by global warming.
Ocean Dumping Act of 1988, PL 100-688	EPA	Amended the Marine Protection, Research, and Sanctuaries Act of 1972 to end all ocean disposal of sewage sludge and industrial waste by December 31, 1991; revised EPA regulation of ocean dumping by establishing dumping fees, permit requirements, and civil penalties for violations.

Bush Administration

Oil Pollution Prevention, Response, Liability, and Compensation Act of 1990, PL 101-380	Transportation Department, Commerce Department	Sharply increased liability limits for oil spill cleanup costs and damages; required double hulls on oil tankers and barges by 2015; required federal government to direct cleanups of major spills; required increased contingency planning and preparedness for spills; preserved states' rights to adopt more stringent liability laws and state oil spill compensation funds.
Pollution Prevention Act of 1990, PL 101-508	EPA	Established Office of Pollution Prevention in EPA to coordinate agency efforts at source reduction; created voluntary program to improve lighting efficiency; stated waste minimization was to be primary means of hazardous waste management; promoted voluntary industry reduction of hazardous waste; mandated source reduction and recycling report to accompany annual toxics release inventory under SARA (see above).

Clean Air Act Amendments of 1990, PL 101-549	EPA	Amended the Clean Air Act of 1970 by setting new requirements and deadlines of three to twenty years for major urban areas to meet federal clean air standards; imposed new, stricter emissions standards for motor vehicles and mandated cleaner fuels; required reduction in emission of sulfur dioxide and nitrogen oxides by power plants to limit acid deposition and created a market system of emission allowances; required regulation to set emission limits for all major sources of toxic or hazardous air pollutants and listed 189 chemicals to be regulated; prohibited the use of chlorofluorocarbons (CFCs) by the year 2000 and set phaseout of other ozone depleting chemicals.
Surface Transportation Efficiency Act of 1991 (Highway Bill), PL 102-240	Transportation Department	Authorized $151 billion over six years for transportation, including $31 billion for mass transit; required statewide and metropolitan long-term transportation planning; authorized states and communities to use transportation funds for public transit that reduces air pollution and energy use consistent with Clean Air Act of 1990; required community planners to analyze land use and energy implications of transportation projects they review.
Energy Policy Act of 1992, PL 102-486	Energy Department	Comprehensive energy act designed to reduce U.S. dependency on imported oil. Mandated restructuring of the electric utility industry to promote competition; encouraged energy conservation and efficiency; promoted renewable energy and alternative fuels for cars; eased licensing requirements for nuclear power plants; authorized extensive energy research and development.

(Continued on next page)

Appendix 1 *(Continued)*

Legislation	Implementing Agency	Key Provisions
The Omnibus Water Act of 1992, PL 102-575	Interior Department	Authorized completion of major water projects in the West; revised the Central Valley Project in California to allow transfer of water rights to urban areas and to encourage conservation through a tiered pricing system that allocates water more flexibly and efficiently; mandated extensive wildlife and environmental protection, mitigation, and restoration programs.

Note: Among major environmental policies due for renewal in 1993 or 1994 are the Endangered Species Act, Clean Water Act, Resource Conservation and Recovery Act, and Superfund (CERCLA).

Appendix 2 Federal Spending on Natural Resources and the Environment, Selected Fiscal Years, 1980-1993 (in millions of dollars)

Budget Item	1980	1981	1983	1985	1987	1989	1991	1993[a] (Est.)
Water resources	4,085 (5,573)	4,079 (4,968)	4,608 (5,149)	4,087 (4,271)	4,107 (4,107)	4,312 (4,011)	4,370 (3,710)	4,432 (3,512)
Conservation and land management	1,302 (1,776)	1,364 (1,661)	1,883 (2,104)	1,446 (1,511)	1,721 (1,721)	3,706 (3,447)	3,912 (3,321)	4,483 (3,552)
Recreational resources	1,642 (2,240)	1,252 (1,525)	1,581 (1,766)	1,574 (1,645)	1,685 (1,685)	1,895 (1,763)	2,482 (2,107)	2,516 (1,994)
Pollution control and abatement	4,672 (6,374)	2,982 (3,632)	3,677 (4,108)	4,303 (4,496)	5,296 (5,296)	5,068 (4,714)	6,150 (5,221)	7,013 (5,557)
Other natural resources	1,395 (1,903)	1,494 (1,820)	1,547 (1,728)	1,934 (2,021)	1,770 (1,770)	2,005 (1,865)	2,309 (1,960)	2,531 (2,006)
Total[b]	13,096 (17,866)	11,171 (13,607)	13,296 (14,856)	13,344 (13,944)	14,579 (14,579)	16,986 (15,801)	19,223 (16,318)	20,976 (16,621)

Sources: Office of Management and Budget, *Historical Tables, Budget of the United States Government, Fiscal Year 1992* (Washington, D.C.: U.S. Government Printing Office, 1991) and Office of Management and Budget, *Budget of the United States Government, fiscal years 1992 and 1993* (Washington, D.C.: U.S. Government Printing Office, 1991 and 1992).

Note: The upper figure represents budget authority in nominal dollars. Actual budget outlays differ only slightly from these amounts. Figures for 1980 are provided to indicate pre-Reagan administration spending bases. The lower figure in parentheses represents budget authority adjusted to 1987 dollars. Figures for 1992 are deflated using an estimate of 4 percent and, for 1993, 3 percent. All other amounts are adjusted to 1987 dollars using implicit price deflators for federal government purchases of nondefense goods and services as calculated by the Bureau of Economic Analysis, Department of Commerce.

[a] FY 1993 estimates are from President Bush's budget issued in January 1992. Revised estimates can be found in President Clinton's FY 1994 budget issued in April 1993.

[b] For comparison, the total budget authority for natural resources and the environment in 1972 was $3.7 billion, or $9.4 billion in 1987 dollars; by 1976 total authority had risen to $6.06 billion, or $11 billion in 1987 dollars. The totals in each column are affected slightly by rounding.

Appendix 3 Budgets of Selected Environmental and Natural Resource Agencies (in millions of dollars)

Agency	1975	1980	1985	1990	1993[a] (Est.)
Environmental Protection Agency Operating Budget [b]	850.1 (1,660.4)	1,268.7 (1,730.8)	1,339.7 (1,399.9)	1,901.3 (1,697.6)	2,535.0 (2,008.7)
Interior Department Total	3,818.0 (7,457.0)	4,578.0 (6,245.6)	5,016.0 (5,241.4)	6,690.0 (5,973.2)	6,333.0 (5,018.2)
Selected Agencies:					
Bureau of Land Management	399.9 (781.1)	918.7 (1,253.3)	799.6 (835.5)	1,226.3 (1,094.9)	1,159.0 (918.4)
Fish and Wildlife Service	207.0 (404.3)	435.3 (593.9)	585.5 (611.8)	1,132.9 (1,011.5)	1,167.0 (924.7)
National Park Service	415.8 (812.1)	531.2 (724.7)	1,005.3 (1,050.5)	1,274.5 (1,137.9)	1,437.0 (1,138.7)
Office of Surface Mining		179.5 (244.9)	377.3 (394.3)	294.8 (263.2)	270.0 (213.9)
Forest Service	955.6 (1,866.4)	2,249.6 (3,069.0)	2,116.4 (2,211.5)	3,473.4 (3,101.3)	3,435.0 (2,721.9)
Council on Environmental Quality	2.5 (4.9)	3.1 (4.2)	0.7 (0.7)	1.5 (1.3)	3.0 (2.4)
Army Corps of Engineers (civilian)	1,744.9 (3,408.0)	3,233.7 (4,411.6)	2,882.8 (3,012.3)	3,164.7 (2,825.6)	4,170.0 (3,304.3)

Sources: Office of Management and Budget, *Budget of the United States Government,* fiscal years 1977, 1982, 1987, 1992, and 1993 (Washington, D.C.: U.S. Government Printing Office, 1976, 1981, 1986, 1991, and 1992).

Note: The upper figure represents budget authority in nominal dollars. Actual budget outlays differ only slightly from these amounts. The lower figure in parentheses represents budget authority adjusted to 1987 dollars. Figures for 1992 are deflated using an estimate of 4 percent and, for 1993, 3 percent. All other amounts are adjusted to 1987 dollars using implicit price deflators for federal government purchases of nondefense goods and services as calculated by the Bureau of Economic Analysis, Department of Commerce.

[a] FY 1993 estimates are from President Bush's budget issued in January 1992. Revised estimates can be found in President Clinton's FY 1994 budget issued in April 1993.

[b] The EPA operating budget is the most meaningful figure. The other two major elements of the total EPA budget are sewage treatment construction grants and Superfund allocations, both of which are excluded from this table. Construction grant authority (not adjusted for inflation) totaled $7.7 billion in 1975, $3.4 billion in 1980, $2.4 billion in 1985, and $1.9 billion in 1990. Spending for 1993 is estimated at $2.5 billion. Superfund authority in 1985 (there was no program in 1975 and 1980) was $0.6 billion and in 1990 was $1.5 billion. Spending for Superfund is estimated at $1.8 billion for FY 1993. The total EPA budget for FY 1993 is estimated at $6.8 billion.

Appendix 4 Employees in Selected Federal Agencies and Departments, 1980 and 1990

Agency/Department	1980	1990
Environmental Protection Agency	13,867	16,013
Excluding Superfund-related Employees[a]	—	12,685
Bureau of Reclamation	—	7,600
Bureau of Land Management	9,655	8,753
Fish and Wildlife Service	7,672	7,124
National Park Service	13,934	17,781
Office of Surface Mining	1,014	1,145
Forest Service	40,606	40,991
Council on Environmental Quality[b]	59	13
Army Corps of Engineers	32,757	28,272

Sources: U.S. Senate Committee on Governmental Affairs, "Organization of Federal Executive Departments and Agencies," January 1, 1990, and earlier years. Figures for the Environmental Protection Agency and Council on Environmental Quality are taken from U.S. Office of Personnel Management, Federal Civilian Workforce, and Office of Management and Budget, *Budget of the United States Government*, fiscal years 1982 and 1990 (Washington, D.C.: U.S. Government Printing Office, 1981 and 1989).

[a] The Superfund program was created in late 1980.
[b] The staff of the Council on Environmental Quality rose to 30 in 1993, with an additional 10 assigned to the council from other federal agencies. The EPA staff in 1993 was 17,915.

Index